STRATEGIC HUMAN RIGHTS LITIGATION: UNDERSTANDING AND MAXIMISING IMPACT

Strategic human rights litigation (SHRL) is a growing area of international practice yet one that remains relatively under-explored. Around the globe, advocates increasingly resort to national, regional and international courts and bodies 'strategically' to protect and advance human rights. This book provides a framework for understanding SHRL and its contribution to various forms of personal, legal, social, political and cultural change, as well as the many tensions and challenges it gives rise to. It suggests a reframing of how we view the impact of SHRL in its multiple dimensions, both positive and negative. Five detailed case studies, drawn predominantly from the author's own experience, explore litigation in a broad range of contexts (genocide in Guatemala; slavery in Niger; forced disappearance in Argentina; torture and detention in the 'war on terror'; and Palestinian land rights) to reveal the complexity of the role of SHRL in the real world. Ultimately, this book considers how impact analysis might influence the development of more effective litigation strategies in the future.

Strategic Human Rights Litigation

Understanding and Maximising Impact

Helen Duffy

·HART·

OXFORD · LONDON · NEW YORK · NEW DELHI · SYDNEY

HART PUBLISHING

Bloomsbury Publishing Plc

Kemp House, Chawley Park, Cumnor Hill, Oxford, OX2 9PH, UK

HART PUBLISHING, the Hart/Stag logo, BLOOMSBURY and the Diana logo are
trademarks of Bloomsbury Publishing Plc

First published in Great Britain 2018

A catalogue record for this book is available from the British Library.

Library of Congress Cataloging-in-Publication data

Names: Duffy, Helen (Law teacher), author.

Title: Strategic human rights litigation / Helen Duffy.

Description: Oxford [UK] ; New York : Hart Publishing, 2018. |
Includes bibliographical references and index.

Identifiers: LCCN 2018009511 (print) | LCCN 2018012286 (ebook) |
ISBN 9781509921997 (Epub) | ISBN 9781509921973 (hardback : alk. paper)

Subjects: LCSH: Human rights. | Human rights—Case studies. | Human rights—Cases.

Classification: LCC K3240 (ebook) | LCC K3240 .D84 2018 (print) | DDC 341.4/8—dc23

LC record available at https://lccn.loc.gov/2018009511

ISBN: HB: 978-1-50992-197-3
        ePDF: 978-1-50992-198-0
        ePub: 978-1-50992-199-7

Typeset by Compuscript Ltd, Shannon

To find out more about our authors and books visit www.hartpublishing.co.uk.
Here you will find extracts, author information, details of forthcoming events
and the option to sign up for our newsletters.

To the human rights defenders around the world who make this work possible, often at great personal cost, and inspire hope

PREFACE: PERSONAL REFLECTION AND ACKNOWLEDGEMENTS

I have been engaged in human rights litigation for around 25 years, in a variety of contexts and roles (within NGOs and more recently in my own practice), on a range of human rights issues and before different national and international fora.[1] I realise my involvement colours my view and I cannot pretend to write this book as a neutral observer. Many of the cases referred to in this study are ones I have been involved in, in one capacity or another,[2] which shapes perspective and influences perceptions. I hope, however, that this unashamedly personal focus also enables me to share some honest reflections on the impact and limitations of this work, and a few lessons learned along the way, by someone who over the years has seen human rights litigation have more and less positive impacts.

While the book partly reflects my own experience, it is deeply informed by others. It benefits from the many informal conversations and structured interviews I have had the privilege to conduct over a number of years—with victims and other persons whose rights were directly affected, civil society representatives and legal practitioners, many of whom have given a great deal to make this litigation possible, as well as with members of government and judicial bodies, funders and others. I am deeply indebted to all those who shared their experience, insights,

---

[1] Legal director of CALDH Guatemala (1995–97) and Interights London (2001–11), when the focus of those organisations was, in large part, to conduct 'paradigmatic' and 'strategic' litigation respectively. My current role at Human Rights in Practice and prior positions involve litigation in the African, European, Inter-American systems and before UN bodies, and occasionally in national courts. At Human Rights Watch (1997–2000) I worked on international justice, including inter alia the *Pinochet* case, and while it would be a strain to call work in the prosecutor's office of the ICTY rights litigation, it had strategic elements in the way the law was developed and applied. My career started with not particularly strategic litigation on behalf of the government in the UK.

[2] In many of the cases mentioned in this book, I was representative of victim(s) (eg counsel or co-counsel in *Mani v Niger*, Judgment No ECW/CCJ/JUD/06/08 of 27 October 2008 (ECOWAS); *Plan de Sanchez v Guatemala*, Judgement of 29 April 2004, Ser C No 105IACtHR; *Abu Zubaydah v Poland* Appl no 7511/13 (24 July 2014) and against *Lithuania* (pending) (ECtHR); *Sabbah and Others Egyptian Initiative for Personal Rights and Interights v Arab Republic of Egypt* Comm 334/06 (ACHPR); *Garzon v Spain* (UNHRC)). In others, I was involved through the organisations I worked for at the relevant time as 'adviser' or assistant to local counsel (eg *Identoba v Georgia* Appl no 73235/12 (12 May 2015) (ECtHR) or third party/*amicus* intervener (eg *R v Pinochet* [1998] UKHL 41; *Rantsev v Russia* Appl no 25965/04 (7 January 2010) (ECtHR); *Kiyutin v Russia* Appl no 2700/10 (10 March 2011) (ECtHR); *Opuz v Turkey* Appl no 33401/02 (9 June 2009) (ECtHR), *Fazenda Brazil v Brazil* (2016) (IACtHR)). See Ch 10 on the different roles, and the implications and possibilities they open up. I have not discussed pending cases.

frustrations and expertise with me. Working for and with remarkable people, some of whose stories are reflected in these pages, has been an honour and a constant education.

My long-standing motivation to write this book was influenced by various factors at different stages, reflecting to some extent my changing appreciation of what litigation was about. One relatively early trigger was the realisation, perhaps obvious to some much earlier, that the carefully crafted legal arguments I felt so committed to, and even well-reasoned judgments, only go so far. Much depended on processes of change that were far from the control of litigators (and often occurring at a distance from the courtroom), yet which were crucially important for the people we represented, for our ability to advise them meaningfully and responsibly, and for the human rights impact of litigation more broadly. In part then, this enquiry began with the gradual recalibration of the emphasis placed on what happened within the legal process, and beyond it.

Most striking for me was the growing realisation that, at least most of the time, many of us involved in human rights litigation just didn't really know what the impact of our cases had been. As the rights litigation industry grew, so did doubts as to whether this was matched by sufficient growth in analysis of the true value of strategic human rights litigation (SHRL). There were many good reasons for this, including lack of time, resources and the inherent challenges in assessing the complex, multi-faceted and long-term question of impact. The fact was, that often busy with the next case or challenge, insufficient time was made available for looking back in order to move forward with greater confidence. Lots, it seemed, was taken on faith as to the inherent worth of the illuminating judicial processes, while experience increasingly brought to the surface a much more nuanced picture and called for greater reflection.

As attention to 'strategic' human rights litigation has increased over time, so has consideration of its impact. First, funders became more attentive to the issue, as part of an increased focus on human rights evaluation in general (with all the controversies inherent in measuring the impact of human rights work). While in many ways positive, this in turn gave rise to doubts. In what may seem like a contradictory sensation to the one outlined above, it seemed to me that too much emphasis came to be placed on *measuring* and *demonstrating* 'results', in an artificial way that missed something about the value of litigation and the variety of ways in which it had a positive influence. Was the impact of SHRL really subject to measurement at all, and if so according to whose matrix? Were some goals, such as contributing to political or social cultural change, for example, really quantifiable? The need to show outputs that surpassed inputs seemed to reduce the litigation process, with its diverse (if uncertain) functions and impact, to a slot machine that had to pay out at least sometimes to keep the investment dripping in. This underscored the need to understand and articulate the nature of the pay-outs in the human rights litigation arcade. This challenge remains relevant, as funder fatigue and scepticism as to the value of litigation grows.

A great deal more thinking and analysis has unfolded in recent years, even since I began this project. Attention has gathered pace substantially with several important studies completed or underway. Often these have focused on a particular theme or jurisdiction; considerable academic literature on the role of the courts in the United States[3] sits alongside valuable reports on economic and social rights litigation in South Africa,[4] constitutional processes in Colombia,[5] and public interest litigation in India[6] for example.[7] Some analysis has considered the role of 'human rights lawyering organisations' or 'cause lawyers' in general, which has at times included the role of litigation.[8] A few studies have explored comparative experiences in litigating particular types of violations,[9] including a significant series of studies sponsored by the Open Society Justice Initiative (with which I have been involved as author of one study on litigating torture in detention).[10] A notable increase in attention has been paid belatedly to one distinct but related aspect of the discussion, namely implementation of judgments.[11]

---

[3] Among abundant literature from the US, see J Lobel, *Success Without Victory: Lost Legal Battles and the Long Road to Justice in America* (New York, NYU Press, 2004); A Neier, *Only Judgment: The Limits of Litigation in Social Change* (London, International Debate Education Association, 2012); M Tushnet, *The NAACP's Legal Strategy against Segregated Education, 1925-1950* (Chapel Hill, UNC Press, 2005); M Klarman, *From the Closet to the Altar: Courts, Backlash, and the Struggle for Same-Sex Marriage* (Oxford, Oxford University Press, 2014).

[4] Several reports impelled by donor foundations, lawyers and practitioners or NGOs stand out in this regard, including: 'Public Interest Legal Services in South Africa Project Report' (Cape Town, SERI, 2015); S Budlender, G Marcus SC and N Ferreira, 'Public Interest Litigation and Social Change in South Africa: Strategies, Tactics and Lessons' (The Atlantic Philanthropies, 2014); G Marcus and N Ferreira, 'A Strategic Evaluation of Public Interest Litigation South Africa' (The Atlantic Philanthropies, 2008). See also analysis by Dugard and Langford relied upon in this book.

[5] See C Rodríguez Garavito and D Rodríguez Franco, *Cortes y cambio social, Cómo la Corte Constitucional transformó el desplazamiento forzado en Colombia* (Bogotá, De Justicia, 2012).

[6] See eg A Bhuwania, *Courting the People: Public Interest Litigation in Post-Emergency India* (New Delhi, Cambridge University Press, 2017).

[7] See eg I Bacik and M Rogan, *Legal Cases that Changed Ireland* (Dublin, Clarus Press, 2016).

[8] R Wilson and J Rasmussen, *Promoting Justice: A Practical Guide to Human Rights Lawyering* (IHRLG, 2001) which included, though did not delve deeply into, an enquiry of what has been achieved through litigation or its limitations. S Scheingold and A Sarat, *Something to Believe In: Politics, Professionalism, and Cause Lawyering* (2004), which coined the term 'cause lawyering' in the US context. Some studies deal with the work of particular NGOs, eg on the work of CELs in Argentina *La Lucha por el Derecho: Litigio Estratégico y Derechos humanos* (Buenos Aires, Siglo Veintiuno, 2008).

[9] See eg *Strategic Litigation of Race Discrimination in Europe: From Principles to Practice* (Nottingham, Russell Press Ltd, 2004); *Litigating Economic, Social and Cultural Rights: Achievements, Challenges, Strategies* (Geneva, COHRE, 2003).

[10] Researched from 2013 to 2017, the 4 studies address: Roma segregation litigation in Europe; the right to education in Brazil, India and South Africa; indigenous rights in Kenya, Malaysia and Paraguay. I am the author of the final study on torture in detention in Argentina, Kenya and Turkey, pending publication.

[11] Though the question of 'impact' considered in this book overlaps with implementation, it is clearly much broader. OSJI, CEJIL and Interights, among others, have all done studies on poor records of implementation of human rights courts and bodies judgments in recent years. A 'European implementation network' was set up to monitor implementation of ECtHR cases in 2016.

This enhanced level of reflection on SHRL is important and overdue, but analysis on what has worked, and importantly what has not, remains patchy. In particular, in a context in which litigation is in many ways increasingly common, but also increasingly challenging, there is a need for those involved in litigation (in whatever role, not only lawyers),[12] and those affected by it, to critically appraise and share their experience, including what we might have done differently and what we can learn collectively for the future. This book is intended as a contribution to that conversation around the impact in the real world, and what it tells us about how to litigate more strategically.

A further motivation for this book was growing concern about the instrumentality of 'victims' within the 'strategic human rights litigation' industry. This problem does not relate exclusively to SHRL, as victims often fare poorly in judicial processes. To some extent these concerns have grown, however, as 'strategic' use of litigation for 'other goals' has been given greater emphasis in international practice. The questions of how litigation impacts on the individuals in whose name cases are (generally) brought, whether the process still 'belongs to' those that bear its name, and how the ethical, professional and moral obligations to the applicants are addressed in the medley of interests at play, are fundamental, yet still somewhat neglected in analysis to date. A related doubt was how often litigators even actually go back to people affected by litigation to enquire into impact on diverse levels and over time.

There is no necessary conflict between 'strategic' and 'client-focused' litigation. Indeed, as we will explore, while there has been a tendency to consider impact on litigants—victims, survivors and family members for example—as distinct and separate from 'strategic' impact, the two are often inherently interlinked. But undoubtedly the role of victims and survivors in SHRL, and the real tensions that can and do arise, raise important ethical, professional, human rights issues that require greater attention.

This book has wanted to be written for a long time and arisen in stages. It began to be researched in 2012 during a brief consultancy that enabled discussions with key actors on how they saw the role and impact of human rights litigation, and the value of this study.[13] They confirmed its potential usefulness and shaped its scope and approach. Though the project languished for a while, as I became immersed in setting up my own practice and in litigation, along the way I was fortunate enough to continue to explore the issue through independent consultancies on SHRL. I am grateful to the Norwegian Refugee Council and OSJI for the opportunities to consider the impact of human rights litigation on land and property rights in Palestine, and torture in detention in Kenya, Argentina and Turkey respectively. Thanks to the Freedom Fund, I had the opportunity to travel to Niger and sit with my client Hadijatou Mani, as well as judges, NGOs,

---

[12] See Ch 2 (challenges) and Ch 10 (developing strategic approaches) on the range of actors and partnerships—going beyond lawyers—engaged in SHRL.

[13] I am grateful to the Hague Institute for Global Justice for supporting that feasibility study in 2012.

government officials and others involved in or affected by her slavery case before the ECOWAS Court and discuss its impact. Particular appreciation is due, however, to the Nuhanovic Foundation; its interest and support (in particular that of Frederiek de Vlaming) made it possible to complete the research and writing of this report during 2016/17. This book also benefited from a dedicated meeting of leading practitioners and NGOs organised by the Nuhanovic Foundation to review a draft of this report in Amsterdam in the spring of 2017. These evolving conversations provided crucial insights for this book, and invaluable inspiration.

While many of the examples in this book are based on personal experience,[14] the study therefore seeks to draw in a broader range of perspectives, ideas and experience, based on many discussions with victims and survivors, lawyers, activists, NGOs, judges, and court and state officials, over a long period of time. Sincere gratitude goes to all those who were interviewed and attended the roundtable, and in particular those who reviewed drafts, including (among many others): Baher Azmy, Adrijana Hanušic Becirovic, Hannah Bosdriesz, Jason Brickhill, Gaston Chillier, Martin Clutterbuck, Fiona de Londras, Max du Plessis, John Dugard, Jim Goldston, Nienke van der Have, Nicole Immler, Jelle Klaas, Viviana Krsticevic, Phil Leach, Joe Margulies, Sibongile Ndashe, Michael O'Boyle, Michael Sfard, Rupert Skilbeck, Steven Watt, Adam Weiss and Liesbeth Zegveld, Many thanks to former students at the University of Leiden and research assistants for Human Rights *in* Practice who provided input at various stages, including Frederieke Poschl, Arturo Esteve, Stephen Greatley-Hirsch, Joyce Man, Manon Beury, and especially Holly Huxtable for her commitment, always running the extra mile with a smile. The report benefited from editing by Kate Clarke of the Nuhanovic Foundation, before diligent review and publication by Hart Publishing. Loving thanks are always overdue to Fabricio, Luca and Maia. And finally to Cath (and Asha) Campbell, for critical review of this book, and uncritical love and support.

---

[14] These detailed studies are at Chapters 5–8. Some such as Guatemala and Rendition are primarily based on personal reflections, building on discussions with other lawyers and activists frustratingly chiselling away at various walls of impunity surrounding the Guatemalan massacres and CIA rendition crimes.

CONTENTS

Part I

1

Introduction

I. Introducing 'Strategic' Human Rights Litigation

This book explores an issue of growing significance in the contemporary practice of human rights law, namely the role, impact and limitations of 'strategic human rights litigation' (SHRL). While there is no fixed definition of SHRL, the term is generally used to mean litigation that pursues goals—or which concerns interests—that are broader than only those of the immediate parties. SHRL uses the courts to advance human rights in a way that reaches beyond the particular victims or applicants at the centre of the particular case. SHRL, sometimes referred to as 'public interest' or simply 'impact' litigation, is a tool invoked increasingly by victims and survivors, human rights activists, lawyers and non-governmental organisations (NGOs) around the world.

A question that underpins this study is what is it exactly that makes some litigation strategic?[1] Is it the goals pursued, and if so, *whose* goals—or strategies—count for this purpose? Is it a feature of the *way* the litigation is conducted, or how it is *used*, 'strategically'? Does it depend on the intention, or even identity, of the public-interest focused actors driving or engaged in it? Or is the question of what difference that litigation actually makes in practice—its impact or influence—central to its classification as 'strategic'?

While all of these considerations may be relevant and important to the SHRL enterprise, the key question explored in this book is the impact or influence of human rights litigation; whatever the goals, strategies or resources involved, did human rights litigation make a difference, and if so what sort of difference, how and why? The focus of this book is on the need to explore and expose the usefulness and limitations of resort to the courts to bring about human rights change. By reference to multiple types of 'human rights' litigation as it unfolds in the world today, on a range of issues in diverse situations and systems, it enquires into the true nature of the impact or influence of human rights litigation.

---

[1] Ch 3, s I queries the basis for stark distinctions between 'strategic' and other types of legal service provisions or victim-focused litigation, primarily defining strategic litigation for the purpose of this book by reference to its impact.

The whole idea of strategic human rights litigation, and the role that the courts *can*, or even *should*, have in bringing about human rights change, has long been somewhat controversial. To an extent, this reflects profound differences of view on the role of the judiciary in democratic society. At one end of the spectrum, the courts can be regarded with an almost religious reverence: solutions are sought, as if from on high, before the ultimate arbiters of truth and right, whose job it is to apply the law without fear and favour and to 'resolve' the problem. Lawyers and litigators may be particularly prone to this view, placing emphasis on the importance of lawyers' pleadings and interpretations of the law and judicial determinations of them, perhaps partly (if unconsciously) to justify our own exclusive role as initiates in the exotic rituals of the court whose carefully crafted legal arguments lead our clients towards the light. The faith of many is ultimately placed on judgment day when the (legally) righteous are rewarded and justice done.

At the other end of the spectrum, there are those who almost demonise the role of the courts, seeing them as anti-democratic, wresting power from elected representatives and their procedures, or as inherently elitist and disconnected from the social struggles within which real change happens. For them, the courts either *should* not (as they are undemocratic), or more commonly *cannot* (as they manifestly lack political power), deliver the meaningful social and political change on which respect for human rights depends. Proponents of both these views have often cited 'landmark' cases such as *Brown v Board of Education*[2] in the US Supreme Court: *Brown* established that segregation in education was unconstitutional in the US, yet—60 years on—complete desegregation remains elusive. *Brown* therefore, like other 'landmark' cases (including some explored in this study) can be cited alternatively as a shining historic victory that changed everything, or as a chimera that achieved nothing. The truth, no doubt, lies somewhere in between.

This book explores, by reference to multiple cases and situations, where, within these extremes of heaven and hell, the role and impact of SHRL lies. Fundamentally, it seeks to recast the way we think about 'success' in this field,[3] by exploring the many different ways in which litigation can and does make a contribution to change.

It will be suggested that, done strategically and used properly, both inside and outside the court, SHRL can have multiple types of impact over extended periods of time. Most obviously, it may provide or contribute to protection, redress and reparation for victims and survivors, including through recognition, compensation, guarantees of non-repetition, rehabilitation or symbolic restorative measures. However, strategic human rights litigation can also catalyse and contribute to much broader changes, of a legal, political, institutional, social or cultural nature.

---

[2] *Brown v Board of Education of Topeka*, US Supreme Court, 347 U.S. 483 (1954).
[3] J Lobel, *Success Without Victory; Lost Legal Battles and the Long Road to Justice in America* (New York, NYU Press, 2004), famously referred to the 'success without victory', through the power of the losing case in the US. See Ch 3.

It may be a vehicle for achieving accountability—whether at the level of the state or its institutions, corporations or the individual. It may help unearth information, contributing to historical clarification and broader processes of reconciliation. It may influence attitudes, discourse and behaviour. It may energise and empower social movements and civil society. It may pursue and strengthen a broad democratic, rule of law agenda.

On the other hand, it may not. Human rights litigation is not a neutral enterprise that at worst does little good, while not doing any harm. Rather, as one interviewee described it, it is 'a hazardous journey, not to be undertaken lightly'. Litigation may have serious repercussions for victims, families and communities, and for human rights causes, if backlash compounds problems rather than presenting solutions. It can lead to the erosion of legal standards due to poor jurisprudence or regressive legislative responses. It may contribute to a veneer of legitimacy that shrouds the reality of justice denied. It may generate 'false expectations and vain promises', and compound original wrongs. In many more cases, there may be reason to question how much really changed beyond the confines of the courtroom, while lengthy and resource-intensive proceedings were depleting resources that could perhaps more effectively have been channelled elsewhere.

For these and other reasons explored in this report, the positive nature and impact of litigation can certainly not be taken for granted. It may be, as one recent report aptly noted, that '*litigation is not an ideology; it is a tool*'.[4] The extent of its impact or influence will invariably depend on how, where, when and perhaps by whom the tool is used.[5]

At the same time, the role of courts that authoritatively determine human rights claims, interpreting and applying the law, is arguably a particular *type* of human rights tool. It has its own particular authority and weight (as well as shortcomings), and care must be taken to 'use' litigation fora in ways that do not undermine the distinctive value of the judicial function. Likewise, care is due to ensure that reaching the 'strategic' potential of litigation does not mean undermining the interests of the victims in whose names, and pursuant to whose right to access justice and reparation, cases are brought. These and other myriad challenges and tensions must be borne in mind in the difficult determinations that must be made as to whether SHRL is an appropriate tool at all in a particular context, and if so how it should be approached.

The central goal of this book is to explore how we might understand the nature and potential of this litigation tool. It will be suggested that understanding impact requires that we jettison the narrow view of the litigation process and its 'outcomes', in favour of an approach that explores the full range of diverse sites or levels of impact—direct or indirect, immediate or incremental, planned or

---

[4] 'Public Interest Legal Services in South Africa Project Report' *Socio Economic Rights Institute of South Africa* (2015).
[5] See Ch 10.

unanticipated, plain or barely discernible. It requires that we consider how 'impact' arises in myriad ways and at multiple stages. It may be positive and negative and sometimes both—at different stages, or if seen from different vantage points. Only by weighing up all the many types of impact that litigation often turns out to have in practice, can we assess its true significance.

It is hoped that the reflections in this book, on understanding impact, and its influence on developing strategy, will prove useful to the growing body of actors engaged in and affected by the rapidly expanding field of human rights litigation, nationally and internationally. This includes victims, survivors, NGOs, private practitioners, law firms and law clinics employing SHRL as a tool to protect human rights across continents and systems, as well as the activists, academics across disciplines, policy-makers, judicial officers and other legal professionals whose work is inherently intertwined with the impact of litigation. It also includes funders, whose support is imperative, some of whom have long supported strategic human rights litigation but shown increasing scepticism towards it, or at least increasingly seek accountability for use of funds in an opaque area where understanding impact can be complex and investment long term and costly.[6] This book hopes to make a contribution to much-needed, and evolving, conversations between all of these actors on the role that litigation can and should play in improving the human rights landscape.

II. Overview of Chapters

Chapter 2 locates the growing field of SHRL within an evolving international landscape that presents both opportunities and challenges. It signals trends in the expansion of human rights litigation before national and international fora, the proliferation of such fora, remedies, substantive human rights law and engaged actors. This richer, more fertile context is undoubtedly offset by serious challenges. Political pressure on judiciaries in many parts of the world, serious deficits in judicial capacity or independence, attacks on human rights defenders including lawyers globally, and geographical gaps in available international human rights fora are among the real challenges that often affect the ability to engage in human rights litigation at all. Myriad impediments stand in the way of victims, survivors and civil society and in practice access to justice very often remains elusive. Despite the challenges, obstacles and dangers, it is a burgeoning field, as survivors, human rights lawyers and activists around the world increasingly seek recourse to litigation to address human rights problems.

---

[6] The resources challenge is one of many flagged in Chs 2 and 9. Not all SHRL is costly, but strategic long-term engagement for maximal impact generally is.

Chapter 3 is the heart of the study, suggesting a framework for understanding and identifying the impact of the growing field of SHRL. It suggests lenses through which we might capture the multi-dimensional and complex nature of litigation's impact, over prolonged periods of time, and in synergy with other action for change—such as advocacy, education, protest and legislative reform for example. It suggests the need to focus not only on what courts say and do, or what people say and do in court, but how the work of the range of actors relevant to the litigation process may influence the discourse, attitudes, legal, political and social contexts in which violations unfold. Looking beyond the plain *outcomes* of litigation, which rarely *provide* a solution for some of the broad-reaching social or political problems that underpin rights violations, it enquires into how it may *contribute* directly and indirectly to change. While acknowledging that many types of impact are simply not susceptible to 'measurement' as such, Chapter 4 identifies and illustrates eight broad categories of impact.

Chapters 5 to 9 present five detailed case studies, based on litigation which I have been engaged in as a lawyer or considered as a consultant. The studies enable a closer critical look at context, and the unique interplay of factors or conditions that have affected the impact of the litigation in diverse situations. Each of the case studies juxtapose the sometimes carefully constructed goals and strategies that guided the litigants, with the broad range of relevant factors that interacted with the litigation process, before, during and after it, and suggest indicators of the positive and negative impact of human rights litigation.

Chapter 10 presents an approach to planning and strategy at the various phases of litigation, formulated on the basis of the experience gained in large part from the case studies. It emphasises the attention that must always be paid to the unique situational, legal, cultural, institutional and other contexts in which the cases arise.[7] Diversity is all the greater on the national level and cautions strongly against a 'one size fits all' formula for strategic litigation. At the same time, while legal strategies must emerge from the individual, local and regional environment, they can and should be informed by an awareness of strategic litigation experience in other contexts. The emphasis in this chapter is therefore on strategies, tactics and approaches that may enhance impact and meet some (by no means all) of the challenges that arise in the SHRL enterprise.[8]

---

[7] There are vast variations between the supranational human rights systems, and diversity is greater on the national level. See Ch 2 below.

[8] See Ch 2 on identifying challenges and Ch 10 on how we might meet some of them through SHRL; it is recognised that many of the obstacles and challenges highlighted in this book as impeding litigation or its effect—political, economic, institutional, legal or practical—require broader solutions, such as judicial, political or institutional reform. Ch 10 focuses on how SHRL in the future might try to meet those challenges that may be influenced by the way we do our litigation work. Issues include: strategic planning, identification of goals and risks, selection of cases, fora and partners, timing, the dynamics of relationships, participation and leadership, remedies sought, early investment in post-judgment implementation, among many others.

By exposing for consideration a range of experience in the litigation of serious human rights violations, and some honest reflections on tensions and limitations that arise in practice, the book ultimately questions how lessons from the past might inform the development of strategic approaches in the future. How can we better understand SHRL, and employ it most effectively, to meet the very real challenges facing human rights work around the world today?

2

The Growing Field of 'Human Rights' Litigation in the World Today: Context, Trends, Opportunities and Challenges

It has been said that we live in an 'age of adjudication' in international law.[1] In no area is this more applicable than in the burgeoning field of human rights litigation, which has changed dramatically in recent decades in a range of ways.

A vastly expanded and evolving practice of human rights litigation has emerged in many states around the world and on the international level. Not only has the volume of litigation grown—often exponentially—but also the range of types of litigation, and the number and spread of available fora and remedies, have increased. Various trends and developments in laws, procedures and practice have created new opportunities to litigate and opened up the space within which to do so strategically, that is, in a way that might amplify its impact for the benefit not only of the victims/claimants bringing the case but also for others.[2] At the same time, enormous challenges beset human rights litigation at this time that often impede the ability to pursue such litigation at all, or stifle its ultimate impact.

This chapter takes a panoramic view across the contemporary landscape of human rights litigation, and the challenges and opportunities it represents, before focusing on the impact of litigating 'strategically' in the chapters that follow.

I. An Expanding Panorama of Human Rights Litigation

A. 'Human Rights' Litigation on the National Level

Great diversity at the national level makes generalisations about the content and form of human rights litigation difficult. Laws, procedures, remedies and legal

---

[1] Judge Christopher Greenwood, keynote speech, opening of the academic year at the Grotius Centre, University of Leiden, 2015.
[2] This potential amplification of the scope and types of impact that litigation can generate is the subject of Ch 10.

cultures all vary, as does legal terminology and the way we refer to what might broadly be considered 'human rights litigation'. If, however, we adopt a purposive and flexible approach, which focuses on courts or human rights adjudicatory bodies being used to advance human rights goals and to have a human rights impact, then a broad array of forms of litigation become relevant. These naturally include the civil claims, administrative actions, judicial review and constitutional challenges, commonly considered as ways to give effect to human rights in domestic systems.

Numerous compelling examples from recent practice also show the creative use of novel legal tools to address deep-rooted structural human rights problems that affect huge numbers of people, such as arbitrary displacement, terrible prison conditions or unjust health and housing policies.[3] César Rodríguez Garavito and Diana Rodríguez Franco, in their excellent book *Cortes y cambio social* ('*Courts and Social Change*') speak of an 'international tendency' towards what they call 'constitutional protagonism' or 'progressive neo-constitutionalism' in respect of rights.[4] Well-known examples of this phenomenon are the 'meta-cases', conducted by the Indian Supreme Court, the South African Constitutional Court and the Colombian Constitutional Court, that have engaged the judiciary in long-term multi-staged litigation processes to oversee the remediation of 'structural' human rights problems.[5] In this evolving model of litigation, courts remain engaged throughout the implementation phase, often for many years: the Colombian Constitutional Court's cases on displacement, ultimately tallied 14 hearings and 84 follow-up decisions—to significant effect.[6]

In many other systems, traditional remedies or causes of action have been given a strategic twist in order to address widespread human rights violations. In Argentina, habeas corpus actions—normally used for the benefit of individual detainees—were innovatively adapted to enable a series of 'collective habeas corpus' actions, forcing the state to engage with the rights of thousands of prisoners held in inhuman conditions of detention, the wide-reaching effects of which are explored elsewhere.[7] Legal devices such as mandamus orders to compel (government) action, and protective orders to prevent it, have been put to good use in various systems. Proceedings based on 'freedom of information' legislation, or in

---

[3] These emerge from the cases from Colombia, Argentina, India and South Africa referred to below.

[4] See CR Garavito and DR Franco, *Cortes y cambio social: Cómo la Corte Constitucional transformó el desplazamiento forzado en Colombia* (Bogotá, De Justicia, 2011); see also for updated and English version CR Garavito and DR Franco, *Radical Deprivation on Trial: The Impact of Judicial Activism on Socioeconomic Rights in the Global South* (Cambridge, Cambridge University Press, 2015).

[5] Ibid.

[6] Ibid.

[7] Innovative litigation challenging prison conditions has effectively created a new remedy in Argentinian law and procedure, and ensured that the issue has a more prominent place on the country's political and human rights agenda. See H Duffy, 'Strategic Litigation Impacts: Torture in Custody', part of Open Society Justice Initiative (OSJI) Study (2017) and 'La lucha por el derecho: Litigio estratégico y derechos humanos' (2008) available at www.cels.org.ar/web/wp-content/uploads/2008/10/La-Lucha-por-el-derecho.pdf.

some systems habeas 'data' cases, are among the forms of litigation used to obtain information otherwise withheld by governments and illuminate the facts surrounding violations.[8]

This ever-broader array of types of national litigation is being creatively employed for human rights ends against a similarly expanding range of *defendants*. The state—or particular manifestations of it—remains the most obvious target for most human rights litigation, particularly on the international level, in accordance with obligations under international law. But for some violations, the focus has shifted to the individualisation of responsibility, including through criminal complaints which have increasingly assumed a central place as the remedy of choice for victims and civil society. The extent to which national criminal processes are controlled by the state, as opposed to accessible to and subject to some influence by victims or civil society, varies from system to system.[9] But trends towards an increasingly participative and instrumental role for victims in many states (as well as internationally), alongside belief in the contribution that accountability makes to reparation and non-repetition, has led to criminal law processes being seen, at least in part, as having a broader human rights dimension.[10]

A growing field of national practice relates to non-state actor responsibility for human rights violations, which has drawn corporate, trade and investment law into the realm of human rights litigation. Customs claims against corporations importing slave labour, and civil claims for exploitation and trafficking that have brought corporations to their knees, signal the human rights potential of such cases, sending powerful messages to would-be corporate violators.[11] Recent cases brought by Dutch lawyers against FIFA to secure human rights standards in respect of preparations for the Qatar World Cup 2022, are another example of the increasingly creative use of litigation against both state and non-state actors.[12]

The development of forms of criminal jurisdiction, including 'universal jurisdiction' (UJ) for serious rights violations—which uncouples jurisdiction from territory and nationality for egregious wrongs—have extended the reach

---

[8] Duffy, 'Strategic Litigation Impacts' (n 7).

[9] Prosecution is generally led by the state, unlike civil claims which are between private parties, but in practice this distinction is more blurred. The degree of victim influence and participation in the criminal process is traditionally considered a classic distinction between common law and civil law systems but trends towards a greater role for victims is seen across these categories of legal system.

[10] Criminal processes have overlapping but also quite different purposes so the convergence of these areas should not be overstated.

[11] A good recent example is the US litigation on slavery and forced labour against Signal International (2016), but there are a growing number of such cases in the field of slavery and human trafficking; 'Ending Impunity, Securing Justice: Using Strategies Litigation to Combat Modern-day Slavery and Human Trafficking' (The Human Trafficking Pro Bono Legal Centre & The Freedom Fund, December 2015) available at www.htprobono.org/wp-content/uploads/2015/12/FF_SL_AW02_WEB. pdf. See information on the Global Legal Action Network's work at www.glanlaw.org/our-work.

[12] The case was brought by Leisbeth Zegveld; for associated publicity, see eg O Gibson, 'Fifa Faces Legal Challenge Over Qatar Migrant Workers' *The Guardian* (10 October 2016) available at www. theguardian.com/football/2016/oct/10/fifa-faces-legal-challenge-over-qatar-migrant-workers-world-cup-2022.

of national judicial mechanisms across borders. This has been an object of hope for many litigants and a target of the efforts of lawyers in many states in recent decades.[13] However, UJ practice has also faced challenges and setbacks. States such as Spain and Belgium that showed leadership in the exercise of UJ in the criminal sphere in the last two decades have seen political pressure slow the advance of this type of litigation following high-profile cases against current or former foreign heads of state or other senior foreign officials. Immunities have protected accused persons from arrest in some cases, while in others, third states declined to comply with requests for extradition. Resistance from various quarters has meanwhile led states such as Spain to curtail the reach of its laws on jurisdiction, requiring a more direct link between the state and the crime. At the same time, recent Argentinian initiatives to prosecute the crimes against humanity committed by Spanish ministers serving under the dictatorship of Spain's General Franco, symbolise that the reach of universal jurisdiction practice may yet continue to spread.

Notwithstanding the challenges to the use of universal jurisdiction, the role and increased relevance of 'foreign' national courts is a distinctive feature of the evolving landscape of human rights litigation. As four of the five case studies in Chapters 5 to 9 illustrate, foreign criminal courts can play a significant role, particularly when justice at home is lacking. In particular they can create a dynamic that impels or incentivises domestic courts in the state where the violations arose to see—and develop—their own legal practices within the broader context of the international effort to address persistent human rights violations.[14] Despite the legal, jurisdictional and other challenges to using foreign courts for civil damages for human rights violations, there are by now many examples of advocates in different states seeking—with at least some success—to bring claims against both states and corporations, for their direct responsibility or for their complicity in violations abroad,[15] broadening the spectrum of litigation further. It is through creative litigation that many novel remedies and procedures have been created, as well as shaped, for the future.

As the volume of domestic rights litigation increases, and types of litigation and remedies continue to evolve, so too do rules and procedures change, sometimes in ways that create opportunities for the strategic use of litigation (as discussed in Chapter 10). An example is the progressive increase in media coverage of litigation

---

[13] As a matter of international law, foreign courts may exercise criminal or civil jurisdiction over certain serious human rights violations, including under the principle of universal jurisdiction (UJ); International Court of Justice (ICJ), *Arrest Warrant Case (Democratic Republic of the Congo v Belgium)* (Judgment) [2002] ICJ Rep 3; *Questions Relating to the Obligation to Prosecute or Extradite (Belgium v Senegal)* (Judgment) [2012] ICJ Rep, p 422.

[14] This has been used to good effect in relation to Argentina, Guatemala and, thus far with less success, in Palestine. See cases studies on Argentina and Guatemala.

[15] See Amnesty International, 'Universal Jurisdiction: A Preliminary Survey of Legislation Around the World—2012 Update' (9 October 2012) with examples, available at www.amnesty.org/en/documents/ior53/019/2012/en/.

processes in various states, which enhance the opportunities for what happens in the courtroom to be seen, resonate and generate impact in the world beyond the court.[16]

B. Available International Mechanisms: Expanding Scope and Outstanding Gaps

On the supranational level, a detailed infrastructure of human rights litigation has been created and transformed, in a relatively short period of time.[17] Yet, not so long ago, the very idea that human rights could be given teeth by allowing individuals to bring claims against the state was considered revolutionary. Anthony Lester in his recent book *Five Ideas to Fight For* (2016) notes that when the European Court of Human Rights (ECtHR) was proposed in 1950, the UK Attorney General Sir Hartley Shawcross wrote that 'the possibility of UK citizens lodging complaints against their government in Strasbourg is wholly opposed to the theory of responsible government'.[18] A Foreign Office Ministerial Brief went further, noting that 'to allow governments to become the object of such potentially vague charges by individuals, is to invite Communists, crooks and cranks of every description to bring actions'.[19] Thankfully, that advice was rejected and the UK joined the Court when it was created in 1959 (a situation that will hopefully continue despite current strains) and human rights litigators and advocates (few of them commies, crooks or cranks) have been bringing cases with increased regularity and developing the human rights system ever since.

Today, there is abundant human rights litigation involving individual (and where possible collective) complaints against states. There has been a proliferation of regional and international courts and bodies that have been created

---

[16] These changes have emerged in numerous states. eg the US has long had cameras in some courts; the UK introduced cameras gradually (see eg O Bowcott, 'Judges to be filmed in English and Welsh Crown Courts' *The Guardian* (25 April 2016) available at www.theguardian.com/global/2016/apr/25/judges-to-be-filmed-in-english-and-welsh-crown-courts). Practice varies and the consequences can be positive and negative. See Chs 3 and 9 on types of social impact that litigation may pursue and the importance of media; such coverage may also create a degree of public 'oversight' of the judicial function, with potentially varying results.

[17] 'Supranational human rights litigation' is the term sometimes used here to apply to cases brought against states to those international regional or sub-regional courts and human rights bodies that receive complaints from individuals or groups, including eg the European Court of Human Rights (ECtHR), African Commission of Human and Peoples Rights (ACommHPR), the African Court of Human and Peoples Rights (ACtHPR), the Inter-American Commission and Court (IACommHR and IACtHR) or the treaty bodies of the UN eg the Human Rights Committee (HRC) or the Committee on Economic Social and Cultural Rights (CESCR). These judicial or quasi-judicial bodies receiving complaints exist alongside a larger body of work implementing human rights standards, including eg enquiry procedures or state reporting of some of these treaty bodies, or by other political bodies (such as eg HR Council or special mechanisms for example).

[18] A Lester, *Five Ideas to Fight For: How Our Freedom is Under Threat and Why it Matters* (London, One World Publications, 2016) 19.

[19] T Bingham, *The Rule of Law* (London, Penguin, 2010).

(or had their jurisdictions expanded) to hear human rights claims. Among these, the ECtHR, the Inter-American Commission of Human Rights (IACommHR), the Inter-American Court of Human Rights (IACtHR), the African Commission on Human and Peoples' Rights (ACommHPR) and the nascent African Court of Justice and Human Rights (ACtJHPR) are the key bodies.[20] There are however also other regional bodies that receive human rights complaints that are often overlooked but whose jurisdictional scope, rules of admissibility and procedure, or advantageous approach or practice, make them important to bear in mind. These include the European Committee of Social Rights (ECSR) and the African Committee of Experts on the Rights and Welfare of the Child for example, with their broad jurisdictional bases and flexible procedures.[21]

On the international level, there are now nine UN treaty bodies with a strong litigation or individual complaints dimension to their broader human rights work.[22] Use of these fora has increased, albeit dependent on states accepting the competence of the body.[23] They currently include the Human Rights Committee; the Committee against Torture; the Committee on Economic, Social and Cultural

---

[20] For the functions of the ECtHR in respect to the European Convention on Human Rights (ECHR), see Art 19 ECHR; for the IACommHR and IACtHR in relation to the American Convention on Human Rights ACHR) see Art 33 ACHR; for the ACommHPR in relation to the African Charter on Human and Peoples' Rights (ACHPR), see Art 45 ACHPR: for the ACtJHR in relation to the ACHR and other regional human rights treaties, see Art 28 Statute of the ACtJHR (Annex to Protocol on the Statute of the ACtJHR, 1 July 2008).

[21] See eg Art 44(1) African Convention on the Rights and Welfare of the Child (ACRWC): 'The Committee may receive communication, from any person, group or non-governmental organization recognized by the Organization of African Unity, by a Member State, or the United Nations relating to any matter covered by this Charter'. Also before the ECSR according to the Additional Protocol to the European Social Charter no exhaustion of domestic remedies is required and collective complaints are possible.

[22] Like the African and Inter-American Commissions (but unlike the Courts), the UN treaty bodies also have monitoring and reporting functions. When they exercise their individual complaints mandate they should act as independent arbitrators, and their functions are often described as 'quasi-judicial': for the functions of the HRC in relation to the International Covenant on Civil and Political Rights (ICCPR), see Art 28 of ICCPR and First Optional Protocol; for the Committee against Torture with respect to the Convention against Torture and Other Cruel, Inhuman and Degrading Treatment or Punishment (CAT), see Art 33 CAT; for the Committee on the Elimination of Discrimination against Women in relation to Convention on Elimination of All Forms of Discrimination Against Women (CEDAW), see Art 17 CEDAW and the Optional Protocol to CEDAW; for the Committee on the Rights of the Child regarding the Convention on the Right of the Child (CRC), see Art 43 CRC and the Third Optional Protocol to CRC; for the Committee on the Rights of Persons with Disabilities in relation to the Convention on the Rights of Persons with Disabilities (CRPD), see Art 36 CRPD and Optional Protocol to CRPD; for the Committee on Enforced Disappearances in relation to the Convention for the Protection of All Persons from Enforced Disappearance (CPED), see Art 29 of CPED; for the Committee on Elimination of Racial Discrimination with respect to the Convention on Elimination of All Kinds of Racial Discrimination (CERD), see Art 9, 11, 14 CERD and for the Committee on Economic, Social and Cultural Rights, which was established under ECOSOC Resolution 1985/17 (28 May 1985), in relation to the International Covenant on Economic Social and Cultural Rights (ICESCR), see Art 16 ICESCR and Optional Protocol to ICESCR. The individual complaint mechanism under the Migrant Workers Convention has not yet entered into force.

[23] eg states must have ratified the Optional Protocol to the ICCPR for complaints to be possible to the UN Human Rights Committee under that convention. See also Art 22(1) CAT; Art 14(1) CERD, Art 31(1) CPED.

Rights; the Committee on the Elimination of Discrimination against Women; the Committee on the Rights of the Child; the Committee on the Rights of Persons with Disabilities; the Committee on Enforced Disappearance of Persons; and the Committee on the Elimination of Racial Discrimination.

While, generally, human rights litigation before this growing range of fora requires an individual victim to bring a case against a state, it is also noteworthy that through the development of rules on procedure and standing, possibilities have emerged to collectivise complaints. Developments such as the *actio popularis* in the African system,[24] or enabling civil society organisations to bring claims in the European system,[25] represent new possibilities and remove some barriers to access justice on the supranational level.

Today, human rights litigation is not, however, limited to courts and bodies with a specific human rights mandate. Courts such as the International Court of Justice (ICJ) or the European Court of Justice (ECJ), although not human rights courts as such, are increasingly addressing human rights matters in the exercise of their jurisdictions.[26] The ICJ has become a key authority on the scope and applicability of human rights in recent years,[27] while the ECJ has had a growing role assessing compatibility with human rights standards on some issues; the latter may indeed have more progressive standards or approaches than its specific human rights law counterparts.[28] These courts are not accessible to

---

[24] The procedure before the African Commission and Court do not require a victim to bring a case: eg r 93 ACommHPR RoP 2010; Art 44 ACRWC and the *Ogoniland Case (Social and Economic Rights Action Center and Center for Economic and Social Rights v Nigeria)* Communication no 155/96, decision of 13–17 October 2001, which the Commission described as the clearest 'demonstration of the usefulness of the action popularis which is wisely allowed under the African commission' (para 49).

[25] In addition to cases in which the NGO may itself be a victim, and therefore applicant, the ECtHR has recognised that NGOs could bring cases on behalf of a deceased individual with no next of kin to bring the claim: *Campeanu v Romania* Appl no 47848/08 (17 July 2014) brought by the Centre for Legal Resources and Interights on behalf of a young man who died through horrific neglect in a care home in Romania. The Grand Chamber shifted its previously narrow approach to victim status.

[26] ECJ is part of the Court of Justice of the European Union (CJEU). Clear examples include the important *Kadi* cases before the ECJ on the lawfulness of EU terrorism lists (Joined Cases 402 and 415/05 *Kadi and Al Barakaat v Council and Commission* [2008] ECR I-6351; Joined Cases C-584/10 P, C-593/10 P and C-595/10 P *Commission at al v Kadi* [2013] ILEC 031 [CJEU]) and a series of human rights focused advisory opinions and contentious cases at the ICJ in recent years (eg *Legal Consequences of the Construction of a Wall in the Occupied Palestinian Territory* (Advisory Opinion) [2004] ICJ Rep 136; *Belgium v Senegal Case* (n 13); *Armed Activities on the Territory of the Congo (Congo v Uganda)* (Judgment) [2005] ICJ Rep 168; *Application of the Convention on the Prevention and Punishment of the Crime of Genocide (Bosnia Herzegovina v Serbia)* (Judgment) [2007] ICJ Rep 43.

[27] B Simma, 'The ICJ and Human Rights' in C Tams and J Sloan (eds), *The Development of International Law by the International Court of Justice* (Oxford, Oxford University Press, 2013) 301.

[28] The EU Charter of Fundamental Rights (CFR) was given binding status through the Lisbon Treaty, in force since 2009, which prompted a more active human rights role for the ECJ. See Art 52(3) CFR which notes that 'the meaning and scope of those rights shall be the same as those laid down by the [ECHR]. This provision shall not prevent Union law providing more extensive protection'. In eg the *Kadi* cases (n 27) it took a particularly robust approach to sanctions and basic human rights, while cases were pending before other fora including the ECtHR. In a range of issues related to labour law, consumer protection, freedom of movement and treatment of refugees, the ECJ has shown the impact it may have on rights protection in Member States in the future.

individuals in the same way as human rights courts, but they certainly are fora in which human rights issues can be adjudicated and determined with impact. The disputed impact of *The Wall* advisory opinion of the ICJ is discussed in the case study on land rights in Palestine.

As the *Hadijatou Mani v Niger* case study in Chapter 5 will highlight, the role of the sub-regional courts in Africa, and the Economic Community of West African States (ECOWAS) court in particular, provide examples of the new opportunities for effective litigation in that part of the world.[29] Although, like the ICJ and ECJ it is not a human rights court as such, ECOWAS member states adopted a Protocol in 2005 expanding the Court's jurisdiction to embrace human rights claims. The case study shows the influence of that case on the ECOWAS Court, while the court's binding authority, rules and procedures have been significant factors shaping the impact of that case.[30]

These bodies focus on determining state responsibility, reflecting the still state-centric nature of the international legal system.[31] The reality that non-state actors often exercise power and influence, and violate rights, sometimes to an equal or greater degree than states do, is increasingly recognised in international practice, but the international architecture of enforcement—including litigation—lags far behind. The lack of parallel procedures allowing individuals to bring claims against non-state actors is a major limitation in the current legal infrastructure that will not readily be overcome. However, just as human rights law and practice has slowly adjusted to recognise corporate human rights responsibility, proceedings such as Investor-State Arbitrations,[32] and the North American Free Trade Agreement (NAFTA) or the Organisation for Economic Co-operation and Development mechanism (OECD), have to some extent provided vehicles for human rights considerations to be brought to bear in the context of a range of disputes concerning investment and trade by non-state as well as state entities.[33]

---

[29] See the *Hadijatou Mani* case (ECOWAS Community Court of Justice, *Hadijatou Mani Koraou v Republic of Niger*, Appl no ECW/CCJ/APP/08/08 (27 October 2008), explored in Ch 5); see also the work of the East African Court of Justice. H Duffy, 'Human Rights Cases in Sub-regional African Courts: Towards Justice for Victims or Just More Fragmentation?' in L van den Herik and C Stahn (eds), *The Diversification and Fragmentation of International Criminal Law* (Leiden, Martinus Nijhoff Publishers, 2012).

[30] eg the decisions of the ECtHR, the IACtHR, the ACtJHR or the ECOWAS Courts are binding while the decisions of the HRC, the IACommHR, and the ACommHPR have traditionally not been so considered, although they give effect to binding treaties. The approach to this question may be evolving through jurisprudence. R van Alebeek and A Nollkaemper, 'The Legal Status of Decisions by Human Rights Treaty Bodies in National Law' in H Keller and G Ulfstein (eds), *UN Human Rights Treaty Bodies: Law and Legitimacy* (Cambridge, Cambridge University Press, 2012) 356.

[31] H Duffy, 'Human Rights Violations by Non-state Actors in the Americas: Can International Law Meet the Challenge?' (CEJIL, 2018 forthcoming).

[32] Convention on the Settlement of Investment Disputes between States and Nationals of Other States.

[33] S Schadendorf, 'Human Rights Arguments in *Amicus Curiae* Submissions: Analysis of ICSID and NAFTA Investor-State Arbitrations' (2013) *Transnational Dispute Management* 1 (2013) available at

Although not addressed in detail here, and extremely selective in their reach, international criminal law fora should not be overlooked. The impact of the International Criminal Court (ICC), for example, may lie in the dynamic that ICC jurisdiction fosters with national processes, as highlighted in two of the case studies on Palestine and the 'war on terror'.[34] The changing role of victims before these fora, and the potential for representation, participation and reparation (however limited),[35] may also influence the extent to which such processes may be seen as human rights processes, broadly understood, albeit with quite distinct objectives, procedures and remedies than complainant-driven human rights litigation.

Despite this progress, there remain glaring gaps in the geographic coverage of the regional human rights systems, and the requirement of state consent for many international human rights bodies. Proposals for a global international human rights court have long been advanced, but never borne fruit.[36] The result is patchy access to existing mechanisms in some parts of the world,[37] notably due to the absence of an Asian or Middle Eastern court of human rights.[38] Some Asian and Middle Eastern states have ratified universal treaties allowing victims to access the United Nations mechanisms, and allow litigation possibilities, but many do not.

www.transnational-dispute-management.com/article.asp?key=1935; See eg Centre for Settlement of Investment Disputes (ICSID), *Técnicas Medioambientales SA v Mexico*, ICSID Case No ARB (AF)/00/2, 29 May 2003 (known as the *Tecmed* case) in relation to expropriation and proportionality with regard to the public interest. See also UK National Contact Point (NCP) for the OECD Guidelines for Multinational Enterprises, *Lawyers for Palestinian Human Rights vs. G4S, Final Statement (March 2015)* available at www.oecdwatch.org/cases/Case_327.

[34] eg ICC jurisdiction arises in relation to eg settlement expansion in Palestine and torture in the war on terror, including in Afghanistan which is under investigation (though the ICC's reach is potentially much broader as many rendition states were parties to the Statute). Part of the ethos of the ICC, like human rights law, is 'positive complementarity'—incentivising states to meet their obligations in the knowledge that where domestic justice fails, the international mechanisms of complementarity could in principle be activated.

[35] See ICC Statute, Art 68 on victim participation, and Art 75 on reparation.

[36] See eg M Nowak, J Kozma, and M Scheinin, 'A World Court of Human Rights: Consolidated Draft Statute and Commentary' (May 2012) available at www.eui.eu/Documents/DepartmentsCentres/Law/Professors/Scheinin/ConsolidatedWorldCourtStatute.pdf. As a result of the lack of international appetite for a world human rights court, emphasis shifted to enhancing effectiveness and coordination between existing bodies. Some scepticism is due as to whether this is happening.

[37] Access to these bodies is sometimes dependent on ratification of particular treaties and (generally) the state accepting the jurisdiction of the mechanism as noted (n 23). As a result, the ability to challenge violations by the US, eg is limited because it has not accepted the jurisdiction of the IACtHR or the HRC, whereas the IACommHR has found it has inherent jurisdiction to consider violations by the US of the Inter-American Declaration of Human Rights

[38] Some Asian states have accepted the jurisdiction of the HRC, which has therefore addressed many individual petitions in cases against Sri Lanka, India and Nepal. Middle Eastern states falling in North Africa are bound by the African Charter mechanisms. The mandate of a new ASEAN Intergovernmental Commission on Human Rights was approved in 2010, representing the first human rights mechanisms in Asia, but it has been criticised for the absence of a formal mechanism of individual complaints; eg 'ASEAN Human Rights Body: Weak Mandate, Weak Protection' fidh Press Release (28 June 2009).

While proposals for additional systems, or new rights of petition within existing systems, are often advanced, resistance is considerable.[39]

SHRL against many of these states (or their representatives) can, therefore, only arise nationally or transnationally in foreign courts. Nevertheless, the impact of SHRL against other states may yet be felt, given the potentially global significance of litigation in shaping international law standards (in an area where the law is substantially developed through jurisprudence).[40] By triggering responses to widespread practices, human rights cases may also influence responses by other states that may not even be under the jurisdiction of the particular mechanism, thus having an impact beyond the states party to the case. Likewise, the standards that emerge from strategic human rights litigation may become relevant in domestic systems which are not part of a regional or universal human rights system, through the comparative interpretation of national laws in domestic courts or legislative processes.[41]

C. Diversification of Actors Engaged in SHRL

The increased opportunities for supranational litigation with the proliferation of new human rights courts and bodies on the international level, each with differing potentials and limitations, is paralleled by the growth and diversification of actors engaging with litigation as a tool for human rights protection.

The considerable number of NGOs nationally and internationally that focus specifically on, or engage with, 'strategic human rights litigation' is a relatively recent phenomenon. When I started with Interights in 2001 there was a handful of organisations focusing on SHRL. When I worked in Guatemala, with the exception of a few national NGOs (one of which was CALDH with which I worked), almost all the litigation work in the Americas was done by the Centro por la Justicia y el Derecho International (Centre for Justice and International Law—CEJIL), which remains a crucial operator in that arena, albeit now alongside others. In the meantime however, although the extent of civil society engagement with human rights generally, and on litigation specifically, and its capacity and effectiveness is obviously context specific,[42] the growth of NGO engagement with human rights issues has been remarkable in its scope.

As human rights law has increased in significance in many domestic systems, so has the involvement of individual private practitioners, sometimes working pro

---

[39] See ibid, on calls for an Asian body to receive individual complaints. Other calls for additional bodies, including in the Middle East and the Pacific, are on-going.

[40] See Ch 4 on Legal Impact.

[41] See below on the growing trans-judicial dialogue, and comparative reference between legal systems generally.

[42] The positive development of international civil society, and its growing interest in litigation as a tool, is tempered by the chilling reality of the attacks and setbacks that human rights defenders face around the world today (see section II on challenges below).

bono on the margins of other practice, sometimes through setting up dedicated human rights practices. In concert with these developments, has been the emergence and growth of law clinics and services, within public service and in academic institutions, across various parts of the globe, often with human rights litigation as a dimension of their work.[43]

In short, both the landscape of SHRL and the personnel engaged in it, have changed dramatically, bringing opportunities as well as perhaps some challenges. The diverse roles played by the different actors continually influence perspectives and approaches to human rights litigation, as discussed below.[44]

D. Developing Law and Broadening 'Trans-judicial' Dialogue

Recent decades have also seen the steady development of substantive international human rights law, which is significant to our enquiry in two obvious ways. First, this legal evolution has been both a goal and a product of (increased) SHRL. It was fully foreseeable that international law generally, and human rights law in particular, would be shaped (and indeed it will continue to be further clarified) by the active role of courts in the interpretation and application of skeletal treaty provisions in the context of particular cases.[45] This is discussed further in Chapter 4 on types and levels of impact.

In turn, the developing law provides the foundation for further effective litigation and the normative 'tools' for its expansion. This can be seen, for example, as the transformation in the changing approach to the 'justiciability' of economic and social rights in the national courts of many states[46] and also internationally.[47]

---

[43] The growth in the phenomenon of law schools active in human rights litigation, which originated in the US but has spread far beyond, contains a very positive dimension in terms of legal education of future practitioners, though it also poses challenges to ensure the quality of legal representation and advice.

[44] See section I.E and Ch 10 on strategic implications of the different litigation roles.

[45] See Chapter 3, section II.

[46] See eg M Farrell, 'The Role of Litigation: Giant Leaps and Baby Steps' (Amnesty International Conference: A Deficit of Protection—Economic, Social and Cultural Rights in Ireland, 22 November 2012). The South African litigation is perhaps the best known with cases such as the *Grootboom* case (*Republic of South Africa v Grootboom*, CCT11/00 [2000] ZACC 19), which sought to compel the government to provide accommodation for the homeless or the *Treatment Action Campaign* case (*Minister of Health v Treatment Action Campaign (TAC)*, No 1 CCT902 [2002] ZACC 16), which compelled the government to make anti-retroviral drugs available to persons living with HIV. In national courts in the global south, see Garavito and Franco, *Radical Deprivation on Trial* (n 4).

[47] The vacuum of mechanisms on the international level has slowly been filled through expansive approaches by some bodies, and the establishment of new ones; eg the ECSR is now operational, receiving collective complaints, while the Committee under the ICESCR can receive individual complaints under an Optional Protocol since 2013. Various African treaty bodies (eg Commission, Court, Committee on the Rights of the Child or ECOWAS) have jurisdiction over economic and social rights. The IACtHR and ECtHR have also given effect to some ESRs, and a strict division between economic and social rights and civil and political rights is increasingly unsustainable. In national courts in the global south, see Garavito and Franco, *Radical Deprivation on Trial* (n 4).

Litigation, including expansive litigation in many parts of the global south, has created a practical impetus that has broken through entrenched debates on whether such rights were inherently less susceptible to judicial intervention.[48] In this domain litigation has played a dynamic role in strengthening and giving effect to the law.[49] Another important development is the increasingly 'holistic' approach of human rights fora to interpreting human rights law in light of other areas of law, such as international humanitarian law (IHL) or the law on peace and security.[50] Growing recognition of the inter-relationship between human rights and environmental law is reflected in, for example, a ground-breaking advisory opinion of the Inter-American Court in 2018.[51] So doing, human rights fora have become significant as interpreters of a broader range of international law norms.[52]

The last two decades have borne witness to increased judicial openness in various forms, which provides opportunities for the cross-fertilisation of experience between systems.[53] There can be no doubt that SHRL has played an important role in transmitting significant legal advances across the borders of the states and regions in which violations took place. While systems vary vastly, it is common in many systems to see an increasingly outward-looking approach to other systems and practices, and a more fluid relationship between national and international law and practice, in various ways. This is reflected in the extent to which some national courts increasingly have regard to international legal standards, whether because they have become part of that state's constitutional or legal orders, or simply as tools in the interpretation and application of national law in national courts even where those standards are not seen as binding on the courts in question.[54] As a former Australian judge has noted, 'once, we saw issues and problems through the prism of a village or nation-state, especially if we were lawyers. Now we see the

---

[48] Not so long ago even among committed human rights lawyers there was resistance to economic and social rights as 'justiciable' but litigation has been donor and beneficiary in the notable shift in the past few years.

[49] The former UN High Commissioner for Human Rights, Mary Robinson refers to human rights having moved from an era of law creation to an era of implementation and enforcement.

[50] In practice, human rights courts have engaged increasingly frequently in recent years in the adjudication of human rights in conflict situations, requiring consideration of IHL. See H Duffy, 'Applicability of IHL' for the Max Planck Trialogues on the Law of Peace and War, Vol 2 (Cambridge, Cambridge University Press, 2018 forthcoming).

[51] See IACtHR, Advisory Opinion on the Environment and Human Rights, 7 February 2018, OC 23/17 (in Spanish).

[52] In theory, for the most part courts and bodies are considering other areas of law as aids in the interpretation of human rights treaties (not applying those areas of law as such). H Duffy, 'IHL Applicability of IHL' ibid, and L van den Herik and H Duffy, 'Human Rights Bodies and International Humanitarian Law: Common but Differentiated Approaches' Leiden Law School Research Paper; Grotius Centre Working Paper 2014/020-IHL in C Buckley, P Leach and A Donald (eds), *Towards Convergence in International Human Rights Law* (Leiden, Brill/Martinus Nijhoff, 2016).

[53] See eg 'Bangalore Principles on the Domestic Application of International Human Rights Norms', *Report of Judicial Colloquium on the Domestic Application of International Human Rights Law*, reprinted (1988) *14 Commonwealth Law Bulletin* 1196.

[54] Many of the 'new' constitutions drawn up in the past 50 years contain references to international law, while legislation in more states incorporates regional or international law in the domestic order.

challenges of our time through the world's eye'.[55] The influence of SHRL in this context is explored further in Chapters 4 and 10.

One important dimension of seeing human rights challenges 'through the world's eye' is the burgeoning phenomenon of 'trans-judicial' dialogue.[56] This judicial borrowing or conversation arises horizontally (between national courts in different states), diagonally (between regional, sub-regional and international bodies) and vertically (between national and international courts).[57] Indeed, the regard of supranational human rights courts and bodies to the decisions of one another, once controversial in some systems, has become commonplace.[58]

The result is that human rights litigation can have a much broader effect on shaping standards beyond its immediately apparent national or regional scope of influence. This opening of systems to international law and comparative practice, and to what a former US Supreme Court justice has called 'the value of a global view of law',[59] greatly increases the significance of human rights litigation for national orders, and the progressive development of international human rights law.

E. Increasing Role for *Amicus Curiae*/Third Party Interventions

Another significant development in recent years that opens up the space for strategic litigation has been the increasing receptivity of courts to '*amicus*' briefs or third-party interventions.[60] Such interventions in human rights litigation across

---

[55] M Kirby, Justice of the High Court of Australia, in *Through the World's Eye* (NSW Australia, Federation Press, 2000).

[56] The phrase was first coined by AM Slaughter, in 'A Typology of Transjudicial Communication' (1994) 29 *University of Richmond Law Review* 99. See also KG Balakrishnan, 'Role of Foreign Precedents in a Country's Legal System' (2010) 22 *National Law School of India Review* 1, dealing with Indian and US courts.

[57] See 'Pluralism or Harmony' (report prepared for the Workshop on 'Judicial Borrowing', sponsored by the Universities of Nottingham (Human Rights Centre) and Middlesex, 23–25 June 2013), on file with author.

[58] The Inter-American system has always been relatively open to standards from elsewhere, whereas at one time the ECtHR frowned upon regard to 'alien' standards, but now frequently draws on other interpretations. Courts look in particular to other systems to interpret comparable provisions, though cases such as *Murillo v Costa Rica (Artavia Murillo et al (In Vitro Fertilization) v Costa Rica)*, Judgement (Preliminary Objections, Merits, Reparations, and Costs) IACtHR Series C No 257 (Ser C) No 257 (28 November 2012) exemplify how even textually distinct provisions will today be interpreted in light of the approach of others courts and bodies as part of a 'contextual' and 'systemic' approach to interpretation. See eg Buckley, Donald and Leach, *Towards Convergence in International Human Rights Law* (n 51).

[59] See Justice Stephen Breyer, *The Court and the World; American Law and the New Global Realities* (New York, Penguin), and www.nytimes.com/2015/09/13/us/politics/justice-breyer-sees-value-in-a-global-view-of-law.html. While some US courts in recent years have famously rejected international sources of law (eg in some war on terror litigation at Ch 7) other cases show that federal and state courts do still draw on comparative practice and international law sources, not just in the context of Alien Tort Claims Statute (ATS) litigation.

[60] The number of states whose courts accept *amicus* briefs has expanded, including in states with no tradition of such interventions, and even where there were no laws or procedures specifically so

international, regional and national courts can allow a range of expertise to be brought in as 'friend of the court', enabling diverse perspectives to influence the litigation process. These contributions fill various roles in practice. They may enhance the court's (or the public's) understanding of the broader significance of a case, giving the litigation a strategic dimension it was not seen to have at the outset and increasing its potential to advance human rights goals.[61] Third-party interventions are often also the vehicle that make possible the judicial comparisons and borrowing, mentioned above. There are examples, nationally and internationally, of *amicus* practice developing from the litigation process, whereby interventions were accepted case by case and led eventually to the role of *amicus* being formalised in the relevant court or body.[62]

In conclusion, the panorama that emerges is of new fora, expanded jurisdictions and a multiplicity of venues for strategic human rights litigation, and an intricate network of regional and international courts and treaty bodies that can hear human rights claims if national remedies fail. The volume of human rights claims has grown exponentially, in part as rights awareness increases, with tens of thousands of supranational cases brought annually.[63] Human rights litigation has expanded into new areas of law and practice, and diversified to reveal a colourful portfolio of rights-focused litigation. As human rights litigation has developed, many of the key prerequisites to effective litigation are now in place, with the existence of adequate substantive law, legal mechanisms, engaged actors and a legal-cultural shift as part of the phenomenon of juridical globalisation. At the same time, as we peruse this rich and fertile landscape, we should be aware of potential blind spots, and acknowledge the very serious contemporary challenges to human rights litigation.

II. Challenges and Limitations to Pursuing Human Rights Litigation

In practice, a vast array of challenges, domestically and internationally, often precludes victims, survivors and human rights advocates from accessing justice at all.

---

providing in domestic systems. On the supranational level, *amicus* interventions are possible before most if not all bodies, and the practice has increased significantly. See A Dolidze, 'Bridging Comparative and International Law: Amicus Curiae Participation as a Vertical Legal Transplant' (2015) 26 *European Journal of International Law* 851.

[61] See Ch 10 on strategic use of such interventions.

[62] The impact and strategic use of third-party interventions is touched on again in Chs 3 and 9 respectively.

[63] The ECtHR alone received 53,500 applications that were allocated to a judicial formation in 2016 (see 'Analysis of Statistics 2016' available at www.echr.coe.int/Documents/Stats_analysis_2016_ENG. pdf). In the same year, the IACommHR received 2,567 individual petitions (see 'Annual Report 2016' available at www.oas.org/en/iachr/docs/annual/2016/TOC.asp). 16 new contentious cases were submitted to the IACtHR in 2016 (see 'Informe Annual' available at www.corteidh.or.cr/tablas/informe2016/).

It can be, and often is, among the goals of SHRL to expose, challenge and overcome some of these obstacles.[64] Indeed, the obstacles, may directly influence the strategy: Chapter 10 looks more closely at how those seeking to use litigation can try to meet some of the challenges in the way they develop litigation strategy to maximise impact.[65] The following are just some of the impediments to bringing human rights litigation that are the backdrop to understanding the potential and limitations of litigation today, on the national and international levels.

A. Impediments to Access to Justice at the National Level

At the national level, multiple impediments stand in the way of victims, survivors, their representatives and civil society bringing human rights cases. These may be legal, political or practical. They range from reprisals and vulnerability, to costs and delays, to corruption and systemic dysfunction, to the more subtle impact of the power dynamics underpinning violations and the justice system itself, or simply the lack of support to bring claims. Together they often impede SHRL from the outset, or eviscerate positive impacts.

i. Legal/Jurisdictional Obstacles

In some cases, obstacles are direct and enshrined in law or judicial practice. One example from the case studies are laws on amnesty that blocked litigation at some point in the Argentinian and Guatemalan contexts, until they were eventually set aside or limited in their scope, in part through litigation. Doctrines of state secrecy used by courts to disallow certain types of claims, sometimes precluding access to court at all, are another. This has been seen most clearly in the rendition and war on terror contexts as discussed in the case study, but also in the doctrine of 'non-justiciability' in the Israeli courts, and the 'act of state' doctrine advanced before UK courts.[66] Broadly interpreted immunities likewise prevent even serious human rights cases from being brought against certain defendants particularly in foreign courts.[67] Very obvious legal obstacles arise from weak legal standards that

---

[64] Examples appear under Ch 4 and the case study chapters.

[65] As noted above, some challenges can be worked around, and turned to advantage, more than others. Some require deep-rooted institutional reform. At a minimum, strategy will need to take into account the challenges as part of a context-specific approach.

[66] See Chs 7, 8 and 9. In most cases of war on terror allegations, brought against the state, state secrecy has blocked litigation entirely, though some cases have been allowed to proceed against private actors—such as Blackwater in Iraq, or psychologists involved in the CIA rendition and torture programme.

[67] Cases against the state, even for serious human rights violations, have been deemed covered by state immunity under international law. Attempts to challenge this as incompatible with human rights law—including in strategic interventions Interights presented with Redress, Amnesty and others— have been largely unsuccessful (see eg ECtHR, *Al Adsani v UK*, Appl no 35763/97 (21 November 2001); *Jones at al v UK*, Appl nos 34256 and 40528/06 (14 January 2014). See also Case Concerning the Arrest Warrant of 11 April 2000 (*DRC v Belgium*) [2002] ICJ. It is different for officials, and certainly for former officials and even former heads of state (as the *Pinochet* case in 1998 famously established.)

do not reflect human rights on the domestic level, the lack of full incorporation of international human rights standards, and varying approaches to the relevance of those standards domestically, based on the relationship between national and international law. Litigation may help shape the law, but it is also undeniably curtailed by the normative tools available and their potential domestic force.

ii. Access to Evidence and Proof

Many challenges arise in the building up and presentation of a compelling case against the state or other powerful defendants, especially where the relevant information rests with the state.[68] These might include situations where access to evidence is denied or limited, especially in cases involving national security or state secrecy, as illustrated by the extraordinary rendition cases. Securing access to information may be a long, painstaking and fruitless quest that needs to precede litigation (though securing such access may also be the object of specific litigation and a significant form of litigation impact, as noted in Chapter 4).

iii. Pressure on Victims and Human Rights Defenders and Closing Civil Society Space

The vulnerability of victims, lawyers, activists and those that support human rights litigation today is evident from the alarming incidence of attacks on litigators and other human rights defenders in recent years.[69] Direct attacks are coupled with legislative changes that in varying ways impede and criminalise activity associated with SHRL. 'Counter-terrorism' laws have expanded to impede and prohibit various forms of association and expression. The application of laws criminalising 'material support' or 'indirect incitement' of terrorism to constrain human rights advocates has had a devastating impact, including on would-be applicants, civil society support and human rights litigators.[70] Defamation laws are also used to sue or indeed prosecute those critical of the state, including those pursuing legal action.[71] In this context, crackdowns on the freedoms of lawyers

---

[68] Human rights courts have flexible rules on evidence and burden of proof that can address this reality, but national systems often do not.

[69] News reports indicate many examples of lethal attacks on human rights lawyers around the globe: eg. in Chechnya (www.hrw.org/news/2016/03/17/russia-rights-defender-attacked-chechnya); LGBT rights activists in parts of Africa (eg *Africa Review*, www.africareview.com/News/Cameroon-gay-activist-killed/-/979180/1916972/-/ao6bf6/-/index.html); and in Latin America (eg N Lakhani, 'Human Rights Lawyer's Home Ransacked in Guatemala in Latest String of Attacks' The Guardian (15 August 2016)).

[70] See H Duffy, *The 'War on Terror' and the Framework of International Law* (Cambridge, Cambridge University Press, 2015) Chs 4 and 7. Turkish human rights lawyer Tahir Elçi was being prosecuted for 'propagandising for terrorism' at the time of his extrajudicial execution, in November 2015. Since then hundreds of lawyers and others have been detained on the same basis.

[71] 'Defamation Laws are Necessary. But They Must be Narrowly Drawn' *The Economist* (13 July 2017).

and activists 'not seen in a generation' have proliferated across the globe.[72] In this context human rights litigation has been portrayed (and prosecuted) as 'inciting subversion of state power',[73] 'insulting government institutions',[74] or 'propagandising for terrorism'.[75] Blocking 'foreign funding' of NGO's, pro-bono lawyers and other activists—on the pretext of security—and manipulating registration requirements have been used to impede this form of human rights work in many states.

Rules on standing may also play a part in limiting the possibility of cases being brought. Requirements that certain types of action can only be brought by a 'victim' of the violation, not others on his or her behalf, collectively or indeed by NGOs acting in the public interest more broadly, may in reality mean that some types of violations affecting vulnerable groups are not brought to court, or where they are, claimants fall away in the course of litigation (see also section B below).[76]

iv. *Judicial Independence, Impartiality and Capacity*

It goes without saying that an independent judiciary is—almost always[77]—a pre-requisite for effective international human rights litigation (though ways to achieve positive impact despite the judiciary are highlighted in the case studies and Chapter 10 below). The independence deficit is a crucial problem in many states today.[78] Even in states where the judiciary enjoys reasonable independence, public disrespect for judges can serve to undermine it: in very recent times, high-profile attacks on 'so-called judges'[79] by the Trump administration in the US, and

---

[72] See eg 'Human Rights Groups Face Global Crackdown "not seen in a generation"' *The Guardian* (26 August 2015) available at www.theguardian.com/law/2015/aug/26/ngos-face-restrictions-laws-human-rights-generation.

[73] See eg, among many others, Chinese human rights lawyer Xie Yang being arrested for 'inciting subversion of state power' in 'China: Human rights lawyer released on bail amid relentless crackdown' *Amnesty International News* (10 May 2017) available at www.amnesty.org/en/latest/news/2017/05/china-human-rights-lawyer-released-on-bail-amid-relentless-crackdown/.

[74] In Bahrain, Mohamed al-Tajer, a human rights lawyer, was charged in 2016 with such incitement; 'Bahrain: Human Rights Lawyer Charged' *Human Rights Watch* (1 December 2016) available at www.hrw.org/news/2016/12/01/bahrain-human-rights-lawyer-charged.

[75] Turkish laws on 'propagandising for terrorism' which have been used against many lawyers, academics and activists in Turkey during 2016–17 as this book was being written.

[76] While difficult to generalise, it is the case that multiple intersecting vulnerabilities and pressures can make it very difficult to pursue claims in practice. For example, in my experience this has regrettably often been the experience trying to bring women's rights claims; experience in the African and Inter American contexts is noted in Ch 10.

[77] There may, as noted below, be occasions on which the litigation serves to highlight the inadequacy of judicial responses and the lack of independence and impartiality.

[78] See Annual Reports of the Special Rapporteur on the Independence of Judges and Lawyers, available at www.ohchr.org/EN/Issues/Judiciary/Pages/Annual.aspx.

[79] A Wang, 'Trump Lashes out at "so-called Judge" who Temporarily Blocked Travel Ban' *The Washington Post* (4 February 2017) available at www.washingtonpost.com/news/the-fix/wp/2017/02/04/trump-lashes-out-at-federal-judge-who-temporarily-blocked-travel-ban/?utm_term=.dd8fa8160316.

strident attacks by both government and the press in the UK, exemplify the problem. Paradoxically, stigmatisation of the international protection of human rights and the use of litigation in particular has been a feature of political discourse in several states, specifically in the counter-terrorism context: in a surprising juxtaposition, the US's 2005 National Defence Strategy identified the use of 'international fora, judicial processes and terrorism' as among 'strategies of the weak'.[80] In particular since 9/11, judiciaries have been publicly denounced by governments for standing up to them on security issues, or even daring to ask them to render account.[81] Pressure has also been applied on judiciaries from foreign states, in a further demonstration of the politicisation of justice.[82]

The case study on Palestinian land rights issues before Israeli courts, shows how goals can be frustrated when the judiciary bows unduly to the executive or military or avoids adjudicating on an issue due to extra-legal considerations. This gave rise to what Sharon Weill identified as patterns of response from the Israeli High Court, that constitute apology, avoidance, and undue deference to the state's discretion.[83] In many situations, special courts or tribunals have even been set up to try certain types of cases, with serious rule of law implications. Questioning their legitimacy or exposing their lack of it, has been the subject of legal challenges, such as the cases challenging US military Commissions touched on in Chapter 7, or the *Taba* case which I argued for Interights in which the Supreme State Security Emergency Court in Egypt was found by the African Commission to lack independence.[84]

The capacity of judges and lack of resources are also often huge challenges. Among the case studies below, this is best illustrated by the *Hadijatou Mani* case study. In this case, the judiciary's own case law may not have been known or available to them.[85]

---

[80] The National Defense Strategy of the United States of America (March 2005) available at www.au.af.mil/au/awc/awcgate/nds/nds2005.pdf, 6.

[81] President Musharraf took exception to the Supreme Court's requests to the Interior Ministry for answers on enforced disappearances: see Human Rights Watch, 'Destroying Legality: Pakistan's Crackdown on Lawyers and Judges' Report (18 December 2007) available at www.hrw.org/report/2007/12/18/destroying-legality/pakistans-crackdown-lawyers-and-judges; For another example in the UK, see the comments of Lord Bingham in *A and Others* [2004] UKHL 56 in the UK House of Lords, Ch 7; *cf* Statement by Home Secretary Teresa May to the Conservative Party Conference, in A Travis 'Tories Promise to Scrap Human Rights Act After Next Election' *The Guardian* (30 September 2013): 'Some judges chose to ignore parliament so I am sending a very clear message to those judges. ... Parliament wants the law on people's side, the public wants the law on the people's side'.

[82] See Ch 7; Wikileaks exposed meetings set up by the US administration to discuss cases pending before Spanish courts, and the COE Commissioner for Human Rights, Thomas Hammamberg, described 'enormous pressure from Washington' on national investigative authorities, which have compromised proceedings aimed at ensuring in war on terror accountability.

[83] S Weill, *The Role of National Courts in Applying International Humanitarian Law* (Oxford, Oxford University Press, 2014). Ch 9.

[84] In the *Taba* case (*Sabbahand Others, Egyptian Initiative for Personal Rights and Interights v Arab Republic of Egypt*, Communication No 334/06 (9th Extra-Ordinary Session, 23 February to 3 March 2011)), one of the objectives of the international litigation was to expose the lack of independence domestically. The case was argued with Hossam Baghat of EIPR; Egypt suspended the executions of the convicts pending retrial.

[85] *Hadijatou Mani* case (n 29); Ch 5.

v. Lack of Legal Aid, Resources and Costs

Resource constraints, resulting in part from the lack of 'legal aid' in many parts of the world, particularly for cases before international courts and bodies, have implications for victims' ability to secure representation, and may limit the way litigation can be done and thus potentially, its quality.[86] In some systems, including within the US, public funding has been restricted for public interest litigation.[87] Even more troubling though is the impact of costs following judgment in certain systems, which makes lodging legal action an intrinsically risky enterprise for lawyers and NGOs that may otherwise be willing and able to take cases pro bono. Domestic systems vary, and some have exceptions for public interest litigation, which may become increasingly common if the importance of such litigation is appreciated.

The challenges posed by the costs of litigation are hardly new: in his book *The Rule of Law* (2011) Lord Bingham cites a complaint from 350 years ago that, in matters of justice '[t]he remedy is worse than the disease. You must spend 10 pounds to recover 5!'.[88] The reality today is that for many reasons equality before courts remains elusive, in line with the old adage that 'Justice is open to all, like the Ritz hotel'. Funding for long-term litigation is key, but often in short supply.

B. Obstacles to Access to Justice at the Supranational Level

Many of the same challenges that confront access to justice domestically arise on the international level. The following are some of the most problematic issues that arise specifically on the international level.

i. Outstanding Gaps

Glaring gaps in the geographic scope of jurisdiction of international and regional human rights courts, mean that the majority of the world's population still has no access to a regional or international remedy at all.[89] Already noted are the lack of a global human rights court (despite proposals) and of a dedicated Asian or Middle Eastern court or human rights mechanism.

---

[86] See *Report of the Special Rapporteur on Independence of Lawyers and Judges*, 'Legal Aid: a Right in Itself' UN Doc A/HRC/23/43 (15 May 2013).

[87] J Stein, *Statement on Litigating the Right to Health, Conference on Litigating for Social Change* (Belfast, October 2016).

[88] Bingham, *The Rule of Law* (n 19).

[89] Reservations, and limited acceptance of UN Committees, noted above, compounds this.

ii. Overload and Delays

Paradoxically, some major challenges are linked to what might be seen as progress: the growing volume of litigation, and number of actors aware of and participating in litigation, has led in some contexts to system overload or at least strain. This is most dramatic before the ECtHR where, at peak overload in 2012, approximately 128,100 applications were pending,[90] a figure that has decreased in very recent years but the volume and backlog remains daunting.[91] The same problems are developing—or foreseen—in other systems.[92] This has implications for delays in rendering decisions[93] and the manner in which cases are handled.[94]

Extremely lengthy international proceedings often seriously compromise the ability to provide effective redress. This is exemplified in cases such as *Atala Riffo* and *Daughters v Chile*. While this case made history by upholding equal parental custody rights of a lesbian woman, the applicant's children had grown by the time the decision was handed down.[95]

Many factors may contribute to delays. For example, a high-level official within the ECtHR spoke of the need for 'more responsible lawyering', arguing that resort to the system must be more selective and more strategic. The major challenge, however, must be the insufficient resources being allocated to meet the growing needs of human rights courts and bodies. Systems vary as regards resources (eg the African system's budget is one eighth that of the ECtHR) but the problem is common to all the existing systems.[96] The IACommHR suffered harsh cutbacks in 2016, a measure that was widely criticised as causing a crisis in

---

[90] ECtHR 'The European Court of Human Rights in Facts & Figures 2012' (June 2013) available at www.echr.coe.int/Documents/Facts_Figures_2012_ENG.pdf.

[91] By the end of 2016 it stood at 79,750 currently 'Pending Cases 2016' *The European Court of Human Rights* (2016) 5, www.echr.coe.int/Documents/Stats_pending_2016_ENG.pdf.

[92] eg in 2015 the IAtCHR received 2,164 new petitions while 9,673 were still pending initial review. See F Ramos, 'The Need for an In-Time Response: The Challenge for the Inter-American Commission on Human Rights for the Next Decade' (2011) 18 *Southwestern Journal of International Law* 159.

[93] Excessive delays characterise some systems, but *cf* the ECOWAS determination in the *Hadijatou Mani* case (n 29), which took 1 year, to delays of up to 10 years at the ECtHR. See with regard to the Inter-American system, A Dulitzky, 'Too Little, Too Late: The Pace of Adjudication of The Inter-American Commission on Human Rights (2013) 35 *Loyola L.A. International & Comparative Law Review* 131.

[94] These may include eg summarily dismissing cases, inadequate consideration or limited judicial reasoning.

[95] *Atala v Chile*, IACtHR, 24 February 2012.

[96] It has been noted that the ECtHR budget is 80 times the budget of the African Commission; see J Sarkin 'The African Commission on Human and People's Rights and the Future African Court of Justice and Human Rights: Comparative lessons from the European Court of Human Rights' (2011) 18 *South African Journal of International Affairs* 284. The IACtHR and IACommHR are similarly underfinanced, and rely on voluntary contributions from member states and other countries outside of the region: see recent report on crisis of funding in the Inter-American system; eg NC Sánchez León, 'The Silent Checkmate Against the IACHR' *Global Rights Blog* (23 May 2016) available at www.dejusticiablog.com/2016/05/23/the-silent-checkmate-against-the-iachr/. Though see also 'IACHR Overcomes its Severe Financial Crisis of 2016 and Thanks Countries and Donors who Made it Possible' IACommHR Press Release (30 September 2016) available at www.oas.org/en/iachr/media_center/PReleases/2016/145.asp, and on-going implications.

the Inter-American system, with implications for the ability to process cases, the way they are processed and potentially even the Commission's independence.[97] Although in the short term, the crisis was averted, the underlying structural deficiencies of the system, which depends on the goodwill of donors, are not resolved.[98] The financial restraints and pressures in the Inter-American system of the IACHR unfold under the political shadow of the 'condemnation of monitored States against their watchdog', particularly dangerous in times of limited financial resources.[99]

iii. *Growing Politicisation of International Human Rights Litigation*

Growing politicisation of human rights litigation in recent years manifests itself in different forms, with troubling reflections across all systems. These arise amidst, and cannot be dissociated from, a much larger phenomenon of pushback against international human rights. In this context 'hardening pleas … to fetter international judges' abound.[100] A clear example is how the work of supranational courts (especially the ECtHR) has been subjected to harsh criticism in sectors of the British media and political echelons.[101] It should not be overlooked though, that criticism of human rights courts and bodies is at the same time, a testament to their effectiveness: it reflects the fact that the decisions of these institutions have gained importance in the domestic legal systems and generated pressure on states to meet their international obligations (which they may eventually do, even if under protest).

In Europe, compliance with judgments of the ECtHR, once considered essentially inevitable,[102] has given way to some (albeit still relatively rare) incidences of shameless non-compliance. Particularly strident pushback has come from the UK, Turkey and Russia, though the political climate at the time of writing suggests the problem may be broader. In the UK, the Courts' decisions on prisoners'

---

[97] The IACommHR had always an insufficient budget, which in 2013 was further decreased while the number of cases is constantly rising. This led to the 2016 'crisis' and the announcement that 40% of the Commission's staff were to be dismissed. See eg Sánchez León, 'The Silent Checkmate Against the IACHR' (n 94) and IACtHR Press Release, 'Severe Financial Crisis of the IACHR Leads to Suspension of Hearings and Imminent Layoff of Nearly Half its Staff' (23 May 2016) available at www.oas.org/en/iachr/media_center/PReleases/2016/069.asp.

[98] The IACommHR receives 6% of the general budget from the Organization of American States and is reliant on the goodwill of donors.

[99] Sánchez León (n 94).

[100] This phrase was used in M Adams et al (eds), *Judging Europe's Judges: The Legitimacy of the Case Law of the European Court of Justice* (London, Hart Publishing, 2017) 1. Not all such pleas are necessarily politically motivated, reflecting legitimate and different views on the judicial role, but in the current climate many cross the line into unacceptable interference with the judicial function.

[101] So far as one level of potential impact in Ch 4 relates to fomenting debate and shaping attitudes, the negative coverage of, eg ECtHR decisions in the British press and the demonisation of applicants, can have a very destructive effect, though open debate on controversial issues can ultimately help air concerns and progress rights protection in the longer term.

[102] The need to comply may have gone unquestioned, at least publicly, though implementation has always been stronger on, eg compensation rather than structural reforms or investigation.

voting rights, security and immigration have proved particularly contentious.[103] Turkey has an increasingly poor record of implementation, and has established a controversial remedy to block access to the ECtHR via means of derogation.[104] In 2015, the Russian Parliament amended the federal law on the Russian Constitutional Court providing the Court with the competence to declare the implementation of judgments of a human rights body impossible on the ground that they are unconstitutional. After the amended law came into force on 14 December 2015 the Russian Constitutional Court applied the law for the first time at the beginning of 2016 when dealing with the implementation of the ECtHR judgment in *Anchugov and Gladkov v Russia*.[105] The similarity in some of the reactions from states is striking, and may suggest a degree of coordination, or at least strong signalling, between member states and a follow-the-leader to the back of the line approach. While in most cases, such as the UK, opposition has remained political, in Russia 'open defiance' has become structural, through the new legislation and judicial decisions applying them. The negative impact of the developments in Russia can already be seen in other countries.[106]

Political push-back is evident across systems. In the Americas, Argentina is the latest once-compliant state to refuse—for the first time—to give effect to a judgment of the Inter-American Court.[107] Perhaps the most extreme example of pushback, which comes from outside Europe this time, relates to the Tribunal of the South African Development Community (SADC tribunal), which was closed down at the instigation of the Zimbabwean government following a high-profile case against it, in which mainly white farmers argued a land redistribution programme violated their rights.[108] While this move by the Zimbabwean government

---

[103] The UK, for the first time, indicated its unwillingness to amend legislation to allow for prisoners to vote (*Hirst v United Kingdom (No 2)* Appl no 74025/01 (6 October 2005); Greens and MT v United Kingdom Appl no 60041/08, (23 November 2010) and demands have become louder for a replacement of the Human Rights Act 1998, which incorporated the ECHR in UK law, with a British Bill of Rights. See for critical assessment of Conservative plans, House of Lords' European Union Committee, *The UK, the EU and a British Bill of Rights* (HL 2015–16, 139); there has also been discussion of derogating in situations of armed conflict in response to claims relating to alleged violations in Iraq and Afghanistan.

[104] See eg Derogation to the Convention on the Protection of Human Rights and Fundamental Freedoms (ETS No 5), Notification—JJ8187C Tr./005-191 (22 July 2016); see for a comment, M Scheinin, 'Turkey's Derogation from the ECHR: What to Expect?' *Blog at EJIL:Talk!* (27 July 2016) available at www.ejiltalk.org/turkeys-derogation-from-the-echr-what-to-expect/ and *Report of the Committee on Legal Affairs and Human Rights of the European Parliament*, 'Implementation of judgments of the European Court of Human Rights, Doc 13864 (9 September 2015) para 16.

[105] *Anchugov and Gladkov v Russia* Appl no 11157/04 (4 July 2013). This is just a last step in a series of events, starting with the *Yukos* judgment of the ECtHR; *Oao Neftyyanaya Kompaniya Yukos v Russia* Appl no 14902/04 (31 July 2014).

[106] Statement of the Council of Europe Commissioner for Human Rights Nils Muižnieks on the non-implementation of the Court's judgments (23 August 2016) available at www.coe.int/et/web/commissioner/-/non-implementation-of-the-court-s-judgments-our-shared-responsibility.

[107] Judgment of the Argentine Supreme Court in Ministerio de Relaciones Exteroires y Culto s/informe sentencia dictada en el caso Fontevechia & D'Amato v Argentina 14 February 2017.

[108] The case dealt with the expropriation of mainly white farmers' property without compensation in Zimbabwe under a government land redistribution programme. Before the Tribunal the farmers

provides a particularly ugly symbol of the politicisation of justice in the region,[109] the recent threats and (limited) withdrawal from the ICC by some states is similarly disturbing.

All these responses may be seen as dramatic manifestations of a broader and more fundamental problem, which is of the lack of respect for, and commitment to, human rights institutions, and to accountability under human rights law.[110] Issues of independence, impartiality and capacity that arise on the international level—from securing independence of international judges from their states,[111] securing adequate nomination, appointment and election procedures, ensuring adequate training and capacity in international human rights law[112] and redressing gender inequality,[113] among others—all have an impact on the standing and legitimacy of the international judicial bodies. The impact of SHRL is necessarily linked to this legitimacy, and to the associated realities of how the justice system in question operates in practice, noted below.

iv. 'Reform' of Human Rights Courts and Bodies: Positive and Negative Consequences

Proposals and initiatives for 'reform' in the European[114] and Inter-American[115] systems in particular, many of which have been justified as necessary to meet the problems of overload and delays, have brought positive results and serious challenges.

There is no doubt that ECtHR reform has reduced backlog and may expedite cases and ensure that judicial attention can be focused on the most urgent ones, yet some developments in the rules and procedures intended to improve efficiency present serious problems in practice. Strict approaches to complex application forms means that even a minor clerical error will lead to applications being

---

sought to prevent state forces from proceeding with the removal of the farmland. On the initiative of the Zimbabwean government the Tribunal's capacity to hear individual applications was suspended in 2012 and terminated following another meeting of the Heads of Government.

[109] See eg F Cowell, 'The Death of the Southern African Development Community Tribunal's Human Rights Jurisdiction' (2013) 13 *Human Rights Law Review* 153.

[110] The threats of withdrawal from the ICC by African states form part of similar problem.

[111] This takes many forms; an extreme example before the African Commission challenged a sitting Attorney General on the Commission; Interights took the case to the Commission (in a sense, against the Commission); see Attorney General, *Botswana v Unity Dow* (124-/1990 (CA No 4)).

[112] See eg ECOWAS Court's decisions in the *Hadijatou Mani* case, and the need it exposed (n 29).

[113] This has recently been highlighted by a campaign for gender equality, GQual run by CEJIL, see www.gqualcampaign.org.

[114] The 'Brighton Declaration' on reform of the ECtHR led to Protocol 15 ECtHR, adopted 13 May 2013. It addresses reform of the ECtHR though many of proposed reforms that would have limited the scope of ECHR practice were rejected.

[115] On 29 June 2011, the Organization of American States Permanent Council created the Special Working Group to Reflect on the Workings of the IAComHR with a view to strengthening the Inter-American Human Rights System (IAHRS) (Special Working Group). A report by the Special Working Group was approved by the Permanent Council in January 2012, and later welcomed by the Organization of American States General Assembly.

sent back, and often out of time, even in important meritorious applications. A stricter and more streamlined approach to admissibility may have reduced excessive repetitive or unfounded claims, but the very high rate of cases deemed inadmissible by a single judge, based on limited information, can appear somewhat arbitrary. As the Human Rights Committee has rightly noted in a quiet rebuke of the ECtHR procedure, the limited (or non-existent) reasoning provided makes it impossible to know if the case is thrown out on procedural or substantive grounds, and whether the ECtHR has really 'considered' the case at all.[116] Interestingly, on this basis, the Committee has concluded that in such circumstances a case may be admissible before it, notwithstanding the rule that where the case has already been considered by one human rights body it is generally not admissible before another body.[117] The refusal to give even a basic indication of why a case is rejected—time limits, procedural irregularity, manifest unreasonableness or no violation of a right under the convention—has a powerful negative impact, on the court's credibility and on victims. In one important case, a client of mine inexplicably received a two-line letter declaring the case inadmissible, without grounds or explanation, with no possibility to seek clarification or appeal. Ironically, such practices show an international court not meeting the most basic standards of justice and due process that it rightly expects of states. The Registry of the ECtHR has committed to addressing this, and the challenges are undeniable, but current practice is part of the problematic reality facing would-be litigants.

In the Inter-American system, the chronic resource problem has translated into (or worsened) procedural problems, which necessarily affect the speed, quality and ultimate impact of human rights processes on several levels. On one view, a lack of clarity in the rules of admissibility and procedure has impeded the Commission's efficiency and transparency.[118] From another, more pragmatic perspective, the lack of staff means that rules of procedure must necessarily adjust.[119] In the African context, it only became apparent to me in the course of a hearing on legally complex and important issues that, in an effort to improve efficiency, the Commissioners themselves were not seeing the applicants' arguments but only a summary (which the applicants and counsel did not see).[120] In all systems, ongoing 'reform' is essential to improve efficiency while still meeting the system's essential human rights goals and basic standards of justice.

---

[116] *Achabal v Spain*, Communication No 1945/200, UN Doc CCPR/C/107/D/1945/2010 (18 June 2013); *Peterson v Germany*, Communication No 1115/2002, UN Doc CCPR/C/80/D/1115/2002 (30 April 2004) para 6.4.

[117] The rule varies slightly between bodies and contexts. Art 5(2)(a) of the Optional Protocol to the ICCPR and the reservation entered by Spain and 17 other states.

[118] Ramos, 'The Need for an In-Time Response' (n 91) at 174.

[119] Ibid, 173.

[120] The case was *Taba* case (n 83) and the hearing in Swaziland concerned inter alia state security courts, mandatory penalties, safeguards against torture. Often only 1judge rapporteur will read the pleadings.

v. Limited Remedies, Reparation and Implementation

Systems vary greatly as to the forms of remedy and reparation they afford. The Inter-American system leads the way in its approach to creative, holistic and case-specific reparation, as the Guatemala case study demonstrates. The African system in turn has led the way in, for example, collective remedies, as cases such as the *Ogoniland* case (cited above in relation to the *actio popularis*) or *Enderois* case show.[121] In keeping with the ECtHR's narrow approach to 'just satisfaction', by contrast, the state is generally bound to pay damages but not *how* to remedy its violation. This informs, and can in practice limit, the types and extent of the impact that can be achieved by the judgment itself. However, as the rendition case study shows, in situations where the Council of Europe's Committee of Ministers is willing to engage fully with the implementation, requiring detailed responses from the state in question, the system may yet enable a broader discussion on reparation through a dynamic dialogue post-judgment.

As regards awards of damages, these are often characterised by a lack of transparency or clear principles. Some quite unprincipled distinctions have crept into practice: in certain terrorism and security-related cases some applicants, found to be victims of unlawful killing or ill-treatment, have nonetheless been denied damages, on apparently dubious bases.[122]

Implementation of decisions is notoriously poor in many systems. Unsurprisingly then, the matter has increasingly become a focal point for attention by civil society organisations.[123] The scale of this problem is hard to ascertain and depends partly on whether implementation is understood to mean simply giving effect to steps specifically ordered by the court (and, as noted, steps required and remedies awarded vary greatly), or whether proper reparation would entail giving some fuller effect to the judgment.[124] As this has been the subject of detailed analysis in recent years it is not addressed in detail in this study, but, it is striking that at least one report suggests that only 15 per cent of remedies ordered by the

---

[121] *Ogoniland* case (n 24). See also eg the broad approach to reparation in the *Enderois* case, *Centre for Minority Rights Development (Kenya) and Minority Rights Group (on behalf of the Enderois Welfare Council) v Kenya* (2010) Communication No 276/03 (25 November 2009).

[122] *McCann v United Kingdom* Appl no 18984/91 (6 October 1995) is the key case here, where IRA suspects killed in Gibraltar were denied damages despite the unlawful nature of their killing, on the basis of their role in the circumstances leading to their death. See also the very disappointing decision on damages in *Mashkadova and Others v Russia* Appl no 18071/05 (6 June 2013); *Matthews v United Kingdom* Appl no 24833/94 (18 February 1999); *cf* the damages award noted in the *Abu Zubaydah* case (*Husayn (Abu Zubaydah) v Poland* Appl no 7511/13 (28 January 2013)), was appropriately significant.

[123] OSJI Report, 'From Judgment to Justice: Implementing International and Regional Human Rights Decisions' November 2010, available at www.opensocietyfoundations.org/reports/judgment-justice-implementing-international-and-regional-human-rights-decisions; *Interights Bulletin on Implementation*. See eg 'Increasing the Impact of Human Rights Litigation: Implementation of Judgments and Decisions' (2010) 16 *Interights Bulletin*. See the formation of the European Implementation Network in 2016.

[124] V Krsticevic, 'A Strategy for Improving the Level of Implementation of Judgements in the Inter-American System' (2010) 16 *Interights Bulletin* 91.

ACommHR have been fully complied with,[125] and another, that only 14 per cent of those ordered by the ACommHPR have been fully implemented.[126] In several systems, these difficulties in implementation have prompted the creation of various mechanisms, and improvements, for follow-up of implementation that may change the landscape going forward.[127] Implementation rates vary not only between systems, but also between types of remedies.

Interestingly but perhaps not so surprisingly, compliance with compensation awards is generally strongest across systems (perhaps as awards tend to be modest in human rights proceedings); by contrast implementation is (perhaps predictably) weakest in decisions ordering proper investigation or stipulating that accountability be established,[128] or demanding guarantees of non-repetition.[129] This no doubt constitutes an important contributing factor in situations where the cycle of violation and litigation is on-going.

vi. The Resources Challenge

Despite proposals to introduce fees, which have thus far been resisted, presenting an international case is not itself costly, and there are examples of groundbreaking judgments with powerful impacts that have been handed down for relatively low cost.[130] In practice, however, building up a good strategic case and ensuring complementarity, action and sustained follow-up—which can be necessary to ensure the case's impact—can be costly. In any case though, the victims most affected by serious abuse are generally not in a position to meet the costs involved in bringing cases at all. There are some limited possibilities for victims

---

[125] F Viljoen, 'State Compliance under the African Charter of Human an Peoples' Rights' (2010) 16 *Interights Bulletin* 60; Krsticevic, 'A Strategy for Improving the Level of Implementation of Judgements in the Inter-American System' (n 122); OSJI, 'From Judgment to Justice' (n 121).

[126] L Louw, 'An Analysis of State Compliance with the Recommendations of the African Commission on Human and Peoples' Rights' (LLD thesis, University of Pretoria, January 2005).

[127] One mechanism at the ACtHPR would provide for a change in the format of the reports that the Commission presents to the Summit of the African Union, as well as various forms of follow-up, time limits to respond and other steps. In Europe, in addition to formal systems, NGOs have specifically been set up to focus on implementation; see B Çalı and N Bruch, 'Monitoring the Implementation of Judgements of the European Court of Human Rights: A Handbook for Non-Governmental Organisations' (University College London, 2011) available at www.ecthrproject.files.wordpress.com/2011/07/monitoringhandbook_calibruch1.pdf.

[128] 50% of the awarded compensations in the IACHR are paid, but only 2% of investigations and prosecutions required by the judgments are undertaken: CEJIL report, *ibid*. In the European system too, almost full compliance with pecuniary just satisfaction awards contrast with poor or incomplete compliance in terms of effective investigations. See also Ninth Annual Report of the Committee of Ministers, Supervision of the Execution of Judgments and Decisions of the European Court of Human Rights (2015). See also case study on *Abu Zubaydah v Poland* in Ch 7.

[129] Ibid; see also an example related the Argentina case study 'Implementación En El Ámbito Nacional de las Decisiones De Los Sistemas Regionales e International De Derechos Humanos—a report by the 'Asociación por los Derechos Civiles (ADC)' *Revista Sur*, 2011 on the disappointingly low level of implementation of measures of non-repetition.

[130] See the *Hadjitou Mani v Niger* process in Ch 5.

to obtain legal aid for human rights cases before the European,[131] African[132] and Inter-American human rights courts,[133] but they must meet requirements that are stringent and often unattainable. In practice, it is only through the support of human rights lawyers and NGOs that these cases can be brought at all, and used effectively. Lagging donor support for litigation has become a huge impediment to SHRL in recent years.

vii. The Burden on Victims: Standing and Status, Vulnerability and Dropping out

Many national legal systems, like most supranational human rights courts and bodies, require that action is brought by a victim of the violation—ie a person directly harmed by the wrong in question. In practice, those directly affected by serious violations are often unable or unwilling to bring such claims, or to sustain them, for a host of reasons related to inter alia powerlessness, pressure, and insecurity of one type or another. Regrettably, this has meant that some types of violations are under-represented in litigation: they are often not brought to court, or where they are, it is not unusual for claimants to fall away in the course of litigation. During my years with CALDH in Guatemala, we prepared multiple claims on behalf of women facing violations of their rights in notorious maquilas (sweatshops). Several of these were lodged but withdrawn. At Interights years later, we devoted a lot of attention and effort to trying to bring women's rights claims before the African Commission, which at that point remarkably had decided no such cases at all. Eventually, we broke through that barrier but the number of cases remains limited.[134] On the other hand, some women's rights cases that were brought, with good effect, in the European system were difficult, fraught processes for the victims involved. As discussed further in Chapter 10, these difficulties can be mitigated to some extent by collective or *actio popularis* claims where possible. As already noted, these are accepted in some contexts, such as in the African system, and the European Economic and Social Rights Committee, where important decisions have addressed issues that are intrinsically collective in nature. Although the ECtHR and ACtHR have to varying degrees shown willingness to abandon

---

[131] See eg. the requirement for legal aid set out in Art 6(3)(c) ECHR; Open Justice Initiative and Public Interest Law Institute, 'European Court of Human Rights Jurisprudence on the Right to Legal Aid' (2006) *Colombia Law School* 4–5.

[132] African Court on Human and Peoples' Rights Legal Aid Policy 2014–2015 at 2, available at http://en.african-court.org/index.php/2016-10-10-11-10-29/office-of-the-registrar/item/27-legal-aid-policy-2014-2015.

[133] As for the IACHR, see Art 2 of the Rules for the Operation of the Victims' Legal Assistance Fund that state that victims who wish to access the Victims' Legal Assistance Fund may be able to do so if they lack the economic resources necessary to cover the cost of litigation before the Inter-American Court, and require use of the resources of the Victims' Legal Assistance Fund their participation in proceedings.

[134] Interights and EIPR (*Al Kheir v Egypt* (Communication No 323/06)) was the first of still few women's rights cases decided by the Commission.

a rigid approach, in the interest of justice, litigation still depends on, and comes at great cost to, individual victims.

By way of conclusion to this chapter, litigation against perpetrators of human rights violations—whether they are states, non-state groups or individuals—has expanded enormously in the last few decades and made impressive advances. It undoubtedly faces considerable obstacles in various forms, including serious political pushback from some states, the curtailing of the independence of the judiciary or undermining of its respected status and legitimacy, funding cuts, inadequate support and protections for victims undertaking the litigation journey, and many challenges to adequate and effective reparations. Despite the challenges, human rights litigation is being invoked at a rate never seen before, and has achieved some remarkable results, for the direct victims of violations and far beyond. In Chapters 3 and 4 we analyse the many, distinct types of impact that can—and do—result from strategic human rights litigation. That analysis will be followed by five case studies demonstrating these impacts.

3

Understanding Impact: Bursting the Bubble on the Champagne Moment

I. Adjusting the Lenses to Capture the Impact of SHRL

There is often a tendency to look at litigation through an unduly narrow frame. Our understanding of the impact of SHRL may depend in large part on the lenses through which we view it, what we are looking at, when and why. We might think of an old *camera obscura*, with its tiny hole that projects a single image into a darkened room. In this narrow frame, the tendency may be to focus on what happens inside the courtroom or the pleadings; as lawyers trained to carefully craft arguments and to analyse, persuade and manoeuvre our clients towards the light, we may be particularly prone to this. Or, even more commonly, the focus may be on judgment day, seen as the culmination of the litigation journey, when fates will be sealed and justice done. In this narrow and static view, the end point is the familiar photo of triumphant lawyers and clients on the steps of the court after judgment is rendered—the proverbial (and sometimes literal) champagne moment celebrating litigation 'success'.

We know of course that the reality is quite different. A winning judgment that remains (as many do) unimplemented may change little. A judgment, whether won or lost, that creates legal or political backlash, may aggravate the situation on the ground. Conversely, a losing case that exposes injustice and catalyses further action may ultimately be transformative. The need to rethink success in human rights litigation is plain: as Jules Lobel noted, we must be able 'to see the success without victory', and conversely recognise that failure may follow fast on victory's heels.[1]

No one frame can capture the complexities of the impact that SHRL can have. In this chapter, I will suggest that to understand more accurately the significance

---

[1] J Lobel, *Success Without Victory; Lost Legal Battles and the Long Road to Justice in America* (New York, NYU Press, 2004).

of human rights litigation, we need to jettison the old *camera obscura* and adopt more modern, sophisticated lenses.

First, we need a high-definition lens to enable us to pick out the detail in the picture and to study the diverse, multi-dimensional sites or levels of impact of SHRL. We need to consider impact on victims, survivors and their families and communities, on perpetrators and institutions, on the law and public policy, on attitudes, discourse, behaviour, and on fundamental principles such as rule of law and democracy.

Second, a long lens, or perhaps a time-lapse function, is needed to see how impact unfolds and evolves over time. We then capture not only the significance of the judgments themselves, but look beyond to see how the spectre of litigation may have begun to influence change before cases are even presented, how impact may arise or continue throughout the process at multiple stages, or only take effect long after judgment.

Third, a wide-angled lens is required to understand litigation in context. This reflects that the impact or influence of litigation will always depend on the context from which it emerges and with which it interacts. Moreover, litigation is always located among other agents for change, such as civil society advocacy, education or legislative reform; they are crucial to the effectiveness of the litigation, and in turn the litigation often feeds into and catalyses these other processes.

Finally, the question of perspective cannot be ignored. It is critical to our choices as litigants, representatives and human rights defenders, to the outcomes we strive for, and it influences how we perceive impact. The starting point should be the perspective of the victim, in whose names cases are brought and to whom the process should, in principle, belong. At a minimum, for legal representatives with ethical duties to our clients, a priority should be to ensure that the immediate victims remain at the centre of our unfolding litigation picture. This does not preclude (with care and attention) a strategic approach that seeks to maximise the impact of litigation for a broader range of beneficiaries. But as litigation unfolds, we need to consider to what extent the process continues to be seen through the applicants' eyes, whether they remain at the centre of our litigation picture, or are they expected to cede room to other factors, such as the impact on other victims and survivors, or the need to protect others in the future?[2]

Beyond the applicants to whom the case belongs, many other actors will bring diverse perspectives. Lawyers are only one set of important actors in SHRL and it should be recalled that there is much to be learned from a multi-disciplinary perspective.[3] As between lawyers and legal actors, those with different roles may also be differently positioned as to the way they consider impact, and the 'strategic litigation' enterprise in general. Private lawyers trained to strictly advance their

---

[2] See Ch 10 on resolving conflicts and ensuring ethical and professional standards are met.
[3] The need for lawyers to reflect self-critically on impact and to avoid assumptions concerning litigation's impact was noted in Ch 1. On the importance of multi-disciplinary litigation teams, see Ch 10.

client's interests may be less inclined to—or even understandably cautious of—the idea of the 'strategic' use of litigation and may not consider it their role to assess 'impact' at all. NGOs and activists on the other hand may be primarily attuned to how the case will affect a broader range of victims, or prevention and protection more generally, or have a specific interest in advancing particular issues or groups, the situation in particular states or regions, or other agendas. Legal academic commentators may tend (at times, but by no means always) to focus on jurisprudential or systemic impacts, or to shy away from questioning impact at all, given the methodological quagmire and its inherent resistance to analysis and proof.

The diverse perspectives brought by multiple actors are potentially complementary in fully understanding the difference that litigation makes, its potential and limitations. In viewing impact, we should endeavour to ensure that the full range of visions are reflected, and acknowledge that you cannot entirely take the photographer out of the photograph.

II. Approaches to Impact and the Meaning of Success

Certain characteristics of SHRL impact come into focus when we view litigation through the three lenses set out (at section I) above.

A. Impact as Multi-dimensional

Litigation can lead or contribute to many diverse levels of impacts in a variety of ways, some of which will be readily apparent, while others require closer enquiry. There are various ways to categorise and explore these levels of impacts, which have been used by commentators looking at the role of the courts in particular issues or contexts. We may consider for example the broad *types* of impact (such as material and non-material, concrete and symbolic impacts, for example),[4] *who or what* is affected (victims, perpetrators, the law, the courts themselves or the public for example), or *how* litigation brings about change (such as through what has been described as the 'unlocking', 'participation', 'reframing' or 'socio-economic' effects of national courts in economic and social rights cases.)[5] This book combines elements of each of these approaches. The framework set out in this study breaks impact down further by considering eight inter-related

---

[4] C Rodríguez Garavito and D Rodríguez Franco, 'Cortes y Cambio Social: Como la Corte Constitucional transformó el desplazamiento forzado en Colombia' (2010) *Centro de Estudios de Derecho, Justicia y Sociedad, Dejusticia*: the OSJI impact studies referred to in the Preface use 3 heads—material, 'legal, judicial and policy' and 'non-material' impact.

[5] See also C Rodríguez Garavito and D Rodríguez Franco, *Radical Deprivation on Trial: the Impact of Judicial Activism on Socioeconomic Rights in the Global South* (Cambridge, Cambridge University Press, 2015).

levels of impact: on victims, law, policy and practice, institutions, information gathering and truth telling, social and cultural change, mobilisation and empowerment, and democracy and the rule of law. On each of these levels, as noted below, it considers how the impact may be positive or negative, or both, when viewed at different stages or from diverse perspectives.

Undoubtedly, impact can also be direct, anticipated, plainly visible and relatively incontrovertible. It may arise as the 'outcome' of a case as seen in examples of victim compensation paid diligently following a court order, the immediate impact of declaratory judgments or the development of the law through jurisprudence. There are examples of each of these direct and irrefutable changes brought about by litigation in the case studies in Chapters 5–9. More often than not, however, impact is indirect and may not have been anticipated or foreseeable at the outset of the process. Perhaps precisely as the link with litigation is more difficult to discern, and certainly to prove,[6] less direct and measurable impacts may tend to go unregistered. This is particularly so where impacts are distinct from the goals of the case, or are less positive in nature, such that there is less incentive for those involved to monitor and expose them.

Or it may simply be that some layers of impact are hidden or disguised at first sight and require more careful enquiry. The contribution of litigation to gradual processes of social, political, legal or cultural change for example—shaping attitudes, discourse and political space for example—are sometimes hardly perceptible and often impossible to quantify. They may nonetheless be among the most important ways in which litigation can help to change the human rights landscape, and understanding the contribution is essential if we are to appreciate the value of the litigation tool.

B. Appreciating the Contribution of Litigation in Context: The Wide-angled View

As noted above, the impact of litigation is impossible to understand out of context. Political and social context, and timing, have an immense influence on the impact that litigation can have. Perhaps the most fundamental dimension of the way we approach litigation impact relates to understanding how it grows from, interacts with and forms part of that broader *context*. Just as politics has often stymied litigation, directly and indirectly, changing political contexts, or moments of political openness and opportunity, have facilitated—or created the space for—effective litigation.[7] In turn, litigation has had a role in contributing to and consolidating

---

[6] See the doubtful measurability of litigation at section III below.

[7] On apartheid South Africa, and the changing role of the judiciary in that context, see R Abel, *Politics by Other Means: Law in the Struggle Against Apartheid* (New York, Routledge, 1995). On interference with judicial processes and impact, see case studies on arbitrary detention and rendition, and land rights in Palestine.

political shifts and opportunities for more progressive litigation in the future.[8] In this complex area, where a vast medley of factors may contribute to change, context is the crucible from which litigation's impact will emerge and understanding it is critical to honest reflection on the role of litigation.

This dynamic relationship between context and litigation impact is clear from across the case studies. The Guatemalan peace process, or the enduring power of the perpetrators of the worst massacres, provides the substrate to the impacts (and limitations) of the Guatemalan genocide litigation in Chapter 6. Global geo-political realities impeding accountability in the 'war on terror' context, or resolution of land rights in Palestine under Israeli occupation, are an integral part of the impact story in those case studies in Chapters 7 and 9. Likewise, the eagerness of the state of Niger to (be seen to) meet its international obligations is the wind in the sails of anti-slavery initiatives in Niger following the *Mani* case at Chapter 5, albeit while the context of entrenched slavery and discrimination provide resistance.

The case studies also reveal a second dimension to the deeply contextual nature of human rights litigation. SHRL is almost always only one agent for change, alongside the other forms of advocacy, legal or political strategies by civil society organisations, activists, survivors, lawyers, international allies and others, that seek to respond to and address human rights violations. Litigation is very often just one component, and not necessarily the most impactful, and we must try then to understand the impact of litigation in this broader frame. The extent to which it contributes to and facilitates, or frustrates, these other processes, is likely to be critical to its ultimate utility. In practice, we often see strategic litigation on entrenched injustice—from apartheid South Africa to impunity in Argentina—prospering following long periods of national and international activism.[9]

It certainly follows naturally from the ambitious nature of some of the goals and impacts that SHRL may pursue as set out at Chapter 4 that they go beyond the aspirations of any case or judicial determination. Litigation may be a catalyst, contributor or facilitator to such change, without necessarily being an identifiable (still less the sole) trigger. What we explore then may be not so much whether litigation provided a *solution* (which will only rarely be the case, given the broad-reaching social or political problems that underpin many rights violations), nor whether change is *caused* by or attributable to it; rather we should consider the *contribution*—perhaps indirect and gradual—that litigation may have made alongside and in relationship with other processes and factors.

---

[8] As noted under section V, litigation may change the information available, the terms of the debate, or alter the political cost-benefit ratio in a way that indirectly influences the political context. See eg Ch 8 case study on Argentinian litigation towards accountability for enforced disappearance during dictatorship.

[9] See Ch 8 and J Dugard and M Langford, 'Art or Science? Synthesising Lessons from Public Interest Litigation and the Dangers of Legal Determinism' (2011) 27 *South African Journal on Human Rights* 39.

Just as litigation's effect cannot be isolated from political and social movements, nor can it be fully understood by isolating particular individual cases or judgments. Impact may only come into focus as we consider clusters or series of cases, which alone may be of minor significance or represent small steps but considered together represent much larger strides forward.[10] A key feature of litigation impact is therefore its cumulative nature. As the massive body of litigation on disappearances in Argentina exemplifies (Chapter 8), it may be part of a multi-staged journey involving a series of strategies that adjusted to opportunities and dodged obstacles to eventually have a wide-reaching impact. Each stage had a discreet impact but its true effect cannot be seen except by standing back and viewing the litigation in the context of the steady progress of the human rights and accountability struggle in that country more broadly. Certainly, it is not always the case: the *Hadijatou Mani v Niger* case study (Chapter 4) presents a prime example of the interactive power of a single case, producing multiple impacts at many stages, albeit in dynamic relationship with many enabling and contributing factors.

C. Impact over Time: The Threat of Litigation, the Power of the Process and the Longer-term View

Assessing impact involves more than a snapshot of any one point of time. Looking only at when a case is won or lost or when judgments are implemented will reveal a very limited sense of impact. Rather, at one end of the spectrum, there are many examples of the *spectre* of litigation generating recognition and reactions of various types. One case study in Chapter 7 illustrates how securing access to lawyers at Guantanamo—opening up the site to the world's view and providing a link between detainees and the world—in *anticipation* of habeas litigation, was perhaps the most significant impact of that litigation, arguably more indeed than the 'historic' Supreme Court ruling that followed or the limited habeas hearings themselves.[11]

The desire to *avoid* litigation can itself be a powerful force for change, sometimes inducing or feeding significant change even before (or indeed absent) a case itself. This has impelled policy change in the hope of rendering the litigation moot, as when truth, justice and reconciliation processes have been pushed forward in part under the shadow of litigation.[12] Settlements out of court have also played an important role. In particular, dynamic settlements or conditional suspension of proceedings can have interesting catalytic effect, as seen by those

---

[10] The tactical implications for litigation—and the advantages of series of cases—are discussed in Ch 10.

[11] See Ch 7 on Litigating the War on Terror.

[12] It has been suggested eg that the Kenyan Nyayo House torture litigation prompted advances in the Kenyan truth, justice and reconciliation process; H Duffy, 'Strategic Litigation Impacts: Torture in Custody' Open Society Justice Initiative (Open Society Foundations, 2017) ('Litigating Torture in Custody' study).

that helped inch towards accountability in Guatemala for example (where massacres litigation before the IACHR was suspended pursuant to an agreement that included promising accountability, and resumed when that agreement was not met).[13] They have led to wide-reaching commitments to strengthen legal frameworks through ratifications or law reform.[14] The terms of settlements can be more far-reaching and significant in some cases than any judgment or remedies award—as the *Khadr* settlement, requiring an apology from the Canadian government, shows.[15] Conversely, the refusal to settle can itself speak volumes.[16]

At the far end of the spectrum, impact may be felt long after judgment is rendered; indeed, there may be no identifiable end point to the process of gradual social change that the litigation pursued at all. This underscores the importance of long-term commitment and the engagement of multiple actors with relevant skills and capacity discussed in Chapter 10.

In between the threat of litigation and the very long-term implementation of judgments, is the often-neglected power of the process. This may take many forms and arise at multiple stages including through preparation, participation and the conduct of proceedings. The case studies highlight evidence and information gathering, the organisation and mobilisation of complainants and others—for litigation purposes but with broader benefits—the role of testimony and the public truth telling function of the litigation itself, among others.[17] Particular moments in the litigation process, especially public hearings, may also catalyse reactions. In my experience of international proceedings, it is quite common for sudden and surprising 'developments' to be announced by governments during or immediately before a hearing, often after years of delay and inertia, as they seek to avoid embarrassing exposure or international condemnation.[18]

---

[13] See the *Dos Erres* settlement and the dynamic with the *Plan de Sánchez* case in Ch 6 on Genocide Litigation in Guatemala.

[14] See eg the friendly settlement in the early inter-state Turkish cases at the European Commission on Human Rights, which provided a framework for political commitments on legislative reform and ratifications or the wide-reaching impact of agreements in relation to prison conditions; Duffy, 'Litigating Torture in Custody' (n 12).

[15] See Arbitrary Detention and Rendition in Ch 7—apology formed a crucial part of the June 2017 settlement of long-running domestic litigation in the *Khadr* case, arguably beyond what courts would have ordered at the end of the process.

[16] See Ch 6; in the *Belhaj* rendition litigation in UK courts the government was willing to pay millions (the government actually paid out 2.2 million pounds in a similar case brought by Sami al-Saadi) but not three pounds and an apology as the applicant sought. The *Belhaj* claim for damages has been allowed to proceed (Supreme Court 2017) and is pending at July 2017.

[17] See eg the *Mani* (slavery) and *Plan de Sánchez* (genocide) case studies, Chs 5 and 6 respectively, which illustrate all of these elements in different ways, or the debate over the role of litigation in the OPT.

[18] Examples of shifting government positions to avoid litigation, or in immediate anticipation of a hearing, are many; see eg *Metwalli v Egypt* before the AfCommHR in which Interights was involved, where a Muslim cleric, imprisoned for views on interfaith marriage and conversion, was released just before the session.

Finally, impact is rarely linear, but reflected in a series of advances and setbacks, as all case studies illustrate. The challenge is often not in achieving, but in sustaining, impact. It is, moreover, commonly incremental in nature, as noted in relation to the contextual view above. Both features underscore the importance of not viewing impact and influence in any single moment but as they evolve over time.

D. Redefining 'Success'

As is already plain, positive impact is about much more than winning or losing a case and we need to shift focus from the steps of the courtroom on judgment day. What happens out of court, or in the proverbial 'court of public opinion' may be more important than what happens in the courtroom, or what is written in the judgment. We need to consider whether there really is 'success without victory', and 'power [in] the losing case'.[19] A case may be successful for example if, as noted below, it forced open political space and debate, and exposed injustice, as a number of the case studies highlight, even if ultimately the claim failed in court.[20]

Judgments that ultimately find against applicants on the basis that the law so provides and the courts must apply it, may do so in terms that send strong messages from the judiciary to the other arms of government, catalysing democratic responses through law reform or policy change. Examples are multiple in the war on terror context, where UK courts have effectively reprimanded their own government, parliament, or indeed other states for action that curtailed rights, even while finding in their favour.[21] Moreover, even judgments that are not only unfavourable but appear unjust may in certain circumstances serve a function: exposing to public criticism and international scrutiny the extent of the denial of justice, or paving the way for international litigation or other forms of pressure for example.[22]

Conversely, a favourable judgment that is not implemented, at the end of a traumatising process, may be a success neither for the applicant nor for the rule of law more broadly. One case often cited in this context is the famous *Grootboom* South Africa Constitutional Court case affirming housing rights under the South African constitution. It was hugely significant in many ways, yet as a former colleague

---

[19] Lobel, *Success Without Victory* (n 1).

[20] See eg Ch8 Land Rights in Palestine case study.

[21] See examples from 'War on Terror' Litigation Ch 7, where courts have reluctantly found against the applicants but have often sent stern reprimands to the executive or to a foreign executive en route. Examples from UK courts include references to 'handing the terrorists a victory that no act of theirs could achieve' by laws that restrict human rights (eg *A & Others v United Kingdom* Appl no 3455/05 (19 February 2009) (ECHR)). In *Binyam Mohamed v Secretary of State for Foreign and Commonwealth Affairs* [2009] EWHC 152 [69], the Court expressed disbelief that a 'democracy' would ask the courts in another state to repress public passages concerning the applicant's torture.

[22] See OPT cases study: will Israeli decisions on non-justiciability have this effect? Judgments that are not implemented can, however, have multiple negative impacts for victims, and for the rule of law, as noted above.

Iain Byrne wrote, it ends with the question '*Did Mrs Grootboom get her House?*'[23] (Of course she did not). Unimplemented judgments still make a difference, but whether they are 'successful' depends on what you ask, who you ask, and when.

Rejection by the state of a judicial decision, or refusal to implement, is a blow for the rule of law. However, even determining when judgments are 'followed' or given effect by states is a complex question. States before international human rights bodies generally state that they will implement a decision, and then may not do so fully (as case studies and implementation proceedings before the Committee of Ministers of the COE testify).[24] The reverse may also be true, whereby states may take the cases more seriously than their policy or posturing allows them to admit.[25] The fall-out from the ICJ judgment in the *Avena* case—wherein the ICJ ordered the United States to provide 'review and reconsideration' of the convictions and sentences of 51 Mexican nationals on death row whose consular rights it had violated—has been cited as an example which illustrates the complexity of the dynamic.[26] The United States announced that it disagreed with the ICJ's interpretation of the Vienna Convention on Consular Rights and the remedies the Court ordered, and withdrew its consent to ICJ jurisdiction over future disputes relating to the Convention. Despite this, a subsequent presidential 'memorandum' explains decisions by reference to the United States 'discharg[ing] its international obligations' and referring to the *Avena* judgment.

Cases may, and often do, create a dynamic between the international judiciary, executive and domestic judiciary that is not apparent from the judgment or post-judgment rhetoric.[27] In this and myriad other ways, impact is nuanced, and cannot be measured in the 'champagne moments' when litigation is 'won' or indeed in the whisky moments when it is lost.

III. Monitoring and (the Challenge of) Measuring Impact

Evaluating effectiveness is essential in order to litigate responsibly and strategically, as discussed later in this book.[28] It is also an essential prerequisite to learning lessons from the past and making choices about where and how to focus work in

---

[23] I Byrne, 'Did Mrs Grootboom get her House?'16(2) *Interights Bulletin* 2010.

[24] *Abu Zubaydah v Poland* Appl no 7511/13 (24 July 2014) before the ECtHR in the rendition study—outstanding commitments have been made through the Council of Europe process of implementation, alongside little visible progress.

[25] See eg the multi-faceted changes following the case despite US opposition: K Alter, L Helfer and M Helfer, 'How Context Shapes the Authority of International Courts' (2016) 79 *Law and Contemporary Problems* 1.

[26] Ibid.

[27] Examples in the case studies include Israeli courts' responses to the Wall Advisory Opinion (ICJ) 2004.

[28] Ch 10.

the future. As mentioned above, increasingly, it is necessary for organisations to account to funders and stakeholders, making monitoring more common and in some ways more important for litigating organisations.[29]

For some forms of direct 'outcomes' from litigation, this may be relatively straightforward.[30] It must also be recognised however that, some of the levels of impact identified below are more resistant to measurement than others. Consider the sort of broad social change that SHRL may pursue, which is a generational process: at what point could one demonstrate with confidence, for example, that attitudes have changed or a rule of law culture has been strengthened? Even if we could, *how* would we show the impact or contribution of litigation to that gradual social change? Some changes may be more readily identified, but similarly difficult to attribute to litigation given that, as noted, the litigation is most commonly a contributor to diverse dimensions of long-term change alongside other processes, rather than the direct producer of them.

It may be partly for this reason that matrices of measurement as such are perceived to be of limited utility and are not much relied upon by SHRL actors. Analyses of impact to date in particular contexts or in relation to particular rights have similarly distanced themselves from any attempt at 'quantification'.[31]

At the same time, these limitations and complexities around measurement make careful enquiry more, not less, important. Even if we cannot prove or attribute impact with any degree of certainty, we may still gain valuable insights from the (often neglected) careful questioning of those most affected, during and after the process, and by drawing into the frame the experience and perspectives of multiple actors.[32] Myriad indicators of progress towards goals can be gleaned from, for example, changes in laws and policies on the subject matter of litigation, the transformation of jurisprudence and subsequent reliance on it, statements by political actors, media coverage and its content, patterns of changing behaviour or incidence of violations towards affected groups, or growing numbers of similar types of cases lodged in the future, among many others.

But caution is undoubtedly due. While efforts to ascertain the impact and influence of litigation is essential, acknowledgement by litigators, supporters and funders that to a large extent, the significance of SHRL is substantially immeasurable, is certainly preferable to distortion. We may never know for sure the full extent to which litigation shaped, contributed to or influenced some types of effective change (and should continue to explore effective theories or approaches

---

[29] See personal reflection on this in the Preface on historic neglect, and see Ch 10 on the importance of this as part of developing sound litigation strategy.

[30] See s II.A above on examples of direct impact which are easier to demonstrate.

[31] See eg OSJI studies noted in the Preface, which adopt a similarly flexible approach to the one adopted here.

[32] In some cases their perceptions are themselves an important form of impact—whether the sense of identity or empowerment of particular victimised groups, or of being subject to oversight by potential perpetrators.

to evaluation of relevance in this particular field).[33] But we can still learn from and reflect on different perspectives and available indicators of progress, however imperfect. In this spirit, the chapters that follow seek to make sensitive enquiries into the impact and influence of litigation in diverse contexts.

IV. Classifications and Distinctions

In order to crystallise the types and levels of impact that litigation may have (identified in the next Chapter, and illustrated in the case studies in subsequent chapters), it is worth clarifying certain distinctions between SHRL impact and other terms closely associated with it.

A. Impact versus Goals

First of all (at the risk of stating the obvious), goals and impact are not the same. Goals are formulated by the parties and their lawyers—whether in a particular case or as part of a broader plan—and are the object of the litigants' intentional efforts and hopes. By contrast, impact emerges, and can be positive and negative, intended and unintended. Certainly, unfolding impacts may influence the (re)formulation of goals as the litigation advances.

The enquiry in this book is above all aimed at understanding what difference SHRL actually makes—its impact—rather than the lofty, or indeed more modest, goals it may pursue at the outset. If we focus on goals and strategies at the outset of litigation, we may risk excluding from our analysis the many cases that have turned out with the benefit of hindsight to have had great impact on multiple levels, perhaps beyond what anyone could have anticipated at the time. We may also risk focusing on contexts where certain types of 'litigation strategies' can be developed, usually by NGO actors, but excluding the opportunity to learn from impact litigation by individuals and their lawyers in contexts where civil society engagement and support is limited for a host of reasons including repression and lack of political space.[34] The focus on 'impact' rather than 'goals' as the essential issue may also reflect the reality, borne out by the case studies, that many of the most striking forms of litigation impact may not have figured as 'goals', or have been foreseen or perhaps even foreseeable, at the outset of the processes.

---

[33] There is no developed theory on how to evaluate litigation as such, for good reason. Various theories are used to evaluate human rights work in general, though their limits are widely acknowledged; the problem is not exclusive to SHRL. 'Theory of change' is referred to in setting up strategy in Ch 10 and has relevant observations on evaluating effectiveness after the fact.

[34] Civil society involvement and support, in various forms, is likely to be critical to the impact of SHRL, as noted in Ch 2 and as the case studies (Chs 4–8) amply illustrate.

An assessment of goals, alongside foreseeable impact—positive and negative—is a critical starting point for any litigation, and must be constantly monitored and reappraised throughout the process (as discussed in Chapter 10). Of course, the goals and impact are linked; not least, the impact on applicants is likely to be closely linked to the satisfaction, or not, of their (evolving) goals. Both goals and impact must be assessed from the varying perspectives of those involved in and affected by the process, as an essential prerequisite to giving meaningful advice and as we seek to avoid the common pitfalls of unfulfilled client expectations concerning the litigation process. While goals and impact do overlap, and in an ideal world might coincide, in the real one we need to mark the distinction between them.

B. Avoiding Sharp Distinctions Between 'Strategic', 'Public Interest' and 'other' Litigation

Some of the controversies surrounding what constitutes SHRL, alluded to in the introduction, are linked to concerns regarding (sometimes dubious) distinctions that are drawn between 'strategic' and other forms of litigation.

The first such distinction is between victim or client-focused litigation and SHRL. In the author's view, it is impossible to fully separate the impact on victims, especially perhaps of massive violations, from the impact on the society of which they form a part. Moreover, generalisations about 'the goals of the victims' as distinct from strategic goals are almost inevitably misleading, not least as victim goals are as variable as the individuals and groups themselves. Victims of serious human rights violations in practice often seek, above all, guarantees of non-repetition—the longer-term social, political or economic change that will ensure the violations do not recur.[35] Victims' goals and broader goals are thus very often one and the same.

Indeed, given the challenges and risks facing those who take up human rights litigation, it should not be surprising perhaps that in practice it is often those victims who are personally committed to the cause at stake, determined to ameliorate the situation for other people, and sufficiently supported to do so, that are the most willing and able to front litigation and stay the course. On the other hand, it is crucial to recognise that their goals will not always be identical to the broader goals of others who may stand to be impacted by the litigation, and careful and separate consideration is due of where they converge and diverge.[36]

---

[35] UNESC 'The right to restitution, compensation and rehabilitation for victims of gross violations of human rights and fundamental freedoms—Final report of the Special Rapporteur Mr. M. Cherif Bassiouni, submitted in accordance with Commission resolution 1999/33' UN Doc (2000) E/CN.4/2000/62.

[36] Ch 10.

However, it would be misleading to characterise victims' goals as necessarily distinct or somehow inherently less strategic. Assumptions about those goals and the impact of victim-centred litigation should be avoided.

Likewise, it is difficult to sustain sharp distinctions between SHRL or 'public interest litigation' on the one hand, and the public provision of 'legal aid' or 'legal services' on the other.[37] As the SERI report on litigation of legal services in South Africa noted, while there is a 'conceptual and theoretical distinction between strategic and clinical legal services … there is not always a clear practical divide'.[38] On the one hand, legal services cases can have as high an impact as proactively selected 'strategic' cases; there are many examples of this among cases recognised globally as strategically significant cases.[39] Legal services can sometimes enable a mass of litigation, or a continuum of legal cases, that may indeed further strategic goals and generate impact more effectively than any single case (as discussed in relation to developing strategy in Chapter 10), muddying the distinction a little more. Moreover, the provision of legal aid itself serves various strategic goals, such as democratising access to justice and strengthening of the judiciary or legal system.

In the South African context it has been noted that a danger arises with the increased focus on public interest or strategic litigation, that legal services are increasingly undervalued, and with them the advancement of a broader social justice agenda.[40] This concern is particularly pronounced where differential approaches are taken to funding or supporting public interest litigation as opposed to legal services. It would be ironic if shorter-term 'strategic' goals were a basis for compromising longer-term human rights or rule of law gains.[41]

While hours of academic industry could be dedicated to definitions and classifications, it may be mostly a distraction for our purposes. It is suggested that strict categorisation of litigation into strategic and others is best avoided, in favour of a flexible approach to 'SHRL' that focuses on impact and enquires into what difference litigation actually makes, and where possible tries to understand why.

---

[37] Such distinctions can be understandable, or indeed promoted, to facilitate organisational definition of goals and methods of work, case selection and prioritisation of resources. See eg the International Law Group's 2001 report. But as noted below they can also be problematic and should be treated cautiously.

[38] 'Public Interest Legal Services in South Africa Project Report' (2015) *Socio Economic Rights Institute of South Africa* 48.

[39] See Ch 10. Many cases recognised as strategically significant started out as individual claims, eg in the Kenya torture litigation, a series of individual claims for compensation, with broad-reaching impact (see Duffy (n 12)). See also 'Public Interest Legal Services in South Africa Project Report' (n 38).

[40] 'Public Interest Legal Services in South Africa Project Report' (n 38) at 49.

[41] This has been suggested in relation to South Africa, eg, where considerable donor attention has been focused on SHRL (see 'Public Interest Legal Services in South Africa Project Report' (n 38)). The untenability of the distinctions was borne out by litigators commenting on how the distinction plays out in several contexts as noted by eg Adam Weiss of the European Roma Rights Centre.

4

Identifying Levels of Impact

The types of impact that arise from or are influenced by litigation are so diverse, complex and often situation-specific that a box-ticking approach would only be misleading. However, despite the undoubted need for caution, experience has shown that it is possible to develop a reasonably sensitive antenna for possible and actual impacts. In this chapter, we turn our attention to identifying and illustrating different types of positive impacts in diverse dimensions—beginning with the potential impacts for victim/claimants, for legal development, policy, society and culture, institutions, democracy and the rule of law—before reflecting on the negative impacts of SHRL. An assessment of potential, limitations and counter-productivity are all critical to deciding whether litigation is an appropriate tool at all, and if so to developing a strategy to enhance the positive impact while taking measures to minimise the risk of negative repercussions (as discussed further in Chapter 10).

I. Victim Impact

Victim or client impact takes many forms, reflecting the variable goals of the particular applicants concerned.[1] It is impossible (and demeaning) to generalise about the impact on 'the victims'. However, the following are among the ways in which SHRL has had a significant impact on those most affected by the violations underpinning litigation.

A. Judicial Recognition and Vindication

Judgments can provide the most obvious form of validation of an individual's or group's experiences, and recognition of the wrongdoing against them. Victims, survivor groups and, perhaps especially, relatives often cite the importance of judicial decisions as a form of acknowledgement. This may be particularly powerful

---

[1] Usually, as discussed in Ch 10, human rights cases are brought by victims as applicants (though this is not always required where eg collective action is possible); this section looks at the impact on those victim applicants.

in circumstances where the victims have themselves been cast as wrongdoers or stigmatised as 'criminals', 'terrorists' or 'enemies', or otherwise tarnished by the suggestions that they are responsible for their own suffering.[2]

The Guantanamo and rendition cases at Chapter 7 offer potent examples of individuals who were presented to the world as 'the worst of the worst'. Their recognition as rights bearers and victims of violations, past and present (in the context of Abu Zubaydah's ongoing arbitrary detention at Guantanamo) has been an important dimension of the impact of those cases.[3] Striking examples from Argentina include the cases of sexual violence during dictatorship. Victims of rape, who were labelled as 'traitors' and accused of romantic involvement with perpetrators, have described the significance of being acknowledged through the judicial process as victims of sexual violence.[4]

B. The Restorative and Empowering Role of the Process

Long before judgment, the litigation process can itself provide victims with a voice. It can, in principle, provide a crucial opportunity for the victim to be heard, accuse and explain, and for others to acknowledge suffering, wrongs and responsibility. While the legal process can be (and often is) alienating, victims have also described it as empowering and energising, playing a role in restoring dignity.[5]

The *Hadjitou Mani v Niger* case is the clearest example, from my experience, of the positive impact of testifying on a victim as described in Chapter 5; a former slave, who was not allowed to look a free person in the eye, found her voice and stature in the course of undoubtedly difficult testimony and felt heard and respected by the ECOWAS Court.[6] Of course this is often not the case, and Mani herself described the insults, threats and degrading treatment she received before national courts. Her widely recognised bravery in confronting the powerful in Niger, including her former master, has however ultimately had an important empowering and vindicating value.[7] Likewise, in Argentina, psychologists accompanying victims and witnesses have noted the psychological importance of participative processes for victims coming to terms with violations. In the *Molina*

---

[2] See the Guatemala study (Ch 6) and misconceptions harboured for a decade by some members of the Plan de Sánchez community as to what had brought the massacres on the communities.

[3] eg *Abu Zubaydah v Poland* (n 24) or *Sabbeh et al v Egypt* (Communication 334/06) where the victims were persons accused of terrorism.

[4] See Ch 8, the *Molina* case (Molina Gregorio, Case No 2086 Argentina Federal Court of Criminal Appeals) in the case study on disappearance in Argentina.

[5] See eg the testimony of Turkish rape survivor Nebahat Akkoç, the applicant in the *Akkoç v Turkey* case, on the importance of the EComHR's fact finding hearing in Ankara: 'No voice was heard here [in Turkey] in litigation whereas with the European Commission, despite the proceeding being a long one, you could see that someone was hearing your voice. This gives you more energy. You find power in yourself to encourage others to pursue the same way'; in Duffy (n 12) at 83.

[6] Case study, *Hadijatou Mani v Niger*, Ch 5.

[7] Ch 5.

case prosecuting sexual violence during dictatorship after many years of neglect of these crimes, the victims describe their ability to speak openly about their wrongs, address the 'guilt' of their sexual violence and confront their attackers and the past, once the cases were underway.[8]

The importance of even *lodging* claims, particularly in a context in which people are powerless, was noteworthy in relation to the Palestinian land rights cases at Chapter 9. When I interviewed the applicant in the *Ja'abari* case, he proudly displayed copies of hundreds of unanswered complaints lodged in respect of intimidation by settlers, as evidence of the abuse and official unresponsiveness.[9] This accords with the description by others of the need to 'do something' in the face of their victimisation and that of their family, and of litigation as 'a form of resistance'.[10]

C. Reparation

i. Compensation

Perhaps the most obvious vehicle for direct impact for victims is the payment of compensation—one important aspect of the reparation to which they are entitled under international law.[11] Compensation has enabled many to re-establish themselves in society and to recover from the losses associated with their victimisation.[12] In the *Mani* case even the very small amount of damages was nonetheless critical in helping her to establish a life free from fear and want, and from her former master. Compensation assumes particular importance in the context of modern-day slavery, where other former slaves during interview cited the lack of economic independence or of any means of sustaining themselves as among the critical factors keeping them in on-going slavery.

Compensation awards can also have a critical symbolic value going beyond financial relief. People affected by serious violations in several states have described how compensation played a role in reinforcing the validation of the judgment in their favour—representing the crucial conversion of words into concrete action,

---

[8] Ch 8.

[9] See below on record-keeping and case study OPT Land rights, Ja'ábari's comment being: 'even a bullet that misses makes a noise. If they do nothing, I have a record'. Interview Hebron, March 2015.

[10] See eg the moving descriptions of the motivations of the family of Aksoy, which gave rise to the first ECtHR finding of torture but led to terrible reprisals in M Goldhaber, *A People's History of the European Court of Human Rights* (New Brunswick, NJ, Rutgers University Press, 2008).

[11] See eg OHCHR Res 60/147 'UN's Basic Principles on the Right to a Remedy and Reparation, including restitution, rehabilitation, compensation, satisfaction and guarantees of non-repetition' (2005) UN Doc A/RES/60/147.

[12] See eg comments of Nebahat Akkoç, the applicant in *Akkoç v Turkey*, ECHR 1996-VI, or the experience of Rumba Kinuthia, a Kenyan lawyer, whose compensation enabled him to return to legal practice and represent other victims of Nyayo House Torture, referred to in Duffy (n 12).

and providing a degree of tangible accountability for the state, institutions and individuals required to pay.[13]

There are, however, other sides to the compensation impact story. In a very practical sense, there is the fraught question of quantum, which can influence impact. Some recent damages awards or settlements for human rights violations have involved very large sums (consider the modern slavery claim before US courts that brought the Signal corporation to its knees or the Mau Mau claims in UK courts for colonial torture in Kenya).[14] A number of other states, including Argentina, have come up with meaningful approaches to quantifying damages that are symbolically significant.[15] But not uncommonly awards are seen by those affected as negligible and disproportionate to the serious suffering to which they respond, limiting their material and symbolic significance.[16]

The real material and symbolic impact of damages awards is obviously eviscerated by non-implementation and on the national level compliance with damages awards varies vastly. For example, a wave of damages awards issued by Kenyan courts against the state for torture in the infamous Nyayo House detention centre played an important role in the vindication of victims and recognition of atrocities of the Moi regime, yet they have thus far not been implemented.[17] Slow processes, inconsistency and a lack of clarity in quantifying damages,[18] and what are sometimes perceived as demeaningly low awards, are widespread problems that clearly undermine impact.[19]

In turn, at the international level, as the various systems adopt different approaches to damages,[20] awards are rarely transparent or predictable. An example are the ECtHR judgments finding there have been violations but refusing to grant compensation—asserting, without explanation, that in all the circumstances

---

[13] The broader impact of payments depends on who pays. It has been suggested that human rights processes involve amounts that come at 'too low a cost' for the state to have any real impact. Corporate claims have been massive, with the impact in the industry.

[14] In *Mutua and Others v Foreign Commonwealth Office* [2012] EWHC 2678 (QB) a settlement of £19.9 million was agreed which included payment to the 5,288 claimants and costs. In *David et al v Signal International LLC* No 2:2008cv01220 5 plaintiffs were awarded $14 million. Note the Mau Mau cases were a collective claim that broke down into more modest sums per applicant.

[15] In Argentina, in an important symbolic as well as practical step, victims received a sum equivalent to the maximum daily wage given to the highest-level personnel of the national government for every day of their detention. Elsewhere amounts have sometimes been described as insultingly low, disproportionate to the wrongs and undermining. As noted below in this section in some security-related and other cases, no compensation is awarded.

[16] International human rights awards are not punitive and can be quite low. National systems vary greatly.

[17] See Duffy (n 12).

[18] eg in some systems, the linkage of awards to income has adversely affected those most in need.

[19] See persistent complaints by applicants from Kenya and Turkey in Duffy (n12.) The Mau Mau claims, where a record award was made, may have been a notable exception, though given the mass of applicants this too reduced to modest sums for each one.

[20] Damages may be in respect of identifiable pecuniary loss resulting from violations or non-pecuniary, moral or non-material damages.

the judgment is itself 'sufficient satisfaction'. In some cases, this is compounded by what appears to be quite unprincipled considerations being brought to bear; this was the case when the ECtHR found in favour of, but refused to award damages to, victims of unlawful killing apparently on account of their status as suspected terrorists, as in the famous *McCann and others v United Kingdom* case.[21] In a case we brought against the Russian Federation in respect of the death of former Chechen leader Maskhadov, and the refusal to return his body to his family on the basis that he was killed in a 'counter-terrorist operation', the Court similarly refused to award damages to his family, causing confusion and frustration.[22] In other cases, such as the Abu Zubaydah and al Nashiri torture cases in Chapter 7, significant compensation was awarded by the ECtHR's standards, with important symbolic value, and there was quite rightly no suggestion that any allegations against them would be in any way relevant.[23]

The symbolism, empowerment and practical significance of compensation have quite often been somewhat sullied by other controversies surrounding monetary payments.[24] Media focus on awards being paid from 'taxpayers' money, rather than on underlying violations, and occasionally adverse reactions by other victims or NGOs, are among the problems the case studies illustrate.[25] The apparent discomfort on the part of some NGOs with supporting compensation can reflect ambivalence as to the value of compensation as a human rights tool and its potentially negative implications for broader strategy. As noted in the Argentina study: 'Human rights organisations feared the State was exchanging money for impunity and silence about the past'.[26] Organisations may also have reservations about being seen to be motivated by or too closely associated with financial advantage, distracting from 'more strategic goals'.[27] All of these factors manifest in mixed

---

[21] *McCann v UK* [1995] ECHR 18984/91.

[22] *Maskhadova and Others v Russia* Appl no 18071/05 (6 June 2013) (ECtHR). *Matthews v UK*, Appl no 24833/94 (18 February 1999) (ECtHR). I was co-counsel on the case with colleagues from Interights.

[23] Ch 7, Litigating the War on Terror. Mr Al Nashiri is being tried by military commission, while our client Abu Zubaydah has not yet been charged.

[24] In addition to seeing this in my own cases, interviews for Duffy (n 12) reveal such issues arising in Kenya, Turkey and Argentina.

[25] This has arisen in eg the UK debate on ECtHR 'payouts' to terrorists; the negative reaction in Poland after the *Zubaydah* case was another indication noted in Ch 7.

[26] C Smulovitz, '"I can't get no satisfaction": Accountability and Justice for Past Human Rights Violations in Argentina' in V Popovski and M Serrano (eds), *Transitional Justice and Democratic Consolidation: Comparing the Effectiveness of the Accountability Mechanisms in Eastern Europe and Latin America* (United Nations University, 2009) in Ch 8.

[27] eg Martín Abregú, Executive Director of CELS has noted that when the reparations law was passed in 1995 (following litigation and other action): 'Economic reparations were very difficult to conceive and discuss by human rights organizations'. There was opposition to supporting victims' claims 'for fear of giving the impression that our center profited from this problem'. Interview held on 1 August 2002; MJ Guembe, 'Economic Reparations for Grave Human Rights Violations: The Argentinian Experience' in P de Greiff (ed), *The Handbook of Reparations* (Oxford, Oxford University Press, 2006).

messaging in respect of victims' rights to compensation, despite it being an essential part of the reparation to which they are entitled under international law.[28]

The complexities and the diversity of victim perspectives on the receipt of reparations (whether through litigation or beyond) is nothing new as reflected in analyses of German post-Second World War reparations schemes for example. Slymovics' work contrasts the feelings of her own family members, Auschwitz survivors, one of whom felt compensation enabled her to 'push back', while the other felt 'unclean' that perpetrators had assuaged guilt through monetary payments.[29] I have seen this in several contexts where compensation from wrong-doers following litigation has led to a deeply regrettable 'sense of guilt' on the part of some victims.[30] Yet for many others, it has been described as 'influencing both individual and collective processes of addressing the past, and in this sense, as having a fundamental value'.[31] Compensation can therefore contribute—but it can also be counter-productive—to the process of reparation.

The case studies also demonstrate how material litigation impact of this type can snowball over time, with what began as discrete compensation claims for specified applicants leading to a broader reparation scheme. This expansion of the beneficiary group was seen in the Guatemala litigation, where the reparations award of the Inter-American Court reached beyond the individuals in whose names the cases were brought. In Argentina, petitions protesting the application of statutes of limitation to preclude damages claims brought by a few individuals to the Argentine courts and IACommHR, triggered one of the largest reparation schemes on the continent benefiting many more affected persons over time.[32]

The ultimate impact of compensation for the victims concerned, and its contribution to other levels of impact, depends therefore on many things: whether compensation is paid, its nature and context of delivery, and whether, in the particular situation, compensation is treated as an important aspect of the right to reparation by victims, courts, communities and civil society. Despite broad recognition of the right—and its potential significance—a more complex picture emerges in assessing the ultimate impact of compensation.

---

[28] eg Duffy (n 12).

[29] See eg S Slyomovics, *How to Accept German Reparations* (Philadelphia, University of Pennsylvania Press, 2014).

[30] See discussion in Ch 8 on Argentina. eg Guembe, 'Economic Reparations for Grave Human Rights Violations' (n 68) notes how ambiguous reactions were not confronted and debated: '[s]adly enough, these objections to the reparations policy did not translate into a dialogue or discussion that could have produced a collective way of addressing the issue. The debate within the human rights movement on this subject was shy, cryptic, and hampered by a strong sense of guilt by the families'; Kenya chapter in Duffy (n 12). See Slyomovics, ibid.

[31] Ibid.

[32] When the Supreme Court upheld the statute of limitations on civil claims in Argentina, in 1989 the IACommHR was engaged in a petition by a group of applicants. The reparation policy evolved from a dynamic back and forth among the government, applicants, the Commission and civil society, eventually covering a broader range of people; the number of victims who qualified for reparation continued to expand under subsequent governments.

ii. Other Concrete Reparation: Restitution, Rectification, Cessation, Protection and Access to Services

A principal goal of human rights remedies, at least in theory, is to put victims back in the situation they would have been in but for the violation. Very often this is possible to a very limited extent only, if at all. In some cases, however, human rights litigation has led directly to orders being issued and implemented, on the restitution of property, the reinstatement of judges wrongfully dismissed,[33] the transfer of land titles,[34] or release from unlawful imprisonment for example.

Litigation at the national or international levels will often, first and foremost, seek the cessation of on-going wrongs and protection.[35] While international courts may have limited direct power to stop violations, examples show they may contribute to bringing an end to on-going violations in various ways. A relatively rare direct example from Interights practice was *Assadnize v Georgia*, where a normally deferential ECtHR ordered that a prisoner be released as there was no other way to remedy the wrong. Persons wrongfully detained may also be released as an indirect result of the pressure and oversight generated by the process. While litigation was pending in the *Hadijatou Mani* case, the applicant was released and the criminal case against her for bigamy, for daring to be free of her master, was effectively dropped. The shadow of litigation, not infrequently, provides a degree of accountability that changes the approach to victims, at least publicly. This is illustrated in the case of torture victim Abu Zubaydah, where extravagant public assertions following his capture, to the effect that he was the 'number three' in Al Qaeda, were dropped once litigation became a possibility and he had access to a lawyer.[36] Judicial oversight can serve as a deterrent to abuse.[37]

At times litigation may not bring violations to a definitive end or resolve them, but simply minimise or delay harm to individuals. In a context in which 'buying time' is described as one of the major tactics and successes of the litigation of land rights in the Occupied Palestinian Territory discussed in Chapter 9, litigation has contributed to significant delays that have slowed eviction and demolitions orders, with broader-reaching implications social and political implications.[38]

---

[33] In *Volkov v Ukraine* Appl no 21722/11 (9 April 2013), the EctHR took the unusual step of ordering that a Supreme Court Judge, Oleksandr Volkov, who had been dismissed due to an alleged breach of oath, should be reinstated. The judge was reinstated on 2 February 2015.

[34] In *Xákmok Kásek Indigenous Community v Paraguay* (24 August 2010) the IACtHR, as a measure of restitution, ordered the state to return 10,700 hectares of land to the Community and to take 'all necessary, legislative, administrative and any other measures' to ensure the right to ownership (paras 281–289).

[35] Protective measures from the state may be counter-productive or not desired by the victim, given the context of distrust and state responsibility or complicity.

[36] See eg *Abu Zubaydah v Poland* (n 24) ECtHR, and *Abu Zubaydah v Lithuania*, Appl No 46454/11, pending www.rightsinpractice.org. As discussed in Ch 7.

[37] This is reflected in international human rights law, eg where judicial review of detention is treated as a safeguard inherent in the prohibition on torture itself. This recognition in law is itself a result of gains achieved through jurisprudential development by courts of IHRL.

[38] Ch 9.

The increasingly important role that litigation has played in the protection of crucial socio-economic and civil and political rights, such as ensuring access to health care and to education[39] or reducing prison overcrowding,[40] is worthy of emphasis for its crucial impact on applicants' lives. When it comes to the willingness to order wide-reaching restorative socio-economic measures such as development, health and psycho-social services and education, based on the need to redress the long-term impact of egregious violations such as genocide, the Inter-American system stands out, as the *Plan de Sánchez v Guatemala* case study illustrates.[41] Access to services may also arise indirectly from the changes in the status or recognition of victims or groups. The Mau Mau litigation in UK courts of colonial torture crimes contributed to a broader debate around the treatment of the formerly banned group in Kenya, and gradually to survivors being registered for social security and health benefits.[42]

iii. Accountability, Investigation and Prosecution

The impact of SHRL on accountability and impunity, linked to broader forms of impact, is highlighted below. It should be noted at the outset, however, that catalysing the independent, effective and thorough investigation required under international human rights law (or reopening an ineffective one) is often a key victim-focused goal, linked to both personal and collective processes of healing and reparation. The importance of seeing perpetrators held to account, even if only by being called to answer in public proceedings (not necessarily only criminal proceedings) can have an important vindicating impact.[43] Even processes that do not result in the convictions and proportionate penalties that they should can have a positive impact for some survivors, and at a minimum expose the deep-rooted impunity that may underpin and sustain the violations.[44]

Hadijatou Mani described the ongoing impunity of her former master as 'confirm[ation] that he was untouchable' (the weakest point in an otherwise positive story of impact and implementation).[45] This is not an unusual tale, as human rights judgments have poor records of implementation with regard to orders for

---

[39] Indian court case *Registrar (Judicial) of High Court of Karntaka v State of Karnataka & Ors*, which a study by Ann Skelton found to have to dramatically reduced the number of out of school children (see A Skelton, 'Strategic Litigation Impacts Equal Access to Quality Education' Open Society Justice Initiative (Open Society Foundations, 2017)) 59). On access to health care, consider eg the role of litigation as one tool for change in the Treatment Action Campaign v Minister of Health litigation in South Africa; see more broadly "How Does Litigation Affect Health Financing", World Health Organisation, Technical Brief series no. 15 (2010).

[40] See collective habeas corpus claims in Argentine courts eg *Verbitsky and Others* discussed in Duffy (n 12) at 45.

[41] See Reparations Judgment and Implementation discussed in the Guatemala case study Ch 6.

[42] See Duffy (n 12).

[43] In Duffy (n 12) there are numerous examples of survivors speaking of the importance of seeing wrongdoers being made 'uncomfortable' (eg *Akkoç* case from Turkey and others from Argentina) even if not ultimately held directly accountable.

[44] Ibid, Turkey testimonies on the importance of the processes notwithstanding impunity.

[45] Interview in Niger 2016.

investigation and accountability.[46] In practice, the accountability goal may be particularly difficult to satisfy, at least in the short to medium term.[47]

iv. Symbolic Reparation of Victims

The *Plan de Sánchez* Reparations Judgment (2004) illustrates the sort of multi-faceted and significant reparations that can emerge from human rights litigation in the Inter-American system. These included 'guarantees of non-repetition by providing for collective memory'—discussed below for their broader social and cultural impact—which can be of huge importance for the survivors. Individual victims have spoken to the importance of their dead being honoured through, for example, museums and monuments established, with individual names carved in stone.[48]

The declaratory role of judgments in acknowledging human suffering and wrongs has been noted, but litigation may also prompt government or institutional recognition of responsibility. Often such recognition and apology only emerge from litigation when there has also been a political transition, such that states 'apologise' on behalf of *previous* administrations, thereby sidestepping genuine *mea culpa*. It can nonetheless involve grappling with institutional responsibility of importance for victims and prevention in the future.

Recognition and apology deserve particular attention in this context, as forms of victim reparation increasingly sought, and awarded, in international law and practice. In the *Plan de Sánchez* case, the state's moves towards acknowledgement and apology were incremental; the state first withdrew its preliminary objections in writing before the hearing; it accepted responsibility publicly during the first public hearing; and, while the reparations judgment was pending, it issued an apology. Another striking example of litigation prompting 'sincere regret' decades after violations was the settlement following cases against the UK government in English courts for torture during the colonial regime in Kenya.[49]

By contrast, as noted in Chapter 7, securing recognition has been an enormous struggle in CIA-led rendition and torture cases. States are chillingly reluctant to recognise victims and apologise for their role in their torture and rendition, perhaps suggesting an unprincipled approach to victimhood that compounds the original wrongs. The *Maher Arar* and *Khadr* cases were notable exceptions where the Canadian government issued public apologies, in the latter case after years of litigation.[50] However, in other cases, apology has increasingly featured as a priority remedy sought through litigation, but to no avail.[51] One recent rendition case in

---

[46] See Ch 2, reports on Implementation.
[47] See eg enormous strides forward, eventually, in Argentina in Ch 8.
[48] See Ch 6 Genocide in Guatemala.
[49] See the Mau Mau litigation in the UK as discussed in Duffy (n 12).
[50] Ch 7.
[51] *Abu Zubaydah v Lithuania* (n 77) seeks remedy and apology.

the UK has been used to good effect to expose the refusal to acknowledge responsibility and apologise: the victims in the *Belhaj* case refused to accept the offer of handsome settlements, insisting instead on only £3 (one for each man, woman and child rendered to Libya) coupled with an apology. No agreement on this basis could be reached.[52] The broader political context is never far from the surface in these cases. In addition to the benefits for victims, the acknowledgement of responsibility and expression of regret can have an important role in institutional learning from mistakes made—often in short supply in the counter-terrorism context.

D. From Victim to Survivor to Complainant to Activist

The potential influence of litigation on the mobilisation of civil society is noted below for its far-reaching social and political impact. However, experience also points to the transformative impact that litigation can have on individual clients themselves. I have seen several examples where applicants become more organised in order to facilitate the litigation, with more wide-reaching positive benefits (eg the associations formed in Guatemala to bring the genocide cases). Another dimension is seen in remarkable examples of victims who later became activists or supporters of other victims to enable them to assert their rights. Among numerous other examples[53] is the *Mani* case, where a woman who was among the most marginalised in society now works with anti-slavery groups and reaches out to empower other women in slavery to secure their freedom.[54]

As noted above, for many survivors, an important part of their motivation in pursuing litigation is to ensure that the crimes do not occur again, that others do not suffer and that lessons are learned. The impact on them is therefore closely linked to the other levels of impact explored below.

II. Legal Impact

One of the clearest and causally most straightforward ways in which human rights litigation has an impact is in the development of legal standards. It does so directly, by shaping jurisprudence and procedures, and indirectly, by exposing problems with national laws and prompting processes of reform.

---

[52] See www.reprieve.org.uk/press/2013_03_04_belhaj_apology_secret_courts. The *Belhaj* claim for damages has been allowed to proceed (Supreme Court 2017) and is pending as at July 2017.

[53] The well-known *Akkoç* torture case against Turkey, where the victim became an activist in the course of the litigation processes, and the mobilisation of families of detainees in Argentina (see also s IV.G below).

[54] Ch 5.

A. Changing National Legislation

In some systems, laws may be declared unconstitutional, or even struck down by the courts, when incompatible with fundamental rights. There are also many examples of reform following promptly and directly on the heels of judgments against the state at the international level, or laws being changed *while* a matter was being litigated. In the post-9/11 context, where rights-restrictive laws swept the globe, courts have often made clear that legislation falls foul of international obligations and national frameworks. As Chapter 7 illustrates, in the European context such cases have proliferated, and states have frequently modified laws and practices in response to ECtHR decisions.

However, while legislative changes may flow directly from a court order, more often legal reform may require a much longer and more multi-faceted process. The *Grootboom* housing rights case (South African Constitutional court) set in train a long process of reform leading to public housing legislation seven years later.[55] Litigation's shorter-term impact may be a greater awareness of the legal inadequacies that have been exposed by the case, playing into a broader advocacy drive for legislative or even constitutional reform.

B. Triggering Enforcement of National Law

In certain situations, adequate laws do exist, but they may not be applied or enforced. Litigation is, in key part, about ensuring that laws are given effect in practice. Cases may expose related underlying issues which need to be addressed, such as a judicial lack of knowledge or understanding of their own laws, or practices and cultures that constrain the application of that law. An example from the case studies is how the *Hadijatou Mani v Niger* case before the ECOWAS Court revealed that exemplary legal provisions on slavery were either unknown or ignored in practice, overshadowed by customary laws. I have also seen litigation expose the refusal of sectors of the state or the public to abide by or give effect to rights they know are enshrined in law, as in the *Tysiac v Poland* case before the ECtHR.[56] In that case, reproductive rights were enshrined in Polish law, but ignored in practice by the medical profession and inadequately supported by the state, such that legal rights had little meaningful effect. International mechanisms may be invoked either to challenge or enforce national law.

---

[55] Public Housing Act 2008, and the *Government of the Republic of South Africa & Ors v Grootboom* above, on the right to adequate housing. As noted above, Ms Grootboom was dead by the time of the legal reform.

[56] *Tysiac v Poland* Appl no 5410/03 (2007) (ECtHR).

C. Developing Legal Standards through National or International Jurisprudence

In practice, international human rights law, set out in skeletal treaties, is given form and content through its interpretation and application by human rights courts and bodies. Bringing cases and securing strong jurisprudence is one way in which the law is strengthened and clarified. SHRL has therefore been used to good effect for decades by 'norm entrepreneurs',[57] with a transformative impact on the dynamic development of international law.

As noted in Chapter 2, while decisions from one system do not strictly speaking apply in another, in practice the increase in judicial cross-fertilisation between systems means that legal developments in one arena increasingly translate into another.[58] Thus litigation at the regional and international levels can have a multiplier effect, rolling out jurisprudential gains across states and ultimately regions.

This global normative impact is illustrated across human rights practice. Take the fundamental doctrine of 'positive obligations' that underpins international human rights law, for example.[59] An early set of cases, spearheaded by the seminal *Velasquez Rodriquez v Honduras* case, interpreted the obligation to 'ensure' the rights in general human rights conventions as enshrining a duty to prevent, investigate, prosecute and provide reparation in international law. As such, they set down what have become the defining norms on the scope and content of IHRL, accepted across international and regional human rights systems. In turn, these normative gains provided the basis for another series of cases that challenged the lawfulness of amnesty laws and related impediments to prosecution in several states, including *Barrios Altos v Peru*, which has been cited around the globe.[60] These cases have in turn triggered legislative and constitutional changes at the national level, and been applied directly in national proceedings (as the Argentina and Guatemala case studies show). They have changed standards internationally and nationally, by providing the basis for courts and bodies around the world to address accountability norms consistently.

Likewise, the emergence of 'new rights'—or rather new interpretations of existing obligations—such as the recognition of a 'right to truth', was born of litigation in the Inter-American system, discussed above, and eventually recognised decades later by the ECtHR in the rendition cases in Chapter 7.[61] In another example of

---

[57] eg H Koh, 'How Is International Human Rights Law Enforced?' (2009) 74 *Indiana Law Journal* 1.

[58] See http://assembly.coe.int/nw/xml/News/News-View-En.asp?newsid=5968&lang=2 referring to developments in Dutch law.

[59] This entails states' obligations not only to refrain from violating rights but to ensure their protection, through prevention and response.

[60] See eg *Barrios Altos v Peru*, Merits, Judgment, Inter-AmCtHR (Ser C) No 75, cited in international and national courts around the globe, including in the Argentinian decisions that led to the amnesty laws being set aside.

[61] *Abu Zubaydah v Poland* (n 24). Discussed in the detention and rendition case study.

this transnational jurisprudential journey reflected in Chapter 5, the ECOWAS Court sitting in Niger relied on the elements of slavery set down by the International Criminal Tribunal for the former Yugoslavia (ICTY) in The Hague, which were then picked up by the Inter-American Court and further consolidated in a case concerning modern-day slavery in Brazil.[62] In this way, different systems collectively contribute to improving and strengthening global human rights standards in a vibrant and multi-dimensional jurisprudential dynamic.[63]

D. Shaping Remedies and Procedures

The impact of SHRL is influenced by the remedies available, which vary among systems.[64] But SHRL itself influences the development of those remedies in sometimes quite remarkable ways. In Argentina during the last decade, innovative legal action sought to use long-standing 'habeas corpus' provisions on behalf of all detainees in the system who were subject to dismal conditions of detention, overcrowding and institutional violence, exposing them to serious risks.[65] The action was, perhaps somewhat surprisingly, accepted by the Federal Supreme Court and a new remedy of 'collective habeas corpus' was born; as such, it has been described as truly 'trailblazing' litigation that broke judicial inertia, established collective habeas corpus as a tool, and influenced subsequent litigation practice addressing structural human rights problems in a range of contexts.[66]

The rapid growth in acceptance of third-party (or *amicus curiae*) interventions in national and international procedures—which open up systems and enlighten judicial processes—has also been prompted by litigation. Originally a child of the common law process, litigants have ventured to use *amicus* interventions increasingly, across legal systems, and through acceptance of such interventions on a case-by-case basis, they have come to be constitute standard procedure in many systems. In some, this constructive litigation opportunism has led to rules on interventions being subsequently formally enshrined in the procedures of the relevant court or body. An international example is found in the African Commission, before which there were originally no formal procedures for

---

[62] *Fazenda Brazil v Brazil* (Case no 12.066, 20 October 2016, IACtHR).

[63] There are today innumerable examples of judicial borrowing; in addition to the case studies, examples from cases I was involved with at Interights include *Opuz v Turkey* on domestic violence, or *MC v Bulgaria* on prosecuting sexual violence, where the ECtHR relied on CEDAW and other standards as a result of strategic interventions, with this as a goal.

[64] See eg Ch 2 comparing limited forms of reparation in the European system to the Inter-American counterpart.

[65] eg Supreme Court of Argentina, *Verbitsky and Ors* (V.856.XXXVIII) Judgment of 3 May 2005. The Federal Supreme Court's decision is wide-reaching and ground-breaking in various ways.

[66] Filippini (2007) in Duffy (n 12). The Supreme Court's recognition of the right to lodge collective habeas corpus action provided a much-needed remedy in cases requiring structural reform, where individual remedies had proved ineffective.

third-party interveners, but a broad reference to the Commission being able to 'hear from ... any ... person capable of enlightening it'.[67] The first couple of third-party interventions were presented in Interights' cases by partner international organisations: CEJIL (in respect of poverty as a ground for waiving the exhaustion requirement, in the case of *John K Modise* in 1994) and the Open Society Justice Initiative (in the case of *Kenneth Good*, on permissible distinctions between citizens and non-citizens). The briefs were accepted, and the rules of procedure later came to reflect and regularise this practice, enabling the adoption of measures for protecting third parties, including witnesses, experts and NGOs.

There are several similar examples before national courts. Although alien to Argentine procedure at that time, requests were made by international NGOs to present *amicus curiae* briefs in 'truth trials' concerning forced disappearance and torture discussed in Chapter 8. These were accepted, paving the way for such interventions in many later cases and opening up an active role for national and international NGOs in bringing comparative human rights arguments to bear on a broad range of issues.[68]

In this and many other ways, national court procedures have been shaped, and subsequent litigation opportunities created, through the practice of litigation with potentially positive, longer-term human rights repercussions.

III. Impact on Policy and Practice

A. Challenging and Changing Policy

The most obvious way in which human rights litigation seeks to bring about change is by challenging policies and practices that violate human rights. States may directly cease an activity and revoke policies as a result of litigation, as happened in the case of the security detention of non-nationals in the UK post-9/11, which ceased due to *A & Ors v UK*, discussed in Chapter 7. This kind of detention was replaced by control orders, which were subsequently also challenged, in an on-going trialogue among the executive, legislature and judiciary.[69]

Achieving change in practices and policies is rarely an overnight event, however compelling the judgment. Certain 'mega-judgments' or 'structural litigation' referred to in Chapter 2, which have involved courts monitoring responses to

---

[67] African Charter on Human and Peoples' Rights (Art 46).

[68] During litigation on the right to truth in Argentina, international NGOs tried this to good effect (*Monica Maria Candelaria Mignone v Argentina*, Case no 2209, 1977 IAComHR); it has since become a common feature of practice in that state and others in the region. Ch 8, case study on Enforced Disappearance in Argentina.

[69] Ch 7 Litigating the War on Terror; for more detail, see Duffy (n 12) Ch 11.

structural human rights problems on an on-going basis, epitomise this.[70] Rather than indicating specific policy measures that the authorities must adopt, the courts established a participative and deliberative framework for the development of policies to address the problem, and a degree of accountability through judicial supervision. One example is the approach of the Colombian Constitutional Court in displacement cases which spanned six years, during which the courts engaged the authorities at multiple stages, with wide-reaching policy ramifications.[71] Another is the litigation of structural issues relating to conditions of detention in Argentina noted above,[72] where the Court imposed specific requirements that the government and legislature: amend criminal legislation; submit detailed reports of conditions of confinement (tellingly so that the judiciary could weigh the 'justification for continuing detention' and whether 'alternatives' were required); convene a dialogue panel, to which *amicus curiae*, prisoners and other sectors of civil society should be invited; and report to the Federal Court on progress every 60 days.[73] As such, the courts remained engaged over a period of years, supervising implementation, forcing policy statements and commitments to be made, and ensuring that issues that the government might prefer to de-prioritise remained on the political agenda.[74]

These structural cases, like friendly settlement procedures internationally, have at times required the establishment of 'platforms for dialogue' on the development of appropriate policy responses. This is an example of how litigation can help create political space and draw a broader range of actors (including victims and civil society) into policy discussions, providing a crucial step towards identifying longer-term solutions that could never be provided by the litigation itself.[75]

Particular policy changes may also arise unexpectedly *during* the litigation, as governments articulate and adjust their positions for the purpose of litigation. The *Al Skeine v UK* case, on the applicability of the ECHR to British troops in Iraq, is illustrative. Under pressure to be consistent with its own litigation position adopted in previous cases, the government shifted its approach to focus on whether and to what extent its human rights obligations applied abroad—that is, from arguing non-applicability to a more nuanced position (which Strasbourg ultimately rejected) that its obligations applied in detention centres but not on the streets it patrolled.[76]

---

[70] Case T 105, CC (2005) in Garavito and Franco, 'Cortes y Cambio Social: Como la Corte Constitucional transformó el desplazamiento forzado en Colombia' (n 4).

[71] Ibid. There were 84 follow-up decisions and 14 hearings.

[72] *Verbitsky and Ors* cases (n 106) in Duffy (n 12).

[73] The Supreme Court of Argentina ordered specific and broad-ranging measures from all branches of government, which provided a road-map for policy reform, with a tight timetable and political pressure.

[74] Ibid; *Verbitsky and Ors* cases (n 106) in Duffy (n 12).

[75] This is linked to the mobilisation and empowerment impact, below. See eg Inter-American Commission on Human Rights (IACHR) Precautionary Measures, No 923–04, *Penitentiaries of Mendoza*, 3 August 2004 available at www.derechos.org/nizkor/arg/doc/carcjul4.html; P Salinas, *La aplicación de la tortura en Argentina. Realidad social y regulación jurídica* (Buenos Aires, Editores del Puerto, 2010).

[76] *Al-Skeini and Others v The United Kingdom* Appl no 55721/07 (1 July 2007) (ECtHR). See also Duffy (n 12) Ch 11.

B. Frustrating Policies

In some contexts, policy change is impossible, either because the courts are unwilling or unable to engage, or the political arms are unwilling to comply. It may be that the best to hope for is that policies are frustrated or impeded, rather than shaped, by the courts. This has been noted in relation to South Africa under apartheid, where anti-apartheid lawyers brought cases with the aim of 'delaying and perhaps frustrating an executive bent upon change'.[77] It resonates also in the land rights cases in Palestine, where 'buying time' is described as one of the major tactics and modest successes. While cases are rarely won, delays have put off hundreds of eviction and demolition orders temporarily, often for prolonged periods of time. While this at first sounds distinctly underwhelming as a goal or achievement, the delay is significant for the individuals involved, and politically. Given the strategic, political, economic, cultural and religious significance of Jerusalem for a Palestinian future state, holding off on the removal of Palestinians from East Jerusalem, and the creation of the 'buffer zone' around Israeli controlled areas, has broader potential impact. The delays in settlement expansion or in the removal of Palestinians from East Jerusalem do not provide solutions in themselves, or achieve the broader social goals they pursue, but they may create time and space for other solutions, from wherever they might emerge.

C. Eroding Impunity

In a great deal of SHRL, one of the goals for victims and others is the pursuit of individual accountability. Accountability is often seen as a crucial form of reparation for survivors, and greatly valued for its potential contribution to non-repetition in the future and to broader rule of law goals. Human rights litigation can, and as the examples show does, impact impunity at different levels.

Cases denouncing inadequate investigations in light of the obligations to investigate, prosecute and punish proportionately are the staple work of human rights courts and tribunals, and have led to changes in policy guidelines and practice in the way particular types of investigation are conducted. In two ECtHR cases in which Interights was an intervener—*MC v Bulgaria* on sexual violence, and *Opuz v Turkey* on domestic violence—the states issued directives on the adequate investigation of crimes, with the real potential to influence the practice and behaviour on the ground.[78]

---

[77] M Chanock, *The Making of South African Legal Culture 1902–1936: Fear, Favour and Prejudice* (Cambridge, Cambridge University Press, 2001) 518.

[78] A directive on the effective investigation and prosecution of crimes of sexual violence was issued following *MC v Bulgaria* Appl no 39272/98 (4 December 2003) (ECtHR), which rejected the domestic requirements of evidence of physical force for a rape charge, or the Victims' Rights Directive following the failure to investigate domestic violence due to lack of victim complaint, in *Opuz v Turkey* Appl no 33401/02 (9 June 2009) (ECtHR).

International proceedings, including implementation proceedings, often provide a forum and context for oversight of domestic accountability processes, and a framework to monitor the genuineness and effectiveness of investigations. These processes often serve at a minimum to force reluctant states to commit publicly to justice and justify delays or obstructions, and on occasion do push defunct investigations forward. This can provide some type of counterweight (albeit often insufficient) to the 'enormous pressure'[79] on authorities *not* to open or advance investigations of powerful perpetrators, as epitomised by the CIA rendition cases.[80] Even as litigation has a relatively weak track record in counteracting impunity, it can considerably alter state discourse around accountability.

The investigation of those responsible may be specifically ordered as a component of the remedies awarded in supranational cases. In the Guatemala cases, the Inter-American Commission and Court specifically required the state to investigate and prosecute massacres of the late 1970s and early 1980s.[81] However, while implementation is a broader problem, it is in relation to accountability that compliance rates are generally poorest. As the Guatemala and Argentina cases demonstrate, such an order is only ever likely to be one small step towards accountability—a tool among others to pressure a reluctant state slowly to edge towards justice. But both cases also show how litigation has been used at many stages to progress along the road towards justice, resulting in numerous prosecutions and convictions in practice. The Guatemalan example reveals multiple prosecutions of, as yet, low-level perpetrators of the *Plan de Sánchez* case.[82]

Likewise, in Argentina, there has been a slow and multi-staged journey towards justice for disappearances during dictatorship. An impressive range of forms of litigation used incrementally, in conjunction with other processes, inched the country towards accountability, and eventually to the unprecedented degree of individual criminal accountability currently underway.[83] Some clarified the duty to investigate and the right to truth; some prompted a reparations process that kept the judiciary involved in the broader discussion; the Inter-American and other foreign courts increased pressure for justice at home. Eventually, the *Simon*

---

[79] See Ch 7: The former COE Human Rights Commissioner Hammamberg refers to such pressure being exerted by Washington on other states not to investigate the war on terror crimes.

[80] See Ch 7 on the US pressure on Eastern European states complicit in the rendition programme; states such as Poland, Lithuania and Romania are now being called upon to investigate and open or are reopening domestic proceedings by supranational courts and bodies.

[81] *Plan de Sánchez Massacre v Guatemala*, Judgment of 19 November 2004, IACHR: '95. More than 22 years after the massacre and 10 after the corresponding investigations were opened, the State has not investigated the facts or identified, prosecuted and punished those responsible. This constitutes a situation of impunity, which contravenes the State's aforementioned obligation, harms the victims, and encourages the chronic repetition of the human rights violations in question ... and this obligation must be complied with seriously and not as a mere formality'.

[82] In Guatemala these have been mostly low-level despite on-going efforts, and some impact, as regards the intellectual authors such as Rios Montt; see the case study in Ch 6.

[83] 1,609 criminal cases were reopened after the amnesty laws were set aside; to date there have been 692 convictions. See Ch7 and Duffy (n 12).

judgment found amnesty laws unconstitutional, and criminal trials got underway in earnest. The role of litigation evolved before getting to this point: By exposing the facts, opening debate, and generating pressure on judges by foreign processes, it cumulatively influenced the political, legal and social landscape in which impunity could exist. Litigation was no magic solution, but an instrument put to good use in diverse ways to combat impunity over a long period of time.

IV. Institutional Impact, Including Judicial Strengthening

Litigation may serve to strengthen institutions, nationally or internationally. There are many examples of human rights institutions being created, or strengthened, to combat a problem exposed—at least in part—through litigation.[84] Whether those institutions can be made to be effective, or are a chimera to obscure the lack of real change, will of course determine their ultimate impact.

A key role of national and international human rights litigation lies specifically in the strengthening of national judiciaries. International human rights courts are not (as is popularly understood) courts of appeal or 'courts of fourth instance',[85] but are duly deferential to their national counterparts, provided they work broadly within the flexible framework of human rights law. The subsidiary system of international human rights litigation provides an opportunity, and incentive, for states to avoid the need for international jurisdiction by discharging their primary role as protectors of human rights and the rule of law, while providing a check on them where they do not.[86] This can bolster the hand of national judges who are friendly to the rule of law. Indeed, the impact of international litigation in supporting national judges, including by protecting judicial independence, is significant.

Where there are national attacks on judicial independence, these may themselves be the subject of international litigation in various forms. Examples from my practice include the *Garzon v Spain* case before the Human Rights Committee, where a judge who was prosecuted for his own judicial decisions could challenge this internationally, or the *Taba* bombings case before the African Commission, where the lack of judicial independence in Egyptian state security courts

---

[84] In very concrete ways, new institutions have been created to give effect to human judgments and to address a particular problem exposed or criticised through litigation: see numerous examples in Duffy (n 12).

[85] The ECtHR reiterates this in these terms repeatedly.

[86] This is reflected in the primordial right to a remedy across international law, eg the ILC Articles on State Responsibility 2001 and all human rights treaties, and in the subsidiarity of international human rights courts and the exhaustion of domestic remedies rule.

was robustly criticised.[87] The crucial importance of judicial independence to the rule of law is clear;[88] SHRL can ensure that where judiciaries succumb, the state can be held accountable internationally, which may provide a small measure of protection or at least strengthen judges' resolve.

International litigation has provided national judges with human rights tools, and may influence national judges' decisions when the issues next come before their courts. In many systems, examples of SHRL has helped open systems up to international and comparative standards, and to considering issues through 'the world's eye'. The growing 'trans-judicial dialogue', evident across several case studies, has encouraged compliance with international rule of law standards domestically.

One of the functions of litigation may be to test and strengthen the human rights machinery itself. The procedures and processes of regional and *international* institutions themselves have been refined and strengthened through practice and by the way that advocates conduct litigation, which may contribute to maintaining or raising standards in courts or bodies themselves. Particularly in the early days of a human rights body's life, an important objective is to ensure there is a suitable flow of cases to develop a functioning and effective body. This was one of a number of objectives that Interights pursued, with some effect, in the early days on the African human rights system. The *Mani* case has been attributed with enhancing the standing of the ECOWAS Court, and gave rise to a line of human rights cases in a previously under-utilised forum.

Litigation may seek to expand particular procedures within systems, enhancing the relevance and effectiveness of those judicial functions. A good example is the gradual expansion, case-by-case, of 'interim' or 'precautionary' measures applied by supranational human rights bodies as an expression of their protective mandate. Finally, SHRL has a role to play in the *education* of judges and other officials. In the *Mani* slavery case, one of the problems that the case exposed was judicial ignorance of rights and the law. By contrast, interviews for this study made clear that, as a result of that case, knowledge of at least the prohibition on slavery has become widespread among judges at different levels. In addition, capacity building of the judiciary, police, prosecution service and other officials has occasionally been reflected directly in reparations orders, or negotiated as part of a friendly settlement.[89] More commonly (as in the *Mani* case),

---

[87] I am counsel in these cases. In the latter, the ACHPR called the state to account for lack of independence of state security courts specifically, which appears to have contributed to some cases being reheard and the process of reform. Many international human rights cases criticise military courts.

[88] Ch 2.

[89] See eg the impact of litigation on legislative reform on torture and ill-treatment in Turkey in Duffy (n 12). In 1982 France, Norway, Denmark, Sweden and the Netherlands brought proceedings against Turkey for violations of the ECHR. Parties agreed to a friendly settlement, and negotiations provided a basis for commitment to reform. Turkey agreed to accede to the European Convention for the Prevention of Torture and the UN Convention Against Torture, agreed to report to the Commission on implementation activities, and also shortened maximum periods of pretrial detention.

capacity building may result indirectly, as other states, organisations or NGOs step up in light of the institutional need exposed by the case. In turn, as a result of unfavourable litigation, the state in question may be keen to appear to be addressing the problem and more open to capacity-building initiatives.[90] As the *Mani* case illustrates, a piece of litigation may expose the need for training among both national judges and their supranational counterparts (in that case, the ECOWAS Court).[91]

Emerging work in comparative politics suggests that the growth of human rights litigation, and in particular the role of NGOs in it, has benefited the courts themselves. One study describes the relationship between the courts and NGOs to be 'reciprocal', whereby the court 'is perceived as an instrument to advance NGO claims' while in turn 'NGO participation provides the court with services or enhanced legitimacy'.[92] While caution is clearly due to protect judicial independence and impartiality, and the perception of the same,[93] the judicial role can itself be supported and enhanced through the development of strong SHRL and the dedication of professionalism and resources to the enterprise.

V. Information, Truth and the Historical Record

Information may be a goal, or more often a valuable by-product, of litigation. Litigation may directly pursue information through 'Freedom of Information Act' litigation in domestic systems, for example.[94] Human rights courts may also, occasionally, exercise a fact-finding function.[95] Less directly and more commonly, litigation processes may prise open facts and contribute more subtly to revealing the truth about the nature of violations and responsibility for them, through submissions by the parties and the dialogue between them and external experts, interveners and courts. Litigation is of course only one way to do this, and not necessarily the most efficient. But its potential to illuminate facts, enhance the understanding

---

[90] See eg widespread training in Turkey as part of the implementation programme of ECHR cases, in Duffy (n 12), or training following the *Mani* judgment, in Ch 5.

[91] See very poor judgment on discrimination (though strong on slavery), and the Danish Institute training programmes that followed.

[92] From HN Haddad, 'Judicial Institutional Builders: NGOs and International Human Rights Courts' (2012) 11 *Journal of Human Rights* 126. It notes also 'civil society provides the court with services, including monitoring, initiating litigation, and documenting violations'.

[93] This is revisited in Ch 10.

[94] See eg Chs 7, 8 and 9.

[95] See eg Art 38 of the ECHR ('The Court shall examine the case together with the representatives of the parties and, if need be, undertake an investigation, for the effective conduct of which the High Contracting Parties shall furnish all necessary facilities'). Similarly, Art 48 of the American Convention on Human Rights provides 'the Commission shall, with the knowledge of the parties, examine the matter set forth in the petition or communication in order to verify the facts. If necessary and advisable, the Commission shall carry out an investigation, for the effective conduct of which it shall request, and the States concerned shall furnish to it, all necessary facilities'.

of those directly affected, as well as society more broadly, and provide tools for further action, should not be underestimated.

Overreaching approaches to national security and state secrecy, particularly in the counter-terrorism context, make access to information particularly challenging, and important. Even in these cases, governments have revealed information to defend their position, respond to judicial prompting, or appear cooperative. In this way, they have placed documents in the public domain which they had previously withheld.[96] Sometimes information may seep out in the litigation process, such as the remarkable revelations on the CIA's rendition programme, which emerged from civil litigation between companies in US courts which had not been subject to the same clampdown on state secrecy grounds as human rights claims as they had fallen under the government's radar.[97]

Information obtained through litigation can contribute incrementally to greater gains, as it is employed as evidence in future cases, or feed other action and advocacy. Even information derived from quite unsuccessful litigation during the dictatorship in Argentina proved invaluable evidence in the junta trials after democracy, just as the 'truth trials' (when criminal trials were precluded by amnesty) informed and re-energised civil society claims for accountability by a broader range of actors. As the series of criminal cases continue to unfold, a broader range of individuals responsible are prosecuted, and to some degree a broader understanding of the wrongs of dictatorship is achieved.[98]

Courts may also call out the authorities on the lack of transparency and the *refusal* to share information in domestic processes, or for overreaching approaches to state secrecy or national security.[99] Litigation may reveal the overreaching nature of secrecy, with its own contribution to the debate on openness and democracy.[100]

Despite its potential to do so, there is certainly no guarantee that litigation will prove to be an effective context for revealing truth. If it comes truth will be slow, and partial. In Turkey it has been suggested that, on occasion, 'false accounts' presented to the judiciary, and to the public through litigation, that went inadequately challenged, consolidated official misinformation.[101] As one interviewee noted, according to the state, detainees were dying through suicide or sickness, or disappeared persons had left the country or joined the PKK; however, over time, the

---

[96] See Ch 7 and the Lithuanian decision to allow documents on the investigation in CIA crimes to be released, announced in the course of the hearing in June 2016.

[97] See eg C Algar, 'US court documents reveal inner workings of CIA renditions' *The Guardian* (31 August 2011) www.theguardian.com/commentisfree/2011/aug/31/documents-reveal-renditions-programme-business.

[98] Ch 7.

[99] See eg *Mohammed Serdar* case in the UK courts (culminating in *Serdar Mohammed v Ministry of Defence* [2017] UKSC 2).

[100] See among others the Guatemala Genocide Study (Ch 6) on the refusal to share military plans alleged to have been destroyed, but which later emerged. Or the Litigating the War on Terror Study (Ch 7), where the extreme refusal of the US to allow Abu Zubaydah to provide information or communication with the ECtHR, even an affidavit, was noted by the Court.

[101] Duffy (n 12).

multiple cases on torture revealed a pattern that ignited public consciousness of the lies being advanced by the state as to the nature and the number of these 'terrorists' who were being tortured in the name of security.[102] The public was thus gradually informed, through litigation, not only of the wrongs, but the terrible extent of the lies and misinformation proffered by the state.[103]

Supranational litigation has been seen to provide a complementary 'truth-telling' process, which may be particularly important in situations like that in Turkey where there have been no truth commissions or similar processes despite massive violations.[104] In practice, however, while litigation can expose facts and failures and shine a light in dark corners, its role in uncovering a fuller 'truth' has been questioned.[105] Litigation is likely to provide at best one small component of a much bigger process to gain understanding and acknowledgement of, and address, the past.[106]

Closely related to the information gathering and truth telling function is the role of litigation in documenting official abuse, destroying the perceived legality of government action, and helping lay the foundation for the future protection of human rights. By exposing and condemning human rights violations, and providing some indication of the reasons for them, it may contribute to the historical record of official practices. This can enable a coming to terms with the past and help build towards non-repetition in the longer term.

The role of the courts in helping, directly and indirectly, to write history and shape narratives comes across in all of the case studies. In Palestine, where so few cases are successful, it is reflected in individual applicants who continue with legal action which had no obvious outcome on the basis that 'Even the bullet that misses makes a noise; if they do nothing I have a record', in the description of litigation as 'holding a mirror to the problems in Palestine', or of judicial archives as 'the great library of the occupation'.[107] The series of land rights cases considered together provide a prism through which the nature of the unjust policies, denial of justice, and their impact on particular individuals, families and communities, can be seen.

---

[102] Ibid: 'In the beginning when police said that a terrorist organisation was found, the press believed that ... because there was a great counterpropaganda ... After a while even the most insensitive came to a point to say "it cannot be that much"'.

[103] Ibid; see cases such as Bedii Tan, Metin Goktepe and Siddik Bilgin which gradually revealed these fallacies as to the nature of victims of torture.

[104] See recognition of the truth-telling value of those processes in S Tanrikulu, 'ECHR as a Truth Telling Commission' in *50 Years of the ECtHR Failure or Success* (Ankara Bar Association, 2009). In Turkey, there has been no truth-telling process, transition or reckoning with the past.

[105] See, however, the view that it has revealed only a much narrower 'fact-finding' function, not a deeper process of truth, in B Cali, 'The Logics of Supranational Human Rights Litigation, Official Acknowledgment, and Human Rights Reform: The Southeast Turkey Cases before the European Court of Human Rights, 1996–2006' (2010) 2 *Law and Social Inquiry* 311.

[106] Interview with Kerem Altıparmak, academic, Ankara University (12 November 2015), Duffy (n 12).

[107] See Ch 9.

The Guatemala case study emphasises how the research and preparation of a case can have a critical function, alongside the revelations through the judicial process itself, in debunking insidious myths, including as to the responsibility of victims for their own misfortune.[108] By informing collective historical narratives it can play a role in breaking down the states of denial that tend to pervade in the face of widespread violations and crimes, and enhance collective learning.[109] As such, the search for information and truth through litigation is closely linked to the question of its social and cultural impact.

VI. Social or Cultural Impact

César Rodríguez-Garavito describes litigation as having a role in 'chang[ing] ideas, perceptions and collective social constructs relating to the litigation's subject matter ... in sociological terms, they imply cultural or ideological alterations with respect to the problem posed by the case'.[110] There are many dimensions to this role, closely associated with other forms of impact, some of which are illustrated below.

A. Reframing Issues, Catalysing Debate and Influencing Attitudes?

Litigation can provide a catalyst for debate on issues that are overlooked or taboo. This is very clearly seen in the case study on slavery, where an entirely new debate emerged around an established, widespread practice protected by a conspiracy of silence. Discussion of the case reverberated around the country, not only in the political echelons, but homes, marketplaces and judicial corridors. Litigation can make a remarkable contribution simply by placing—or keeping—in the public eye unwelcome issues that affect the least powerful and threaten the status quo.[111] The role of litigation in generating awareness of violations, causes and contributors—closely linked to its function in unlocking information and revealing the truth noted above—is an important prerequisite to pressuring for change and learning from the past.

The *terms* of the debate may also be influenced by litigation. Proceedings in court inherently reframe issues in legal rather than purely political terms. The legal

---

[108] See legal philosopher Jaime Molamud Goti on the importance of clarifying that victims are 'not responsible for their own disgrace'. An example of an international judgment of this type is *El Masri v Macedonia* Appl no 9630/09 (13 December 2012) (ECtHR) where the Court, in a judgment on rendition, recognised the wrongs and victimisation, and awarded compensation to the individual.

[109] S Cohen, *States of Denial: Knowing about Atrocities and Suffering* (Cambridge, Polity, 2000).

[110] C Rodríguez-Garavito, 'Beyond the Courtroom: The Impact of Judicial Activism on Socioeconomic Rights in Latin America' (2011) 89 *Texas Law Review* 1669, 1680.

[111] See cases studies in Chs 4–8. Slavery, conditions of detention, rendition, inequality and high-level impunity for torture were all issues that not only the authorities but also some sectors of the public sought to keep behind closed doors. Litigation made this at least more difficult.

paradigm may influence the context, tone, content and quality of the discussion. This can be particularly important in the context of vitriolic debates on issues such as terrorism and security, though as experience shows legal action cannot be guaranteed a positive presentation in the media.[112] The reframing in court proceedings can add weight, influencing the seriousness with which issues are taken. In Guatemala, litigation played an important role, alongside other processes, in awakening an appreciation of the massacres as 'genocide'.

The *Hadijatou v Mani* slavery case is one example where several sources attest to attitudes (in judicial halls and the marketplace) having been directly shaped by litigation and ensuing coverage and debate. Similarly, litigation against torture in detention has been described as contributing to public awareness, and over time a greater degree of public condemnation of the phenomenon (although much still depends on who tortures whom).[113] In various contexts, survivors who dared to expose and litigate such violations have challenged the notion that such practices are ordinary, and at a minimum 'denormalised' them.[114] It may nonetheless prove among its most significant contributions, not only for the individuals but in shaping public attitudes that ultimately bear upon repetition.

B. The Humanising Power of the Litigation Narrative

Court cases can serve to tell real people's stories, individualising and providing an often-graphic illustration of what human rights violations mean in practice. This can help move public debate laws, policies and practices beyond the level of abstract, political questions. In respect of at least some applicants, litigation can expose and challenge assumptions and prejudices—towards groups or individuals that often underpin violations. Judicial determinations can themselves carry weight in public perception, reframing demonised individuals as applicants, victims and rights-bearing human beings.[115]

In the face of egregious violations to human dignity, the 'humanising' goal of litigation may be central. It cannot be taken for granted though and is particularly challenging in contexts such as counter-terrorism and others where prejudice vis-a-vis individual applicants can be prevalent and stubborn.

---

[112] See Rendition case study noting negative press associated with legal action in this field, as well as more positive presentations.

[113] See interviews in Duffy (n 12): interview in Istanbul with Şebnem Korur Fincancı, academic and medical practitioner.

[114] Ibid.

[115] It is in the face of tense politicalised debate, as has characterised the political debate around terrorism in many states, that the discipline of dispassionate legal and principled arguments, and judicial responses, is most needed, but where shaping public perceptions appears most challenging. This will be explored in the case studies of the UK counter-terrorism cases in Ch 7. See also controversies regarding 'sympathetic victims' in Ch 10.

C. Recognition, Reconciliation and Restoration of Culture

Undoubtedly, litigation can be divisive just as it can be restorative, but what emerges from much discussion on the impact of litigation is that it can, and sometimes does, facilitate healing processes. To the extent that, as noted above, it has clarified truth, provoked apologies and consolidated 'collective memory' in particular contexts, litigation has also been associated with 'individual and collective processes of coming to terms with the past'.[116]

The opening of museums, monuments that bear the names of the dead, and commemorative events that honour them, as reflected in Chapters 6 and 8, may be important manifestations of this impact. Their significance is reflected in the inscription on the chapel which was built in Plan de Sánchez, Guatemala as part of the reparation associated with the massacre at the same site: 'Memory, truth, justice and reparations form the fundamental base of the restitution of the social fabric and an authentic reconciliation'.

The litigation of colonial crimes provides another telling example of processes that have been described by litigants as beginning to heal very old wounds.[117] The Mau Mau torture case brought to British courts, and the associated settlement, was described as 'the beginning of reconciliation between the Mau Mau freedom fighters of Kenya and the British government'.[118] The reconciliatory impact cannot be dissociated from the other more concrete consequences of the legal action, which included financial compensation, a memorial, welfare for Mau Mau veterans and a lifting of the ban on the organisation.

Given the cultural impact of certain violations, the corresponding need for reparation that restores culture is emphasised in litigation on issues such as genocide in Guatemala and indigenous rights more broadly.[119] In the former, the desecration of Mayan culture was inherently linked to the genocide by the state, and strongly reflected in the reparations judgment. Though implementation has been incomplete, specific and concrete measures have been taken to 'promote' the Mayan culture and language. Likewise, the documentation and presentation in court of the 'historical, cultural, social and religious precepts' of indigenous groups, in famous cases such as Enderois litigation before the African Commission, has been described as 'an important vehicle to capture … cultural heritage', regenerating the 'cultural pride of the communities'.[120]

---

[116] See esp the Guatemala and Argentina studies (Chs 5 and 7).

[117] Duffy (n 12) citing members of the Mau Mau movement, in relation to the Mau Mau case concerning UK colonial crimes in Kenya.

[118] Mau Mau representative Gitu Kahengeri, cited in Duffy (n 12). The settlement agreement included a payment in respect of 5,228 claimants, as well as a substantial sum in costs, to the total value of £19.9 million. But it also led to the construction of a memorial in Nairobi and welfare for Mau Mau War Veterans.

[119] J Gilbert, 'Indigenous People Land Rights' (2017) Open Society Justice Initiative 59, 60 www.opensocietyfoundations.org/sites/default/files/slip-land-rights-20170424.pdf.

[120] Ibid.

VII. Mobilisation and Empowerment

Many international studies identify politically aware, mobilised and organised groups as factors that are often key (albeit not essential) to the longer-term strategic success of litigation initiatives.[121] In turn, it can equally be said that litigation is a 'political and politicising process' that itself, empowers and enables.[122]

This is particularly important where cases bring to public attention issues that affect marginalised social groups or persons subject to prejudice and discrimination, as is so often the case with the full range of human rights violations. Strategic litigation can contribute to giving a public voice to that group, as well as highlighting that issue. In so doing it may enhance the confidence and standing of the group, or their representatives,[123] and in turn their leverage and capacity to defend themselves and represent others in the future. It may influence the resources at their disposal, as illustrated in some of the case studies.

Litigation processes can contribute to the creation or strengthening of social structures within affected groups, that enhances the effectiveness of other, non-litigation strategies.[124] In Palestine, litigation by groups such as the Sheikh Jarrah communities of East Jerusalem vitalised a strong community voice. In Guatemala, an association of victims that came together principally for the purpose of preparing litigation has endured as a collective and enhanced the ability of the survivors to assert their rights. This was described by one interviewee as perhaps the most significant contribution of the massacre cases in the longer term.[125] In Argentina, it has been suggested that the largely shared priority of the struggle against impunity through litigation contributed to the cohesion of the whole human rights movement in that state. The need for regional and international coordination has contributed in turn to international networks which have enhanced other human rights advocacy work.[126]

---

[121] S Budlender, G Marcus SC and N Ferreira, *Public Interest Litigation and Social Change in South Africa: Strategies, Tactics and Lessons* (The Atlantic Philanthropies, 2014); G Marcus and N Ferreira, *A Strategic Evaluation of Public Interest Litigation South Africa* (The Atlantic Philanthropies, 2008). See eg study on why litigation on human rights issues in US and India reaped differential results, and the Atlantic Philanthropies report analysis of the factors contributing to impact in eg the well-known *Grootboom* housing case in South Africa, which includes social mobilisation as a key factor. My analysis of Guatemala reaches similar conclusions, to the effect that one of the most important outcomes of the litigation processes was the longer-term social organisation and mobilisation. See also MJ Guembe's analysis of dictatorship-related litigation in Argentina, Ch7.

[122] Dugard and Langford, 'Art or Science?' (n 9).

[123] Interview Maitre Chaibou, co-counsel in the *Mani* case in Niger, noting that cases from his office, or involving Timidria, the antislavery NGO, are now taken seriously and cannot be ignored.

[124] See Chs 5 and 8 on Guatemala and Palestine respectively. As noted, several analyses of public interest cases have noted the significance of mobilisation for litigation. Beyond that, the formation of litigation support groups can itself have other broader benefits for the community, as noted in eg the study on Guatemala.

[125] Interview with Paul Se.

[126] Shared objectives in relation to the criminal prosecutions of previous regimes in Latin American and beyond has led to complex networks and partnerships between human rights organisations, and sometimes state actors.

Litigation can have a crucial mobilising effect on other victims of the impugned practices. Indeed, there are many cases where victims have themselves become human rights defenders following litigation, as seen in the *Mani* case in Niger in Chapter 5, where Mani took on the challenge of litigation to secure her freedom and later became an advocate for those still enslaved.[127] In Niger, the research and interviews brought to light remarkable evidence of how news of the litigation swept into many dark corners of the country, and inspired other victims to come forward and to seek help.[128]

It has been observed by Dugard and Langford in the South African context that an increasingly common critique of litigation is that 'rights-based approaches have traditionally neglected the dimension of power—that is to say that rights discourse has over-emphasised the agency of actors and under-emphasised the structures of dominating power [whether these are social, political or economic]'.[129] To the extent that litigation can, in effect, target this underlying reality, its positive impact should not be underestimated. More broadly, it has been suggested that the human rights litigation process is fundamentally about the transfer of power from the executive to individuals, so far as it reviews executive action against the benchmark of human rights.[130] This is linked to empowerment, but also strengthening democracy, the last level of impact highlighted in this report.

VIII. Democracy and the Rule of Law Impact

An essential ingredient of democratic legitimacy is the willingness to govern within the law. Judicial oversight and accountability are inherent to that enterprise. While strategic litigation may therefore seek to be instrumental in myriad forms of change, its intrinsic value as an instrument of the rule of law should not be underestimated. It can reinforce the importance of law, seek to give it real effect, and contribute to the stabilisation of a legal system.

Through litigation, states are called to account—at least to some extent: to explain, clarify or change their positions. This can arise throughout the legal

---

[127] Duffy (n 12) revealed examples from Turkey and Argentina and Kenya on this. See s V.A. In the case of *Akkoç v Turkey*, 2 women suffering extreme vulnerability and abuse as slaves regained their role in society and became advocates for others in similar positions of vulnerability.

[128] Interviews Niger. Affirmed in Special Rapporteur on Slavery's Report of 2015 (UN Doc A/HRC/30/35).

[129] Dugard and Langford (n 9).

[130] Then Dame Mary Arden stated in a 2005 case that 'the decision in the A case should not be misinterpreted as a transfer of power from the executive to the judiciary. The position is that the judiciary now has the important task of reviewing executive action against the benchmark of human rights. Thus, the transfer of power is not to the judiciary but to the individual'; (2005) 121 *Law Quarterly Review* 623624; TH Smith 'Balancing Liberty and Security? A Legal Analysis of United Kingdom Anti-Terrorist Legislation' (2007) 13 *European Journal of Criminal Policy and Research* 73.

process, questions to parties and the broader debate, as well as through the ultimate judicial decision. As the unfolding litigation stories in Latin America may attest, the existence of robust judiciaries, and the willingness of government to be criticised and challenged within the framework of law, is itself a test of democratic maturity. Following transitions to democracy, SHRL can therefore play a particularly important role. Analysis of the role of litigation in post-totalitarian countries of Central and Eastern Europe suggests that strategic litigation has proved to be a useful tool in developing human rights protection.[131] In the Palestinian context some have suggested that resort to the courts is about investing in and building that democracy for the future.[132] This reflects discussion in Argentina on the extent to which the swath of accountability litigation has, over time, contributed to the reassertion of the significance of the judiciary, thereby 'consolidating the transition to democracy'.[133]

IX. Negative Impact

Despite its potential, human rights litigation is not an outcome-neutral enterprise. The real negative impact that strategic (and especially 'unstrategic') litigation can have underscores the importance of ensuring that litigation is done carefully and selectively. There are many ways in which litigation can be—and has in practice been—counter-productive or damaging, many of which are flagged already and explored in the case studies that now follow. Indeed, most dimensions of positive impact, have a potential flip side; litigation can have (and, as case studies show, have had) detrimental effects on victims, the legal framework, policies and practices, on public attitudes and social movements.

The abundant and shocking examples around the world today of the negative consequences that flow from bringing legal action for applicants and those associated with them cannot be neglected in any responsible discussion on SHRL impact.[134] The stories behind the cases reveal brutal reprisals, as epitomised by the ground-breaking *Aksoy v Turkey* case, which is known for its jurisprudential impact on 'torture' standards, but which led to the applicant being re-tortured and ultimately killed, and his father repeatedly tortured and castrated, for refusing

---

[131] See eg *Assenov v Bulgaria* Appl no 90/1997/874/1086 (28 October 1998) (ECtHR) and examples in 'Access to Justice in Central and Eastern Europe' (Public Interest Law Initiative, 2003).

[132] Interviews for land rights case study.

[133] See eg L Fillipini on criminal processes as consolidating democracy in Ch7, Argentina Case Study. For a recent questioning of the extent to which the focus on criminal law has gone far enough to build social cohesion and democratic foundations, see M Goti 'Crímenes de Estado, Dilemas de la Justicia' (Buenos Aries, Hammurabi, 2016).

[134] See M Forst, Report of the Special Rapporteur on the Situation of Human Rights Defenders, 29 December 2014 (A/HRC/28/63).

to cede to threats to withdraw complaints.[135] Some of the case studies explored here, such as the Argentinian dictatorship cases, have similarly involved the disappearance and torture of complainants and witnesses.[136] In Palestine, individuals have been arrested for lodging complaints. Many other applicants elsewhere report similar consequences, or public vilification for 'betraying their country' through complaining to a foreign court.[137] The growing practice of bringing criminal complaints against lawyers and others for supporting 'terrorist' applicants is one of the many sinister implications that SHRL has in the world today.[138] This reality underscores the often multiple vulnerabilities of those applicants subject to on-going violations, who most need the protection of SHRL but often cannot secure it.[139]

The litigation process can also be traumatising, as noted above, in more and less insidious ways. Victims may feel marginalised or disrespected within elitist judicial or 'lawyer-led' processes. Beyond the direct treatment of victims throughout the processes is the simple fact of unfulfilled expectations, and a sense of being, once again, the victim of injustice when litigation 'fails'.[140] Given the range of negative consequences, unsurprisingly, in many cases, victims withdraw their claims, and the potential of litigation for them and others is never realised.[141] Perhaps more remarkable is the determination that so many show, despite all odds, to pursue justice before the courts. Other broader negative consequences include the consolidation of poor jurisprudence or the adoption of clarifying legislation that further restricts rights.[142]

The potential for political backlash against issues, groups or institutions even of 'winning cases' makes careful evaluation of prospects and timing essential. The political and social reverberations from the IACtHR's advisory opinion on gender equality and same sex marriage requested by the government of Costa Rica, with

---

[135] See the excellent book Goldhaber, *A Peoples History of the European Court of Human Rights* (n 51) one of relatively few studies that seeks to tell the human stories behind ECtHR cases and their real consequences.

[136] eg dictatorship witness Jorge Julio López in Argentina provides an example, or see more recently cases on torture in detention today where reprisals have arisen in Argentina; Duffy (n 12).

[137] This has arisen recurrently in Turkey; see Duffy (n 12). Interview Ayse Bingol and Nebahat Akkoç, the applicant in the *Akkoç v Turkey* case.

[138] Interview with Tahir Elçi for Duffy (n 12), whose case *Tahir Elci and others v Turkey* Appl no 23145/93 and 25091/94 (13 November 2003) (ECtHR) focused specifically on torture and intimidation of lawyers. Elci was tragically executed shortly after this interview in November 2015.

[139] eg those in continuing detention, or on-going enslavement, who seek to litigate assume great risks. The death of the *Opuz* (n 119) applicants, after complaints had been made, show the challenges arising from ineffectiveness of complaints procedures to secure protection.

[140] Unjust outcomes may involve not only losing the case, eg the victim may win on some points but be denied basic compensation on dubious grounds. This arose in the *Maskhadova and Others v Russia* Appl no 18071/05 (6 June 2013) (ECtHR), case where I represented the family members with Interights colleagues.

[141] See Ch 2 above. I have had strong claims dropped by women in Guatemala, in the war on terror context, and in women's rights cases across systems and in Turkey. See also Interview with Öztürk Türkdoğan, president of the Human Rights Association and Ayse Bingol, 11 December 2015; Duffy (n 12).

[142] See Ch 7 and Ch 9.

potential implications for the outcome of national elections in that country, provide dramatic illustration.[143] At the same time, similar controversies arose around the impact of same sex marriage litigation in US courts, where it has been argued that short-term backlash ceded to longer-term progress.[144] Nonetheless, pushback in popular opinion may worsen the discrimination that so often underpins violations, and compound underlying problems. Negative outcomes from litigation may, in turn, reaffirm an unfavourable law or practice and make it more resistant (or impossible) to challenge in subsequent cases, depending on the legal system,[145] thereby entrenching the problem. Undermining of the judicial role by government, press or others, where litigation does support 'unpopular' causes, is often a risk.

Litigation is necessarily limited by particular facts, applicants, laws and the jurisdiction of particular courts. It may occasionally reframe debate in unduly limited, and less helpful ways. It may close debate down while it is subject to litigation, with potentially chilling effects on other strategies for change.[146]

Finally, litigation risks providing a veneer of legitimacy around practices, policies or indeed the legal system as a whole. A finding against applicants can be misunderstood or manipulated to undermine causes and social movements. Acquittals or adverse rulings can, and often have, been portrayed as proving that allegations were 'fabricated' or baseless.[147] A court's rejection or even refusal to exercise jurisdiction can be seen as a determination that the claim was unmeritorious (whatever the basis for the court's ruling which may be quite different).[148] More broadly, as explored in the case studies, deep concerns can emerge as to the long-term impact of the 'legitimising' role of litigation. Intractable debates and profound concerns have arisen in Palestinian context as to the role of legal challenges in 'beautifying' the occupation in Palestine—creating an impression at home and abroad that there is a fair and functioning legal system wherein justice can be served while, for certain rights issues at least, this is highly questionable.[149]

---

[143] Advisory Opinion, IACHR No 24 on Gender Identity, Equality and Non-Discrimination, 9 January 2018.

[144] Eg M. Klarman, From the Closet to the Alter, Courts, Backlash and the Struggle for Same-Sex Marriage (Oxford, OUP, 2014).

[145] A direct and curious example is Art 26 of the Irish Constitution, under which the President may refer a proposed bill of doubtful constitutionality to the Supreme Court prior to its enactment into law; however, if the bill is found to be constitutional by the Court, the subsequent statute is immune from constitutional challenge.

[146] Reporting while litigation is pending may be limited, or governments may refuse to answer questions on the basis that issues are 'sub judice', pending judicial resolution. One peace activist at the roundtable discussion of the draft of this study suggested that a downside of acclaimed litigation in Dutch courts of the Srebrenica massacre had impeded the broader political discussion around responsibility for example.

[147] There are numerous examples of this from Turkey, see Duffy (n 12).

[148] In my experience this is most problematic where opaque admissibility procedures (as before the ECtHR eg—see Ch 2) mean cases can be thrown out without reasons.

[149] See case study in Ch 9 on Palestine for structural issue, courts responses, associated debate; see discussion on the proposals of a boycott of the Israeli courts that were ultimately rejected; see M Sfard, *The Wall and the Gate* (forthcoming, 2018).

There are shadows of these debates and concerns around some of the war on terror litigation, notably the dysfunctional Guantanamo habeas hearings.[150] One lawyer who practised during apartheid described the feeling of 'being tarnished by the need to speak in terms of laws they despise'.[151] While litigation may seek to improve the legal and political landscape it is also constrained by it, posing unenviable dilemmas for those considering SHRL.

It should also be recalled, however, that impact, whether negative or positive, is complex, often a matter of perspective, and rarely linear. Today's setback may be a stepping stone towards tomorrow's progress, and vice versa.

---

[150] Ch 7, Litigating the War on Terror. Since 2010, Guantanamo habeas proceedings have ground to an effective halt, leading to questions as to whether they merely create an illusion of judicial oversight.
[151] He described the dilemma as follows: 'A specter is haunting lawyers working against injustice—the specter of legitimation. Those who seek to challenge unjust states by using the law of those states against them are very likely to feel tarnished by the need to speak in terms of laws they despise. This sense of personal taint is bad enough, and sometimes may simply be intolerable'; S Ellmann, 'Struggle and Legitimation' (1995) 20 *Law & Social Inquiry* 339.

Part II

5

Case Study—*Hadijatou Mani v Niger*: Slavery before the ECOWAS Court

I. Introduction

The *Hadijatou Mani v Niger* (the *Mani*) case presents a set of circumstances faced by thousands of women living as *wahiya* or 'fifth wives' in Niger.[1] Hadijatou was born into servile status and sold (with witnesses and associated contractual formalities) into sexual slavery at age 12. What is exceptional in Hadijatou Mani's case, however, is that she escaped slavery, and went on to pursue—and eventually achieve—a measure of justice. The litigation of her case before the West Africa Community Court of Justice of the Economic Community of West African States (ECOWAS Court) has been extolled as historic.[2] This study is an attempt to better understand the true impact of this case—for Hadijatou herself, for others subject to the same violations in Niger, and on the enabling environment that sustains the on-going scourge of slavery-related practices in West Africa.

I was co-counsel in the *Mani* case before the ECOWAS Court, representing Hadijatou alongside Ibrahima Kane (also of Interights and one of our lawyers on the Africa programme) and Abdourahman Chaibou, a private lawyer in Niamey. I have written two earlier papers on this case,[3] but for the purposes of this

---

[1] Estimates are elusive and vary starkly. Anti-Slavery International (ASI) has often cited 43,000, a figure based on a study done by Timidria, a Nigerien anti-slavery organisation, in 2003. Other sources cite figures as high as 160,000. Local anti-slavery groups have suggested that the practice may be on the decline, following in part the publicity emanating from this case; however, it may simply be better hidden. See eg 'Report of the Special Rapporteur on contemporary forms of slavery, including its causes and consequences', Urmila Bhoola, Mission to the Niger (2015).

[2] *Mme Hadijatou Mani Koroua v The Republic of Niger*, 27 October 2008, No ECW/CCJ/JUD/06/08 (Judgment). See eg 'Former Slave Wins Historic Case Against Niger Government' *The Telegraph* (28 October 2008); 'Free at Last: Female Slave Who Dared to Take Niger to Court' *The Times* (28 October 2008); 'Court Rules Niger Failed by Allowing Girl's Slavery' *New York Times* (27 October 2008); 'Une Cour Regionale Africaine Condamne le Niger pour Esclavage' *Le Monde* (27 October 2008). In B Kampmark, 'A Little Case of Slavery: Niger and Hadijatou Mani', Hadijatou's role is compared to Rosa Parks' refusal to move seats on a segregated bus in the US, available at www.factsandarts.com/articles/a-little-case-of-slavery-niger-and-hadijatou-mani.

[3] 'Hadijatou Mani v Niger: Slavery Unveiled by the ECOWAS Court' (2009) *Human Rights Law Review* 151–70, and H Duffy, 'Human Rights Litigation in Sub-regional African Courts: Towards Justice for Victims or Just More Fragmentation?' in L van den Herik and C Stahn (eds), *The Diversification*

study I wanted to go back and explore more deeply, with Hadijatou herself and others, the true nature of the impact eight years on. I suspected it would expose a much more nuanced picture than appeared in the euphoric post-judgment era. I visited Niger from 20–25 April 2016 with partners from civil society groups active on slavery in the region (Anti-Slavery International (ASI) and Minority Rights Groups International (MRG));[4] our consultations with victims and survivors, government representatives, lawyers, paralegals, judges at various levels of the court system and members of civil society groups, during that trip, have provided the material for this study.[5]

The following sections sketch the background and context of the litigation, indicate some of the layers of impact that the case presented, suggesting en route various factors that may have contributed to impact, or impeded it, and some of the lessons we might learn from this experience for the future.

II. Background

A. Slavery in Niger and beyond

The practices underlying this case are unequivocally prohibited, not only under international law—where slavery violates one of the most fundamental norms of the international order and carries state and individual responsibility[6]—but also in the Nigerien domestic system. Slavery was officially abolished in French West Africa in 1905, prohibited by the first Constitution of Niger after independence in 1960 and criminalised in Niger's penal code in 2003.

The gap between law and reality is such that slavery and related practices are nonetheless widespread and remain deeply entrenched in Nigerien society. While more prevalent in some areas than others, slavery is spread throughout much

---

and Fragmentation of International Criminal Law (Leiden, Martinus Nijhoff, 2012) 163–84. Some of the description below is drawn from this work.

  [4] I travelled with colleagues from ASI and Minority Rights Group International. I am very grateful to Sarah Mathewson, Emanuelle Treameau (ASI) and Lucy Claridge (MRG) for their input and support and to the Freedom Fund which funded the trip to explore impact and the value and feasibility of future cases.

  [5] In Niger we interviewed: Hadijatou Mani in her village; former slaves (fifth wives) through 2 sessions in the town of Dogueraoua, and in a village inhabited by former slaves and their descendants, Zongo Ablo; several judges in the capital Niamey and in the town of Konni including the head of the local courts, the court of cassation and court of appeal; lawyers and civil society actors, notably Timidria and Mr Chaibou, the lawyer who has conducted all of the slavery-related cases supported by Timidria and sponsored by ASI; various government officials from the Ministry of Justice; and nascent 'agences' dedicated to slavery and trafficking.

  [6] It constitutes a particularly egregious human rights violation, enshrining obligations *erga omnes*, and giving rise to individual criminal responsibility if carried out on a widespread or systemic basis.

of the state in both urban and rural areas, and though often associated with the Tuareg and their complex caste system, slavery and the entrenched discrimination and exploitation of persons of 'slave descent' transcends the 26 ethnic groups that exist in Niger today. The true scale of the problem is unclear,[7] but there is little doubt that the *Mani* case that emerged in 2007/08 was emblematic of a widespread, if rarely acknowledged, phenomenon in Niger and neighbouring states.

Her experience also formed part of a much bigger global problem than is often recognised, with recent estimates putting victims of modern day-slavery at over 45 million.[8] In Niger, as elsewhere, slavery is sustained—and rendered particularly resistant to change—by its inherent nexus with profit and deep structural inequalities, among other complex factors.[9] As one scholar noted, by way of background to the *Mani* case:

> Scholars can't quite agree on what came first: racism or economic justification, but the truth, as always, lies somewhere in between. In Niger, the institution persists as if it were genetic—those whose ancestors were slaves bear the mark of it for their lives. The mark, like Cain, is virtually impossible to shrug off. As the people who assumed power after independence came from a slave-owning pedigree, there was little surprise in its durability in Niger. A country blighted by military regimes and a dominant agricultural sector did little to eliminate its perceived worth.[10]

B. Hadijatou Mani's Slave Status and 'Liberation'

The facts of the *Mani* case represent as clear a case of slavery as they come. As such, the case did not shift the boundaries of the law or our understanding of the prohibition, as some other slavery and trafficking case have done.[11] Rather, it gave

---

[7] See n 1 on varying estimates.

[8] In 2016, the Global Slavery Index estimates that 45.8 million people are in some form of modern slavery in 167 countries.

[9] The ambiguous role of customary law and obscure relationship between 'slavery' and 'marriage' emerge throughout the *Mani* case; broader factors of relevance include extreme degrees of poverty and under-development, low education and deficits in the rule of law infrastructure some of which are highlighted below.

[10] See Kampmark, 'A Little Case of Slavery' (n 2). It also notes:

> There was very little peculiar about keeping it going on in Niger after its independence in 1960. Slavery is very much a case of economic self-interest and the preservation of racial inequalities ... Niger is not the only state responsible for allowing this 'peculiar institution' to persist, a term coined by American scholars who examined the intricate workings of slavery in the Deep South. Other West African states—Mauritania, Mali, Burkina Faso—continue to either condone or turn a blind eye to the practice.

[11] See the overview in 'The Regional Litigation of Modern Day Slavery: a Nascent Contribution' (2016) 14(2) *Journal of International Criminal Studies*. Cases such as *Rantsev v Cyprus and Russia* Appl no 25965/04 (2010) (ECHR) or *Trabalhadores do Brazil v Brazil* Case no 12.066 (2016) (IACHR), where I intervened with colleagues as third party or *amicus intervenor*, helped shaped our understanding of modern slavery more given more complex sets of facts. But see jurisprudential impact (s IV.F) below.

a compelling human face to the problem, exposed its nature and the tolerance of it—indeed the flagrant disregard for the prohibition, as well as the many legal, institutional and social obstacles that stood in the way of giving that prohibition practical effect.

Hadijatou Mani was born the daughter of a slave and inherited her mother's servile status.[12] When she was around 12, despite her mother's opposition, she was sold by her mother's owner to El Hadj Souleymane Naroua for the sum of 240,000 CFA (equivalent to around 300 Euros). The extent of the acceptance and assumed legitimacy of the practice of slavery is revealed in clear terms by the fact that her sale, like her subsequent liberation, was governed by contracts of purchase and transfer certificates. These were transactions with certain attendant formalities, officiated and witnessed by several people, including village chiefs, not carried out under cover of night without trace or evidence. Just like her sister before her, whom we also met in Niger, and very many more girls across Niger, Hadijatou was duly bought and paid for and dispatched to her new owner.

From the age of 13 she was subject to a seven days a week routine of harsh unremunerated labour, rape, humiliation and punishments when she tried to escape. Later, during her testimony to the ECOWAS Court, she would describe the physical, sexual and emotional abuse and the degradation of being reminded constantly by her master and others that she was a slave. She depicted a life that she summed up as being treated 'like a goat'. Her new master had four wives, whom Hadijatou also served, and seven other *wahiya* or *sadaka*[13] ('fifth wives' or female domestic slaves).

In an unusual turn of events, after 10 years of captivity in 2005, her master decided to 'liberate' Hadijatou in order to make her one of his four wives. He duly provided her with a signed 'liberation certificate' (which later provided the ECOWAS Court with compelling evidence), that specified that 'I, El Hadj Souleymane Naroua have liberated Mme Hadijatou Koroua on this day 18 August and she is now free and is no-one's slave'.[14] The certificate was signed by the 'chef du village', 'the master' and the 'beneficiary'. A striking amount of weight seems to be placed on these certificates by victims and civil society groups, as if the right to freedom was enshrined in or could depend on these pseudo-legal documents. Yet in her 'liberation certificate', Hadijatou saw her right to be free and, armed

---

[12] Her sisters, one of whom we interviewed in Niger, were similarly sold.

[13] The Court describes the practice of *sadaka* or *wahiya* as 'acquiring a young girl, generally in servile conditions, to serve both domestically and as a concubine'; Judgment (n 2) at para 8. The form of slavery in practice in Hadijatou Mani's case was *wahiya or sadaka*, which consists of acquiring a young girl as a slave, sometimes referred to as one of the 'fifth wives', ie as a supplement to the four a man can legally marry in accordance with Islam's Recommendations as interpreted in Niger. The *sadaka* does housework and is at the '*master*'s service' for sexual relations at any time. See also paras 9 and 10 of the judgment (n 2).

[14] On file with author.

with it, she refused to marry her former master and tried to leave. This provoked two parallel lines of legal cases in Niger—her prosecution at her former master's instigation, for bigamy (on the basis that she had gone with another man of her choice, with whom she still lives today) and her own attempt to secure recognition of her right to be free.

C. Futile Attempts at Justice in Niger

The litigation at the domestic level (in which we were not involved) went in bizarre and bewildering directions, demonstrating an overarching problem—the lack of capacity, independence and/or regard for or understanding of the law by those whose job it is to give it effect. It also exposed judicial approaches to slavery, and the obscure relationship between slavery and marriage in the eyes of the courts.[15] In brief, her former master, Naroua, argued that Hadijatou and he were de facto married. The first instance local Tribunal Civil et Coutumier ruled in Hadijatou's favour, not based on the prohibition on slavery, but rather on the fact that the requirements of marriage under customary law had not been met. Naroua appealed, and the Tribunal de Grande Instance (TGI) reversed the decision, ruling that under Niger's customary law a female slave is de facto married to her master once she is released. Hadijatou brought the case before the Supreme Court, which sent the case back to the TGI on the basis of procedural irregularities, again without reference to the fundamental nature of the rights at stake.

In parallel, and following the same logic, a complaint for bigamy proceeded against Hadijatou. She, her new husband and her brother (who had assisted in her marriage) were sentenced to six months' imprisonment and a fine of 50,000 CFA each.[16] They appealed their convictions before the Court of Appeal in Niamey, which deferred the case until the decision of the divorce judge was rendered.[17] The acceptance of slavery throughout society, including by the judiciary in Niger, as well as the lack of independence and impartiality, is illustrated in the banality of the responses of the courts and the police when the facts of Hadijatou's case came to their attention.[18]

[15] Former slaves have been treated as de facto married to their former master upon liberation (as Naroua argued), while a defence to charges of slavery includes marrying the 'slave'. This is one of numerous issues that needs to be addressed in Niger.

[16] Decision of 2 May 2007 by the Correctional Tribunal of the TGI.

[17] Decision of 9 July 2007; as discussed below, we were assured in Niger that the prosecution has been de facto dropped, but this charge has never been formally resolved.

[18] As noted below, the police imprisoned Hadijatou for bigamy when she left her master, rather than protecting her in accordance with anti-slavery laws. The customary courts ignored domestic legal provisions and applied customary laws that condone and regulate slavery.

III. The *Hadijatou Mani* Case before the ECOWAS Court

The case came to Interights via informal networks, through local anti-slavery activists at Timidria, and international networks including Anti-Slavery International (ASI). At this point in time Hadijatou was in a situation of extreme vulnerability; subject to reprisals and intimidation by her former master, imprisonment by the authorities for daring to assert her freedom, with a pending prosecuted for bigamy and an uncertain appeal pending. She required urgent action to be taken on her behalf.

The *Mani* case was plainly important not only for the applicant but more broadly, and there was quite rightly little doubt that we should do it. The main goal was to seek immediate protection. That the case could have broader potential impact was also immediately apparent, given the nature of the violations and the prevalence of the problem it epitomised, but secondary to meeting the client's very immediate needs. Nonetheless, while in this case the decision whether to take the case was straightforward, there were real challenges and strategic dilemmas, regarding *how* and *where*.

First, a highly significant consideration in a case like this was ensuring victim protection and effective representation from a prison in rural Niger. A major *sine qua non* was gaining personal access to Hadijatou in order to receive her consent and instructions, and ensuring her support and full engagement before, during and after the case. The role and commitment of NGOs like Timidria and ASI was essential in this and at all stages of the process. The case, and the impact it ultimately had, was principally a result of the network of local, national and international civil society, supported by, and working hand in glove with the team of three lawyers with national, regional and international experience.

Second was the question of *where* to take the case. The obvious forum would have been the African Commission on Human and Peoples' Rights (ACHPR) where Interights frequently litigated. This would in some ways have been a safe and familiar terrain, but there was justifiable cause for concern regarding effectiveness, and whether the ACHPR would be willing or able to act on an expedited basis.[19] There was also a novel option on the table. A couple of years earlier, in 2005, the ECOWAS Court had adopted a protocol extending its jurisdiction 'to determine cases of violations of human rights that occur in any member state' which had yet to be fully tested.[20] This development was part of the emergence

---

[19] The Commission could in theory have requested provisional measures but whether they would have done so in a case like this, and whether they would ultimately have been adhered to was in doubt.

[20] The Court's Protocol provides jurisdiction 'to determine cases of violations of human rights that occur in any member state' without qualification, and potentially embraces economic and social as well as civil and political rights. See Supplementary Protocol A/SP.1/01/05 of 19 January 2005, Art 9(4).

of new sub-regional fora in Africa.[21] These nascent human rights courts were, however, relatively unknown, compared to the ACHPR or the United Nations (UN) committees that could have received individual complaints on Niger, and there were (ultimately well-founded)[22] concerns about lack of experience in human rights law. I recall feeling considerable wariness about being 'experimental' with such a sensitive and urgent case. On the other hand, all avenues involved risks and pitfalls, and the ECOWAS Court's rules and processes compared very favourably to those of other available fora on various grounds;[23] on balance, the benefits were considered to outweigh the risks. After some angst and deliberation, the ECOWAS Court was chosen for its lighter case load, and potential weight, providing the promise of faster handling of this urgent case, hopefully greater impact in Niger in the short term, and ultimately a binding judgment with greater prospect of implementation.[24] The choice of forum in this case was, on reflection, an absolutely critical one that transformed the nature of the *Mani* case and its wide-reaching impact (as discussed at section IV).

On 14 December 2007, we filed a submission before the ECOWAS Community Court of Justice on behalf of Hadijatou Mani Koroua,[25] arguing that the state was responsible for serious violations of her human rights including slavery, discrimination on grounds of gender and social origin, arbitrary detention and denial of family rights. The respondent state argued that the case was inadmissible as it was pending before Nigerien courts, and that as the applicant and Souleymane Naroua were in fact married this was therefore a private matter and not one for the state. The Court joined the issues of admissibility and merits.

In *Ugokwe v Nigeria*, Judgment No ECW/CCJ/APP/02/05 of 7 October 2005, para 29, the Court noted 'the inclusion and recognition of the African Charter in Article 4 of the Treaty of the Community behoves on the Court by Article 19 of the Protocol to bring in the application of those rights catalogued in the African Charter'. The Charter covers a broad range of civil, political, economic and social rights.

[21] At around the same time, the Community (SADC) Tribunal's jurisdictional influence in the human rights arena was also being tested (with ultimately notorious results as, following its decision regarding unlawful evictions in Zimbabwe (*Mike Campbell (Pvt) Ltd & Others v Republic of Zimbabwe*, 28 November 2008), the tribunal was suspended under pressure from Zimbabwe).

[22] See s IV.F (impact on legal standards) below, noting that to some extent this concern was borne out by the approach taken to certain basic human rights principles, though on balance the decision was the right one.

[23] The then recently established African Court did not have jurisdiction.

[24] Rules of the ECOWAS Court, Art 62. There is no rule of exhaustion of domestic remedies, which potentially mattered given that the Supreme Court had sent the case back to the lower courts. Cases can take several years before the ACHPR (as before the ECtHR in the European context). Hearings before the Commission are generally private, so neither the press nor public have access, and in any event neither hearings nor the issuance of decisions are scheduled in advance. Ultimately, they lead to recommendations of the Commission rather than binding judgments. This Court with its speedy, public process and binding judgments compared favourably—on paper at least.

[25] *Hadijatou Mani v Republic of Niger*, Requete (on file with author) based on Art 9(4) of Supplementary Protocol A/SP.1/01/05 of 19 January 2005 amending Protocol A/P.1/7/91 of 6 July 1991, which provides that the ECOWAS Court has the jurisdiction 'to determine cases of violations of human rights that occur in any member state'.

At a preliminary hearing held at the seat of the ECOWAS Court in Abuja, Nigeria, in January 2008, we asked the Court to exercise its power to sit outside its own seat, in the state where the violations occurred. We hoped that this would have a positive impact for Hadijatou and in Niger more broadly, but we could not be sure, and it increased the stakes. The government did not formally oppose but expressed concern about a 'possible negative media effect and politicisation of the trial'.[26] The Court agreed to exercise its discretion to hear the case in Niamey, the capital of Niger, citing the nature of the case, the applicant's circumstances and the need to secure the attendance of witnesses.[27]

The dividends paid by this decision went beyond what any of us could have anticipated. The critical faculty of the Court to sit in the state where the violations arose, and for an indigent victim, witnesses, civil society, journalists and the general public to access the Court and engage with the process, proved crucial to the impact of the case. The hearing of the case in Niger made possible active participation by the applicant, led to a degree of engagement by relevant actors in Niger and stimulated public debate on slavery in Niger, in a way that has transformed the significance of the case.[28]

The merits hearing was held in Niamey from 7 through 11 April 2008, during which the Court heard the applicant, witnesses,[29] the counsel for the applicant and the respondent state. The Supreme Court was decked out with a full military welcome for the ECOWAS Court, which was treated, oddly, as visiting dignitaries, with grandees from across government and the state holding a reception for the Court and appearing in Court for the hearing. This caused some discomfort for some of us, given our sense of the judicial role, but it reflected the state's public engagement, and keenness to assume a respectful posture, which was crucial in the process and continued (to its credit) after judgment. The hearing generated much interest within Nigerien society and was well attended by a diverse public and the press.[30] The media attention was critical to the ability of the case to have a multiplying effect across Niger and beyond.[31]

On 27 October 2008, the ECOWAS Court rendered judgment in *Hadijatou Mani Koroua v Niger*. The Court found the state of Niger in violation of its international obligations to protect Hadijatou Mani from slavery, and awarded

---

[26]   ECOWAS Court, Judgment (n 2) at para 32.

[27]   Ibid. ECOWAS Court, Decision, Case No ECW/CCJ/APP/08/08, 24 January 2008 (on file with author).

[28]   See s IV.

[29]   Witnesses for the applicant were a witness to Hadijatou's original sale, the person who transferred Hadijatou from her 'seller' to her new master and a member of the anti-slavery NGO Timidria who was a witness to the conditions in which she lived when he met her, to obtaining her liberation certificate and to government attempts to 'clear the mess up' by having Hadijatou lawfully marry her former master despite the latter's refusal on the basis that, he argued, they were already married. The state's witnesses were a village chief and canton chief who testified against the prevalence of slavery in Niger and a sociologist who testified to the practice of slavery beyond Niger.

[30]   The courtroom was full each day. In attendance were the president of the parliament, Supreme Court judges, the foreign minister, the National Guard and members of Nigerien civil society.

[31]   See s IV; there was quite extensive coverage inside Niger and internationally.

Hadijatou compensation.[32] It was undoubtedly a proverbial 'champagne moment'. The *Hadijatou Mani* judgment was immediately hailed as 'historic' and a 'landmark' judgment.[33] As always, the epithets attached to cases have to be taken with a pinch of salt, in favour of enquiry over time as to where the significance of the case really lay, for whom and why. Exploring the impact of the *Mani* case in Niger revealed areas of limited progress, but also dimensions of impact that went far beyond those we had, or perhaps could have, anticipated at the time of bringing the litigation and even those that met the eye on judgment day.

I visited Hadijatou in her home, a small hut in Daltoudou, that she shares with her family. She described the importance of the case on multiple levels, as set out below. Some of these were associated with the judgment and its immediate implementation, but many were not. Notable importance was placed on the *process* of litigation and on unfolding broader reactions and gradual shifts some years later. In broader discussions with others affected by the decision, what was most striking was the extent to which the *Mani* case is known across Nigerien society and that many actors, from those most affected by slavery, to government, members of the judiciary, civil society or the public, have firm views on its significance and multi-dimensional impact.

IV. The Impact of the *Mani* Case

This section breaks down some of the indications of impact—on the applicant, on judicial and other practices and on policy, broader debate and social change—that were brought to our attention in relation to the case. The impacts considered here reflect the perspectives of those interviewed and are rarely verifiable and still less quantifiable in objective terms.[34] Nevertheless, there are strong indicators that the case had a profound impact on many people in diverse and sometimes surprising ways and at various stages.

A. Victim Impact in the Context of Slavery

i. *Judgment as Recognition*

The *Mani* judgment reached definitive conclusions regarding the existence of slavery in Niger, and acknowledged Hadijatou's story and suffering, and the violations of her rights. For the first time, a court of law found that she was right, and

---

[32] Judgment (n 2).

[33] See eg 'Niger Guilty in Landmark Slavery Case' *The Guardian* (28 October 2008); *the Times* referred to the case as 'historic'.

[34] As ever, it is impossible with some longer-term impacts to know if impact was 'caused' directly by a case. There is also difficulty obtaining sufficient information to really differentiate to what extent there have been changes in what are by their nature clandestine practices, from a situation in which there is simply less visibility surrounding practices.

that she had been wronged. First and foremost, the ECOWAS judgment recognised and recorded the factors surrounding her victimisation, breaking through the myths of marriage and bigamy to identify slavery and call it by its name. It reflected the reality of slavery as experienced by one person and sustained by many. Indirectly it identified the responsibility of the many state and non-state actors that had made it possible, from her former master, to the chiefs that officiate and benefit, to the police and the courts that failed so starkly in their obligations of protection. It sets out the facts related to her sale and transfer, psychological and physical abuse, sexual exploitation, harsh labour, physical violence, insults, threats and humiliation, and her master's role in establishing control over her movements, even after the issuance of the 'liberation certificate'.[35] The Court concluded that 'there is no doubt that the applicant, Hadijatou Mani Koroua, was held in slavery for nearly nine years, in violation of the legal prohibition of this practice'.[36] In Niger we heard from other former slaves as to the importance—not only to Hadijatou but also to them—of recognition of the widespread practice of the *wahiya* in Niger, and its unlawfulness. The positive impact of acknowledgement was felt across a greater number of victims of practices that had been the subject of taboo for generations.

ii. Critical Compensation

The vindication of Hadijatou in the ECOWAS Court's finding was accompanied by compensation. She was awarded 10,000,000 CFA (approximately 15,244 Euros) in compensation in the judgment itself; importantly (and to the government's credit), this was paid immediately following the ECOWAS Court's judgment. In a case such as this, where the violations have kept the victims destitute and without property (or the right to own), compensation assumes particular symbolic as well as practical significance. It was critical to her reintegration into society as it enabled Hadijatou to buy a few animals, a basic house and to be self-supporting. Discussions with other victims of slavery highlighted the economic realities of dependency, as preventing many from seeking freedom, the significance of monetary relief is readily apparent.[37]

iii. The Power of the Process

a. Cessation and the Chilling Effect of Litigation on Hadijatou's Situation

When the case first came to us, among Hadijatou's immediate needs were to be released from prison and for the harassment by her former master and the state to cease. Although we were concerned that no legal action could ever unfold fast

---

[35] Judgment (n 2) at para 76.

[36] Ibid, para 80.

[37] Interview with former slaves, Zongo Ablo, where they referred to complete dependence, the lack of skills, education and the inability to sustain themselves and their families as among the factors that sustain slavery.

enough to meet these needs, it is noteworthy that in this case the effects began to be felt once the ECOWAS case was filed, before any hearing and long before judgment. Hadijatou was in fact released from prison very shortly after filing, and the charges of bigamy pending against her were effectively dropped.[38] Hadijatou Mani reports that she was not pursued by her master once the ECOWAS Court's proceeding got underway. The case thus illustrates the preventative potential of litigation itself, even before it is fully underway—still less resolved.

b. Participation and Public Recognition

During the hearing of her case, Hadijatou took the difficult decision to testify before the ECOWAS Court, and a full public gallery, sitting in the Supreme Court building in Niamey. This decision, which was ultimately a decision for her, was a controversial one within the team, but on reflection made a decisive difference to the impact of the case on the victim, perhaps also on the Court and on broader public opinion. Plainly terrified, with her baby strapped to her back, Hadijatou took the stand twice to give her evidence. She described her ordeal at the hands of her former master, visibly growing in stature and confidence as she stated her case and accused those responsible.

On arriving in Niger and before meeting Hadijatou I was told that she would not look me in the eye: the tradition was that slaves were not allowed to look free people in the eye and old habits die hard. This proved true at the first few meetings as the legal team worked with her to prepare for the hearing, heads bowed. As Hadijatou gave her evidence, however, (and despite being interrupted on several occasions—through multiple translation problems from Housa to French) it was remarkable to watch her persist and assert herself, gradually standing taller and finding her voice. I have never seen a process of giving testimony before a Court be so visibly empowering. Leaving the Court that day was the first time I saw her smile and look me in the eyes.

When asked recently about the significance of the ECOWAS process, Hadijatou emphasises the importance of this testimony and interaction with the ECOWAS judges. She felt 'heard' and 'respected' by the Court. This was plainly surprising to her, in light of her earlier (and sadly not untypical) experience of testifying before the national courts, where she was variously threatened, insulted and ignored. In the context of the ECOWAS hearing, someone who testified that she had 'been treated like a goat' felt that her experience, and her worth, were recognised.

The publicity surrounding her case has had a defining influence on the impact of the case. Considerable media attention initially prompted by the hearing and judgment brought considerable further attention, and unusual forms of recognition, to Hadijatou herself in the months and years that followed. She has been visited in her remote village by film crews, journalists and human rights activists

---

[38] The charges have not been pursued, and by all accounts will not be although we are still waiting for them to be formally dropped.

and officials, and was honoured for her courage in various contexts, including being awarded the US State Department's 'International Woman of Courage' award in Washington DC in 2009. She made the trip to DC, accompanied by Timidria and ASI. She was named by the Time Magazine as one of the top 100 most influential people in 2009. It should not be overlooked that this attention could have had terrible consequences for the victim, her community and relationships. The fact that we could see no real indications of that are (like so much of this story) to the credit of Hadijatou and the role of the NGO Timidria in providing support and protection—a reminder of the importance of such support structures.

Apparently more important to Hadijatou than international attention was the recognition within her area of the country. She describes with apparent satisfaction how other women have congratulated her for her courage and talked to her about their situations. When her case was first brought back in 2008 she said that her aims were for her children to be free people, and for no one else to suffer. Recognition by others that she has helped them was clearly empowering and restorative. In her own words, she feels good that she has 'opened the door' for others.

Reparation for Hadijatou seems to have taken many forms at different stages; cessation upon filing the case, satisfaction and empowerment of active participation during the process, to vindication through the judgment; payment of direct compensation shortly thereafter, to recognition for her suffering and her courage on an on-going way in the months and years that followed. Given her goals that others would not have to suffer under slavery as she had, the impact on Hadijatou is closely associated with the broader question of the impact of her case on practice and policy of slavery itself.

B. Out of the Shadows: Social and Political Impact

i. Exposing and Naming Slavery

The description of the case as historic may be justified by the fact that it was the first international case to expose the widespread yet largely unacknowledged practice of slavery in Niger. The most significant dimension of impact may be the dramatic shift in public acknowledgement and debate (an essential prerequisite to other forms of change such as the associated movement in public policy discussed below). The *Mani* judgment played a particular role in recognising slavery, contributing to an objective assessment of slavery as a matter of fact in the historical record of the country. It puts the existence of slavery beyond plausible deniability.

The process of breaking through the 'state of denial'[39] and enabling debate on the topic was naturally not an overnight happening and is on-going: it began already in the early stages of the hearing—due to the media coverage, gradually unfolded throughout the process and continued following the judgment. But a

---

[39] S Cohen, *States of Denial: Knowing about Atrocities and Suffering* (Cambridge, Polity Press, 2001).

crucial stage in the journey was the hearing. On the night following the first day of hearings, 7 April 2008, slavery was discussed for the first time on national radio in Niger. When questioned during his testimony to the Court the next day, a sociologist (brought as a witness by the state) referred, remarkably, to the day the ECOWAS hearing started as one of the two most important days in the history of the country, the other being independence.

ii. From State Acknowledgement to Shaping Policy

The official rhetoric on slavery has also changed dramatically since the *Mani* case, with an impact on government positions and policy. For a long time, the Nigerien government denied slavery in Niger, a denial that persisted during the *Mani v Niger* proceedings themselves, where it was claimed among other things that *if* slavery existed it was an isolated problem. In the immediate wake of the judgment, this denial softened.[40] Over time, a more direct acknowledgement of slavery and its nature and impact has emerged. This is reflected in statements by high-level officials describing the practice as a 'plague poisoning our society',[41] and stating that the campaign against slavery was 'one of the authorities' major challenges, as the practice of slavery was one of the worst forms of denial of human dignity'.[42] In short, there is a stark contrast between what is said about slavery today, and the complete cloak of silence that surrounded it in 2007.

More concretely, this has translated into a series of 'enforcement efforts' in the past decade, as recognised by for example the US State department.[43] A series of administrative measures has also been put in place to address slavery,[44] though many of these appear to be linked to trafficking, perhaps reflecting pressure to adhere to the Palermo Protocol or greater resources being available for implementation of the Palermo Protocol than other forms of slavery.[45] There is

---

[40] There was no immediate explicit acknowledgement of slavery following judgment, though it agreed to implement, with more explicit openness coming over time. ILO, Observation (CEACR) on the Forced Labour Convention, 1930 (No 29)—adopted 2010, published 100th ILC session (2011) available at www.ilo.org/dyn/normlex/en/f?p=1000:13100:0::NO:13100:P13100_COMMENT_ID:2327461.

[41] Ada, Minister of Labour in 2014 at ILO, 'Le Niger signe pour mettre fin à l'esclavage moderne' (5 June 2015) available at www.ilo.org/global/standards/information-resources-and-publications/news/WCMS_373598/lang--fr/index.htm.

[42] ILO, Observation (CEACR) on the Forced Labour Convention, 1930 (No 29)—adopted 2013, published 103rd ILC session (2014) available at www.ilo.org/dyn/normlex/en/f?p=1000:13100:0::NO:13100:P13100_COMMENT_ID:3149830.

[43] US Department of State, Trafficking in Persons Report 2008, at 196, available at www.state.gov/j/tip/rls/tiprpt/2008/index.htm.

[44] eg Order 2010-86 (in accordance with the Palermo Protocol) creating institutional mechanisms in order to fight against trafficking in persons, including slavery but only in the context of trafficking; Décret 2012-082/PRN/MJ establishing the organisation, membership and modus operandi of the National Coordination Committee to Combat Trafficking in Persons; Décret 2012-083/PRN/MJ establishing the organisation, membership and modus operandi of the National Agency for Combating Trafficking in Persons; and Arrêté 2011-046/MI/S/D/AR/DGPN creating a central service for minors and women.

[45] These measures have been supported by a series of practices, such as training police officers on trafficking and gender in human rights, communications campaigns, national and international fora on peace and security and a National Anti-Trafficking Action Plan (2014–18).

therefore also a sharp divide between the period when the government washed its hands of any responsibility for 'private matters' and the plans of action and policies it openly endorses today. To be sure, eradicating slavery will require a great deal more concerted action by the government and the international community. The progress that has been made unquestionably reflects the influence of many factors and many other forms of action against slavery and trafficking around the globe in recent years. That notwithstanding, it is widely considered that the ECOWAS Court played a crucial role in forcing official acknowledgement and impelling the state's response: 'it is certainly significant that the verdict came from within the West African legal system, shaming the government of Niger into action'.[46]

iii. Impact on the Practice of Slavery?

It is more difficult, if not impossible, to reliably assess the broader impact of the case on slavery practices in West Africa. Perhaps unsurprisingly, reliable information on rates of slavery is scarce, vastly variable, and fluctuating, making it accordingly difficult to obtain. We did hear several accounts from victims and some paralegals that the practice of *wahiya* has diminished, which several interviewees attribute directly to the case, though this is impossible to ascertain.

Some others questioned whether the practice has reduced, or at least by how much, or is simply less visible now. Judges, lawyers and victims consistently referred to people being more 'afraid' that cases might be brought against them after the *Mani* case. Village chiefs are said to be less public in their involvement. Slaves are less visible publicly than 10 years ago. Whether this means the practice has gone further underground, or diminished, is unclear.

While an overarching assessment of shifting practice may be unwise in light of available data, there are indications that the case led in particular instances to individuals being liberated or seeking justice, that it has emboldened NGOs, and that there are nascent shoots of accountability, and changes in the legal and institutional context that provide less promising environments for slavery to thrive in, than those that were in place in 2007.

C. Empowerment and Mobilisation

i. Claims by Victims and Survivors of Slavery

In Niger we heard from women, former slaves, of the importance of the case for them, in providing hope, encouragement, a recalibration of the relationship of power in their own situations and in some cases directly motivating them to

---

[46] See Kampmark (n 2).

take steps to assert their rights. Some had travelled to Niamey to see the case themselves, others had seen the case on TV, but all of them had heard people talking about it. In this context, the importance of the world knowing about the case, and the role of the media and civil society in this, had particular value.

Several reports in Niger and neighbouring states with parallel problems, suggest that a greater number of women have come forward to anti-slavery organisations seeking their own 'liberation' after the *Hadijatou Mani* case.[47] In some cases, we heard striking accounts of women who had been trafficked from Niger to neighbouring Nigeria who heard news of the judgment. One such woman recalled directly threatening her master that he had to return her to Niger or have such a case brought again him. Other women reported escaping from slavery, emboldened by hearing of the *Mani* case, while some heard former masters being 'advised' that there could be trouble from keeping slaves. Others did not seek their freedom, for fear 'those involved are still too powerful' or for economic dependency reasons. But they spoke of feeling moved and inspired by Hadijatou, a *wahiya* like them who had the amazing courage to stand up and explain what was happening to them all.[48]

A more surprising form of impact emerged from accounts by Hadijatou and other former slaves of their sense of being treated very differently by other people after the case, which they, at least, attributed to the case. One of the women interviewed in the village of Zongo Ablo (a collective of former slaves) described their abuse at market for example, and stated simply that 'they don't call us names anymore'. While there may or may not be an empirical basis to assert any such shift, the impact on these women was real and remarkable.

In addition to the women motivated to seek help from anti-slavery organisations, some (though relatively few) pursued legal action. Following the *Mani* decision, NGOs such as Timidria have continued to take legal proceedings on behalf of slaves and/or former slaves and they may have had a greater measure of success than previously.[49] When others were asked why they had not done so, the tone was more sombre, suggesting that despite the victory that Hadijatou's case represented for them, they still felt, perhaps quite rightly, that those in power remain 'untouchable' and justice elusive. Several of them, as well as judges and activists, also described owners and chiefs now being afraid, intimidated into hiding their ownership of slaves or participation in the practice.

These various manifestations of impact of the case suggest that it played a role in generating increased *resistance*, or giving people more confidence in asserting their rights. It was this mobilising effect of the case that prompted the admittedly very far-reaching claim that 'its significance parallels the defiance of Rosa Parks

---

[47] See eg 2015 Report of the Special Rapporteur on contemporary forms of slavery (n 1).
[48] See n 5.
[49] See ASI website for information.

who refused to move from her front seat in a segregated bus in Montgomery City in 1955. We can always hope'.[50]

ii. Activists and Civil Society

Another striking form of impact relates to the empowerment, and mobilisation, of civil society anti-slavery actors more broadly. The movement found a face and a voice for change in the form of Hadijatou herself. Following on from her own active involvement in the process, Hadijatou began to work with Timidria, fulfilling an important role by reaching out to other slaves to assist them to secure their liberation. Here, the litigation can be seen to have brought about a dynamic transformation, the empowerment of the victim directly enabling the empowerment of others.

The *Mani* case put Timidria and its work on the map and had an important impact on its status: the harassment of its members, a feature of practice only a decade ago, has waned.[51] In turn, numerous accounts suggest the standing of this and other anti-slavery groups has grown. Voices from within civil society groups, litigators and the judiciary confirmed that its members now 'had to be listened to' by judges and others. Indeed, the cases brought by the activists and lawyers involved in the *Mani* case have a different profile and are taken more seriously than previously.[52] Here too, we see the impact of the case resonating far beyond the confines of the Court, emboldening the spirit of others committed to the struggle against the entrenched practice of slavery.

D. Limited Impact on Accountability

The ECOWAS Court recalled that the state is obliged to meet its obligations to investigate and hold to account those responsible for the crime of slavery under national law. In practice impunity is pervasive in Niger. The authorities remain reluctant to prosecute slavery cases and, in the few exceptional cases where there have been charges, the penalties are significantly lower than provided in the criminal code.

It was noteworthy and exceptional when, following the ruling of the ECOWAS Court, Hadijatou's master was prosecuted and convicted.[53] He was however sentenced to a 12-month prison term, and ordered to pay 1,200 Euros in damages

---

[50] Kampmark (n 2).

[51] Examples include the 2005 decision by the government to cancel a public ceremony celebrating the emancipation of 7,000 slaves and the arrest of anti-slavery activists.

[52] eg Hadijatou Mani's Nigerien lawyer, M Chaibou, considered that cases brought by him, on slavery and other human rights issues, are now treated with caution and respect by judges.

[53] Cour d'Appel de Niamey, *Haoulata Ibrahim v Seidimou Hiyar*, 25 July 2006.

to Hadijatou and a fine of 500,000 CFA to the government. Naroua complained that the sentence was excessive and filed an appeal before the Court of Appeals of Niamey, while a counter-appeal supported by human rights NGOs argued that the sentence was not a proportionate penalty under international law. On appeal, Naroua was sentenced to a three-year suspended sentence and ordered to pay Hadijatou half the original amount. Hadijatou highlighted the continuing impunity of her former master as the 'disappointing' aspect of the case. The fact that her former master continues to own slaves, and to live freely, is the clearest and most troubling indicator of the extent of the pervasive impunity in Niger and a stark reminder that that impunity continues to delimit the impact of this case and similar legal actions to date.

The lack of concrete statistics, or available case records, makes it difficult to monitor broader trends with respect to impunity.[54] Following the criminalisation of slavery in 2003, the government did not encourage the application of the law because it considered that talking about it compromised the country's image. The *Mani* case may have shifted that equation, having exposed definitively the practice and triggered many government responses and commitments, as highlighted above.

NGOs, lawyers and judges interviewed suggest there has been some energising of accountability efforts, but results remain scarce. There have been more allegations of slavery-related crimes in recent times. Nonetheless, investigations tend to falter and when they do get to court, convictions are extremely rare, and penalties inconsequential.[55] In interviews, the Prosecutor's Office blames NGOs for not doing enough to investigate, while the judges blame the prosecutors. Meanwhile, the perception of victims and civil society is that certain members of Nigerien society remain, as victims have stated, 'untouchable', and it appears that prosecutors and judges lack the resources, independence and determination that change will require. When it comes to impunity, changes in practice unfold through baby-steps and thus far consist of a few notable exceptions. The need for a 'fundamental shift of mentality on accountability' is an outstanding deficit in the full implementation of the *Mani* judgment.

---

[54] This was reflected in interviews, and in the fact that eg International Labour Office, notably, has repeatedly asked the Nigerien government to provide copies of the judicial decisions handed down under ss 270-1 to 270-5 of the Penal Code, in vain. ILO, Observation (CEACR) on the Forced Labour Convention, 1930 (No 29)—adopted 2013, published 103rd ILC session (2014) available at www.ilo.org/dyn/normlex/en/f?p=1000:13100:0::NO:13100:P13100_COMMENT_ID:3149830. There is more available information on trafficking, which does suggest a distinct shift in the investigation and prosecution of trafficking in the period since the *Mani* case, linked to initiatives to enforce the Palermo Protocol; eg US Department of State, Trafficking in Persons Report 2008, at 196, available at www.state.gov/j/tip/rls/tiprpt/2008/index.htm and US Department of State, Trafficking in Persons Report 2015, at 264, available at www.state.gov/documents/organization/243561.pdf.

[55] This is out of line with Niger's slavery law, and far from the proportionate penalties for slavery required by international law.

E. Strengthening Institutions

i. Domestic Institution Building, Including Judicial Impact

The case exposed the fundamental failure of the judiciary to protect, and to apply (or even to know) its own law, when cases came before it. It highlighted underlying problems that require longer-term responses, such as the lack of independence, capacity and resources of the judiciary.

The particular role of customary courts, and their disregard for written international and domestic law prohibiting slavery, was put under the spotlight by this case. Unfortunately, as one commentator noted 'the court refused to tackle the issue of customary laws which do much to legitimise slavery. That sacred cow will be allowed to live just that much longer'.[56] Despite this, it could be argued that the case has at least forced recognition of the incompatibility, for which the state can be held to account. In turn, this has opened up discussion about the need for greater judicial attention to clarifying custom, though what will come of that remains uncertain.[57]

The extent of the impact of the case on the judiciary is difficult to assess, and several conflicting indications arose from our enquiry. Judges are clearly all aware of the *Mani* case which is said to have had an impact on the way they approach slavery-related cases, initiating a more 'cautious' approach than previously adopted. The judge who decided against Hadijatou was much criticised internally afterwards, and reportedly found his career development blocked as a result of the case. This is arguably a significant form of impact in itself, and has not gone unnoticed within the judiciary. A review of domestic cases to date suggests some progress in Nigerien courts, however imperfect, but also outstanding areas that require urgent attention if access to justice is to be more meaningful.[58]

When interviewees were asked whether and why the *Mani* case would be handled differently today they gave tellingly different answers. Some interviewees were emphatic that it would, as judges would now know about the case and the law, but others were less sure, and one judge noted honestly that the influence of powerful parties may yet be a stronger factor than knowledge of the law.[59] The fact that many judges themselves have slaves is a reminder perhaps that legal change may follow longer-term social, practical and institutional change.

What is not in dispute is that there is now an enhanced level of awareness, and a sense of judicial accountability, that changes the context. There is an openness to discuss, at least, the question of customary law and customary courts and a

---

[56] Kampmark (n 2).

[57] Ibid.

[58] Presentation and interview with M Chaibou, and discussion with ASI on the strategic impact of domestic cases to date, Niamey, 2016.

[59] Another noted discretion of the judges still remains paramount and makes predictions difficult.

willingness to consider the need for external training and support. There is recognition of some of the other challenges the system must rise to meet, and of the fact that there may be an international cost to failing to do so. Yet, resource constraints are huge and access to justice greatly impeded by a drastically inadequate supply of lawyers in the country. There are 127 lawyers—of whom only nine are women and only one has experience in slavery cases—for 10 million inhabitants. The mountain of challenges facing the justice system in Niger, and its progress with respect to this issue in particular, will require long-term solutions that go beyond the power of any one case. Nevertheless, the open resistance encountered before the *Mani* judgment sits in stark contrast to the tone of the conversation today, when there is openness to discussing the challenges for the Nigerien justice system in its handling of slavery-related cases.

Other institutional changes relate to the development of mechanisms of enforcement. As the *Mani* case brought to light a country with a reasonably strong legal framework but a shocking lack of implementation, these developments are an important step forward. They include the establishment of the National Human Rights Commission,[60] which includes the fight against slavery in its mandate, and an Agency to fight human trafficking.[61] It is not possible to ascertain with any certainty the operative effect of the *Mani* case on these changes, many of which were impelled by other international legal developments, such as the Palermo Protocol. But it would be hard to deny that the case contributed to a climate that became increasingly favourable to the adoption of the state policies, institutions and measures (a whole series between 2010 and 2012) designed to address the systemic lack of institutional structures needed to address slavery-related practices and to restore the state's reputation.

ii. Supranational Impact: Launching the Rights Jurisdiction of the ECOWAS Court

The *Mani* case heralded the emergence of new and expanding sub-regional human rights fora in the African continent. The proliferation of courts and fora is the subject of criticism in some quarters, as contributing to fragmentation in international law.[62] I have argued elsewhere that this concern is short-sighted as the additional fora offer at least a better chance of a much-needed remedy where there may otherwise be none, as the *Mani* case highlights.[63]

This case demonstrated the potential positive influence of binding, effective human rights fora on the human rights landscape and the capacity to make an essential contribution to the credibility and effectiveness of the rule of

---

[60] Law no 2012-44 of 24 August 2012 establishing the National Human Rights Commission.

[61] Décret 2012-083/PRN/MJ establishing the organisation, membership and modus operandi of the National Agency for Combating Trafficking in Persons.

[62] Duffy, 'Human Rights Litigation in Sub-regional African Courts' (n 3).

[63] Ibid.

international law in parts of Africa. The decision catalysed recourse to the Court, as borne out by the relative flood of cases in the years that followed this—its first and most celebrated, human rights case.[64] The reputation and authority of the ECOWAS Court has been reinforced by the case, and perhaps by the fact that Niger implemented the Court's decision and swiftly paid Hadijatou's compensation. The *Mani* judgment, and the few others by the ECOWAS Court that preceded it, have served to entrench the jurisdiction of that Court over a broad range of human rights. Since the ECOWAS judgment, the East African Court of Justice has also shown its willingness to exercise jurisdiction over significant human rights issues—suggesting a potential cross-over impact on its sister sub-regional jurisdiction.[65]

At the same time, weaknesses in the Court's approach, outlined above, also highlight challenges to be met if the potential of this court as a human rights forum is to be fully realised. Moreover, the fact that this case suggests that human rights might be better protected through sub-regional courts than the traditional, domestic human rights mechanisms has in turn provoked some debate on the role and deficiencies in those procedures, and underscored the need for reform. The case may have contributed in a small way to an important debate on the state of access to justice for victims in the region.

F. ECOWAS and the Law of Modern Day Slavery

The *Mani* case emerged from a refusal to apply protections in domestic law, not from deficits in the internal legal framework as such. Unsurprisingly then, legislation was not a major aspect of implementation in the immediate aftermath of the judgment. However, a number of new laws have emerged over time, to clarify or strengthen the framework or create enforcement mechanisms to give meaningful effect to prohibitions enshrined in law as noted above. Niger has gone out of its way, perhaps influenced by the reputation for slavery consolidated by the *Mani* judgment, to be at the forefront of international efforts to combat modern-day slavery, and to modify its law and policy accordingly.[66]

---

[64] ECOWAS had decided 13 cases in the 4 years prior to the *Mani* case and has decided 100 cases in the 7 years since. Among the other significant human rights cases, see *SERAP v Federal Republic of Nigeria and Universal Basic Education Commission* ECW/CCJ/APP/08/08.

[65] The Court is the judicial body of the sub-regional organisation the East African Community, and its jurisdiction is based on the East African Treaty of 1999. See www.claiminghumanrights.org/eac. html. However, it has taken a very restrictive approach to time limits that has thwarted its consideration of several cases; see eg *MLU v Attorney General of Kenya* (Mt. Elgon appeal). 2011.

[66] In addition to changes noted above, see eg the modification of the Labour Code prohibiting forced labour (Art 4) and the worse forms of child labour (Art 107), following the decision by Niger on 14 May 2015, Niger became the first state to ratify the 2014 Protocol related to the 1930 Convention on Forced Labour (no 29). Of course, what matters more is what the state does, not only what it says, or signs. The little used criminal law on slavery was itself passed in the context of the 33rd session of the African Commission on Human and Peoples' Rights which took place in Niamey Niger, to little real effect.

In terms of impact on international standards, the *Mani* case was one of the first slavery cases at the international level. As such it contributed to an, as yet, small body of jurisprudence on the prohibition of slavery-like practices.[67] At the same time, it would be overreaching to consider the case as having had a profound jurisprudential impact on legal standards as such: while this case was perhaps as clear a case of slavery as they come, it did not test the limits of what constitutes slavery as some other cases have done,[68] nor did it expand the realm of states' positive obligations in any significant way. Moreover, as a legal document address-ing state responsibility, it would be generous to describe the *Mani* judgment as having its strengths and its serious weaknesses, giving rise to a somewhat debat-able impact—either positive and/or negative—on legal standards. A few issues addressed in that judgment, of potential relevance to its lasting procedural or jurisprudential impact for future cases, are worth highlighting.

i. Admissibility: Clarifying Non-applicability of the 'Exhaustion of Local Remedies' Rule

The respondent state had sought to have the case thrown out through various preliminary objections to admissibility, the most significant of which was the non-exhaustion of domestic remedies, on the basis that the matter was 'pending' in Niger.[69] It argued, by reference to the practice of other human rights bodies and the principle of subsidiarity that a rule requiring exhaustion of domestic remedies was enshrined in customary law, and should be developed through the Court's practice despite the absence of any such explicit rule in the ECOWAS context. The Court upheld the applicant's arguments[70] that 'the rule of exhaustion of domestic remedies is not applicable before the Court',[71] a clarification that may prove sig-nificant in future cases.[72]

---

[67] Judgment (n 2).

[68] See by contrast eg the recent *Fazenda Brazil v Brazil* IACHR decision of 15 December 2016 or *Rantsev*, in both of which I was intervener as Human Rights in Practice precisely because of their jurisprudential development. These cases tested the limits of the definitions of modern-day slavery, clarified and gave content to norms.

[69] See section C, where it is noted that the Supreme Court had sent the matter back for retrial domestically on technical grounds, while Hadijatou remained imprisoned for asserting her right to be free and marry a man of her choice.

[70] The delays and the approach of the authorities—their inability or unwillingness to appreciate the nature of the violations or to address them—were inconsistent with the idea that there was an effective remedy available to be pursued in Niger. See Applicant's Memoire en Response (on file with author).

[71] Judgment (n 2) at para 49. It cited Art 10(d)(ii) of Supplementary Protocol A/SP.1/01/05 on the ECOWAS Court which provides: 'Access to the Court is open to the following: [...] d) individuals on application for relief for violation of their human rights; the submission of application for which shall: i) not be anonymous; nor i) be made whilst the same matter has been instituted before another Inter-national Court for adjudication'.

[72] The applicant had also argued that, in any event, such a rule would not be a bar to admissibility in the circumstances of this case where all reasonable efforts had been made to secure justice in Niger and the system had demonstrated its inability or unwillingness to provide an effective remedy. But this finding could prove significant for other cases where the facts were different.

ii. Nature and Definitions of Slavery

The judgment reaffirms the legal nature of the long-established, absolute prohibition of slavery in international law:[73] it noted the comments of the International Court of Justice in the *Barcelona Traction* case which endorsed the *erga omnes* nature of states' obligations in relation to slavery[74]—that is, that they are owed to the community of nations as a whole.[75] While well established as a matter of international law, the Court's recognition of the *erga omnes* nature of these obligations serves as a valuable reiteration of the implications, for third states, of the existence of slavery, as exposed in this judgment. Under the international law of state responsibility, *erga omnes* obligations reflect agreed-upon shared interests, and imply, in certain circumstances a more specific obligation, to cooperate to bring an end to such egregious violations.[76]

Perhaps more importantly in terms of impact on legal standards, the Court endorsed the applicant's arguments as to the nature and definitions of slavery in contemporary international law and practice. As a starting point it took the definition of slavery provided in Article 1 of the Slavery Convention of 1926 wherein 'Slavery is the status or condition of a person over whom any or all of the powers attaching to the right of ownership are exercised'.[77] The Court then considered more recent approaches, reflecting the practice of international criminal tribunals, and citing, in particular, decisions of the International Criminal Tribunal for the former Yugoslavia (ICTY)[78] to the effect that the key question relates to the actual degree of power or control exercised over an individual.[79] As such, the ECOWAS Court's judgment makes a contribution to the strikingly small body of jurisprudence on the elements of modern day slavery in international law.[80]

In Hadijatou's case the Court found that the circumstances of her sale and transfer and the conditions in which she subsequently lived, as set out in her

---

[73] Judgment (n 2) at para 75.

[74] *Case Concerning the Barcelona Traction, Light and Power Company, Limited (Belgium v Spain)*, Second Phase, Judgment of 5 February 1970 [1970] ICJ Rep 3, paras 33–34.

[75] Judgment (n 2) at para 81.

[76] On the implications of *erga omnes* status for all states, see 'Commentary to Article 48 of the ILC Articles on Responsibility of States for Internationally Wrongful Acts' in J Crawford, *The International Law Commission's Articles on State Responsibility; Introduction, Text and Commentaries* (Cambridge, Cambridge University Press, 2002) 276–80.

[77] Judgment (n 2) at para 74.

[78] *Prosecutor v Kunarac et al*, Judgment, Case No IT-96-23 & IT-96-23/1-A, A. Ch., 12 June 2002, para 119.

[79] Ibid. 'These [...] include the 'control of someone's movement, control of physical environment, psychological control, measures taken to prevent or deter escape, force, threat of force or coercion, duration, assertion of exclusivity, subjection to cruel treatment and abuse, control of sexuality and forced labour'.

[80] H Duffy, 'Litigating Modern Day Slavery in Regional Courts: A Nascent Contribution' (2016) 14(2) *Journal of International Criminal Justice* 375–403.

testimony to the Court, met *all* of the '*indicators* of slavery' in international law. As mentioned previously, the facts of the *Mani* case did not challenge the boundaries of the definitions of slavery, but it helped solidify a universal approach to the modern definition of slavery, and as such has been cited since, in other factually more challenging cases (in for example the Inter-American system).[81] The state had not sought to refute the allegations concerning her purchase or conditions of life in her master's house, but had sought to use the institution of marriage to throw a cloak of legitimacy over the practice of slavery.[82] The Court declined to engage in any discussion of the claimed 'marriage', which was rejected implicitly in the findings that this was a clear case of slavery, and that the state was legally responsible for its failure to have protected the victim from it.[83]

The judgment emphasised the failure of the domestic judiciary to condemn the practice of slavery when Hadijatou's case came to its notice.[84] Indeed it places significant emphasis on the positive obligations of the judge, acting on *his or her own initiative*,[85] in the public interest, to condemn and to initiate a process of punishing those responsible, wherever facts indicating slavery came to their attention,[86] as part of the obligation to take 'adequate measures to ensure that acts of slavery are repressed'.[87] The Court described the failure to react as amounting to judicial acceptance—or at least tolerance of—the practice of slavery, highlighting systemic challenges to be met and that slavery is to be prevented, and responded to within a rule of law framework, in the future.[88]

[81]   See eg *Fazenda Brazil* (n 68).

[82]   The respondent state argued before the Court 'that the applicant was [...] El Hadj Souleymane Naroua's wife, with whom she lived with more or less happiness as any couple until 2005, and that children were born from this union'; Judgment (n 2) at para 78. The applicant pointed out that there was no evidence of marriage, or to establish consent, or to refute that she was in any event a child at the time of the transaction, incapable—as international and African standards make clear—of providing such consent or of entering into a valid marriage. See eg 1956 Supplementary Slavery Convention, Art 2, regarding the appropriate minimum ages for marriage and procedures that allow spouses to freely express consent; and 1990 African Charter on the Rights and Welfare of the Child Article OAU Doc CAB/LEG/24.9/49 (1990), Art 21(2) (ratified by Niger on 11 December 1999).

[83]   eg Judgment (n 2) at para 85.

[84]   The judgment criticised the fact that the national judge, instead of denouncing the applicant's status as a slave of its own motion, found that there were circumstances where it was lawful under customary law. The ECOWAS Court noted that the judge found that 'the marriage of a free man with a slave woman is lawful, as long as he cannot afford to marry a free woman and if he fears to fall into fornication'. Judgment (n 2) at para 83.

[85]   The state argued during the proceedings that this case had been brought not as a slavery case but as 'divorce' proceedings, as the domestic court documents suggest. The applicant contended otherwise and the Court accepted in its summary that her case had challenged her enslavement. In any event, the Court's emphasis here on the *proprio motu* power of the authorities suggests that either way the obligation is on the judge to react to the facts that come to his attention.

[86]   Judgment (n 2) at para 82, refers to the fact that in a case such as that of Hadijatou Mani Koroua, the national judge should have dealt with this slavery case on its own motion and initiated a criminal procedure.

[87]   Ibid, para 86.

[88]   Ibid, para 84.

iii. Weak Approach to Discrimination and other Violations

While giving due consideration to the issue of slavery, the Court's neglect of other issues, and its decision in relation to other violations of human rights, and discrimination in particular, is anomalous.[89] Slavery, in particular sexual slavery, is inherently and obviously linked to the question of equality. To be sure, the judgment acknowledges that the practice of *wahiya or sadaka* involves young girls being kept under the control—and for the 'service'—of their male masters, which includes providing sexual services and enduring domestic violence,[90] and that it reflects discrimination on the ground of social origin.[91] However, it concludes, somewhat bizarrely, that these violations are attributable to the individuals directly responsible (in this case her former master), not to the state. This conflicts both with established international law on states' responsibilities for human rights violations,[92] and with the Court's own recognition of the state's responsibility, as mentioned above.[93] Also out of step with international human rights law[94] was the Court's determination that Hadijatou's two-month detention and sentencing on bigamy charges did not amount to arbitrary or unlawful detention.[95]

To my knowledge the judgment has not been relied upon by any court as providing support for a narrower reading of international law, perhaps as it was so plainly an untenable approach. But the *potential* for negative impact on jurisprudential standards is there, even if, to date, these sections of the decision do not seem to have had such effect. In short, while the decision to resort to a tribunal with relatively little experience in human rights reaped ample dividends in the form of the many impacts highlighted above, it may not have been cost free in

---

[89] The reasons are a matter of speculation: perhaps the Court was of the view that it had addressed the factual substance of the applicant's case through its slavery claim, or wanted to make some findings in favour of a cooperative state.

[90] Judgment (n 2) at paras 10 and 76.

[91] See ibid, paras 62–71. The judgment does not explicitly recognise discrimination on the ground of gender, as opposed to discrimination on the ground of social origin.

[92] As noted above, this is well established as a matter of general human rights law which enshrines the positive duties to protect individuals from serious human rights violations and has been elaborated on in some detail by the Committee on the Elimination of All Forms of Discrimination Against Women.

[93] The Court had explicitly noted that although slavery was attributable to a particular individual acting in the context of 'custom' and for 'individual' purposes, the victim had the right to be protected by the Nigerien authorities, be they administrative or judicial. It also acknowledged state responsibility for 'all human rights violations' that stem from the state's tolerance, passivity or inactivity in respect of slavery; Judgment (n 2) at para 85.

[94] The Court found that the detention could not be held unlawful as it was authorised by a court and therefore had a legal basis, whether ill-founded or not whereas international law requires an assessment not just of the existence of a law or a judicial decision authorising detention but of its 'quality', including compatibility with the basic international and national legal principles of foreseeability and accessibility. The Court failed to address other arguments.

[95] Judgment (n 2) at paras 90–91. The Court found that it was based on a judicial decision and that '[t]his decision, whether ill-founded or not (and it was not for the court to assess), constitutes a legal basis'.

terms of the quality of the legal analysis set down in the judgment. This does not seem significantly to have altered the outcome, but it signals room for capacity building and for improvements that could made by judiciaries themselves.

iv. Trans-judicial Dialogue and Modern Day Slavery

On a more positive note, the judgment of the ECOWAS Court contributes to the growing phenomenon of 'trans-judicial communication'[96] between human rights jurisdictions. At least on the central issue of slavery in international law,[97] the judgment illustrates and reinforces the cross-fertilisation from international criminal law into the human rights field, and between human rights courts across continents. The case represents a global journey of long-established, yet little used, norms relating to slavery: formulated over a century ago, they have found recent application in the criminal decisions of, for example, the ICTY in The Hague, which in turn encouraged reliance upon them by the ECOWAS Court sitting, on this occasion, in Niamey, Niger. From there, the *Mani* decision has gone on to influence human rights courts in Europe and Central America contributing to the clarification of the elements of modern-day slavery and states' obligations in their own case law.[98]

V. Conclusions

Unlike the other case studies, the *Hadijatou Mani v Niger* case was not part of a cluster of litigation. The *Mani* case is a prime example of how a single case involving a single person, that was cheap, urgent, speedy and unplanned, can ricochet and trigger a broad range of multi-dimensional impacts.[99] It speaks for the importance of flexibility in the strategic litigation planning of organisations,[100] such that

---

[96] See A-M Slaughter, 'A Typology of Transjudicial Communication' (1994) 29 *University of Richmond Law Review* 99, 102. The Court refers to the few existing decisions on slavery emanating from other jurisdictions, illustrating a well-functioning trans-judicial dialogue between human rights courts and tribunals.

[97] On some issues the Court's approach was dangerously myopic; see the issue of discrimination above.

[98] This is notably so in several European courts' decisions to grant (or not) refugee status to alleged victims of slavery, or in the recent *Fazenda Brazil v Brazil* judgment (n 68) on the definition of modern-day slavery and positive obligations.

[99] To take a single case was not a strategic decision, but a resource-related reality and there is certainly much to be said for follow-up litigation to build on the foundation of the *Mani* case and to maximise its impact. See Ch 10.

[100] When the case came to Interights, there was no focus on slavery and trafficking, no obvious person to do it, and no specific funding—issues that can be strongly influential in whether to take on work—but luckily there was enough flexibility that I could take on the case, alongside Ibrahima Kane, and dedicate the serious amount of time this exceptional case required, but organisational and funding factors can pose challenges to this flexibility.

they can respond to the urgent needs and invaluable opportunities for enabling change, that cases such as this represent. The case confirms the vital nature of flexible funding for this kind of litigation, when it happens—as life often does—to outwit the parameters of well-considered strategic plans and grant proposals.

Were we to think of landmark judgments as only those that change the law, then the *Mani* case does not stand out. Yet there are many reasons, other than the content of the judgment (thought it had its value) why it deserves its acclaim as a historic or landmark case.[101] It represents a process that was first and foremost always about the victim in the middle of it, which had a transformative effect on her life. But it was also an opportunity seized to embark on a process that could—and would in fact—generate a chain reaction of responses and reactions on multiple levels, over time, resonating throughout Niger and beyond. It was the first international case to expose the widespread yet largely unacknowledged practice of slavery in Niger, and one of the first slavery cases to be brought or won at the international level.[102] It appears to have triggered attitudinal and behavioural changes in market places, corridors of power and courtrooms, movements in public policy, and at least a slight recalibration of power dynamics in a profoundly unequal and unjust context. It threw light in dark corners, where slavery continues and impunity prevails. It made clear the need for greater national and international engagement and support that may bring further progress down the line.

There is a long way to go to eradicate slavery in Niger and the *Hadijatou Mani* case was no panacea. But the conspiracy of silence has been ruptured, slavery is acknowledged and the subject of plans and policies, Hadijatou's dignity in some way restored, and activists—on whom the ultimate success of this work will largely depend—are mobilised and empowered for the struggle ahead.

---

[101] It made a modest contribution to legal developments around the elements of slavery, but problems with approaches to discrimination are noted above.

[102] *Prosecutor v Kunarac et al* (n 79) resulted in criminal prosecutions and convictions for sexual slavery at the International Criminal Tribunal for the former Yugoslavia (ICTY); *Siliadin v France* (2006) Appl no 73316/01 43 EHRR 16 before the ECtHR gave rise to findings not of slavery but 'forced labour'; and in *Malawi African Association and Others v Mauritania*, Comm Nos 54/91, 61/91, 98/93, 164/97 to 196/97 and 210/98 (2000) the ACHPR found 'conditions analogous to slavery'. See also the subsequent judgment and appeals decision of the Special Court for Sierra Leone concerning sexual slavery and forced marriage: *Prosecutor v Brima, Kamara and Kanu*, Appeals Chamber, SCSL- 2004-16/A, 22 February 2008.

6

Case Study—*Plan de Sánchez v Guatemala*: Genocide in the Inter-American System

I. Introduction

Guatemala was the site of one of the longest running non-international armed conflicts in history, spanning a terrible 36 years from 1960 to its formal conclusion with the peace accords of December 1996. Under the rationale of depleting the guerilla support base by '*quitando el agua al pez*' (removing the water from the fish), hundreds of massacres were committed against rural, predominantly indigenous communities in the late 1970s and especially the early 1980s. One of these massacres took place in the small *aldea* of Plan de Sánchez, during which 268 indigenous villagers lost their lives in one morning, on 18 July 1982.

From the mid-1990s I worked for the 'Centre for Legal Action in Human Rights in Guatemala' (Centro para Acción Legal en Derechos Humanos, CALDH) on a range of human rights issues and litigation, predominantly preparing and presenting cases to the Inter-American system. Over time I focused my work on the massacres, working with a multi-disciplinary team from CALDH and other NGOs, and representing the community of Plan de Sánchez before the Inter-American Commission on Human Rights (IACommHR/the Commission). The case progressed from there to the Inter-American Court on Human Rights (IACtHR/the Court) which handed down the *Plan de Sánchez v Guatemala* judgment in 2004.[1]

This case study considers the strengths and weaknesses of that litigation process, its possible impact and its limitations. It first provides the context of the litigation—the background to the massacres, broader conflict and transition in Guatemala—, and looks at the various types of human rights litigation that were undertaken at different stages, of which the *Plan de Sánchez* case was an early example (II). The next section sets the *Plan de Sánchez* case within this context (III), while the one that follows, the heart of the study, considers the ways in which the case may have contributed to change on multiple dimensions (IV).

---

[1] IACtHR, *Plan de Sánchez Massacre v Guatemala*, Judgment (Merits) IACtHR Ser C No 105 (29 April 2004).

While fully recognising the impossibility of establishing the specific contribution that this particular process may have made in the context of a long and multi-faceted struggle, it offers reflections on its possible significance, based on my own experience and discussions with other researchers and activists involved in or affected by this work more recently.

This study is intended to encourage consideration of the impact of the process from several temporal perspectives. The significance of such processes is often considered in terms of the broader struggle against impunity—and for accountability—in Guatemala. Indeed, this case has been cited as belonging to the 'foundational phase' of important, on-going, criminal accountability processes for genocide in Guatemala.[2] One might also evaluate its contribution to developments in domestic investigation and prosecution practices more generally in Guatemala today. Alternatively, we may consider the significance of the case by reference to the IACtHR's comprehensive reparations judgment over a decade ago.[3] The impact of that judgment, and its gradual implementation, for victims, for subsequent policy, legislation and practice and for the whole process of transition, are all, unquestionably, a key part of the picture. I would suggest, however, that to appreciate the full significance of the case, we must cast our eye further back in time, to the very earliest days of the preparation of case. In this way we will not lose sight of the informational and mobilising power that the process had—from its very inception, throughout the research, preparation and participation phases, and including its multiple consequences—right up to the present day. Such a comprehensive view is often missing from post-process analyses of impact.

II. Background

The 36-year Guatemalan armed conflict carried an estimated death toll of around 200,000. According to the UN truth commission set up following the accords ('Comisión d'Esclaricimiento Historico', Commission for Historical Clarification, CEH), 93 per cent of those deaths were attributable to the armed forces and 83 per cent of the victims were indigenous Maya.[4] The Guatemalan Army reportedly razed 626 villages across the country, and left an estimated

---

[2] See Chapter 4 section IV.C.iii for legal impact, as well as prosecution of low-level officials and the historic, if frustrated, trial of Ríos Montt. See also H Bosdriesz, 'The Contribution of the Inter-American Court of Human Rights to Domestic Accountability Efforts for Serious Crimes: Fact or Fiction?' (Human Rights Integration Network Conference, The Global Challenge of Human Rights Integration-Towards a Users' Perspective, Ghent, December 2015) available at www.hrintegration.be/conferences.

[3] See *Plan de Sánchez Massacre v Guatemala*, Judgment (Reparations) IACtHR Ser C No 116 (19 November 2004).

[4] See CEH, 'Guatemala: Memory of Silence', *Report of the Commission for Historical Clarification—Conclusions and Recommendations* (25 February 1999) p 34, para 82, available at www.aaas.org/sites/default/files/migrate/uploads/mos_en.pdf.

1.5 million displaced.[5] One such village was the small *aldea* of Plan de Sánchez, Baja Verapaz department, in the Guatemala mountains. On the morning of 18 July 1982, the army and local 'volunteer' civil patrols, 'Patrullas de Autodefensa' (PACs), murdered, raped, razed crops, dwellings and infrastructure, wiping out 268 indigenous villagers and Plan de Sánchez itself. Survivors fled, forced off the land they would return to and try to rebuild years later.

Although the Guatemalan conflict itself came to an end in 1996, the massacres ceased earlier, with the return to civilian rule following the military coup of 1983, which would be marked in 1985 by the adoption of a strong, rights-friendly constitution. That notwithstanding, political transition was never very solid: the twin forces that had supported the dictatorial regimes of the late 1970s and early 1980s—the military and a powerful private sector representing a tiny economic elite known as the 'Comité Coordinador de Asociaciones Agrícolas, Comerciales, Industriales y Financieras' (CACIF)—continued to dominate Guatemalan politics.[6] This could be seen most strikingly in the re-emergence and political success of General Efraín Ríos Montt, who had been head of the military during the worst period of massacres, and founded the 'Frente Republicano de Guatemala' (Guatemalan Republican Front, FRG) in 1989. Unsurprisingly, during the 1990s complete secrecy continued to shroud the military policies pursuant to which the massacres had unfolded ('Plan Victoria 82' and 'Sofía'). Nevertheless, a painstakingly slow process of enquiry by journalists and NGOs did get underway in the early 1990s[7] that would eventually bear fruit and provide evidence for legal action. That litigation would in turn help uncover more information, paving the way for future legal and political action.[8]

Guatemalan civil society groups grew out of the harsh repression of the 1980s in an effort to provide protection and support.[9] Threats against them and against judges and lawyers involved in human rights cases have long impeded human

---

[5] Internal Displacement Monitoring Centre, 'Guatemala: Internal Displacement in Brief—As of December 2011' (2011) available at www.internal-displacement.org/americas/guatemala/summary.

[6] This elite is often seen as represented by 'CACIF' agricultural and financial association; see www.cacif.org.gt.

[7] Many collaborators with CALDH in the preparation of cases included the Instituto de Estudios Comparados de Ciencias Penales/Guatemala (ICCPG), the Fundación de Antropología Forense de Guatemala (FAFG) and internationally eg the American Association for the Advancement of Science in the US.

[8] eg during the criminal trials for genocide, the Justice and Reconciliation Association ('Asociación Justicia y Reconciliación', AJR) demanded that the Guatemalan Army hand over the campaign plans dubbed 'Victoria 82' (Victory 82) and 'Firmeza 83' (Firmness 83) and for an operation labelled 'Sofía'. The army gave the Courts of Justice the first two (in a more complete form than they had given to the CEH), but claimed that the file on Operation Plan 'Sofía' had been lost. At the end of 2009, US-based analyst Kate Doyle received one of the original copies of that plan; available in Spanish at www.alainet.org/es/active/52081.

[9] See 'Grupo de Apoyo Mutuo' (later 'Asociación de Familiares de Detenidos y Desaparecidos de Guatemala'), said to be inspired by 'Madres' and 'Abuelas de la Plaza de Mayo' in Argentina (cited in the Argentina case study in Ch 8). It was set up in the 1980s and followed by other human rights groups to seek information on the disappeared, and later to pursue justice.

rights work,[10] and have been a feature of the cases concerning the massacres in Guatemala specifically.[11] Guatemalan civil society also suffered itself the effects of a long and divisive conflict, wherein divisions within the armed and political opposition contributed to fragmentation among NGOs too. This made broad-based, coordinated civil society work on the genocide or other issues challenging, notwithstanding pockets of intense and fruitful cooperation on particular cases or groups of cases.

The economic inequality and injustice that had underpinned the conflict in the first place had of course not been resolved by the 1990s, and the implications of privilege, power and prejudice were never far beneath the surface. (This remains the case today.) Weighty obstacles to justice invariably emerge in a context in which the most disenfranchised seek to call to account the most powerful economically, politically and militarily.[12]

Unsurprisingly then, by the time I moved to Guatemala, in January 1995—on the 10-year anniversary of the scintillatingly progressive constitution—there had been no reckoning with the past, little public discussion and hardly any real attempt to secure truth, justice or reparation for the thousands of victims of the massacres. At the same time, it was a moment of real opportunity and considerable optimism: the negotiations between the government, military and the guerrillas (represented by the high command of the 'Unidad Revolucionaria Nacional Guatemalteca' (URNG), an umbrella organisation in which the various guerrilla movements active in Guatemala had come together) had been on-going since the mid-80s and were well underway.[13] (To be sure, details of how questions of justice,

---

[10] The killing of a judge and a police officer in the course of the investigation of the extrajudicial execution of anthropologist Myrna Mack in the early 1990s, or of Bishop Gerardi following the Archbishop's report noted below (n 24) were notorious examples. For more information on on-going threats to prosecutors and judges who years later would dare to prosecute senior military/political figures such as Ríos Montt, see eg US Department of State, 'Guatemala 2016 Human Rights Report', *Country Reports on Human Rights Practices for 2016* (2016) available at www.state.gov/documents/ organization/265802.pdf; and Human Rights Watch, 'Guatemala: Events of 2015' (2015) available at www.hrw.org/world-report/2016/country-chapters/guatemala.

[11] Judges involved in the high-level prosecutions of those responsible for the massacres were subject to threats and to precautionary measures from the IACommHR on 28 June 2013. The Commission considered that they were 'at risk as a result of their judicial activities in various processes related to organised crime, cases against soldiers accused of serious violations of human rights, as the massacre of Plan de Sánchez and Las Dos Erres among others'; see IACommHR, 'Precautionary Measures in favor of Judges Iris Yassmín Barrios Aguilar, Patricia Isabel Bustamante García and Pablo Xitumul Paz, judges on the First Criminal Sentencing Court for matters relating to Drug Trafficking and Major Crimes against the Environment, responsible for trying José Efraín Ríos Montt and José Mauricio Rodríguez Sánchez, for the crime of genocide', PM 125/13, *Iris Yassmín Barrios Aguilar et al, Guatemala* (28 June 2013).

[12] Notably, just 1 year after the peace accords, the elections were won by the FRG, founded by the former general and dictator Efraín Ríos Montt, who became president of the Guatemalan Parliament.

[13] The negotiations started in the late 1980s as part of the larger process to bring peace to Central America, and the UN became more actively involved when the UN Mission for the Verification of Human Rights and Compliance with the Comprehensive Agreement on Human Rights in Guatemala (later UN Verification Mission in Guatemala, MINUGUA) was established through UNGA Res 48/267 (19 September 1994) UN Doc A/RES/48/267; see www.un.org/en/peacekeeping/missions/past/ minuguabackgr.html for more information.

impunity or amnesty would be handled—or the indigenous accords—had not yet been fully fleshed out).

In this respect, the timing of the original filing of the massacres cases was significant:[14] the *Plan de Sánchez* petition was lodged in July 1996, six months before the peace accords were signed. It therefore had the opportunity both to reflect and to feed into live political issues of the moment.[15] To some extent the petition became a means to underscore and publicise the international obligations set out in the brief, and to give a voice to the victims and petitioners in the wider political context as well as before the Commission itself.

The timing was also relevant, for the wave of movements for accountability that was just gathering steam, at the same time, elsewhere in the world.[16] There was a growing alertness internationally to getting the inter-relationship between peace and justice right, and to the perils of pursuing the former at the expense of the latter, experiences in Argentina and elsewhere in the region, as well as developments beyond it.[17] The political and legal uncertainty of the moment effectively enhanced the potential significance of legal action. The context was an outward-looking Guatemala in which a long-suffering civil society movement was armed with a series of legal and political tools, on both national and the international levels. There was reason to be optimistic as we prepared the *Plan de Sánchez* case in 1995 and presented the petition in 1996.

While the genocide litigation was still in its infancy, the landscape changed again. First, the negotiation of an amnesty law led to the passing of the 'National Reconciliation Law' in 1996 as part of the peace accords.[18] Ultimately, although the potential for misinterpretation and application of the amnesty remained matters for concern (and indeed the law was later challenged),[19] the amnesty was certainly far narrower, and more reflective of the state's international obligations, than previous amnesties in the region had been. It 'extinguished criminal responsibility' for crimes committed during the civil war by members of the insurgency

---

[14] Some reports suggest that the case was filed after frustration with the peace accords and the Reconciliation law, but in fact it began earlier, 6 months before the accords, based on the de facto impunity in Guatemala. This was controversial among some who felt that litigation should not 'interfere' with the peace process.

[15] Discussions as to the nature and limits of international legal obligations to investigate had particular political significance and currency in the context of the negotiations of the amnesty laws.

[16] See K Sikkink, *The Justice Cascade: How Human Rights Prosecutions Are Changing World Politics* (New York, Norton, 2011).

[17] The conflict having drawn to end in the former Yugoslavia, and the genocide in Rwanda had just led to the establishment of international tribunals ICTY (through UNSC Res 827 (25 May 1993) UN Doc S/RES/1373), and ICTR (through UNSC Res 955 (8 November 1994) UN Doc S/RES/955).

[18] Ley de Reconciliación Nacional, Decreto No 145-1996, Diario de Centro America No 54 (27 December 1996).

[19] This law would later be challenged domestically, unsuccessfully, as noted below in s IV.C.i; the incompatibility of amnesty for serious crimes under international law would be key to the Guatemalan Constitutional Court's decision in October 1997 to uphold the law as capable of interpretation and application 'in a way consistent with international law' and therefore constitutional; see Corte de Constitucionalidad de la República de Guatemala (Guatemalan Constitutional Court), Decision Nos 8-97 and 20-97, 7 October 1997, IV. The amnesty is now at the heart of another case pending before the IACommH.

and the state forces,[20] but it notably enshrined exceptions for genocide, enforced disappearance, torture and other crimes in respect of which responsibility cannot be 'extinguished' under international law.[21] Of concern to some of us however—though given much less attention—were the existing amnesty laws that (were not repealed and) provided blanket amnesty. As we feared, these would come to be invoked later on.[22] But discussions about the nature and limits of the international legal obligation to investigate had greater significance and currency in the context of the negotiation of the peace accords. Consequently, questions with regard to the interpretation of the new amnesty (or 'reconciliation') law—now in tension with the existing amnesty laws—disappeared below the radar.

Meanwhile, other legal developments were providing tools for subsequent litigation, in particular, the growing number of ratifications by Guatemala of human rights treaties, which under the stellar terms of the new constitution, had the highest rank in the legal order. In turn, in 1996, shortly after massacres cases including *Plan de Sánchez v Guatemala* were first lodged before the IACommHR, the CEH was established under the 1996 peace accords—a crucially important, although limited, endeavour. It reached significant findings and uncovered important information, but it could not 'name names' (identify those responsible) and its limited dissemination and endorsement by the state has been said to have 'flouted the peace accords' on which its establishment was based.[23] An unofficial parallel truth enquiry was established through the Archbishop's human rights office—an important NGO in Guatemala—under the leadership of Bishop Gerardi, in part to address these limitations.[24] In a detailed report (entitled '*Nunca Mas*', suggesting again the influence of the earlier Argentinian commission by the same name, as noted in the Argentina case study),[25] it did the naming and shaming that the official commission could not. Both made a contribution towards the search for the truth and, seen from the perspective of litigation that followed, both provided invaluable sources of information and evidence. The fact that, two days after the report was published, Bishop Gerardi was murdered sends a chilling reminder of the challenges of working for justice in Guatemala that are an inescapable part

---

[20] See also E Braid and N Roht-Ariazza, 'De Facto and De Jure Amnesty Laws: The Central American Case' in F Lessa and LA Payne (eds), *Amnesty in the Age of Human Rights Accountability: Comparative and International Perspectives* (Cambridge, Cambridge University Press, 2012) 185.

[21] National Reconciliation Law (n 18) Art 8.

[22] See H Duffy, 'Las Amnistías Vigentes en Guatemala; el Arma Secreta de la Impunidad en las Negociaciones de la Paz' (November 1996) *Revista el Debate* (in Spanish). They would later be invoked by defendants when the National Reconciliation Law was denied.

[23] Impunity Watch/Convergencia por los Derechos Humanos, 'La Persistencia de la Verdad: A diez años del informe de la CEH' (25 February 2009) 17–20, available at www.impunitywatch.org/docs/La_persistencia_de_la_verdad-CEH.pdf (in Spanish).

[24] Proyecto Interdiocesano de Recuperación de la Memoria Histórica, 'Guatemala: Nunca Más' (24 April 1998) available at www.derechoshumanos.net/lesahumanidad/informes/guatemala/informeREMHI-Tomo1.htm (in Spanish).

[25] See Ch 8 on Argentina.

of the context. Some of the challenges facing those seeking to work on justice in Guatemala at that time persist, if in changed form, to the present day.[26]

It was in this changing and challenging landscape that the *Plan de Sánchez* case was prepared and presented in the mid-1990s—one of a number of legal steps, within a broader faltering movement towards truth and justice in Guatemala.

Litigation in relation to the massacres unfolded at different stages before various fora—domestic Guatemalan courts, foreign courts exercising universal or extraterritorial jurisdiction and supranational courts, especially the Inter-American system. This was not so much part of a highly coordinated and multi-faceted long-term legal strategy, as a largely uncoordinated but broadly complementary set of legal actions, by different actors working on different cases in different contexts. Nonetheless, the diversity and multiplicity of litigation is relevant to its overall impact, because a particular piece of litigation can benefit from the dynamic that arises between different approaches to similar facts, that could not have arisen from any one in isolation.

The first type of legal action of relevance involved fruitless attempts, during the mid-1990s, to impel the Guatemalan authorities to investigate and ensure accountability for the massacres. This was the focus of efforts when I joined CALDH in 1995, which had been formed five years previously by Guatemalan former labour lawyer Frank Larue, supported at that time by US and later by several other international colleagues.[27] They set up office in Guatemala City in the early 1990s and developed relationships with local civil society groups, political actors and communities who had suffered in various ways from the repression of the early 1980s—including through the massacres—and began discussions about justice and accountability. The legal work described below had its roots in these connections and conversations. By 1995, requests to the authorities to investigate and prosecute had been made, but had fallen on deaf ears.[28] I joined colleagues in sitting in public ministry waiting rooms and on hold, to find that files were 'missing' that day. Relevant officials were always on a break. If you proved obstinate, trips got longer and excuses more elaborate. It was clear that little would move regarding the massacres in Guatemala without serious external pressure and support.

This inertia provided the impetus for the cases to be taken to the Inter-American system, including the *Plan de Sánchez v Guatemala* case presented to the IACommHR in July 1996, and ultimately decided by the IACtHR in 2004. While it is this case that is the subject of this study—and it will be discussed in more detail below[29]—it should be noted that it unfolded alongside other important cases, related to other massacres, in other regions of the country, presented

---

[26] See n 11 on precautionary measures resulting from threats to judges and civil society.

[27] The original US lawyers were Anna Gallagher and Wallie Mason.

[28] Perhaps the first was made in relation to Rio Negro in 1993, and others including Plan de Sánchez had followed, but met with little results.

[29] See section III.

at roughly the same time, namely the *Dos Erres v Guatemala* case brought by the Center for Justice and International Law (CEJIL), which led to a 2009 judgment of the Court.[30] While this dual approach may have had less to do with strategic planning than with a lack of coordination and communication between NGOs, the parallel cases actually created a useful dynamic, each benefiting from advances and responding to setbacks in the other, as noted further below. Much more recently, cases have gone to the Commission and Court on other massacres, building on previous decisions and pushing forward for more comprehensive and effective implementation.[31]

In turn, while both of these cases were pending before the Commission, other NGOs took different types of litigation transnationally. This included ventures to seek investigation and prosecution of Guatemalan perpetrators by Spanish courts under its universal jurisdiction laws.[32] The effects of these, like other universal jurisdiction claims brought in Spain and elsewhere, are difficult to pinpoint. Although ultimately unsuccessful, these initiatives did generate international attention and spark discussion at a formative stage in Guatemala, as to where and how justice should best be done, and about the reality and implications of impunity in Guatemala. These actions have also been described as 'lending legitimacy to the demands of victims groups' and are particularly significant in Guatemala where threats and intimidation, and the on-going power of those responsible, have undermined and thwarted civil society.[33]

Finally, and most important of all, has been legal action within Guatemala, especially a growing number of low-level prosecutions and—most recently—the prosecution of the former president, Ríos Montt, and other high-level officials. Several processes have unfolded before Guatemala's courts since the bleak period of the filing of the *Plan de Sánchez* petition, when there was plainly no prospect of justice at home. These have tested the limits of the amnesty laws, clarifying the relevance of international standards on investigation and accountability—relying strongly on Inter-American standards. What emerges from this longer-term impact on justice in Guatemala, is how a dynamic exchange between cases, nationally and internationally, has gradually helped to move justice forward.

---

[30] See IACtHR, *Las Dos Erres Massacre v Guatemala*, Judgment (Preliminary Objections, Merits, Reparations, and Costs) IACtHR Ser C No 211 (24 November 2009).

[31] See eg *Members of the Village of Chichupac and Neighboring Communities of the Municipality of Rabinal v Guatemala*, No 12.588, referred to the Court by the Commission on 16 September 2014; see for details IACtHR Press Release No 100/24 (17 September 2017) available at www.oas.org/en/iachr/media_center/preleases/2014/100.asp.

[32] The first of several attempts was brought by the Menchu Foundation in 1999, while the *Plan de Sánchez* case was pending. Several others have been brought since but have not prevailed.

[33] See eg L Skeen, 'Universal Jurisdiction: Spain Steps Down' Comment on Global Policy Forum (24 August 2009) available at www.globalpolicy.org/international-justice/universal-jurisdiction-6-31/48104.html.

III. The *Plan de Sánchez* Case

In January 1995, when I joined the CALDH legal team, the focus was on collecting information, and on community relations and seeking criminal investigation. The need to seek greater international engagement was clear and we had naïvely optimistic discussions about a possible case before the International Court of Justice, the potential and relative merits of UN bodies and other fora, before settling on proceeding to the IACommHR as the most realistic forum before which to present—as soon as possible—the case against Guatemala.

A. Developing Community Relations

As a young and relatively inexperienced lawyer working on these issues in Guatemala, I not infrequently look back and shudder at my naïve faith in the legal process, and all that I would now do differently to engage more effectively the tools at our disposal. But one thing we did right was the amount of time we spent on meetings and workshops with communities. While we lacked training and preparation, we did intuitively what we could to develop relationships and trust, seeking out ways to have difficult conversations that were nevertheless open, honest, safe and meaningful, and mindful of cultural, political and security challenges along the way. The composition of the team as it was, multidisciplinary and consisting of committed Guatemalans and internationals, with people who spent considerable time with communities, was an essential aspect of making those conversations feasible.

Over a period of just over a year, during multiple trips, workshops and meetings in the community and outside, we discussed whether they would be interested in pursuing justice in some form or another. We tried to explain the possibilities and limitations of a completely alien international system. With the benefit of hindsight, and considering ideal conditions (neither of which ever exist) we should have had psycho-social support for the victims and communities who were being asked, indirectly, to confront—and were beginning to speak up about—traumatic experiences and on-going terror, for the first time. As is often the case though, there was little we could have done to meaningfully address the inevitable fear and insecurity.

A related challenge, as always, was how to handle community representation while ensuring so far as possible that all had a voice.[34] Informal community support and representation groups were formed by community members, facilitating

---

[34] This was done through smaller and larger meetings, an effort to draw in men and women, while trying to ensure that questions of representation were made by the right people, in consultation, and not by us.

the case preparation and providing a crucial form of mutual support. In time, some of the same survivors and community members would form part of an effective Justice and Reconciliation Association ('Asociación Justicia y Reconciliación', AJR)[35] active in the criminal prosecutions of some of those responsible for the massacres many years later.[36]

B. Researching and Preparing the Case

Challenges arose from the outset in advising clients in a context in which our knowledge and ability to predict what could go wrong, or right, was limited. We could not know about possible negative implications, including for security, that might flow from bringing the case, and we could offer no real protection. We did not know either what they really stood to gain from the process. At that stage in the Inter-American system, jurisprudence was less developed on impunity issues or reparations than it is today, and in the context of a Commission that was a political operator and therefore somewhat unpredictable, it was particularly difficult to know what we could expect. The approach was therefore to err on the side of caution, in a way that made international litigation sound distinctly unrewarding. As noted below,[37] when we were asked if the claimants could secure socio-economic support as an outcome, I was highly sceptical and advised that they most likely would not. I was pleased to be wrong many years later, when the *Plan de Sánchez* judgment would turn out to include far-reaching socio-economic measures. As lawyers we are often are pressed to predict the future; we must ensure that we *advise* rather than predict, and do so cautiously, while being aware that impact may well go beyond what we could possibly have foreseen.

An early area of focus in the preparation of the *Plan de Sánchez* case was on securing better access to information, to enhance our own, and, more importantly, the community's understanding, of what had happened in 1982. This was crucial, given that at this point there was no truth commission as yet, and secrecy and repression were the rule. The research involved Guatemalan experts carrying out basic investigative work, but given the challenges noted above in a context where access to files was extremely limited and difficult within Guatemala, it required international support from journalists, NGOs and solidarity networks. Piecing together available information on different massacres, a pattern emerged that showed how the Plan de Sánchez massacre unfolded in the context of a broader systemic state policy.

Alongside gaining this historical and political contextual overview, the evidence of those affected was critical. Many witnesses' testimonies were taken from

---

[35] See n 8 for more information.
[36] See section IV.A.iii.
[37] See section IV.B.ii.

communities and eyewitnesses. Survivors and others affected shared their personal experiences. This process, which again, ideally would be done with a greater level of support, was moving and for some cathartic. The collection of witness statements, which would (as would all the evidence) be developed for criminal cases, spoke powerfully, recording for the first time the real personal impact of the massacre of 28 July 1982.

C. Filing the Case

The *Plan de Sánchez* petition was filed before the IACommHR on 25 October 1996. We argued violations of multiple rights, committed as part of a policy of genocide against the indigenous population. The massacre was described in detail through the voices of victims. Placing their accounts in the context of the broader state policy brought to light, despite limited available evidence, the widespread and systematic nature of the massacres. We argued that the state was obliged to investigate, prosecute, punish and provide reparations, which it had woefully failed to do, and that there was no available and effective domestic remedy in Guatemala at that time.

The filing itself had few public reverberations. This was partly due to what was, with hindsight, an unduly limited public strategy at the time. This reflected a lack of experience and a different sense than now of the significance of publicity in effecting change. But there was also a degree of fear and ambivalence among some involved, as to whether the sensitivity of the case was such that publicising it would help or hinder, strengthen or render vulnerable those in whose name the case was brought. On reflection, these questions were among the key questions to resolve prior to filing and would have deserved greater strategic clarity. Easy to say and less easy to do when so much is uncertain as to the implications of the case on people's lives.

As was typical, the case took years to conclude. But already in the first year, through preliminary (private) hearings and direct channels of communication with the government (through the 'Comisión Precidencial Coordinadora de la Política Ejecutivo en Materia de Derechos Humanos', which represented the State before the Commission and Court), the case generated discussions internally within government and an opportunity to engage with it, in a conversation on responses to the massacres. It was not until 11 March 1999 that the IACommHR would decide on admissibility.[38] Its report on the merits, and recommendation to transfer the case to the Court, followed a few years later.[39]

---

[38] Decision adopted by the IACommHR during its 102nd Regular Session, Admissibility Report No 33/99, *Case 11.763* (Plan de Sánchez Massacre) (11 March 1999).

[39] IACommHR, Petition against the Republic of Guatemala in Relation to *Case No 11.763* (Plan de Sánchez Massacre), 31 July 2002; see also *Plan de Sánchez*, Judgment (Merits) (n 1) at para 9.

D. Judgment and Implementation

The judgment itself handed down in 2004 found multiple violations and called on the state to take a broad range of measures of reparation, in a landmark judgment on reparations in the Inter-American system, including individual measures for identified victims and collective reparations, as outlined in the following section. It gave rise to a long (and on-going) process of interaction between survivors, civil society, the state and the Inter-American system, through the implementation procedure before the Court.[40] More broadly it fed into a conversation around the nature of the wrongs in Guatemala, and necessary responses, including accountability and coming to terms with the past. It was followed by, and to some degree reflected in, ensuing domestic processes, including challenges to amnesty laws, and ultimately the long awaited criminal cases against individual perpetrators described below.

IV. The Impact of the *Plan de Sánchez* Litigation

A. The Power of the Process

i. Research, Preparation, Confronting the Truth

When we think of impact we tend to focus on judgment day, or on how the implementation of judgments changed lives or influenced law, policy or practices. Like other cases though, the *Plan de Sánchez* case shows the power of the process itself, even from the very earliest days of the preparation of the case. The processes of discussion with the communities described above,[41] provided a vehicle for victims' stories to be heard, and collected, for the first time.

The research on the pattern of massacres that had swept the country—however imperfect and incomplete at that point—proved powerful in discussions with the community. Information pulled together indicated the nature of the sweeps across the country, bringing a very different perspective on the massacre to those most affected by it. It was chillingly apparent, as conversations began to open up, how many of the community harboured doubts about who had been responsible. Were family or personal conflicts to blame for triggering this terrible onslaught of violence? The information gathered and shared helped to dispel some of the myths and uncertainties about what had befallen them and why. This was particularly helpful in a context where illusions and recriminations were not uncommon and

---

[40] See eg IACtHR, *Plan de Sánchez Massacre v Guatemala*, Monitoring Compliance with Judgment, Order of 1 July 2009, available at www.corteidh.or.cr/docs/supervisiones/sanchez_01_07_09_ing.pdf; *Plan de Sánchez Massacre v Guatemala*, Monitoring Compliance with Judgment, Order of 21 February 2011, available at www.corteidh.or.cr/docs/supervisiones/sanchez_21_02_11_ing.pdf (only in Spanish).

[41] See s III.A.

fear and suppression widespread. The great importance of this part of the process was that it encouraged members of the community to share their own stories and hear those of others, in most cases for the first time, revealing to them that they were not 'responsible for their own misfortune'.[42]

ii. Setting the Record Straight

The research and consultation phase served an important restorative purpose, but provided as well as, of course, an evidentiary base for the case itself. The case preparation effectively created the beginnings of a historical record, which would be developed by subsequent legal and political action, by truth commissions and by the unfolding litigation process and judgments themselves. The litigation process was a catalyst to important specific revelations from the state's side, when, within the framework of the criminal trials for genocide in the country, long-standing efforts to access military plans finally resulted in the army giving the Guatemalan Courts of Justice the first two [military] plans in a more complete form than they had given to the CEH.[43]

The refusal of the State to share information was—as it often is—illuminating, and exposed the fallacy of official positions: the government claimed for example, before the Commission and Court, that one of the military plans—'Operation Plan Sofía'—had been lost, whereas it was later uncovered by a US NGO. The gradual uncovering of erstwhile secret details, coupled with the sheer mass of testimony, contributed to a growing historical record of violations in Guatemala. This was particularly important before the complementary but much broader process by the CEH. By the time the *Plan de Sánchez* case proceeded from the Commission to the Court, the CEH would in turn feed into the evidence presented to the Court, as it would again in subsequent criminal cases within Guatemala. Litigation has been part of a gradual and on-going process of uncovering the truth, and with time, turning that information to evidence and to growing demands for justice.

iii. Organisation and Mobilisation

Meanwhile, the community organised itself for the purposes of representation and support. The Justice and Reconciliation Association (AJR) was formed for the purpose of pursuing justice in domestic courts;[44] eventually, this would be supplemented by the 'Coordinación de Acompañamiento Internacional en Guatemala' (Coordination of International Accompaniment in Guatemala, CAIG).[45] The AJR has served to give a voice, visibility and profile to victims and communities,

---

[42] Malumud Goti, cited in Ch 3.

[43] The applicants sought disclosure of the Guatemalan Army's military campaign plans 'Victoria 82', 'Firmeza 83' and operation 'Sofía'; see n 8 for more information.

[44] See n 8 for more information.

[45] This victim-based organisation comprised, but went far beyond, the survivors and representatives of Plan de Sánchez. Several victims in the *Plan de Sánchez* case were witnesses in the *Montt* trial. See for more information in Spanish: www.acoguate.org/acompanamiento-internacional/.

and to facilitate their participation in discussions relevant to justice, with benefits that go beyond the cases themselves. This is an obvious manifestation of the broader positive mobilising impact that the search for justice in Guatemala has had on Guatemalan civil society. It has enhanced the international profile of key actors and organisations from within civil society, as well as of the prosecutor's office and to some extent the judiciary.[46] The beneficial effects of the search for justice on civil society, and in particular the organisation of groups from within communities or survivors, was described by one interviewee—a lawyer involved in the cases—as perhaps the most important impact of the litigation on genocide in Guatemala.[47]

iv. Recognition and Apology

Recognition of wrongs is often considered a function of courts and an important impact of judgment. The *Plan de Sánchez* case shows how recognition by the state authorities themselves can arise during the litigation process, before judgment was rendered, prompted—as is often the case—by the impending public exposure of the hearing before the Court. The state's movement toward recognition and expressions of regret unfolded incrementally, throughout the process. Firstly, the Guatemalan state withdrew its preliminary objections and accepted responsibility in writing before the hearing, and publicly during the first hearing in Court.[48] In due course, the judgment itself provided objective, judicial recognition of individual victims, identifying by name the 268 victims, one by one. The Court found multiple violations and provided detailed descriptions of the atrocities carried out against them on July 1982.

Following judgment, and while the Reparations judgment was pending, the State issued an apology.[49] As the Reparation judgment notes:

> The State expressed its profound regret for the events suffered by the Plan de Sánchez community on July 18, 1982, and apologized to the victims, the survivors and the next of kin, as an initial manifestation of respect, reparation and guarantee of non-repetition. In this regard, it requested the Inter-American Court to weigh the significance of the act of justice performed by the State in acknowledging its international responsibility. It also expressed its determination to repair the damage caused to the victims, survivors and next of kin for the suffering inflicted upon them by the violation of their human rights.[50]

The Court later recognised the importance of this as a 'contribution to the proceedings and to the development of the effectiveness of the Inter-American

---

[46] eg Claudia Paz y Paz has been honoured in various contexts for the importance of her role as independent and determined prosecutor of the genocide cases.

[47] Interview with Pauls Seils, the Hague 2016.

[48] *Plan de Sánchez*, Judgment (Merits) (n 1) at paras 30–33.

[49] See IACommHR, Press Release No 12/00, 17 August 2000, available at www.cidh.org/Comunicados/English/2000/Press12-00.htm.

[50] IACtHR, *Plan de Sánchez*, Judgment (Reparations) (n 3) at para 92.

Convention'.[51] As the quote above shows, clearly such recognition was explicitly linked to an attempt to relieve its reparation obligations, which led some to question how 'genuine' such apologies really are. However, in *Plan de Sánchez*, the apologies were eventually linked with other steps, such as the public acts of recognition on-site, monuments to commemorate the dead and moves towards non-repetition, giving them credibility, and power, as restorative steps.

Such apologetic engagement by authorities with communities has not always taken place elsewhere in Guatemala. It is an illustration of the impact of the process that this did happen in Baja Verapaz. However, in that case it seemed to operate to limit further impact, in that it was not rolled out into a broader programme of apology or acknowledgement.[52] A level of dejection by some of these other community members has been reported by one researcher.[53] As noted next below, the scope of this recognition and apology and their impact were also somewhat tempered by the refusal of the State to categorise the massacres in Guatemala as cases of genocide.[54]

v. *Acknowledging the Nature of the Wrongs: Naming Genocide in Guatemala*

The *Plan de Sánchez* process contributed to an appreciation of the egregious violations in Guatemala as genocide. The sensitivity surrounding the label of genocide, 'the mother of all crimes', is borne out by the state's persistent objection, throughout the process, even after it acknowledged the massacres themselves and its responsibility. When I started on these cases in the mid-90s there had been no recognition in political contexts at all—neither by the government nor the URNG in the peace negotiations for example, nor by international bodies—of the genocide and its impact on the indigenous population of Guatemala. In this context, the legal debate as the case was being prepared, and the eventual presentation of substantiated legal claims of genocide, had particular significance.

I took the view that the evidence emerging pointed to these massacres as properly amounting to genocide.[55] Intense discussions unfolded within and between NGOs, and I recall the controversy and the appropriate seriousness with which

---

[51] *Plan de Sánchez*, Judgment (Merits) (n 1) at para 50.

[52] Research by Lieselotte Viaene suggests that in other communities investigated by her, there has been a lack of engagement by the state—by those responsible for perpetration: 1 victim complained that 'we […] have a cross with all the names of our deceased. And the government has never come to look at this cross, even though it is standing there. There they would see the names of our dead mothers, of the parents, the elders, our grandfathers and grandmothers who were murdered' in L Viaene, 'Life Is Priceless: Mayan Q'eqchi' Voices on the Guatemalan National Reparations Program' (2010) 4 *International Journal of Transitional Justice* 4, 21.

[53] Ibid.

[54] IACommHR Country Report, *Situation of Human Rights in Guatemala: Diversity, Inequality and Exclusion, OEA/Ser.L/V/II/Doc. 43/15* (31 December 2015) para 3.

[55] The controversy revolved around whether the indigenous victims should be seen as 'political groups', not covered by the convention, as well as issues of subjective intent. It is now well recognised that there was genocide in Guatemala, and IACommHR processes made an important contribution.

NGOs and activists discussed the classification question. I believe that it was in the *Plan de Sánchez* petition that genocide was formally alleged for the first time. Over time, the conversation opened out and a number of authorities gradually lent their weight to it, but for some people this very early framing of the narrative and legal understanding of the Guatemalan crimes, and its impact on the impetus towards justice in Guatemala, is one of the most significant indirect contributions of this process.[56]

The IACommHR's report found that the massacre was committed 'within the framework of a genocidal policy of the Guatemalan State, carried out with the intention of totally or partially destroying the Mayan indigenous people'.[57] The Commission has adapted this approach in subsequent cases in relation to the massacres.[58]

The state objected to the Court's consideration of the genocide claim on jurisdictional grounds. The Court warily agreed. Nervous about its mandate and allegations of jurisdictional over-reach in other contexts,[59] the Court held it could not find that the violations amounted to genocide on grounds of its limited competence.[60] It did however refer to 'the issue of genocide' mentioned both by the IACommHR and by the representatives of the victims and noted:

> facts such as those stated, which gravely affected the members of the Maya Achí people in their identity and values and that took place within a pattern of massacres, constitute an aggravated impact that entails international responsibility of the State, which this Court will take into account when it decides on reparations.[61]

While less clear than the Commission therefore, it implicitly recognised the nature of the wrongs and the gravity of what had happened in Guatemala and its impact on forms of reparation. The reference to genocide as a relevant argument resonated in other cases coming to the Court later, even where genocide had not been presented as a key dimension of those cases.[62] It provoked debate around the

---

[56] Discussions with eg Frank la Rue and Mario Maldonado.

[57] IACommHR, Petition (n 39) at para 3.

[58] See *Village of Chichupac and Neighboring Communities Case* (n 31).

[59] See eg the *Abella* decision of the Commission (*Juan Carlos Abella v Argentina*, Case 11.137, Report No 55/97) finding violations of international humanitarian law, criticism thereof and the more conservative approach to interpretation of the American Convention in light of broader international law by the Court in *Las Palmeras* case of 6 December 2001 (IACtHR Ser C No 90).

[60] *Plan de Sánchez*, Judgment (Merits) (n 1) at para 50: 'With respect to the issue of genocide mentioned both by the Commission and by the representatives of the victims and their next of kin, the Court notes that in adjudicatory matters it is only competent to find violations of the American Convention on Human Rights and of other instruments of the inter-American system for the protection of human rights that enable it to do so'.

[61] Ibid.

[62] IACtHR, *Las Dos Erres Case* (Merits) (n 30), Concurring Opinion of Ad Hoc Judge Ramón Cadena Rámila, para 3. Although the facts were different and the community affected in the Petén region was not an indigenous community, ad hoc Judge Cadena Rámila, however, expressed a view in which genocide, although part of a convention over which the Inter-American Court lacks jurisdiction, could still be considered as aggravating circumstances in the decision of a case.

Court's willingness to look to broader international law as an interpretative tool in the future, including as an aggravating factor in finding violation of the American Convention on Human Rights, as was reflected in more detail in a separate opinion in the *Plan de Sánchez* case.[63]

B. Reparation and Implementation

The Court's judgment provided a crucial form of objective recognition of the nature of the wrongs committed against the community of Plan de Sánchez (and others).

i. Developing Collective as well as Individual Reparations

The reparations order has been described as 'ground-breaking'.[64] The Court's emphasis on collective as well as individual reparation, and on the fact of collective reparation being owed to affected persons beyond the particular petitioners identified in the case, is particularly significant. This reflected the profound and terrible nature of the personal, social and cultural impact of the violations themselves, carried out under the scorched earth policy. Indeed, in this respect, the judgment was described as contributing to the 're-conceptualisation of reparation in the Inter-American system', and clearly had a normative impact.[65] These 'community-based' or collective reparations took many forms as sketched out below.[66]

ii. Socio-economic Measures, Health and Education

At the start of the process, back in 1995, when we asked applicants about their goals for the case, they thought about it for a while and said they needed schools, hospitals and crops. The Court in the *Plan de Sánchez* order extremely wide-reaching reparation taking the need of the applicants into account. But these measures were notably ordered not only for Plan de Sánchez but also for other affected communities. They reflected the structural impact on the community life, culture, production and infrastructure, with symbolic as well as deep-rooted practical significance.

---

[63] *Plan de Sánchez*, Judgment (Merits) (n 1), Separate Opinion of Judge Sergio Garcia-Ramirez, para 9.

[64] See eg C Evans, *The Right to Reparation in International Law for Victims of Armed Conflict* (Cambridge, Cambridge University Press, 2012) 158.

[65] LM Balasco, 'Reparative Development: Re-conceptualising Reparations in Transitional Justice Processes' (2017) 17 *Conflict, Security and Development* 1. The author refers to it as 1 of 4 particularly important Guatemalan cases in this respect.

[66] While these steps are monitored as part of on-going implementation of the judgment, even before the judgment was rendered, some forms of satisfaction such as acknowledgement of wrongs and honouring the dead were well underway as noted above in s IV.A.

They included community infrastructure (roads, sewage systems), a housing program, education and the provision of teachers, medical treatment and psychosocial support for victims. The Court's approach to reparation in this case proved to be a precursor to a now more expansive body of jurisprudence from the Inter-American system, generally showing a holistic approach to repairing massive violations, with generational effect.[67]

The state committed itself to implementing this judgment, and has taken noteworthy measures towards compliance, as recorded in the on-going monitoring by the Court itself.[68] In particular, the state reported that the Ministry of Public Health and Social Welfare, from one year after the judgment, had been 'providing collective, family and individual medical and psychological treatment to the residents of the Plan de Sánchez village, and neighboring communities, through two psychologists and one nursing assistant'. However, the Commission and victims have called for a 'more comprehensive' approach, more information and better access to medicine for example. Hence, implementation remains incomplete in some respects and the Court has resolved to continue to monitor progress.[69]

Through the state's process of implementation, the Court's monitoring and the Commission's active participation, a platform for dialogue with the community as to the adequacy of the provision of basic economic and social rights has been created. Those discussions and the on-going engagement of the survivor community are themselves particularly valuable types of impact to flow from the international human rights judgment.[70] They also contributed to a broader debate that eventually resulted in a more comprehensive reparations scheme in Guatemala.[71]

iii. Satisfaction and Guarantees of Non-repetition

The Court emphasised that reparation needed to go beyond material compensation. Including 'satisfaction seeking to repair the non-pecuniary damage ... which have public repercussions', which it found to 'have particular relevance in this case, owing to the extreme gravity of the facts and the collective nature of the damage produced'.[72] The symbolic measures ordered by the Court were therefore

---

[67] See eg *Plan de Sánchez*, Judgment (Reparations) (n 3) at paras 100–01.

[68] Monitoring Compliance with *Plan de Sánchez* Judgment (n 40) at para 30; Monitoring Compliance with Judgment (n 40) at para 15.

[69] Ibid.

[70] The Court noted inadequate compliance with lack of personnel to provide the services needed; Monitoring Compliance with Judgment (n 40) at para 26. In 2011, it noted that infrastructure improvements and bilingual education programmes were not fully effective; Monitoring Compliance with Judgment (40) at para 27.

[71] A broader reparation scheme was set up by the state of inevitable broader impact that any of the IACtHR judgments. Those judgments may, however, have highlighted the need for such programmes.

[72] *Plan de Sánchez*, Judgment (Reparations) (n 3) at para 93.

extensive, with strong public and collective dimensions. The Court ordered the following:

— *A public act organised by the state in the community itself,* acknowledging the State's responsibility, and commemorating those executed in the massacre.[73] The high level public act of acknowledgement was part of a process of reparation, closely linked to guarantees of non-repetition.

— *Translation* of the judgments of the Court into the Maya Achí language, and publication and dissemination of the pertinent parts of the judgment. In this respect, the Court noted in follow-up proceedings years after judgment that the translation and partial dissemination of the judgments had been carried out, while urging that the judgment be published and made available throughout the affected municipality of Rabinal.[74] In this way, the Court sought to bridge the gap between what happens in the courtroom in Costa Rica and in the Guatemalan communities most affected.

— *Monument to 'historical memory':* Importantly, the Court paved the way for engaging with a sometimes neglected aspect of reparation—guarantees of non-repetition through acknowledging wrongs and honouring the memory of the dead. The Court held that the state must provide resources for 'collective memory' to contribute to raising public awareness, to prevent the recurrence of events like those that occurred in this case, and to keep alive the memories of the deceased.[75] This included the construction of a memorial chapel for the victims of the massacre, and the Court has since found that the state should provide a certain amount of money 'for the maintenance and improvements to the infrastructure of the chapel in which the victims pay tribute to those who were executed'.[76] Its example may also have catalysed other such monuments, which have proliferated in Guatemala since this one appeared. The restorative function of such monuments has been recorded by several survivors and researchers. As one survivor noted, 'we do not want to let the names of our friends be forgotten by not mentioning them, we have to mention them, because they are not to blame'.[77]

iv. Cultural and Linguistic Reparation

The reparations judgment required the state to take a range of measures directed at the promotion and protection of Maya Achí culture. In the judgment on merits

---

[73] Ibid, 100–01.

[74] IACtHR, *Plan de Sánchez Massacre v Guatemala*, Monitoring Compliance with Judgment, Order of 5 August 2008, paras 12, 14, available at www.corteidh.or.cr/docs/supervisiones/sanchez_05_08_08_ing.pdf.

[75] *Plan de Sánchez,* Judgment (Reparations) (n 3) at para 104.

[76] The Court monitored compliance of the payment for infrastructure maintenance; Monitoring Compliance with Judgment (n 40) at para 22.

[77] Viaene, 'Life Is Priceless' (n 51) at 20.

the Court had noted that it would consider the 'facts [...] which gravely affected the members of the Maya Achí people [...] when it decides on reparations'.[78] In the reparations judgment, it explained its reasoning:

> Given that the victims in this case are members of the Mayan people, this Court considers that an important component of the individual reparation is the reparation that the Court will now grant to the members of the community as a whole.[79]

The Court recognised that when the collectivity involves indigenous people, the harm produced threatens their cultural foundations and the social fabric of society and cannot be understood only in terms of the suffering of individual petitioners. It therefore required measures to strengthen training, education and related institutions to this end.[80] The Court has since taken a similarly progressive and creative view of reparations in other cases in relation to cultural harm.[81] In its follow-up reporting on implementation, the Court performs an on-going role in acknowledging the nature and impact of the wrongs, and in empowering the victim and survivor communities, and strengthening their institutions. As such, the judgment has served to keep on the agenda the fundamental underlying discrimination and historic injustice against indigenous Guatemalans.

v. Compensation

The Court also ordered the payment of compensation, in what appeared to be very substantial sums. Though the amounts awarded were in reality quite modest when shared among the many applicants, these awards were nevertheless significant. By 2007, the Court found that the State had 'settl[ed] 66.66% of the sum of compensation awarded for pecuniary and non-pecuniary damage'.[82] The receipt of compensation can have complex effects, for those directly involved and also for others. It was reported that compensation has on occasion led to 'a sentiment of guilt among those with access to the money [...] towards relatives who were

---

[78] *Plan de Sánchez*, Judgment (Merits) (n 1) at para 51.

[79] *Plan de Sánchez* Judgment (Reparations) (n 3) at para 86.

[80] This concerned in particular the obligation to 'study and dissemination of the Maya Achí culture in the affected communities through the Guatemalan Academy of Mayan Languages or a similar organization' and to 'provide teaching personnel trained in intercultural and bilingual teaching for primary, secondary and comprehensive schooling in the affected communities', *Plan de Sánchez*, Judgment (Reparations) (n 3) at para 110.

[81] See among others the line of cases addressing indigenous rights in the Inter-American system, eg *Moiwana Community v Suriname*, Judgment (Preliminary Objections, Merits, Reparations and Costs) IACtHR Ser C No 124 (15 June 2005); *Saramaka People v Suriname*, Judgment (Preliminary Objections, Merits, Reparations, and Costs) IACtHR Ser C No, 172 (28 November 2007); *Kichwa Indigenous People of Sarayaku v Ecuador*, Judgment (Merits and Reparations) IACtHR Ser C No 245 (27 June 2012); *Río Negro Massacre v Guatemala*, Judgment (Preliminary Objections, Merits, Reparations, and Costs), IACtHR Ser C No 250 (4 September 2012).

[82] IACtHR, *Plan de Sánchez Massacre v Guatemala*, Monitoring Compliance with Judgment, Order of 28 November 2007, para 2, available at www.corteidh.or.cr/docs/supervisiones/sanchez_28_11_07_ing.pdf. It left open for further compliance monitoring the payment in full of compensation and costs.

killed but also towards those who, for bureaucratic reasons have not obtained compensation'.[83] It can also have both a symbolic value and a significant practical importance in enabling victims of genocide to re-establish sustainable modest sources of livelihood and rebuild their lives.

vi. Duty to Investigate and Accountability

Notably, the first non-material aspect of reparation that the Court referred to in the judgment was investigation and accountability. The significance was encapsulated in these terms:

> More than 22 years after the massacre and 10 after the corresponding investigations were opened, the State has not investigated the facts or identified, prosecuted and punished those responsible. This constitutes a situation of impunity, which contravenes the State's aforementioned obligation, harms the victims, and encourages the chronic repetition of the human rights violations in question.[84]

The nature of some of these failures, and the insecurity, impotence and anguish caused to victims were set out.[85] The practical implications for accountability in Guatemala are discussed further below, but the obligations of the state, and concrete dimension of its failure, were set down in clear terms.

C. Impact on Impunity and the On-going Quest for Justice in Guatemala

A central goal of the international case, and of the civil groups involved in it, was always to combat the deeply entrenched impunity in Guatemala. An important aspect of both the Commission's report, and especially the judgments on merits and reparations of the Court, was the firm determination that the state was obliged to investigate, and to identify, prosecute and punish those responsible.[86] The processes had exposed, and objectively confirmed the state's abject failure to meet these obligations and the various impediments that stood in the way of it doing so. Through implementation, the state was forced to account for it, and struggled to look active, but results were limited. Through more recent cases in the Guatemalan courts, victims and NGOs have sought, with some faltering 'success' (as noted below), to bring these international obligations to bear in the domestic system. This has been accompanied, and made possible by, multi-faceted action and factors coinciding to try to strengthen and put pressure on the system and

---

[83] See Balasco, 'Reparative Development: Re-conceptualising Reparations in Transitional Justice Processes' (n 64).

[84] *Plan de Sánchez*, Judgment (Reparations) (n 3) at para 95.

[85] Ibid, 94.

[86] eg *Plan de Sánchez*, Judgment (Merits) (n 1) at para 2; *Plan de Sánchez*, Judgment (Reparations) (n 3) at paras 24, 49(6), 49(8), 49(9), 49(18), 49(19) and 87.

make justice a real possibility. At various stages these supranational cases have provided tools to civil society to use domestically in pushing for investigation, and in forming domestic legal challenges to impunity. An interesting dynamic also arose in this respect between international massacre cases that is worthy of note. Following the judgment in *Plan de Sánchez*, the parties to the *Dos Erres Massacre* case agreed to a friendly settlement and the case was effectively 'suspended', subject to compliance with the terms of this agreement, which included that investigations be conducted and accountability established. When it became clear however, that impunity continued to prevail in practice, the applicants reverted to the Court, which resumed the exercise of jurisdiction and handed down a strongly worded judgment in 2009, creating increased pressure on the state to deliver on justice.

i. Clarifying Accountability Obligations, and Reducing the Scope of Amnesty

The IACtHR's jurisprudence has had a decisive influence on domestic standards in Guatemala. This has taken several forms, as seen in decisions of the Constitutional and Supreme Courts to remove obstacles to accountability. The Courts have upheld the doctrine on continuing crimes and interpretation of enforced disappearance.[87] Most tellingly for present purposes, they have found that the authorities must investigate and hold to account those responsible for the massacres and they have rejected the applicability of the 1996 National Reconciliation Law (amnesty law) to such cases.

This transposition of international standards was certainly not automatic but has come about gradually. Guatemalan courts' have waivered, their approach evolving erratically over time, reflecting a dynamic relationship between the regional and national systems. The Guatemalan courts had reached several conflicting decisions regarding the applicability of the 1996 amnesty law before the *Plan de Sánchez* decision came down. For example, in 2001, the Constitutional Court had decided that the amnesty *was* applicable to military officers involved in the Dos Erres massacre (admittedly in the context of allegations of threats to members of the Court).[88] After the *Plan de Sánchez* case was handed down with clear accountability obligations, and with civil society pressing ahead for accountability domestically, the *Dos Erres* case was, as noted above, suspended pursuant to a friendly settlement. However, as is often the case in international human rights litigation, faltering advance was most apparent in respect of the accountability aspect of the *Plan de Sánchez* judgment of 2004 on which implementation was

---

[87] This has been interpreted as meaning that the crime continues until such time as the remains of the victims are found, as one example. See Bosdriesz, 'The Contribution of the Inter-American Court of Human Rights to Domestic Accountability Efforts for Serious Crimes (n 2) at 17–18.

[88] According to Bosdriesz, the 'decision was taken only a week after one of the CC judges involved in the case left the country as a result of threats made against him'. See Bosdriesz (n 2) at 18.

weakest. The IACtHR re-seized the matter in the *Dos Erres* judgment of 2009, condemning the state's approach to the amnesty law, and the broader lack of investigation and undue delays, already exposed by the *Plan de Sánchez* case.[89]

On 8 February 2010, the Guatemalan Supreme Court decided that the Inter-American Court's judgment in the *Dos Erres* was 'self-executing' and ordered, inter alia, that suspects be apprehended and prosecuted, without application of the amnesty law.[90] Just a month later, the Constitutional Court of Guatemala upheld a Supreme Court decision to deny amnesty to another military officer.[91] In 2012, the Guatemalan courts were called on to apply the 1996 amnesty law, provoking litigation in which I intervened as *amicus*, with other international lawyers,[92] and the Court accepted that the amnesty law could not apply in any case which concerns grave violations of human rights, with specific reference to the IACtHR's jurisprudence.[93] The exception for genocide, torture and enforced disappearances had been expressly stated in the language of the law, pursuant to the negotiations, but ambiguity and uncertainty had remained, and the government has maintained support for the amnesty laws.[94] It was therefore ultimately through the Guatemalan courts, citing the binding nature of the IACtHR's rulings, that the narrower interpretation of the amnesty law was upheld.[95]

Although, strictly speaking, beyond the scope of this report, it is noteworthy that the amnesty issue was not definitively settled there, but reared its head again in the *Montt* trial (2013) and subsequently. As this latest development shows, it is not a linear process, however, but a series of advances and setbacks informed as ever by a range of powerful external factors. Nevertheless, accountability standards have undoubtedly been improved in Guatemalan justice system and the influence of the IACtHR's jurisprudence on the massacres cases, while inconsistent, is certainly evident.

---

[89] *Las Dos Erres Case* (Merits) (n 30) at para 133.

[90] Corte Suprema de Justicia de Guatemala (Guatemalan Supreme Court), 'Solicitud de Ejecución de Sentencia de la Corte Interamericana de Derechos Humanos', No MP001/2006/96951, Judgment of 8 February 2010 (in Spanish).

[91] Guatemalan Constitutional Court, Decision of 18 March 2010, No expediente 4837-2009 (in Spanish).

[92] See for a summary of the involvement of Human Rights in Practice in the case www.rightsinpractice.org/legaladvice-litigation.html#4; the *amicus curiae* brief is available in Spanish at www.rightsinpractice.org/doc-html/RIOS%20MONTT%20AMICUS%20SPANISH.pdf.

[93] See eg Guatemalan Supreme Court, Judgment of 8 August 2012, No expedientes 1143-2012 and 1173-2012, and Judgment of 10 April 2013, No expedientes 1758-2012 and 1779-2012 (in Spanish). IACommHR Country Report (n 53) at paras 432–35.

[94] Art 8 of the Law on National Reconciliation expressly excluded genocide, torture, forced disappearance 'or those offenses that are imprescriptible or that do not allow for the extinction of criminal liability as per domestic law or the international treaties ratified by Guatemala'. See also paras 442–43 of the IACommHR Country Report (n 53). The IACommHR expressed concern with regard to the support of amnesty for grave human rights violations (para 442), and the classification of the situation in the country as genocide remained a matter of dispute with the Guatemalan government.

[95] Ibid, paras 435–36.

ii. Prosecuting at Low Levels

Given the entrenched nature of impunity in Guatemala it is noteworthy that several prosecutions and convictions in relation to the Plan de Sánchez massacre eventually took place. Almost exactly 30 years after the massacre, in 2012 there were five convictions that were upheld by the Guatemalan courts on appeal. The defendants were former military commissioner Lucas Tecú and civil patrolmen Santos Rosales García, Eusebio Galeano, Julián Acoi and Mario Acoj, direct perpetrators of the massacre.[96] They were sentenced to 7,860 years in prison (30 years for each victim).[97] These trials both reflected and consolidated the positive impact achieved by the *Plan de Sánchez* case, especially by confirming the facts uncovered by it and the recognition to which the victims were entitled. They also generated further momentum towards a fuller justice, as reflected in the terms of the criminal judgment itself. Significantly, although that case concerned low-level perpetrators, it called for the public ministry to continue to investigate 'the intellectual authors'.[98] Prosecutions have also unfolded in relation to other massacres[99] including Dos Erres in relation to which the Supreme Court ordered the investigation following the IACtHR's judgment.[100] Multiple arrest warrants were issued and some individuals have been arrested abroad through international cooperation, and held to account.[101]

iii. Faltering Advances towards Accountability at the Highest Levels

Attempts at higher level accountability, while on-going and thus far elusive, have gained significant momentum and themselves had considerable effect in recent years. In 2012, the same year as the Plan de Sánchez direct perpetrators were sentenced, charges for genocide and crimes against humanity were filed against Efraín Ríos Montt and José Mauricio Rodríguez Sánchez. This is the first time a former head of state has been prosecuted for crimes against humanity in the courts of the country where the crimes were committed. Hearings took place in a Guatemalan courtroom, with some of the most powerful characters in Guatemalan history

---

[96] CALDH, 'Historica condena por massacre de Plan de Sánchez', website of the Network in Solidarity with the People of Guatemala (20 March 2012) available at www.nisgua.org/historica-condena-por-masacre-de-plan-de-sanchez/.

[97] IACommHR Country Report (n 53) at para 3.

[98] Bosdriesz (n 2) at 24.

[99] In an early example, members of the civil patrols PACs were prosecuted after the peace accords, but then 'broken out of jail' in a symbol of impunity. See L Arriaza and N Roht-Arriaza, 'Social Repair at the Local Level: the Case of Guatemala' in K McEvoy and L McGregor (eds), *Transitonal Justice from Below: Grassroots Activism and the Struggle for Change* (Oxford, Hart Publishing, 2008) 151–53. It ordered the state 'to effectively direct the investigations so as to identify, prosecute, and punish those responsible for the crimes committed in Dos Erres, and remove all obstacles, de facto and de jure, which maintain the case in impunity'.

[100] Developments arise in relation to the *Dos Erres* judgment; as noted above in n 90, the Guatemalan Supreme Court ordered that the competent court continue with the prosecution.

[101] There were 17 arrest warrants. US authorities in 2009 reportedly arrested 3 ex-military who had been involved in this massacre; 'Capturan en EE.UU a tres implicados en masacre de las Dos Erres' *Prensa Libre* (5 May 2010).

sitting in the dock. Multiple witnesses provided testimony as victims or witnesses, speaking to the genocidal policy that desecrated communities, cultures and traditions. International trial observers followed and reported daily, a website was established, and the world watched an important display of justice for genocide, conducted where it is often said it can be done best, at home.

Of particular note was the level of participation in the Montt trial. First and foremost were the more than 90 victims and survivors of the genocide in the Ixil who gave testimony to their treatment like 'animals', and to the individual, collective and cultural impact of the crimes. Some of the questioning from the Court and the defence has been criticised, as has the adequacy of the measures of victim protection and the limited efforts to integrate the indigenous dimension into the trial process.[102] Nonetheless, witnesses have described the importance of the process on many levels: to honour the memory of their dead,[103] 'to tell their stories before a national audience for the first time',[104] to demand respect that they deserve ('we are poor ... but we deserve respect')[105] and, as the Court's judgment eventually reflected, as 'a cry for justice and a demand that these events are never repeated'.[106]

Ríos Montt was convicted on 10 May 2013. Euphoria was well founded, but short-lived. The judgment was overturned in its entirety 10 days later and a retrial was ordered.[107] Lawyers on behalf of Ríos Montt argued that Montt, like Pinochet before him, lacks the mental capacity to stand trial.[108] Rios Montt died, in April 2018, as this book was being finalised. He was never fully held to account for his crimes. While the frustration for victims and civil society is clear, the general's obituaries, replete with references to genocide and human rights violations, leave little doubt as to the impact on his legacy and on the historical narrative. There is room for debate as to whether he entirely escaped justice. Meanwhile just weeks after his death, former high ranking military officers were convicted in relation to one case of rape and disappearance in the early eighties, holding promise for further accountability.

---

[102] E Patterson, 'The Rios Montt Trial—Have Efforts Been Made to Integrate the Mayan Perspective?' *International Justice Monitor* (9 April 2013) www.ijmonitor.org/2013/04/elisabeth-patterson-the-rios-montt-trial-have-efforts-been-made-to-integrate-the-mayan-perspective/.

[103] eg International Justice Monitor, '"They viewed us as if we were not people": Witness testimony continues for a fourth day in Rios Montt trial' (23 March 2013) www.ijmonitor.org/2013/03/they-viewed-us-as-if-we-were-not-people-witness-testimony-continues-for-a-fourth-day-in-rios-montt-trial/. International Crisis Group, 'Justice on trial in Guatemala: The Ríos Montt Case' Latin America Report No. 50 (23 September 2013) 6.

[104] International Crisis Group, ibid, 3.

[105] Ibid, 6.

[106] Open Society Justice Initiative, *Judging a Dictator: The Trial of Guatemala's Ríos Montt* (2013) 49.

[107] IACommHR Country Report (n 53) at paras 427–28.

[108] The High Risk Tribunal 'B' ordered a private trial (behind closed doors and with no press presence) for January 2016 for the purposes of applying security measures and corrections measures (such as confinement to his home or a healthcare facility, due to his health). However, after various interruptions, Presiding Judge María Elena Castellanos declared on 16 March 2016 that retrial proceedings in the *Maya Ixil Genocide* case should start, disregarding pending motions. Montt was not present and, on 3 June 2016, the First Court of Appeals suspended the case indefinitely. On March 2017, a new trial against Montt for crimes committed during the Dos Erres massacre was ordered. See the Trial International webpage available at www.trialinternational.org/latest-post/efrain-rios-montt/.

The process can hardly be seen as a failure. Victims described the importance of their giving testimony, of the crimes being recognised as genocide in the conviction, of the reduction of all-powerful military and political strongman as a form of accountability in itself. Since 2013, a steady stream of investigations and prosecutions for grave crimes committed during Guatemala's conflict have continued, in what has aptly been described as a 'two steps forward, one step back' advance.[109] These shoots—however imperfect—of accountability are the culmination of a long, multi-staged process to which litigation lent its weight, within a much broader movement for change.

V. Conclusions

It has been a long, winding and incomplete journey towards justice in Guatemala. There has been remarkable progress, offset by notorious challenges and setbacks. While assessment of the strengths and weakness of efforts to secure justice in Guatemala inevitably vary, it is clear that we have travelled a long way from the Guatemala of the mid-1990s that I landed in, with the apparently impenetrable wall of silence, denial and/or impunity surrounding massacres such as Plan de Sánchez and the genocide of which it formed part.

Myriad factors have contributed to that movement. Massive investment of resources by NGOs, including CALDH and others, the power of specific individuals, such as survivors, victims' representatives or prosecutors, and international support of various forms, are among the factors contributing to the progress. In turn, security challenges,[110] systemic inequality, or the role of 'veto players'[111] are among the factors that limit this progress.

The approach to reparations in the *Plan de Sánchez* case was remarkable in the breadth of its recognition of beneficiaries and its ambition for impact. It contributed to international standards in relation to reparations; the Inter-American jurisprudence on reparations has become a reference point for courts and tribunals, across human rights systems and now in international criminal law.[112] It has recognised the pressing need for reparation to comprise a full array of compensation, recognition, remorse, commemoration, translation, outreach,

---

[109] T Reisman, 'Human Rights Trials in Guatemala: "Two Steps Forward, One Step Back"' *International Justice Monitor* (2 May 2017) available at www.ijmonitor.org/2017/05/human-rights-trials-in-guatemala-two-steps-forward-one-step-back/.

[110] Judges involved specifically in *Plan de Sánchez* and other cases subject to threats were covered by precautionary measures; see n 11 and IACommHR Country Report (n 53) at paras 223ff.

[111] F Lessa et al, 'Overcoming Impunity: Pathways to Accountability in Latin America' (2014) 8 *International Journal of Transitional Justice* (2014) 75. The authors define 'veto players' as 'those actors who oppose accountability for, or investigation into, past human rights violations' at 78.

[112] *Prosecutor v Thomas Lubanga Dyilo* (Order for Reparations) ICC-01/04-01/06-3129-AnxA (3 March 2015).

socio-economic support, the development of infrastructure, education, health, psycho-social measures, cultural redress and investment, in response to wrongs as egregious as genocide. By setting down the need for a structural approach to reparation in this case and others of a similar nature, the approach aims at genuine restitution that takes into account the nature and impact of the violations. It has been observed that 'the transitional justice/development nexus could not be clearer in these important rulings. Each case is an assertion by the Court that the State must not only compensate but also assist in restoring and rebuilding [for] victims [...] families and communities'.[113]

Implementation of this judgment is on-going, and likely to remain so for some time. A checklist approach to implementation does not tell the whole impact story. As one commentator noted, even if one sees full compliance as low on these cases, there may have been 'low compliance but high impact' from cases such as *Plan de Sánchez*.[114] Through the on-going process of implementation, there are platforms for engagement and for victims and representatives to have a voice and contribute to discussion on how the impact of this important judgment can be maximised and given real effect.

While the judgment and implementation are crucial, this case study suggests that the impact of these processes can be understood long before the judgment, reflecting the power of the process itself, from its inception: when *conversations* with communities began; when they began organising themselves for the purpose of litigation, with lasting benefits; when they began to *share* and to confront experiences for the first time; when researchers, lawyers, journalists and academics began to draw together *evidence* and share it with the community, and dispel insidious notions of blame.

Conversely, the importance of litigation such as this may lie in its—sometimes almost indiscernible—contribution to the building of a different future in the much longer term. In the Guatemalan context, where longstanding challenges are formidable and new ones emerge constantly, progress is undoubtedly difficult to identify or to sustain. But the inscription on the wall of the chapel constructed on the massacre site in the Plan de Sánchez community to honour the dead speaks to the hope enshrined in these processes:

> Memory, truth, justice and reparations form the fundamental base of the restitution of the social fabric and an authentic reconciliation.

---

[113] See Balasco (n 64) at 7.
[114] Bosdriesz (n 2) at 3.

7

Case Study—Arbitrary Detention, Torture and Extraordinary Rendition: Litigating the 'War on Terror'

I. Introduction

The post-9/11 world of counter-terrorism has been a global breeding ground for human rights violations. The most notorious of these, and those that have given rise to some of the most voluminous litigation, are arbitrary deprivations of liberty—including in Guantánamo Bay and previously in the UK—and torture and rendition, led by the CIA but made possible by a 'global spider's web' of support.

This case study raises the question of the impact and the shortcomings of some of the litigation challenging the lawfulness of detention and seeking reparation for torture and rendition victims, as it has unfolded in national courts (notably in the US and the UK) and on the supranational level. These cases illustrate the particular obstacles and challenges to litigation, and invite reflection on their impact in the face of heightened terrorist threats and national security concerns, crises and conflicts (real or perceived).[1] These are cases in which I have been involved in various capacities, as counsel and/or intervener, alongside a throng of human rights litigators and advocates around the world.

The first cluster of cases relates to arbitrary detention. Perhaps the most famous piece of litigation in the war on terror context was the Guantánamo 'habeas' litigation. Since 2002, detainees have been engaged in the painstaking process of claiming their right to habeas corpus, challenging the 'legal black hole'[2] in which they were held without judicial review of the lawfulness of their detention. It has been a long, multi-staged litigation journey that culminated in a *quintessential* champagne moment. In 2008, in the *Boumidiene* case, the US Supreme Court

---

[1] H Duffy, *War on Terror and the Framework of International Law*, 2nd edn (Cambridge, Cambridge University Press, 2015).

[2] English judge Lord Steyn first coined this phrase; J Steyn, 'Guantánamo Bay: The Legal Black Hole' (2004) 53 *International and Comparative Law Quarterly* 1.

found that all Guantánamo detainees had the constitutional right to challenge the lawfulness of their detention. *Boumidiene* was hailed as a historic victory for the rule of law.[3] It has also been lambasted as a 'pyrrhic victory'.[4] The first section below reflects on the nature and impact of this historic cluster of cases. This is followed by brief consideration of the different trajectory, and impact, of litigation in UK courts challenging restrictions on liberty on security grounds.[5]

The second group of cases concerns reparation for victims of the extraordinary rendition programme (ERP), with an emphasis on the case of one of my clients, Zayn al-Abidin Muhammad Husayn Abu Zubaydah (Abu Zubaydah), whom I represent alongside his US counsel in international proceedings. This study briefly explores the response of US courts, where claims by CIA rendition victims have generally been directly thrown out on 'state secrecy' and other grounds. It then highlights how national and international proceedings have had more traction elsewhere. This includes a long line of torture and rendition litigation in UK and Canadian courts. This reveals, among other things, UK government attempts to restrict access to justice on various grounds, including the 'act of state' doctrine, and the unfolding trialogue between the government, courts and legislative arms of the state. Given the on-going nature of some of the wrongs, the case study also flags the role of the courts in compelling states to intervene on the part of persons unlawfully detained as a result of their unlawful cooperation. This litigation exposes the practical and political challenges to enforcement (when the individuals are in foreign custody) and varying ways in which judiciaries respond to their own powerlessness.

The focus turns finally to one of a growing body of *international* cases seeking accountability for cooperation. The case of *Abu Zubaydah v Poland* before the ECtHR, whose 2014 judgment represented the first time that states had been held to account for allowing CIA 'black site' detention on their territories, and the first time that Abu Zubaydah was able to secure any judgment in his favour throughout 12 years of on-going arbitrary detention. This study explores the various impacts, and obvious shortcomings, of this litigation.

This short survey of a much larger body of litigation is far from conclusive but may serve to raise questions relevant for future litigation in an area where violations are flagrant and widespread, and practical, political and legal challenges acute.

---

[3] See fuller discussion in Duffy, *War on Terror and the Framework of International Law* (n 1) Chs 8 and 11.

[4] J Lobell in F Davis and F De Londras (eds), *Critical Debates on Counter-Terrorism Judicial Review* (Cambridge, Cambridge University Press, 2014). A pyrrhic victory is one in which the victor's losses are as great as those of the defeated (so called after Pyrrhus, who defeated the Romans at Asculum in 279 BC but suffered excessive losses). See also F de Londras, Ch 1, *Counter-terrorism judicial review as regulatory constitutionalism* in Davis and De Londras.

[5] This includes national and international judicial interventions in the *A & Others* case. Considering the UK and US experience offers some comparative value—the difference of approach between UK and US has been commented upon in eg DD Cole, 'The Brits Do It Better' *New York Review of Books* (12 June 2008) 68.

II. Litigating Arbitrary Detention

This section provides a brief survey of a few clusters of litigation before various courts, highlighting evolving approaches to the judicial role in overseeing the lawfulness of detention. It points to some of the challenges and certain indicators of impact that emerged at each stage and concludes with a consideration of the overarching observations and questions on the strategic impact of this litigation.

A. Guantánamo Habeas Corpus Litigation in US Courts

The anomaly of Guantánamo Bay—a detention centre set up specifically to detain 'enemy combatants' in the 'war on terror' beyond the protection of the law—requires little introduction.[6] Similarly, the series of cases brought by US lawyers and advocates on behalf of detainees to assert their right to habeas corpus and challenge the lawfulness of their detention is perhaps one of the best-known clusters of human rights litigation ever conducted—certainly in the war on terror context (by way of shorthand, I will refer to these collectively as the 'habeas litigation'). The trajectory of the habeas litigation was far from linear but took the form of a long game of legal ping-pong (with detainees as the ball) between the judicial and political branches, over a period of six years. Detainees' claims were bolstered by massive international support and expert interventions from many quarters. I was among the early interveners in this process, presenting an *amicus* brief to US courts on international standards pertaining to the Guatánamo detainees.[7] By the time this litigation made its way to the Supreme Court, the habeas litigation had become an international cause célèbre.

The Supreme Court's famous *Boumediene* judgment in 2008, often taken as the end-point in that process, was hailed as an historic, landmark, human rights victory. Yet, jubilation was tempered by the fact that it had taken six years to reach a decision on a remedy that is intended to provide relief within hours, days or maybe, in the most exceptional circumstances, weeks. Moreover, despite the victory of principle, and the fact that the habeas proceedings exposed the lack of a legal basis for detention, the system has meanwhile ground to a halt. Courts have found that while they have power to review the lawfulness of detention, they have no power to order release. Moreover, standards of review have been altered to the point where, as a dissenting US judge noted, each time a detainee has proved his case the 'goalposts have moved', and that 'it is hard to see what

---

[6] See Duffy (n 1) Ch 8.
[7] Intervener in *Al Odah, Khaled et al v USA, et al* (Case 02-5251) on behalf of Interights. See www.gpo.gov/fdsys/granule/USCOURTS-caDC-02-05251/USCOURTS-caDC-02-05251-0.

is left of the Supreme Court's command in Boumidiene that habeas review be meaningful'.[8]

Was this litigation then an historic victory or rather an epic failure? What form does 'success' take in cases such as these, and at what cost? This section sketches out the development of the habeas cases in US courts in the lead up to and including *Boumediene*, and then considers their impact at multiple stages.

i. The Multi-staged Guantánamo Litigation

a. First Round of Litigation

The first round of habeas litigation took place in 2004, when a series of cases made its way through US courts. In *Hamdi v Rumsfeld*,[9] the Supreme Court held that US nationals had certain constitutional rights, including having 'a meaningful opportunity to contest the factual basis for their detention, before a neutral decision-maker'. Justice Sandra Day O'Connor famously cautioned, on behalf of the Court, that: '[w]e have long since made clear that a state of war is not a blank check for the President when it comes to the rights of the Nation's citizens'.[10] This 2004 case was seen to represent an important marker of executive accountability, albeit in the limited number of cases in which the detainees happened to be US nationals.

When it came to the habeas corpus right of the vast majority of detainees, non-nationals detained outside the US, however, the Supreme Court in *Rasul & Ors v. Bush*[11] took a distinct and far more cautious approach. It refrained from framing the issue as one of constitutional rights and indeed, even from recognising international law, despite copious *amicus curiae* briefs on the point. Rather, the Court reached its decision based on a statute conferring jurisdiction on courts, finding that there was nothing in legislation that precluded the courts from exercising habeas review.

The government's response to these judgments is a reminder of how litigation can act as a catalyst to executive and legislative action, for better or worse. By the time judgment was handed down, one US national had already been released and the other was transferred to the regular court system.[12] For the hundreds of non-nationals detained at Guantánamo, the response was quite different. First, the executive introduced the Combatant Status Review Tribunals and Administrative Review Boards in an apparent attempt to provide an alternative that would enable

---

[8] J David Tatel, dissenting in *Latif v Obama*, 132 S. Ct. 2741 (2012), denying cert. to 666 F.3d 746, decided 20 June 2012.

[9] *Yaser Esam Hamdi and Esam Fouad Hamdi as next friend of Yaser Esam Hamdi, Petitioners v Donald H Rumsfeld, Secretary of Defense, et al* 542 U.S. 507 (2004), 536 decided 28 June 2004 (*Hamdi v Rumsfeld*).

[10] *Hamdi v Rumsfeld* (n 9).

[11] *Shafiq Rasul, et al, Petitioners v George W Bush, President of the United States, et al; Fawzi Khalid Abdullah Fahad al Odah, et al, Petitioners v United States, et al* 542 U.S. 466, decided 28 June 2004.

[12] See notes on *Padilla* and *Hamdi*, in Duffy (n 1) Ch 8.

the right of habeas corpus to be side-stepped—despite these being non-judicial mechanisms that lacked basic procedural rights associated with habeas corpus. This provided cover for congressional follow-up in the form of the Detainee Treatment Act 2005 (DTA): in addition to some positive provisions on the treatment of detainees, the DTA made explicit that there was *no* right of habeas corpus for Guantánamo detainees.

b. Second Round of Litigation

This led to a second round at the Supreme Court in the case of *Hamdan v Rumsfeld*.[13] The US government claimed that the DTA had stripped *Hamdan* of his right to habeas corpus. In its June 2006 judgment, the Court again refrained from addressing the question of whether there was a constitutional right to habeas corpus that rendered the DTA's provisions unconstitutional. It found instead that the Act did not apply to Hamdan anyway, as his case was on-going at the time the DTA was adopted.

Having determined that it had jurisdiction, the Court went on to find that basic due process guarantees contained in Common Article 3 of the Geneva Conventions, incorporated into US law by the Uniform Code of Military Justice (UCMJ)[14] statute, applied to all detainees. The decision that the military commissions were unlawful because they violated these basic provisions was an important and positive decision in terms of rights protection. It is noteworthy, however, that the issue of arbitrary detention in *Hamdan* is not framed in terms of 'individual rights' but as a separation of powers issue, addressing whether the President had acted in a way that exceeded congressional limits.

Nonetheless, there had been a finding by the Supreme Court that the executive's conduct violated international and domestic law. The US government again faced the quandary of how to respond to this judicial reproach. With the 2006 Military Commission Act, Congress responded in two ways. First, it determined that the relevant international law—the Geneva Conventions—could no longer be relied upon as a source of rights in habeas corpus or other civil proceedings against US personnel. This response did not deal with the problem by bringing policy into line with law as litigators might have hoped. Rather, the law was identified as the problem and international sources of law that could be relied upon in court removed. Secondly, it provided that courts would not have jurisdiction to hear habeas corpus applications (or any other action) by any person determined to be an enemy combatant or awaiting such determination, thus extending the jurisdiction-stripping provisions of the DTA beyond Guantánamo to detentions anywhere.[15]

---

[13] *Salim Ahmed Hamdan, Petitioner v Donald H Rumsfeld & Others*, 548 U.S. 557 (2006).

[14] Uniform Code of Military Justice, UCMJ, 64 Stat 109, 10 U.S.C. Ch 47.

[15] S 7(1) MCA: '(e)(1) No court, justice, or judge shall have jurisdiction to hear or consider an application for a writ of habeas corpus filed by or on behalf of an alien detained by the United States who has been determined by the United States to have been properly detained as an enemy combatant

c. Third Round of Litigation

Notwithstanding the accumulation of several Supreme Court judgments on related matters, the basic question—whether constitutional due process and habeas corpus protections apply to non-nationals detained outside US territory— remained unanswered until June 2008.[16] In *Boumediene v Bush*[17] there seemed to be no further possibility of constitutional avoidance and the question was finally answered in the affirmative: the US Supreme Court ruled that 'enemy combatants' held by the US at Guantánamo Bay do have the right, under the US Constitution, to challenge their detention before regular courts. The Court also ruled that the procedures for review of detainees' status under the 2005 DTA were not an adequate and effective substitute for habeas corpus. It therefore declared unconstitutional Section 7 of the 2006 Military Commissions Act, which denied habeas corpus to any detained foreign 'enemy combatant'.

The recognition that all detainees are entitled to this basic right, irrespective of their nationality, designation as 'enemy combatants', and offshore location, was hailed as a victory for the rule of law. The judgment itself was a close 5:4 decision, with some strident dissents that graphically demonstrate the extent of the antipathy of certain judges towards the exercise of judicial powers in relation to what they saw as issues of security for executive determination.[18] In addition, as noted above, the simple fact that it took a whole six years to decide that detainees are entitled to a protection that should guarantee judicial access within hours, days, or maybe weeks, tempered the sense that this litigation was a complete success. Perhaps even more striking though, was what happened next, as regards the implementation of the right to habeas that had been recognised by the apex court.

d. Implementation, or Aftermath?

In the first few years of habeas review for Guantánamo detainees, a clear majority of cases saw the lawfulness of detention successfully challenged.[19] This had ancillary positive impacts as it exposed the lack of justification for detentions by

---

or is awaiting such determination'. Sub-section (2) stipulates that the courts cannot 'hear or consider any other action against the United States or its agents relating to any aspect of the detention, transfer, treatment, trial, or conditions of confinement' of an enemy combatant covered by the Order.

[16] Little clarity was provided by the lower courts. In 2 cases—*Al Odah* and *Boumediene*—the district courts reached different outcomes, and on 20 February 2007, the DC Circuit Court of Appeals ruled 2-1 that the Guantánamo detainees have no constitutional right to habeas corpus review of their detentions in federal court.

[17] *Lakhdar Boumediene, et al, Petitioners v George W Bush, President of the United States, et al* 553 U.S.

[18] Notably Justice Scalia's assertion of the 'disastrous consequences' of the majority judgment, which he claimed, 'will almost certainly cause more Americans to be killed'. Dissenting judgment of Scalia J, p 2.

[19] A 'scorecard' maintained by the Centre for Constitutional Rights as of September 2011, indicated approximately 75% of success at that time. However, see shift in 2010 noted in Seton Hall, 'No Hearing Habeas: D.C. Circuit Restricts Meaningful Review' (1 May 2012).

the executive and affirmed the importance of judicial review. This trend came to be reversed, however, when superior courts began to criticise the lower courts undertaking the habeas reviews for their willingness to question the government's assessments.[20] In 2010, the Appeals Court in the case of *al Adahi v Obama* effectively changed the test for evaluating evidence in these cases: it suggested that 'some evidence to support the order', was all that was required—rather than 'a preponderance of evidence'—the test more often applied, and in fact not challenged by either party in this case.[21] Decisions since then have not grappled with or tested the facts, in deference to government assessments, and the right to appeal to the Supreme Court has been refused.[22] Alongside pre-existing procedural concerns,[23] this has led many to question whether this litigation now provides any 'meaningful' review at all.[24]

A second crucial factor that seriously impeded the impact of habeas litigation was the decision of the US courts that, while detainees had the right to challenge their detention, the courts had no power to order their release into the United States.[25] This conclusion raised the fundamental question whether there was any point in having habeas litigation, if it was a right that could secure no remedy. Where successful litigants remained detained, what do such decisions do to the authority of courts?

ii. Reflection on the Impact of the Habeas Litigation

The *Boumediene* victory was an important juncture in a long and fraught litigation journey. Yet, as we have seen, assessing its impact exclusively by reference to the

---

[20] Some suggest the turning point was a decision of 2010 in which the Court of Appeals of the DC Circuit criticised in strident terms the lower court's evaluation of the appeals from the United States District Court for the District of Columbia (NO. 1: 05-CV-00280-GK); Seton Hall, 'No Hearing Habeas' Report (n 19) attributes the refusal to grant habeas in all but 1 case thereafter to this decision. See MP Denbeaux: 'Since Al-Adahi, judges are effectively robo-signing denials and rubber-stamping government allegations. The Supreme Court gaveth and the Appeals Court taketh away' available at http://law.shu.edu/about/news_events/releases.cfm?id=289524.

[21] *Mohamad al Adahi v Obama*, Case No 09-533 (Court of Appeals, DC Circuit) 3, 13 July 2010. Although a 'preponderance of evidence' test was contested by neither of the parties, *propio motu* (and *obiter*) the Court advanced (at p 5) that: 'For years, in habeas proceedings contesting orders of deportation, the government had to produce only some evidence to support the order'.

[22] Seton Hall (n 19).

[23] eg it has been described as 'almost impossible' for detainees to question intelligence use by the government. See also 'Goodbye to Gitmo', http://opinionator.blogs.nytimes.com/tag/habeas-corpus/.

[24] See eg Seton Hall (n 19). Judge David S Tatel's dissent (2:1) in the Appeals Court hearing of *Latif v Obama* Case No 10–5319 (Court of Appeals, DC Circuit), 14 October 2011 (n 8).

[25] *Kiyemba v Obama* 559 U.S. 131 (2010) https://ccrjustice.org/home/what-we-do/our-cases/kiyemba-v-obama. 22 Uighurs, Chinese nationals, were detained in the course of the Afghan conflict and sent to Guantánamo. The military knew as of 2003 that many were not affiliated with al Qaeda. They could not be repatriated given the threats to their lives in China. In 2008, a district court ordered them to be released into the US but an Appeals Court again overturned in 2009. The last of them were released in 2014.

judgment itself, would provide only partial insight into the effects, positive and negative, of this litigation before and after. The promise of habeas review contained in *Boumidiene* ultimately provided little meaningful opportunity to challenge the lawfulness of detention, at least post 2010, and resulted in short-lived, moral victories in court that could not procure the remedy of their release.

In an almost absurd twist, one powerfully negative impact of this litigation was the transferal of individuals, among whom was our client Abu Zubaydah,[26] out of Guantánamo to other jurisdictions, in *anticipation* of the *Boumediene* decision.[27] Sustaining the policy of 'exporting' detainees, was the limited geographic scope of the principle established in the *Boumidiene* judgment: it applied only to Guantánamo detainees, not to detainees wherever held.[28] This meant that even after the historic victory of principle that the *Boumidiene* case represented, judges described detainees held elsewhere, in the infamous Baghram airbase in Afghanistan for example, as being held in a 'black hole', a 'law-free zone'.[29] Moving individuals out of Guantánamo, to avoid the reach of human rights protections strengthened by the litigation, could be seen as an indication of the importance of habeas review. It is in any case a troubling circumvention of the role of courts, made possible by the patchwork approach to the protection of the most basic rights of the human person.

The right to habeas for Guantánamo detainees established in *Boumidiene* was, moreover, too little too late for all those we now know were being tortured and whose most fundamental rights were violated for years, enabled by the absence of judicial review. The impact of the *Boumediene* judgment, or habeas hearings, varied for different detainees, some getting favourable decisions and being released or relocated. Even then though, as in the case of *Boumediene* himself, the positive impact was often diminished by the devastating consequences of the passage of time before the right was recognised—not only for detainees but for others: 'Had I been brought before a court when I was seized, my children's lives would not have been torn apart, and my family would not have been thrown into poverty'.[30]

---

[26] See eg *Abu Zubaydah v Lithuania* Appl no 46454/11, 31 May 2018.

[27] See Duffy (n 1) Ch 8 Guantánamo, and Ch 10 Extraordinary Rendition.

[28] *Al Maqaleh et al v Gates, Secretary, United States Department of Defense*, 605 F.3d 84 (D.C. Cir. 2010). Argued 7 Jan 2010—Decided 21 May 2010. In a 15 February 2011 decision Judge Bates issued a ruling in favour of Mr al-Maqaleh, allowing him to file his Amended Petition and to present additional facts and arguments regarding the Court's jurisdiction. See Duffy (n 1) 'War and Human Rights' in 'War on Terror' (2015) Ch 7.

[29] Justice Bates reviewing the lawfulness of the men's cases in January 2009. See Editorial, 'Backward at Bagram' *New York Times* (1 June 2010) at A26. This description resonates with that of Guantánamo. Likewise, on the same day that the US Supreme Court handed down its judgment in *Boumediene*, it also handed down *Munaf v Geren*, in which it acknowledged that persons detained in Iraq also had the right to habeas corpus, but found that the US courts could not administer it as that fell to Iraqi courts; *Munaf et al v Geren* 553 US 674.

[30] Letter to *New York Times* (7 January 2012) www.nytimes.com/2012/01/08/opinion/sunday/my-guantanamo-nightmare.html.

The impact on the individual certainly goes beyond the question of release.[31] For Boumediene, there is value in the principles underpinning the case that bore his name. But his satisfaction has been overshadowed by the continuing nature of the violations and denial of justice for others:

> I'm told that my Supreme Court case is now read in law schools. Perhaps one day that will give me satisfaction, but so long as Guantánamo stays open and innocent men remain there, my thoughts will be with those left behind in that place of suffering and injustice.[32]

As of today, with the habeas system effectively ground to a halt, detainees such as Abu Zubaydah have still had no habeas review, 15 years after his arbitrary detention began.

On one view, then, as Jules Lobel has stated, it was a pyrrhic victory, that risks legitimising a profoundly unjust system by creating an illusion of judicial review that does not exist. While many *were* released, he attributes this to *other* action, such as hunger strikes and the associated mobilisation. That notwithstanding, we should consider several other important ramifications of this litigation before swinging from hailing the historic victory to decrying the complete failure.

Most obvious, perhaps, is the expressive value of the judgment, in shattering the underlying assumption that anyone can be held in legal limbo. The reassertion of the principle, while not enough, is important, particularly given the extent to which states around the world relied on the Guantánamo model to justify or divert attention from their own violations. The reassertion of the basic right of habeas corpus, that no one is above the law, and no-one below it—even in the face of terrorism—resonated around the world.

Less obvious, yet perhaps the key contribution of the Guantánamo habeas litigation, was that the US was forced to provide detainees with access to lawyers—in order to *prepare* for the litigation. In so doing, the rest of the world was effectively given access to information about the detainees, who these people—described generically as 'the worst of the worst'—*really* were, and the terrible torture many had endured. And things began to change, not enough, to be sure, but significantly nevertheless. Many cases of mistaken identities and entirely empty files emerged. Allegations against our client, that he was the 'no. 3 Al Qaeda' or even a member of Al Qaeda at all, were dropped. Thus, the mere spectre of judicial review, and the indirect oversight that lawyers could provide, appear to have had a catalytic impact, forcing re-evaluation of some individual cases and compelling some slight measure of accountability, even before the litigation got underway.

Guantánamo litigation contributed to political debate nationally and internationally as Guantánamo came increasingly widely and vociferously to be rejected

---

[31] See eg Bakker Qassim letter to Obama in 2009 after his release and relocation to Albania in 2006 following military review: www.andyworthington.co.uk/2009/03/27/a-letter-to-barack-obama-from-a-guantanamo-uighur/.

[32] Letter to *New York Times* (n 30).

as a 'monstrous failure … [and] affront to the rule of law'—and thus it is destined to be remembered.[33] A shift in international opinion and the growing isolation of the American position, were accompanied by increasing internal opposition in the US.[34] Many factors contributed to this attitudinal shift, but the judgments from the Supreme Court provided formal indicators of the denial of justice. The massive enterprise of Guantánamo litigation itself also allowed a broader range of voices to be heard, including from unusual quarters such as through interventions from the UK House of Lords and military lawyers.[35] The courts' own authoritative voice was heard, and provided tools for advocacy and political action.

The courts clearly could not 'solve' the underlying political problem that allows violations at Guantánamo to continue to exist nearly a decade after *Boumidiene*. Rarely did they provide judicial solutions for particular individuals who could access habeas. At the end of the day, the site remains open and detainees such as Abu Zubaydah are still held in arbitrary detention. However, if the habeas litigation did not provide solutions, it did change the context in which the struggle for solutions continues.

While Guantánamo Bay remains open and its future uncertain, it is difficult to be enthusiastic about the extent to which litigation contributed to change in policy and practice. But there have been many shifts in policy, and in detention standards and practices at the site, not to mention the sharp reduction in numbers of detainees, to which the litigation may have contributed, directly and indirectly, in various ways. Perhaps most critically, for the detainees it triggered access to lawyers, and through them, to the world. It exposed facts, myths and spurious justifications, and helped maintain international attention despite 'Guantánamo fatigue'. It influenced the terms and the tenor of the conversation. It provided a lightning rod for international attention, intense media engagement, and statements by other states or international institutions following judgment, helping to counter Guantánamo fatigue and bolster opposition.[36] Alongside other forms of action, it helped to increase the pressure on foreign governments to intervene, on international organisations to condemn and on the US to reduce detainees (which are down from 779 to 41).

On the spectrum between success and failure, it is not easy to locate this litigation. But one might tentatively conclude that the greatest impact of litigation on behalf of Guantánamo detainees lay not so much in that champagne moment of 2008, but in the disguised contributions it has made along the way. Its ultimate

---

[33] Statement by Lord Steyn; see Duffy (n 1) Ch 8 for the steady if somewhat slow rejection and isolation of the US on Guantánamo.

[34] As regards public opinion, on one view hunger strikes by prisoners did more to attract attention, ignite action and change policy than judicial determinations; Lobell in Davis and de Londras, *Critical Debates on Counter-Terrorism Judicial Review* (n 4).

[35] See Duffy (n 1) Ch 8. For the text of the Israeli experts, see https://ccrjustice.org/sites/default/files/assets/files/Brief%20of%20Amici%20Curiae%20Specialists%20in%20Israeli%20Military%20Law%20and%20Constitutional%20Law%20in%20Support%20of%20Petitioners.pdf.

[36] On how this opposition unfolded over time, see Duffy (n 1) Ch 8.

contribution to the on-going challenge of ensuring cessation and non-repetition of this 'dark chapter in American history', remains to be seen.[37]

B. [Not] the UK's Guantánamo: Litigating Unlawful Deprivation of Liberty in UK Courts

While the Guantánamo habeas litigation was in its infancy, parallel cases were making their way through the English courts, resulting in the famous *A & Others* case before the House of Lords (The '*Belmarsh* judgment'),[38] and on to the European Court of Human Rights (ECtHR) in 2004.[39] This section reflects briefly on this related but different story of litigation and its impact.

The cases concerned the policy of detaining non-UK nationals based on their suspected involvement in international terrorism. The detainees were persons who could not be deported for legal reasons, pursuant to the 2001 Anti-Terrorism, Crime and Security Act.[40] In order to allow their detention, the UK had derogated from its obligations in respect of the right to liberty under Article 5 of the European Convention on Human Rights (ECHR). The case raised different issues from those before US courts as the right of habeas corpus was not, as such, in dispute in the UK, where regular independent review was provided by the Special Immigration Appeals Commission ('SIAC')—a court of law—albeit on the basis of controversial rules and procedures.[41] The case, which made its way up to the House of Lords (then the highest court of appeal in the UK), concerned the lawfulness of this derogation from the ECHR, and the detention of non-nationals on security grounds.

The majority deferred to the government's assessment of the existence of an 'emergency' justifying derogation but found that the detention of non-nationals could not be justified as *strictly required* by that emergency. The judgment notes: 'If derogation is not *strictly required* in the case of one group [nationals], it cannot

---

[37] See the 11 January 2017 letter from members of Congress to President Obama calling on him to close Guantánamo before President-elect Trump assumed office.

[38] Based on their detention in Belmarsh Prison.

[39] *A and others v Secretary of State for the Home Department, X and another v Secretary of State for the Home Department* [2004] UKHL 56 (*A & Ors (Derogation)*).

[40] Removal was not possible on human rights grounds—given the real risk of ill-treatment in their states of origin. See ss 21 to 32 of the UK's Anti-terrorism, Crime and Security Act 2001 which:

> allow[s] the detention of those the Secretary of State has certified as threats to national security and who are suspected of being international terrorists where their removal is not possible at the present time. These provisions change the current law, which allows detention with a view to removal only where removal is a realistic option within a reasonable period of time.

[41] Controversial rules related to, eg, access to counsel and to evidence. See eg UK's Parliamentary Constitutional Affairs Committee, *The operation of the Special Immigration Appeals Commission (SIAC) and the use of Special Advocates* (HC 2004–05, 323-II) See also eg 'Ian Macdonald QC resigns from SIAC' (1 November 2004) available at www.gardencourtchambers.co.uk/news/news_detail.cfm?iNewsID=268.

be strictly required in the case of the other group [non-nationals] that presents the same threat'.[42] The Court therefore found a violation of the rights to liberty and to non-discrimination, provided for under Articles 5 and 14 of the ECHR (and codified in the UK Human Rights Act of 1998).

The positive impact of this case was multi-dimensional. The first level relates to the clear judicial assertion of principle as to the need for a strict approach to the protection of the right to liberty and careful but challenging judicial oversight. Still on the normative level, the case did what much of the debate and indeed litigation elsewhere—including the US litigation referred to earlier—had neglected to do: it signalled the centrality of the issue of equality. This is particularly significant in a context of frequent reliance on divisions and distinctions based on nationality as well as other grounds as a basis for inferior treatment, which, as the House of Lords made clear, has no basis in law.[43]

Judicial consternation, manifest in unusually pointed rhetorical flourishes such as Lord Hoffmann's famous rebuke that 'the real threat to the nation comes not from terrorism but from laws such as these', fed debate on the proper limits of counter-terrorism.[44] The case is also more broadly constitutionally significant in its assessment of the proper judicial role and the limits of due judicial deference. In a powerful passage Lord Bingham famously rejects the Attorney General's submissions in this respect, noting:

> I do not in particular accept the distinction ... between democratic institutions and the courts ... [T]he function of independent judges ... [is] a cardinal feature of the modern democratic state, a cornerstone of the rule of law itself. The Attorney General is fully entitled to insist on the proper limits of judicial authority, but he is wrong to stigmatise judicial decision-making as in some way undemocratic.

---

[42] *A & Ors (Derogation)* (n 39) Lord Bingham, at [132]:

> I would hold that the indefinite detention of foreign nationals without trial has not been shown to be strictly required, as the same threat from British nationals whom the government is unable or unwilling to prosecute is being met by other measures which do not require them to be detained indefinitely without trial. The distinction which the government seeks to draw between these two groups—British nationals and foreign nationals—raises an issue of discrimination. But, as the distinction is irrational, it goes to the heart of the issue about proportionality also. It proceeds on the misconception that it is a sufficient answer to the question whether the derogation is strictly required that the two groups have different rights in the immigration context. So they do. But the derogation is from the right to liberty. The right to liberty is the same for each group. If derogation is not strictly required in the case of one group, it cannot be strictly required in the case of the other group that presents the same threat.

[43] The onus is on the state to demonstrate that discrimination on the ground of nationality is justified, which it was unable to do in this case, resulting in a finding that it had also violated the right to equality. On nationality-based distinctions, see eg UN Human Rights Committee General Comment No 15: The position of aliens under the Covenant [1986] in UN Doc HRI/GEN/1/Rev.6 (2003), at 140; Inter-American Commission on Human Rights, *Precautionary Measures in Guantánamo Bay*.

[44] *A & Ors (Derogation)* (n 39) Lord Hoffmann, at [96] and [97].

The case has been lauded as 'a powerful statement by the highest court in the land of what it means to live in a society where the executive is subject to the rule of law'.[45] It has been held up as a rare case in which a court effectively overruled the government's assessment of security threats and the necessary measures to be taken,[46] and as one of the 'finest assertions of civil liberties by a UK court [since 1765]'.[47]

As is often the case, however, there is another side to the impact story. Though the Lords issued a certificate of incompatibility, the offending legislation was not struck down and the detainees' situation did not immediately change. With nine of them still in detention, the case proceeded to Strasbourg, and the Grand Chamber of the ECtHR handed down a unanimous decision that was significant for its assessment of issues relating to derogation and the right to liberty and equality, and also for its own role in assessing politically sensitive issues in the national security context.[48] On the lawfulness of that derogation, the ECtHR showed extreme deference in this case to the national authorities' determination of the existence of an emergency. It noted:

> it was for each Government, as the guardian of their own people's safety, to make their own assessment on the basis of the facts known to them. Weight must, therefore, attach to the judgment of the United Kingdom's executive and Parliament on this question. In addition, significant weight must be accorded to the views of the national courts, who were better placed to assess the evidence relating to the existence of an emergency.[49]

It is perhaps open to debate, in an age of exceptionalism and overreaching claims of emergency and conflict, whether such deference is appropriate. The Court did, however, engage in close scrutiny of the permissible grounds of detention. It considered each case in detail on its facts, to assess the true reason for the detention. It found (in all but one case) that the detainees were not persons 'against whom action [was] being taken with a view to deportation or extradition,'[50]—as the government had argued, in line with one of the criteria in the Convention—since

---

[45] Speech by Arden LJ (Clifford Chance Lecture, 27 January 2005) in M du Plessis 'Terrorism and National Security: The Role of the Judiciary in a Democratic Society European' (2007) 4 *Human Rights Law Review* 327.

[46] A Tomkins, 'Readings of A v. Secretary of State for the Home Department' (2005) *Public Law* 259, 259.

[47] C Gearty, 'Human Rights in an Age of Counter-Terrorism: Injurious, Irrelevant or Indispensable?' (2005) 58(1) *Current Legal Problems* 25–46, who describes it as 'the finest assertion of civil liberties that has emerged from a British court since at least *Entick v Carrington*' (see *Entick v Carrington* [1765] EWHC KB J98).

[48] *A and others v United Kingdom* Appl. no 3455/05 (2009) (ECtHR). 11 of the 'certified' individuals applied to the ECtHR as, despite their victory at the national level and the House of Lords issuing a 'declaration of incompatibility', the offending legislation had not been struck down and their situation had not changed; 9 were still in detention whilst the other 2 had chosen voluntarily to leave the UK rather than remain in detention and they had been denied the right to claim compensation in the UK. See S Shah, 'From Westminster to Strasbourg: A and others v United Kingdom' (2009) 9(3) *Human Rights Law Review* 473–88.

[49] *A and Others v United Kingdom* (n 48), para 180.

[50] Ibid, para 170.

their deportation was impossible. Instead they were detained because of the perceived *threat* that the individuals represented. While acknowledging that 'national authorities enjoy a wide margin of appreciation under Article 15 in assessing whether the life of their nation is threatened by a public emergency',[51] the Court was rigorous in its approach to the necessity of the *particular* measures taken in response. It ultimately agreed with the House of Lords' assessment that, as the measures were limited to non-nationals, they could not be necessary, and were discriminatory.[52] It rejected the government's claims of judicial overreach: 'as the House of Lords held, the question of proportionality is ultimately a judicial decision, particularly in a case such as the present where the applicants were deprived of their fundamental right to liberty over a long period of time'.[53]

Its decision on the right to challenge the lawfulness of detention in the context of proceedings marked by controversial procedures, such as the use of special advocates and reliance on secret evidence, was also significant. While acknowledging that 'there may be restrictions on the right to a fully adversarial procedure', the critical test was whether, in all the circumstances, there was in fact an opportunity to mount a meaningful challenge to detention.[54] The Court concluded that detention could be justified in five cases but not in another four.[55]

Whether or not one agrees with the Court's conclusions as to the SIAC proceedings' compliance with Convention standards, there is no doubt about this case's normative contribution. The ECtHR's approach balanced its deference to national assessments of security imperatives, and to national courts' responsibility for weighing up proportionality in particular cases, with a cautious but fairly robust approach to its own oversight role. The impact on international standards and judicial approaches is borne out by the abundant citation of this case in other jurisprudence and academic commentary.

Perhaps most critical to any impact assessment of the *Belmarsh* litigation was the executive's response. In the course of the litigation, the UK government changed its law and practice. The derogation and offending legislation were withdrawn, and new legislation reflecting new policies, was adopted. This provided inter alia, for 'control orders' rather than imprisonment for persons suspected of involvement in international terrorism.[56]

---

[51] Ibid, para 180.

[52] Ibid, para 190.

[53] Ibid, para 184: 'In any event, having regard to the careful way in which the House of Lords approached the issues, it cannot be said that inadequate weight was given to the views of the executive or of Parliament'; see para 220 on permissible restrictions to a fully adversarial procedure, and the need to 'counterbalance'.

[54] Ibid, para 205. Among the prerequisites was that the applicant have 'sufficient information' to be able to defend himself and to give instructions to the special advocates.

[55] Ibid, 212–24.

[56] Control orders were preventative measures, intended to protect members of the public from the risk of terrorism by imposing restraints on those suspected of involvement in terrorism-related activity. They were replaced with Terrorism Prevention and Investigation Measures (TPIMs). See *Final Report of the Independent Reviewer of Terrorism Measures* (2012) and C Walker and A Horne, 'Lessons

Subsequent cases challenged, in turn, those control orders, clarifying that control sometimes amounted to 'deprivation of liberty' in fact,[57] and revealing the impact of such orders on real people's lives. These cases demonstrated the need for—and indeed the willingness of—the courts to engage once again, on a case-by-case basis, with the difficult issue of striking an acceptable balance between individual rights and public safety. In many cases, judicial review of control orders led to withdrawal or amendment of an order.[58] Ultimately, the careful and thorough review of control orders may have contributed to their relatively limited use in practice, to incremental modifications in the system, and ultimately to the replacement of control orders with other temporary 'prevention and investigation measures'.[59]

While UK policy has rightly been subject to much criticism, what is clear is that there has been a dynamic dialogue between the judiciary and the executive that has gradually contributed, in a predominantly positive way, to limiting the human rights violations in relation to deprivations of liberty. Policy remains problematic but it has certainly been responsive to, and in significant measure shaped by, the decisions of the courts in this area. While national courts have played a decisive role, the existence of the ECtHR has plainly bolstered the role of domestic courts and encouraged a dynamic response by the executive branch in the UK. It also impelled strident reaction against the Convention and the Strasbourg Court by the British press, some politicians and sectors of the public, with as yet uncertain long-term consequences.[60]

III. Litigating Rendition and Torture

Torture and secret detention in the CIA's extraordinary rendition programme (ERP) shows the depths to which states have stooped in the name of security

---

Learned from Political Constitutionalism? Comparing the Enactment of Control Orders and Terrorism Prevention and Investigation Measures by the UK Parliament' (2014) *Public Law* 267.

[57] eg an early case on point was *Secretary of State for the Home Department (Appellant) v JJ and others (FC) (Respondents)* [2007] UKHL 45, decided 31 October 2007, on limits and degree of control over aspects of daily life as amounting to unlawful 'detention'. On control order litigation in Australian courts, see *Thomas v Mowbray* [2007] HCA 33 (High Court of Australia, 2 August 2007). See also C Walker, 'The Reshaping of Control Orders in the United Kingdom: Time for a Fairer Go, Australia!' (2013) 37 *Melbourne University Law Review* 143.

[58] See the UK's Independent Reviewer report 'Control Orders in 2011' noting that review 'though not always prompt, was thorough and careful'. https://terrorismlegislationreviewer.independent.gov. uk/wp-content/uploads/2013/04/control-orders-2011.pdf.

[59] PTA 2005 was repealed and replaced by the Terrorism Prevention and Investigation Measures Act 2011. Report of Independent Expert (n 58), who notes similarities and differences, which were motivated by 'civil liberties concerns'. In addition, comparable restrictions to those imposed by control orders can still be imposed by the executive under asset freezing and immigration/nationality powers.

[60] The impact on the inability to expel non-nationals has been the source of much controversy; see eg debate around the case of Abu Qatada in the UK.

post 9/11, and the dark side of willing international cooperation.[61] The removal of 'high value detainees' from the protection of the law, to enable systematic torture, has led to the ERP being referred to as an international criminal conspiracy of enforced disappearance of persons.[62] A mass of evidence, gathered by journalists, NGOs, a variety of truth-finding processes, and litigation processes has revealed the responsibility of many states, non-state actors and individuals. Despite this, secrecy, denial and impunity remain prevalent, reparation, including acknowledgement and apology almost non-existent,[63] and the struggle for accountability and/or real commitment to learning lessons and ensuring non-repetition, has been uphill.[64] Political reluctance, and pressure, has rendered litigation all the more challenging and all the more important. Victims have turned to litigation in domestic courts and, where those options failed, to supranational fora.

One of those victims, Abu Zubaydah, has been variously described as the 'guinea pig' for the CIA's 'enhanced interrogation techniques', 'the first high value detainee' to be taken into the programme and subjected to all of the CIAs torture techniques, and the 'A-Z of where we went wrong'.[65] Documentary evidence shows clearly his systematic torture and rendition across secret 'black sites' around the globe, and the commitments given to those engaged in his torture that the world would never know, justice would never arrive and he would be held "incommunicado for the remainder of his life".[66] True to assurances given before he was tortured, he remains arbitrarily detained in Guantánamo today, 16 years after his capture, without charge or trial. In this bleak context, the following section reflects on the relevance of litigation on behalf of Zubaydah and others like him, nationally and internationally.

A.   Damages Litigation in Domestic Courts in the US and UK

As is well known, a broad approach to the doctrine of 'state secrecy' has led to numerous damages claims brought by rendition victims against the state being thrown out in US courts.[67] In US law a privilege applies to state secrets when the

---

[61] For more detail on the programme, responsibility and international law, see Duffy (n 1) Ch 10.

[62] Ibid, Ch 10, referring to UN reports and others.

[63] Apologies remain rare: one was forthcoming following the Canadian *Maher Arar* inquiry. The *Khadr* settlement of July 2017 by the Canadian government included an apology. Otherwise, while payments have been made they have generally been *ex gratia* and on the condition of not pursuing litigation'; see eg *Habib v Omar Suleiman* (April 2011); 'Ex-Gitmo Australian sues Former Egyptian officials' *Egypt Independent* (15 June 2011) www.egyptindependent.com/news/ex-gitmo-australian-sues-former-egyptian-officials.

[64] Duffy in Davis and De Londras (n 4).

[65] Former FBI agent Ali Soufan described the case of Abu Zubaydah as 'the A to Z of where we went wrong as a nation'; see www.miamiherald.com/news/nation-world/world/americas/guantanamo/article81232607.html; Duffy (n 1) for more details.

[66] Cables sent between the first black site where he was tortured and CIA headquarters show that assurances were sought, and granted, to the effect that he "would remain incommunicado for the remainder of his life". The US Senate Intelligence report summary, 9 December 2014 makes this clear; see H Duffy, CIA Torture report, Opinion, *The Guardian* (14 December 2014).

[67] See also eg immunities. See Duffy in Davis and De Londras (n 4) for a fuller discussion on challenges and obstacles.

court is satisfied there is a 'reasonable danger that compulsion of the evidence will expose military matters which, in the interests of national security, should not be divulged'.[68] In successive claims before US courts, for damages in respect of torture and rendition, the government has argued that the 'entire aim of the case is to establish state secrets', and the Courts have dismissed most claims in their entirety on this basis.[69] The Supreme Court has refused, without giving reasons, to review this issue.[70]

Litigation that results in the case being thrown out in this way, completely precluding access to justice, can hardly be seen as successful. It has, however, shone a harsh light on the denial of justice in US courts, and been a lightning rod for criticism of them, including from international bodies that have found the US to be violating the obligation to allow victims to 'follow suit' in respect of their torture and rendition. Despite deep frustration with the limited results of damages litigation, advocates suggest that the US rendition litigation had an indirect impact on multiple levels: it gave visibility to victims and their stories throughout the world, generated public debate about the legality, morality and efficacy of torture, and contributed indirectly to political repudiation of the CIA programme.[71] Litigation to date has provoked debate, and legislative proposals, at least questioning the use (and abuse) of state privilege.[72]

Within the litigation itself, cases that have been thrown out on state secrecy or immunities grounds have also provoked a growing degree of internal judicial disaffection. Over time, slightly more robust judicial positions have emerged, majorities in favour of dismissal have narrowed and stronger dissents have been issued, such as Judge Guido Calabresi's dissent in the case that threw out Maher Arar's claim: 'I believe that when the history of this distinguished court is written,

---

[68] *United States v Reynolds* 345 US 1, 10 (1953).

[69] eg *El-Masri v United States* 305, followed by *Mohamed v Jeppesen Dataplan Inc* 614 F.3d 1070 (9th Cir 2010) (*en banc*). The *El-Masri* case was the first of a number in which the Court ruled that the protection against disclosure was absolute, followed by the case of Binyam Mohamed and four others against a private company Jeppesen Dataplan. Albeit in a narrow decision Canadian Maher Arar's case was dismissed on 'Bivens' grounds—special factors counselled against recognition of a remedy.

[70] eg in the Supreme Court: *El Masri v United States* Case No 06-1613. In the district court: *El Masri v Tenet*, Case 1:05-cv-01417-TSE-TRJ. For details of the petition lodged before the Inter-American Commission on Human Rights, see www.aclu.org/pdfs/safefree/elmasri_iachr_20080409.pdf.

[71] President Obama campaigned on a promise to end the extraordinary rendition program; on his second full day in office he signed an Executive Order (EO) permanently shuttering the CIA's overseas prisons and prohibiting abusive interrogations. Certain provisions of the EO were subsequently enacted as law in the McCain-Feinstein Anti-Torture Amendment Act. See also D Luban, 'Trump and Torture' *Just Security* (21 March 2016).

[72] Although the Obama administration continued the practice of asserting overbroad secrecy claims in an attempt to terminate civil litigation, members of Congress, citing the *El-Masri* case, introduced legislation in both houses to reform the state secrets privilege so that it can no longer be used as a de facto immunity doctrine for the executive branch, and the administration introduced guidelines on invoking state secrets (US Dept of Justice: 23 September 2009. The DoJ under the Trump administration did not seek to block the *Salim* litigation on secrecy grounds, but invoked the guidelines to protect certain information. http://bit.ly/2zssV6I.

today's majority decision will be viewed with dismay'.[73] The majority suggested that the 'separation of powers' doctrine required such deference to the executive, while a strong dissent countered that it is because of the separation of powers that courts must uphold the law and challenge the executive in situations such as this. Significantly, a more recent US case against psychologists Mitchell and Jessen alleged to have designed the torture techniques was allowed to proceed, and eventually settled on the eve of trial.[74]

The trajectory, while far from reassuring, may suggest a softening of approach for at least some defendants over time. For now, the inertia of US courts underscores the importance of using alternative approaches and fora to highlight the plight of rendition and torture victims such as Abu Zubadayah.

B. Litigation Relating to Cooperation with the US in Foreign Courts

A defining feature of the ERP has been a global spider's web involving an estimated 57 states, providing various forms of support for, and engagement in, the programme. Increasingly, foreign courts have been called on to provide relief in respect of the role and responsibility of the many other states for their varying forms of cooperation with the US. These cases have helped to expose facts, catalyse debate and generate pressure. Judicial involvement with these issues in the UK has taken many twists and turns, and it goes beyond this short study to consider the various impacts, both positive and negative, of that growing line of jurisprudence. Nevertheless, a few aspects are worth highlighting.

First, as regards cooperation in respect of torture and rendition specifically, the UK government has sought to block access to the courts on various grounds: it has argued that its cooperation with the US or other states involve 'acts of state', that review of these activities would have problematic implications for foreign relations, and that such matters simply lie beyond the purview of the courts. The courts, for their part, have rejected the idea that cooperation in rendition and torture cases concerns an act of state, and reasserted their role in determining tort claims for violations of basic human rights in this context.[75] A 2017 decision of

---

[73] Judge Guido Calabresi's dissent was 1 of 4. On 2 November 2009, the Second Circuit Court of Appeals *en banc* affirmed the district court's decision dismissing the case on immunity grounds. On 14 June 2010, the Supreme Court denied Mr Arar's petition for *certiorari*. For relevant documents see http://ccrjustice.org/arar. The Appeals Court upheld and the Supreme Court once again refused, despite the constitutional implications for human rights and the judicial function, to consider the case.

[74] *Salim and Others v Mitchell*, trial was set for 5 September 2017; see 'On Eve of Trial, Psychologists Agree to Historic Settlement in ACLU Case on Behalf of Three Torture Victims' (17 August 2017). Related issues arise in pending litigation against military contractors CACI for aiding and abetting the torture and cruel treatment of men held at the infamous Abu Ghraib prison in Iraq.

[75] *Cf Rahmatullah (No 2) v Ministry of Defence and another* [2017] UKSC 1. See Counter-terrorism Judicial Review as Regulatory Constitutionalism in Davis and de Londras, n 4, p 35–55.

the UK Supreme Court found that cooperation by the Secret Intelligence Service, with foreign states, in securing unlawful detention, rendition and torture was not subject to state immunity, and that government and officials sued could not rely on the doctrine of 'foreign act of state' to preclude civil claims on the basis that other states were involved.[76] Moreover, it was suggested by several of the judges that, even if there were any such rule precluding judicial review of such governmental action, a 'public policy exception' arose for claimants allegedly detained, kidnapped and tortured.[77]

Second, on national security grounds, the government has successfully pressed for certain modifications to the basic principles and procedures involved in the determination of torture in detention cases.[78] For example, the introduction of 'closed material proceedings' to hear civil cases involving classified information emerged from lengthy litigation proceedings and dynamics that paralleled in some ways the back-and-forth between judicial and political branches in the US habeas cases. In the case brought by Bisher Al-Rawi and five other former Guantánamo Bay detainees against the UK government, for its role in their overseas torture, the government asked the Court to recognise a common law rule such that all classified information would be heard in a closed material proceeding to which the plaintiffs would not have access[79] other than through a 'special advocate', who from that moment on may no longer have contact with the plaintiff.[80] The divisional court originally upheld the possibility that a court could order a closed material procedure for part (or, conceivably, even the whole) of the trial.[81] However, the Court of Appeal reversed that decision and the Supreme Court affirmed the reversal,[82] ruling that courts could not order a 'closed material procedure', allowing the government to rely on secret material in closed session without statutory authority.

Just as in the habeas litigation, cases can act as legislative catalysts, for better and for worse: in this case it prompted the executive to seek and obtain such

---

[76] Ibid. Courts recognised the rule by which a domestic court will treat as non-justiciable—or will refrain from adjudicating on—certain categories of sovereign act by a foreign state abroad, but the mere fact that the case raised issues concerning foreign states conduct could not be enough.

[77] Lord Neuberger (n 75); see also Lord Mance in *Belhaj and another (Respondents) v Straw and others (Appellants)* [2017] UKSC 3.

[78] Such concerns have been held to justify the refusal to allow the disclosure of information or documents despite the impact on human rights; eg *Binyam Mohamad v Secretary of State for Foreign and Commonwealth Affairs* [2009] EWHC 152.

[79] A 'closed material procedure' is a procedure in which a party is permitted to rely on pleadings and evidence without disclosing such material to other parties if disclosure would be contrary to the public interest. Disclosure is deemed contrary to the public interest 'if it is made contrary to the interests of national security, the international relations of the United Kingdom, the detection and prevention of crime, or in any other circumstances where disclosure is likely to harm the public interest'.

[80] *Al Rawi and Ors v The Security Service & Ors* [2009] EWHC 2959 (QB), [2].

[81] Ibid.

[82] *Al Rawi and Ors v Security Service & Ors* [2010] EWCA Civ 482, [70]; and [2011] UKSC 34. See www.amnesty.org/en/region/uk/report-2012.

statutory authority. The UK Justice and Security Act 2013 incorporates a broad procedure for closed civil proceedings in national security cases, in which only one party has access to the court or to the evidence. Such procedures, and the government's inclination to overuse what should be exceptional procedures, have been widely criticised, including by the Supreme Court.[83] But the fact remains that, in the hearing of sensitive national security cases, justice in civil proceedings has moved behind closed doors.[84] Moreover, similar procedures are now being used, even more troublingly, in the criminal sphere.[85] Long-established principles of open justice are being incrementally eroded, despite apparent judicial victories.

A third group of cases from British—and in one case Canadian—courts raises the important issue of the *on-going* responsibility of cooperating states, following their unlawful cooperation, to seek the protection of detainees. Here too, the states in question have argued that this issue lies beyond the courts, being within the domain of the 'foreign affairs prerogative'. In respect of the notorious detention in Guantánamo of Omar Khadr, who was 15 at the time, Canadian officials shared information with their US counterparts leading to his long-term arbitrary detention. The Canadian Supreme Court was asked to compel the Canadian government to make representations on his behalf.[86] The Court found that, notwithstanding the 'foreign affairs prerogative' argued by the government, the court *could* make such an order. While it was sensitive to the argument that the executive was better placed to make such decisions, it held that 'it is for the courts to determine the legal and constitutional limits within which such decisions are to be taken'.[87] However, taking into account inter alia that such representations on the detainee's behalf would not necessarily succeed, and that the Court was not fully appraised of the nature of the diplomatic exchanges in question, no mandatory relief was granted.[88] Although an important assertion of the role and powers of the court in principle, the Court's refusal to risk non-implementation may be seen as a sign of its weakness, leaving Khadr with 'declaratory relief' only—from this particular round of litigation.

When similar issues arose in the *Rahmatullah* case in UK courts, concerning a Pakistani citizen captured by the UK in Iraq and transferred to US custody

---

[83] *Bank Mellat (Appellant) v HM. Treasury (Respondent) (No 1)* [2013] UKSC 38; see dissent of Lord Hope.

[84] The government introduced a 'Justice and Security Bill' with 'closed material procedures' in the absence of claimants and their lawyers to cases where an individual claims the UK security services were involved in his torture.

[85] Erol Incedal's trial for terrorism ended in 2016 and he was cleared by a jury; the press was substantially excluded from the trial and subject to similar restrictive reporting regimes that had been tested first through the civil courts.

[86] The *Khadr* litigation had various dimensions. One preliminary one involved finding that, although the US was responsible for Khadr's on-going detention, there was sufficient 'causal connection' with Canada for the Charter to apply and the Court found a violation of Art 7; *Canada (Prime Minister) v Khadr* p 2010 SCR 44, para 37.

[87] Ibid, para 37; see discussion in De Londras, *Counter-terrorism judicial review as regulatory constitutionalism*, in Davis and de Londras, n 4.

[88] *Canada (Prime Minister) v Khadr* (n 86) at para 47. De Londras, *Counter-terrorism judicial review as regulatory constitutionalism* (n 4) and *Detention in the 'War on Terror' Can Human Rights Fight Back?* (n 87) 39.

and detention in Afghanistan, the Court agreed to issue a writ of habeas corpus requiring representations to the US.[89] It did so despite government arguments that the court could not impede or compel foreign relations, and moreover that such a request to the US to hand over the detainee would be futile. Ultimately the writ was issued but the US refused to hand Rahmatullah over, and the notable show of judicial muscle did not have its desired result.[90] As the Court of Appeal noted in subsequent proceedings, defending its decision to issue the writ, 'it performed its minimum function of requiring the UK government to account for its responsibility for the applicant's detention and to attempt to get him released'.[91]

Thus, the courts in the *Khadr* case ultimately declined to order that representations be made, partly on the somewhat feeble basis that they would not be able to enforce them. The *Rahmatullah* court did it anyway, but indeed its request was not enforced. The lack of impact on US decision-making may be seen to expose the futility of some of this litigation. While the reach of domestic courts to address violations in the context of foreign affairs remains limited,[92] it has been suggested that these cases ensure at least that 'the foreign area is not left entirely unregulated'.[93] This litigation has influenced legal standards, and the approach to doctrinal questions around the foreign relations exception and the role of the courts in rights adjudication more broadly, by suggesting that doctrine—once sacrosanct—is not absolute, and recalibrating its relationship to human rights considerations. Damages claims are however proceeding through UK and Canadian, and to a very narrow extent US courts, the ultimate effect of which remains uncertain. Though, as ever, it is impossible to ascertain with precision the indirect impact of this litigation, it had at least an exposing and irritant effect, and may have contributed to putting pressure on states to provide redress and to take necessary measures of reform in respect of their intelligence agencies and cooperation for the future.[94]

---

[89] Para 56, Master of Rolls, *obiter*. And *SS Foreign and Commonwealth v Rahmatullah* (n 75); though the Court noted it was not an instruction to order his return.

[90] De Londras (n 87) at 43.

[91] *Cf Rahmatullah (No 2) v Ministry of Defence and another* (n 77), Lord Justice Neuberger, [17]. The government and its officials could not ultimately be sued in relation to its own role in the detention and treatment of this applicant and others detained in Iraq and Afghanistan, on the basis of sovereign acts carried out under the 'act of state' doctrine: see www.supremecourt.uk/cases/docs/uksc-2015-0002-judgment.pdf.

[92] De Londras (n 87) has referred to these cases (and the *Munaf* case noted above), as examples of how the courts will show 'muscularity' on internal issues, but remain deferential in fact on external matters.

[93] While still maintaining a foreign affairs exception, the 'internal' questions on the state's own conduct and control enable the court to exercise jurisdiction and seek to hold the state to account, even though in fact it inevitably has implications for the 'external' foreign relations. These 'soft findings' have 'important regulatory on government action'; De Londras (n 87) at 50.

[94] It is noteworthy, however, that rules on cooperation with foreign states have changed within the UK and Canada post-rendition. See eg Duffy (n 1) Ch 12, Conclusions.

Finally, 'settlements' arise from litigation which may in some situations have an impact that goes beyond that of a judgment. This may have been so in *Khadr's* case, where the settlement of the long-running litigation recently prompted comprehensive reparations, including a rare apology and recognition from the state.[95] The refusal to settle can also send powerful messages, and present advocacy opportunities. In the *Belhaj* case before UK courts, the victim refused a large financial settlement stating publicly that instead he would settle for an apology and one pound, as token compensation for each of the three defendants.[96] The UK refused and his case proceeded to the significant judgment noted above (rejecting state immunity and foreign act of state as barring proceedings). Thus, while acknowledgements and apologies can be a crucial dimension of reparation, and have expressive value more broadly, they remain the rare exceptions. This reflects an unprincipled distinction that is often made between 'deserving and undeserving victims' that undermines the rule of law approach to violations and compounds the original injustice.[97]

C. Supranational Rendition Litigation: The Impact and Limitations of *Abu Zubaydah v Poland*

Despite some advances in national courts, recognition by governments and access to effective remedies through national courts remains extremely scarce. Where reparation claims have been blocked in domestic courts, and where (with the exception of Italian trials in absentia in the Abu Omar case),[98] states have failed to investigate and hold individuals to account as required by human rights law, victims have pursued justice elsewhere. Attempts to engage transnational litigation possibilities, including access to courts on grounds of universal jurisdiction, have been subject to non-cooperation and political interference, and have, thus far, not borne fruit.[99]

Due to the extensive engagement of European states in the CIA programme, it is unsurprising that the ECtHR has played a particularly significant role in this area. Several judgments have now been handed down by the European Court finding

---

[95] See also the *Salim* settlement in the psychologists case, referred to above (n 74).

[96] See www.reprieve.org.uk/press/2013_03_04_belhaj_apology_secret_courts/.

[97] On the distinction between 'undeserving' or 'suspect' camps of victims of counter-terrorism and innocent victims of terrorism, see Duffy in Davis and De Londras (n 4). See much more limited practice on apologies from Canada in this field, eg most recently the *Khadr* settlement June 2017 including apology.

[98] See Italian prosecutions of CIA and Italian agents for Abu Omar's abduction but limited, as yet, accountability discussed in Duffy (n 1) and 'Accountability for Counter-Terrorism: Challenges and Potential in the role of the Courts' in Davis and De Londras (n 4).

[99] Criminal court responses, including initiatives investigating and potentially prosecuting US agents and officials elsewhere, are not addressed here but see eg Duffy in Davis and De Londras (n 4), on the role of Spanish and other courts in prosecuting in respect of Guantánamo.

that European states breached their obligations by cooperating in various ways with the CIA. Perhaps the most striking form of such participation was in the establishment of CIA-run 'black site detention centres' on other states' territories. The first judgments on black site detention abroad were handed down in 2014 against Poland, in favour of our client Zayn Al-Abidin Muhammad Husayn and Abd Al Rahim Hussayn Muhammad Al Nashiri.

There have been judgments addressing various other forms of cooperation handed down before 2014,[100] and since,[101] including on behalf of Abu Zubaydah and al Nashiri against Lithuania,[102] and Romania.[103] Cases against the US (which has not meaningfully engaged with the process) are also pending in the Inter-American system.[104] The African system looks set to consider the cooperation of African states.[105]

In the *Abu Zubaydah v Poland* (and the parallel *al Nashiri v Poland*) case the ECtHR rendered unusually lengthy, detailed and strident judgments, finding Poland responsible for the torture, secret detention and unlawful transfer of the applicants. By allowing its territory to be used by the US for a secret detention site, it incurred international responsibility and was bound to make 'just satisfaction' to the victims. Poland facilitated and created the conditions for their secret detention, resulting in torture and arbitrary detention, and the violation of his rights to fair trial and private and family life. The judgments were immediately hailed as 'landmark' cases when they were handed down in 2014.[106]

But how much difference did these cases actually make and why? Perceptions of the impact of this litigation vary quite strikingly. For some (perhaps more commonly external commentators) there is reason to extol the virtues of far-reaching and historic judicial responses in the face of extreme executive excess, and to consider that it is precisely in face of such abuse that the role of courts has assumed

---

[100] The first, in 2012, was *El-Masri v Macedonia* Appl no 39630/09 (13 December 2012) (ECtHR), which condemned Macedonia for its role in detaining Mr el-Masri at the behest of the US and transferring him to the CIA who subsequently transferred him to Afghanistan.

[101] In 2016 this was followed by a judgment *Nasr and Ghali v Italy* Appl no 44883/09 (23 February 2016) (ECtHR) concerning the abduction of Abu Omar from the streets of Milan.

[102] *Abu Zubaydah v Lithuania* (n 26) was heard in June 2016. Judgment was rendered on 31 May 2018, shortly before this book went to print. It unanimously found Lithuania in violation of the applicant's rights, and follows in relevant parts the Poland judgment.

[103] *Al Nashiri v Romania* Appl no 33234/12, 31 May 2018.

[104] Eg *Khaled El Masri v United States*, P-419-08, Inter-American Commission on Human Rights. In several cases concerning El Masri, Padilla and Iraqi and Afghan detainees, the US has responded arguing the Commission's lack of competence as its human rights obligations do not apply abroad or during conflict.

[105] Eg Extraordinary rendition case *al-Asad v Djibouti* 383/10 is before the African Commission on Human Rights (author was adviser to counsel), while another case concerning Kenyan/Ugandan rendition was brought to the East African Court of Justice. *Omar Awadh Omar and 6 Others (Applicants) v The Attorney-General Republic of Kenya, The Attorney-General Republic of Uganda and the Secretary-General East African Community (Respondents)* Appl no 4 of 2011 East African Court of Justice, First Instance Division.

[106] See eg Amnesty USA, 'Landmark Rulings Expose Poland's Role in CIA Secret Detention and Torture' (28 July 2014) www.amnestyusa.org/news/press-releases/landmark-rulings-expose-poland-s-role-in-cia-secret-detention-and-torture.

particular significance as the guardians of human rights. One colleague—my co-counsel on rendition cases—when asked what impact he thought the rendition litigation has had, said 'none at all'. This section offers a few observations on the impact and limitations of some of this litigation as I have seen it unfold through my involvement in rendition cases.[107]

i. *Jurisprudential Impact of the Judgment*

One obvious level of impact, which can be seen from the face of the *Abu Zubaydah v Poland* judgment itself, is normative or jurisprudential. In some ways it expanded the law and in others consolidated existing standards, on issues such as the right to truth, or the prohibition on transfer (to the risk of unfair trial or arbitrary detention), on procedural protection in detention, burdens of proof and the nature of the obligations to conduct an effective, thorough investigation and accountability. As such, judgments such as *Abu Zubaydah v Poland* locate the clandestine world of international cooperation within a legal framework and seek to clarify that framework en route. This case was, however, less about progressive development of the law and more about exposing and seeking to address flagrant violations.

ii. *Responsibility and Accountability of the State*

Poland, like many other states, had long denied all knowledge of, or responsibility for, unlawful secret detention on its territory. A growing flood of information was met with a wall of secrecy and denial. Plausible deniability effectively ended in 2014, when the Court found it established beyond reasonable doubt that Abu Zubaydah *was* transferred into Poland on 5 December 2002 and made clear that even by that early stage in the life of the ERP, cooperating states *knew* (or should have known) of the risks, yet Poland failed to prevent, protect or respond. The judgment constituted objective recognition of Polish responsibility and made it more difficult to continue simply denying all knowledge—a shift that is seen in the different approach by the state at the implementation stage (noted below). The Court found additional violations arising out of Poland's refusal to engage with the allegations and to share information with the Court, and found that 'investigative secrecy' could not provide a pretext to avoid meeting its obligations or cooperating with the Court.

Before judgment itself, a litigation *process* such as this one calls governments to account in various ways. It forces them to establish a position and offer explanations and justifications through their written submissions (which are generally public). Where there are hearings, such as those that have been held in camera and in public session at the ECtHR in the two *Zubaydah* cases, governments

---

[107] As noted above, I represent Abu Zubaydah against Poland and Lithuania before the ECtHR along with US counsel, and on behalf of Interights was co-counsel in al Asad v Dijbouti, and intervener in el Masri v Macedonia.

face direct questioning by the court and a degree of public scrutiny. To an extent these processes have therefore themselves compelled greater transparency around investigations, or at least accountability for the lack of openness, which is particularly valuable in an area shrouded in extreme secrecy. One small example of the power of the hearing process arose when the government of Lithuania, which had claimed 'investigative secrecy' in respect of all documents submitted to the ECtHR concerning its purported investigation, when questioned by the Court at the public hearing, agreed to lift this claim and make information (albeit limited and heavily redacted) available publicly.

In addition, in the Polish case the government was called to account for the implementation of the judgment, before the Committee of Ministers. The implementation process has long been neglected by lawyers and activists and is only now beginning to be seen as an integral part of the litigation process, but its significance is illustrated by these cases. The Committee—a political body with the ultimate authority to remove states from the Council of Europe[108]—has actively engaged and elicited detailed responses from the Polish state (as noted further below). Notably, this political process goes beyond simply implementing the operative part of the ECtHR judgments. Encompassing progress with the prosecution, legislative developments and institutional reform, it has provided a context for broader dialogue on dealing with the underlying problems that gave rise to this case. In reports on the Polish action plan, the Committee for example

> considered that most of the measures set out in the action plan do not address the root causes of the issues identified in the Court's judgments, namely a blatant disregard of the legal framework governing the actions of State agents, and urged the authorities to address these issues.

Indirectly, the judgment also alluded to the responsibility of the multiple non-state actors who facilitated and made possible the ERP. Although the judgment was explicitly only directed at Polish responsibility, one commentator observed that the 'judgment may be interpreted as an accusation against the US', and by necessary inference the many other states who made the programme possible through other forms of cooperation.[109]

iii. Victim Reparation

The ECtHR could do little to address the egregious on-going violations of Abu Zubaydah's rights, and victim impact was always going to be limited. In addition,

---

[108] See Art 8 of the Statute of the Council of Europe:

> Any member of the Council of Europe which has seriously violated Article 3 [including respect for the enjoyment of human rights] may be suspended from its rights of representation and requested by the Committee of Ministers to withdraw under Article 7. If such member does not comply with this request, the Committee may decide that it has ceased to be a member of the Council as from such date as the Committee may determine.

[109] A Bodner, 'Poland: Trust no one but the Law' *Open Democracy* (26 February 2015) www.opendemocracy.net/can-europe-make-it/adam-bodnar/poland-trust-no-one-but-law-0.

the Court generally takes a narrow approach to reparation, mostly awarding 'just satisfaction', which tends to be limited to basic financial damages awards on behalf of victims (this contrasts starkly with the holistic approach to reparations of the Inter-American system—as discussed in the Guatemala/*Plan de Sanchez* case study).

In the *Abu Zubaydah* and *al Nashiri v Poland* cases, the court ordered an unusually high award of 100,000 Euros each, reflecting its view on the gravity of the wrongs, and which the government committed to paying. While practically, that may be of little benefit to a client still deprived of liberty at Guantanamo, there is also symbolic importance in such a significant damages award. On the other hand, at least on one view, money was never what mattered in these cases, and indeed the compensation payment may have been counter-productive to the debate in Poland, generating considerable hostility to the idea of paying 'terrorists' and diverting attention from the central issues in the case. Nonetheless, the Polish government committed promptly to paying and funds have been transferred.[110]

The importance of recognition, and satisfaction, in a case such as this should not be underestimated. Despite abundant and detailed information on the torture of Abu Zudaydah, from incontrovertible sources such as internal CIA documentation and cables, insiders involved in his torture, and memoranda authorising the use of all 'enhanced interrogation techniques' on him, it was in the ECtHR judgment that he was recognised for the first time as a victim of human rights violations. The vindication of a court can be particularly important in cases such as this where clients have been vilified through false public allegations against him, and dehumanised through their abuse.

The limitations on access to Abu Zubaydah and on the telling of his story—due to excessive secrecy that precludes all communication with the outside world—led to him being described in the judgment as 'a man without a voice'.[111] It is not possible for him to share his own experience of the case directly, just as it was not possible for him to share his testimony with the European Court. This must limit the empowering power of the process in cases such as these. However, lawyers who have met with rendition victims, speak of the validation that can come from being represented, and—despite the impediments—have their stories heard and the truth recognised.[112] In this particularly toxic environment where individuals are degraded during their torture and thereafter, a process that recognises the victim and his suffering, past and present, and wrongdoers' responsibility, can have a restorative role. That said, it is impossible to make generalisations about such things; the litigation process has also been retraumatising for torture and

---

[110] In the case of our client, owing to his placement on the United Nations Resolution 1267 list, imposing individual sanctions (including asset freezes), though in December 2017 he was delisted, recognising that he was not a member of al Qaeda and posed no danger. On those designated on to be on the Al-Qaida or ISIL sanctions lists, this was paid into trust. He has since been delisted.

[111] *Abu Zabaydah v Poland* Appl no 7511/13 (2014) (ECtHR) para 453.

[112] Consultations with colleagues in relation to the feedback of several rendition detainees.

rendition victims[113] and there is every basis for growing frustration, and a sense of accumulating injustice.

iv. Representations Regarding On-going Violations

The ECtHR case could do little to remedy the continuing violations of Abu Zubaydah's rights through on-going arbitrary detention at Guantanamo. However, the judgments, while focused on Polish responsibility, were noteworthy for their indirect condemnation of the applicants' current situation. Zubaydah's detention without charge or trial at Guantánamo Bay was described by the ECtHR as 'a flagrant denial of justice'.[114] In its first consideration of the judgment after it was rendered in 2014, the Committee of Ministers took the unusual step of calling on Poland to seek assurances from the US that neither Abu Zubaydah nor Al-Nashiri would be subjected to the death penalty (more relevant for Mr Al-Nashiri who is being tried by military commission) and to seek assurances that the applicants would not be exposed to further denials of justice. This led to a series of exchanges between the Polish government and the US, in which the latter made clear that it could not provide such assurances and that it was not subject to the provisions of the ECtHR.[115]

The Committee of Ministers expressed satisfaction with the actions of the Polish authorities in making and following up on such requests but also expressed concerns over the US lack of response. It urged Poland to address its requests to higher political levels. The Secretary General of the Council of Europe was invited to transmit the US' response to the Permanent Observer of the US to the Council of Europe.[116] A new request for diplomatic assurances, prepared by the Office of the President of Poland, was sent to the US Embassy in Warsaw on 18 July 2016.[117] The Court built on this approach in the subsequent Lithuania case. In that case the judgment itself reflects the important principle that states' obligations to provide redress include making representations to the US to seek to bring to an end injustices to which they have contributed.

v. Legislative and Institutional Reform

Concrete measures by Poland to respond to the ECtHR judgment are set out in successive action plans[118] on which the state reports periodically. Developments

---

[113] Depositions and other pre-trial procedures, as well as the trial itself, have caused victims and survivors to re-live traumatic events and in some respects seems to have exacerbated symptoms of post-traumatic stress disorder. See eg L Siems, 'These CIA Torture Victims May Finally Have a Chance at Justice ... but have had to Relive their Torment' *The Nation* (26 June 2017).

[114] *Abu Zabaydah v Poland*, Judgment (n 110).

[115] On 19 February 2016, Poland indicated it had been informed by the US that diplomatic assurances could not be provided given that the ECHR and decisions of the ECtHR do not reflect the obligations of the US under international law.

[116] This was done on 17 March 2016.

[117] Council of Europe, 'Communication from the authorities (19/07/2016) in the group of cases Al Nashiri v. Poland (Application No. 28761/11)' DH-DD(2016)834, https://rm.coe.int/CoERMPublicCommonSearchServices/DisplayDCTMContent?documentId=09000016806940c6.

[118] Council of Europe, 'Updated action plan 1 as to the measures to comply with the judgments in the cases of Al Nashiri and AbuZubaydah v. Poland' DH-DD(2016)627' https://rm.coe.int/CoERMPublicCommonSearchServices/DisplayDCTMContent?documentId=0900001680650b7f.

cited include legislative change to ensure greater information is made available in relation to on-going investigations that were previously covered by blanket secrecy,[119] the establishment of (controversial) measures on enhanced oversight of special services,[120] the appointment of a new Minister as Coordinator of Special Services and the bolstering of parliamentary control over the activities of the intelligence services via a 'Parliamentary Commission for Special Services'. The efficiency or impact of these measures remains to be seen, and will depend on political action and factors beyond litigation. But the case exemplifies how judgments can at least catalyse a process of internal reflection and develop a platform for reform. More broadly, reports of proposals for reform and greater oversight of intelligence agencies in Poland and beyond, if they come to pass, point to the potential for more significant, and much-needed, change for the future.[121]

vi. Investigation and Impunity

The judgment was clear in its findings that, despite its claims to the contrary, Poland had not and was not conducting the thorough, effective and independent investigation required by the Convention. Some benchmarks that the state must meet are provided in the judgment itself. However, the impact on impunity remains questionable and the Committee continues to express concern about the lack of investigative progress condemned in the judgment. There is little indication to date that this has changed.

These cases, and in particular the implementation processes, have served to reveal the lack of cooperation and indeed continued obstruction by the United States. Litigation in both Poland and Lithuania has forced governments to state openly that requests for mutual legal assistance have been issued to the US, but either ignored or denied.[122] Both governments have used this failure to cooperate as justification for their own failure to proceed more effectively with the investigations. Politicisation and obstruction of justice remaining the norm in these cases across states poses a real challenge to the rule of law.

vii. Broader Visibility, Debate and Social Impact?

The extent to which the case has shaped attitudes or responses on a social level is, as ever, much more difficult to ascertain. Social and political impact do not

---

[119] Ibid, 16. Entering into law on 4 March 2016, Art 12(2) states the General Prosecutor and heads of prosecution organisational units (or others empowered by them) may submit to the media information on pending preparatory proceedings or information concerning prosecution activities, excluding classified information.

[120] Although presented as compliance with the judgment, the amendments to the Police Act adopted on 15 January 2016 have been described by Amnesty as 'a major blow to human rights'; Amnesty International, 'Poland: New surveillance law a major blow to human rights' (29 January 2016) www.amnesty.org/download/Documents/EUR3733572016ENGLISH.pdf.

[121] Duffy (n 1) Ch 12.

[122] Several applications were submitted to the US and denied. Romania, UK and UAE authorities have also been asked to cooperate in the provision of information and hearing of witnesses.

happen overnight, but as a result of longer-term and multi-faceted action. These cases have certainly been widely cited in the publications of NGOs, Amnesty International,[123] Strasbourg Observers,[124] Human Rights Watch,[125] Just Security,[126] Open Democracy[127] and by the European Parliament. In particular, the European Parliament has repeatedly cited the Poland cases, in combination with the US Senate Intelligence Committee Report,[128] in calling for further transparency and accountability.[129]

The case before the ECtHR captured media attention and contributed to a broadening of debate. Immediately following the decision against Poland, references to the cases in both academic journals[130] and the news[131] were abundant. While focus is most often on accountability of the US, there are also indications of broader reflection on the history of the countries and the implications of these judgments for their societies. Examples include reflections on how Stare Kiejkuty, a Polish military area used as a CIA black site, had been used by the Soviets, then the Nazis, before the CIA, reflecting a dark history of abuses by foreign states and the importance of non-repetition. Films and artistic work in Poland, Lithuania and elsewhere, have broadened the reach and nature of that reflection and discussion. Some coverage fuels resentments about use of 'taxpayers' money' to compensate 'terrorists', revealing key challenges that arise in reparation in the national

---

[123] Amnesty USA, 'Landmark Rulings Expose Poland's Role in CIA Secret Detention and Torture' (28 July 2014).

[124] A Singh, 'Landmark European Court Decision Sends Clear Message on Ending Impunity for European Complicity in CIA Torture' *Strasbourg Observers* (9 September 2014) https://strasbourgobservers.com/2014/09/10/landmark-european-court-decision-sends-clear-message-on-ending-impunity-for-european-complicity-in-cia-torture/.

[125] 'Poland: Landmark Rulings on CIA Torture Complicity' *Human Rights Watch* (24 July 2014) www.hrw.org/news/2014/07/24/poland-landmark-rulings-cia-torture-complicity.

[126] R Parekh, 'European Court of Human Rights rules against Poland in CIA "black site" case' *Just Security* (24 July 2014) www.justsecurity.org/13205/european-court-human-rights-rules-poland-cia-black-site-case/.

[127] Bodner, 'Poland: Trust no one but the Law' (n 109).

[128] The 'Feinstein Report' issued by the US Senate Intelligence Committee on 9 December 2014 documents CIA abuses between 2001 and 2009; 'Senate Intelligence Committee Study on CIA Detention and *Interrogation* Program'.

[129] European Parliament Directorate General for Internal Policies, 'A quest for accountability? EU and Member State inquiries into the CIA Rendition and Secret Detention Programme' (September 2015) www.ceps.eu/system/files/Quest%20for%20Accountability.pdf is published by the Directorate General for Internal Policies: Policy Department C Citizen's Rights and Constitutional Affairs.

[130] See S Cunningham, 'Al Nashiri v. Poland and Husayn (Abu Zubaydah) v. Poland' (2015) 26(1) *King's Law Journal* 1; A Deeks, 'Checks and Balances from Abroad' (2013) 83(1) *University of Chicago Law Review* 65–88; H Carey, 'The Domestic Politics of Protecting Human Rights in Counter-Terrorism' (2013) 27(3) *East European Politics & Societies and Cultures* 429–65.

[131] See A Goldman, 'European Court Finds Poland Complicit in CIA "Torture," Orders Detainee Compensation' *The Washington Post* (24 July 2014) www.washingtonpost.com/world/national-security/european-court-finds-poland-complicit-in-cia-torture-orders-detainee-compensation/2014/07/24/7ce81f02-133a-11e4-98ee-daea85133bc9_story.html; D Smith, 'Abu Zubaydah, detainee tortured by CIA, makes case for Guantánamo release' *The Guardian* (23 August 2016) www.theguardian.com/us-news/2016/aug/23/abu-zubaydah-guantanamo-bay-cia-torture.

security context. Others focus on the human story, on the cruel nature of the treatment and continued detention of the applicant and shared responsibility for the on-going injustice of his situation.[132]

In conclusion, while impact may be observed on various levels, it is overshadowed by the overwhelming inadequacy of the response to the rendition and torture programme in general, and to on-going violations of Abu Zubaydah's rights. His litigation has not, and could not, resolve this. But it may have contributed to keeping him, and others like him, in the public eye, despite being detained far beyond it. It may have played a small role, alongside many other factors, in keeping the issue of forgotten 'forever prisoners' on the agenda.[133] It may also have contributed to historical clarification of the wrongs, and the shared nature of the responsibility for them. It has exposed the inadequacy to date of domestic investigations and the need for legislative and institutional reforms. While actual changes to the law and institutions in Poland are at best questionable, the process has provided a platform for international oversight and engagement towards more meaningful change.

It is too early to assess the cumulative impact of these processes. Whether their potential is realised will depend on the use to which these judgments and processes are put, and on the generation of continuing momentum. This in turn will depend on the role and commitment of civil society actors and of other states—individually and collectively—to force Poland and other states to make its commitments a reality. Lack of political will to meet the challenges and resist pressure, fatigue and competing priorities all threaten the realisation of this potential.

IV. Conclusions

Caution is due in trying to draw conclusions from such wide-ranging practice, in diverse legal systems, but a few tentative observations on this litigation and how we might approach impact may be helpful. First, the practice explored makes clear the nature and extent of the gaps, challenges and limitations in pursuing litigation in this field. Legal or jurisdictional impediments are epitomised in the use of state-secrecy to block US courts, though attempts elsewhere to divest judiciaries of their oversight role remind us it is a broader phenomenon. Glaring gaps in the international legal system mean patchy access to supranational mechanisms; while the dynamic between the ECHR and national judiciaries influenced developments

---

[132] See article by co-counsel AL Jacobsen and J Margulies, 'The "guinea pig" for U.S. torture is languishing at Guantánamo' *The Washington Post* (7 October 2016).

[133] See M Koren 'Who Is Left at Guantánamo? And who can never leave?' www.theatlantic.com/politics/archive/2016/05/guanatanamo-bay-forever-prisoners/482289. Other factors, such as the hunger strike (see Lobell, in Davis and de Londras (n 4)), or the military hearings in Guantánamo, were likely a greater 'magnet' for attention, but the cases played a role in continuing this momentum and diversifying attention.

in the UK, there is no comparable binding, international court with jurisdiction over the US and several other states involved in rendition.[134] These are supplemented by inordinate practical and political challenges involved in representing people some of whom are unable to communicate with the public, lawyers or courts.[135] Never far from the surface are the political challenges, including 'enormous pressure' from Washington on other states not to meet their obligations in respect of justice in torture and rendition cases.[136]

The war on terror has in turn been a trying time for the courts themselves, with an inevitable impact on human rights litigation. Judicial independence has been compromised through 'special' courts, pressure on and criticism of 'so-called' judges who stand up to the state on national security,[137] or the stigmatisation of the judicial role as 'undemocratic' and as 'a strategy of the weak'.[138] Litigation has prompted some European states to threaten withdrawal from the ECtHR, and refusal to implement.[139] Meanwhile, the climate of fear and secrecy in which many litigators, lawyers, human rights defenders, judges and victims operate makes human rights litigation difficult or even perilous.[140] As governments further restrict—and push back against—the judicial role in the US and UK, it remains to be seen whether the courts recoil or become more assertive in their defence of basic rights.

So how then should we consider the impact of litigation in such a challenging and changing field? We might begin, as many do, by considering the *normative* value of the 'historic' judgments themselves. Judgments in this field have at times clarified important principles, among them universality, while their value may lie in simply reasserting basic standards increasingly cast in doubt in the name of security. The *legislature* has also been prodded into action by the courts—albeit at times to improve and at others to weaken rights protections.[141] Litigation has catalysed changes in law, policies and practice, sometimes quite directly,

---

[134] eg Thailand was the first site of Abu Zubaydah's torture and there is no available regional mechanism. Cases against the US have been brought before the IACommHR but the processes afforded little weight.

[135] See impediments on Abu Zubaydah due to presumptive classification, addressed in his ECHR proceedings; see Duffy (n 1) Ch 10.

[136] Ibid, Ch 10.

[137] A Wang, 'Trump lashes out at "so-called judge" who temporarily blocked travel ban' *The Washington Post* (4 February 2017).

[138] 'Our strength as a nation state will continue to be challenged by those who employ a strategy of the weak using international fora, judicial processes, and terrorism' (National Defense Strategy for the United States of America, 2005).

[139] Part of the backlash is highlighted in C 2.

[140] Extreme examples today include in Turkey, where litigators and judges have been prosecuted (Duffy (n 1) Ch 4) and judges have reportedly been dismissed for finding against the state (2,700 judges were removed following the coup, and during 2017 removals continued following unfavourable decisions). See statement of MICT on conviction of Judge Aydin Sefa Akay by Turkish criminal court, 15 June 2017.

[141] *A & Ors* (n 48) was a broadly favourable legislative change; Guantánamo and closed material proceedings not.

as in the wake of the *Belmarsh* judgment, or by 'chipping away', in conjunction with a host of other forms of action, at UK control orders or the arbitrariness of Guantanamo.[142]

Crucially, litigation has helped to secure access to detainees and to information which changes the context of the conversation in significant ways. Gaining *access to lawyers* for Guantánamo detainees (formally for the purpose of preparing habeas litigation) is often overlooked but is perhaps the most significant impact of any of the litigation reviewed. The course of litigation process has prized open facts and uncovered a 'treasure trove' of now public documentation on what states knew, and their role in torture and rendition, of particular importance in face of a wall of state secrecy.[143] At times, access to information was the goal of 'freedom of information' litigation,[144] courts compelled the government to share information with plaintiffs or defendants,[145] or information emerged through discovery processes (as in the *Richmor* or *Salim* litigation).[146] This unearthing of information is part of the historical recording of some of the most egregious violations in the history of several countries, encouraging us to learn from the mistakes of the war on terror.

Litigation has drawn attention to issues, given them a human face and a legal framework for discussion. Feeding into conversations around appropriate responses to international terrorism, and its limits, and the value of law and democracy, may prove vital to longer-term reckoning with the past. There is cause for careful reflection on whether litigation influenced attitudes and public perceptions: whether it contributed to the shift in public opinion (national and international) on Guantánamo that preceded the policy shift, or the controversial, and sobering, question whether there has been any such shift in light of revelations of systematic torture. At a minimum, litigation enhanced awareness of practices and clarified their unlawfulness in all circumstances.

---

[142] See eg C Walker, *Blackstone's Guide to the Anti-Terrorism Legislation*, Oxford, Oxford University Press, 2014) 238; Liberty, 'From War to Law' (2010) 19 on impact of litigation on UK policy on control orders.

[143] Canadian litigation has shown, eg that Canadian officials 'not only knew Abdullah Almalki, Ahmad Abou-Elmaati and Muayyed Nureddin would likely be tortured at the hands of Syrian intelligence officers, they supplied them with interrogation questions'; *The Attorney General of Canada v Abdullah Almalki* 2015 FC 1278.

[144] See eg through FOIA (Freedom of Information Act) litigation on rendition and torture in Eastern Europe states and the US, in Duffy (n 1) Ch 10.

[145] *Canada (Justice) v Khadr*, 2008 SCC 28. On 23 May 2008, the Court took the unusual step of ordering Canadian officials to allow Mr Kadhr access to records of his interrogations with Canadian agents, for use in preparing his defence before the Guantánamo Military Commission. In the *Mohamed* case, UK courts required the government to provide Mohamed with information that may be relevant to a commission trial planned at the time by the US *Binyam Mohamed v Foreign and Commonwealth Office* 30 July 2009, revised 16 October 2009.

[146] The discovery process in *Salim et al v Michel and Jeppsen* resulted in the production of hundreds of documents on the CIA's detention and interrogation program that were previously withheld under FOIA. *Richmor* litigation was between rendition flight contractors used by the government; it went beneath the radar and led to a vast amount of information being available through the discovery process. This was then used in eg *Abu Zubaydah v Lithuania*.

At a minimum, it has forced the executive to render account under the law, in opaque areas such as international cooperation and counter-terrorism, both inside the court process and beyond it.[147] Judges, and judgments, have been among the persuasive voices in those conversations. They have sent messages to the government, legislature and to their judicial peers, also transnationally, as in the unusually robust judicial rebukes from English courts to US counterparts.[148] Litigation has in turn drawn a broader range of voices into the judicial process and broader debate—and opened up systems to the cross-fertilisation of ideas—through an unprecedented array of *amicus* interveners from around the globe in the Guantánamo[149] and rendition litigation.[150] Sometimes the *implementation* process (as in the Abu *Zubaydah* case before the Committee of Ministers) has provided a valuable platform for dialogue on what is required of all arms of the state to redress wrongs, and to ensure *non-repetition* through in legal, institutional and policy change.

The litigation has also forced reflection on the fraught issue of the correct balance between the executive, legislative and judicial democratic functions.[151] On one view, judicial deference has (as in the past), been the order of the day, at great cost; at what price in terms of judicial efficiency in the administration of justice—and protection of individuals—came the virtue of judicial restraint during six years of habeas litigation?[152] On another view, courts in diverse systems—whether promptly, or as a matter of last resort—have broken the historical pattern of extreme deference in the counter-terrorism field: 'executive unilateralism is being challenged by national courts in what could perhaps be a globally coordinated move'.[153] The truth may lie somewhere in between.[154] Courts have been

---

[147] Even in earlier cases before *Boumidience*, SCOTUS refusal to shield Guantánamo from judicial scrutiny in *Rasul, Hamdi* and *Hamdan*, with the latter sending the message that even the Commander-in-Chief/President is subject to the restraint of law. See E Benvenisti, *Counterterrorism: Democracy's Challenge* (Oxford, Hart, 2008) 30.

[148] This concerned the injustice of Guantánamo detentions and overreaching secrecy impeding the proper administration of justice in respectively; *R (Abbasi) v Secretary of State for Foreign and Commonwealth Affairs* and the Appeals Court in the *Binyam Mohamad* case. The latter noted: 'we did not consider that a democracy governed by the rule of law would expect a court in another democracy to suppress a summary of the evidence contained in reports by its own officials or officials of another State where the evidence was relevant to allegations of torture and cruel, inhuman or degrading treatment, politically embarrassing though it might be'.

[149] *Amicus* interventions appeared from such diverse quarters as the British House of Lords or Israeli military.

[150] *Amicus* interventions by eg UN Special Rapporteur on Terrorism and Human Rights and several NGOs were presented in the *al Nashiri* and *Zubaydah* cases highlighting the broader significance of the case.

[151] See eg careful and difficult 'balancing' by the judiciary in cases concerning access to secret evidence.

[152] See also eg *A & Ors* (n 48), deference on the existence of an emergency and Lord Hoffmann's dissent in the House of Lords that the nation was not under threat from al Qaeda.

[153] Benvenisti, *Counterterrorism: Democracy's Challenge* (n 146) 254. See JE Rytter, in Davis and de Londras (n 4) on an unusual level of development of the law by the judiciary in Denmark in the national security context in recent years. *A & Others* (n 39) is the clearest example from the UK.

[154] See eg the *Khadr*, or the Guantánamo litigation above. Benvenisti, ibid, sees post-9/11 decisions of SCOTUS/UKHL as less of a break in convention and more 'a dampening or flattening of that pattern' at 62.

significantly robust in principle, but rather more timid in implementation and forcing executive action,[155] leading some to conclude that they resonate loudly but their impact is 'perhaps more rhetorical than real'.[156] Undoubtedly, litigation has reinvigorated debate within judiciaries, with the 'potential for judges to educate the public about the real meaning of democracy'.[157]

Finally, and perhaps most importantly, is the impact on the individual victims and survivors. While victims such as Abu Zubaydah remain in Guantánamo, with no meaningful opportunity to defend himself, no charges and no reasonable prospect of release, it goes without saying that impact is inadequate. But cases have at least told the victims' stories, and so far as possible, enabled the voiceless to be heard. They have provided often-graphic illustrations of what euphemisms such as 'extraordinary rendition' and 'enhanced interrogation techniques' mean to real human beings. Media attention to filings, hearings and judgments has brought those realities to a broader audience. Judgments in turn validate those stories and experiences. Litigation has provided a vehicle for at least some recognition of wrongdoing and 'reparation', while *settlements* have played a role in advancing the long-neglected role apology. While arbitrary detention, torture and rendition have sought to put certain people beyond the reach of the law, litigation can—as one English judge put it—transfer power from the executive to the individual.[158] The humanising power of the process sits alongside more concrete and direct forms of impact where individuals have been compensated, released, afforded legal representation or had control orders modified or lifted for example.[159]

The cases explored here are replete with examples of more negative impact: the circumvention of law's reach by transferring detainees from Guantánamo, in anticipation of habeas review;[160] the lack of enforcement of judgments;[161] unfavourable media coverage providing a vehicle for further antipathy; or

---

[155] See the Uighur cases (n 25), where the courts were not willing to order release, or *Khadr* where little prospect of enforcement influenced the decision to uphold the right but not to issue an order to give effect to it.

[156] Benvenisti (n 146) 8–61.

[157] Du Plessis, 'Terrorism and National Security' (n 45).

[158] Dame Mary Arden: 'the decision in the *A* case should not be misinterpreted as a transfer of power from the executive to the judiciary. The position is that the judiciary now has the important task of reviewing executive action against the benchmark of human rights. Thus, the transfer of power is not to the judiciary but to the individual' (2005) 121 *Law Quarterly Review* 623–24; ATH Smith, 'Balancing Liberty and Security? A Legal Analysis of United Kingdom Anti-Terrorist Legislation' (2007) *European Journal on Criminal Policy and Research*.

[159] eg *Abu Zubaydah v Poland* compensation.

[160] One troubling consequence of litigation of torture in detention more broadly may be moving people further from any legal protection; eg in H Duffy, 'Strategic Litigation Impacts: Torture in Custody' Open Society Justice Initiative (Open Society Foundations, 2017), interviewees suggested detention beyond official places of detention in police vans, streets and elsewhere was one of the consequences of improved oversight of detention, including through the courts. Some interviewees also suggested that the use of lethal use of force as an alternative impelled by, among other things, by habeas litigation; see also D Jenkins, 'When Good Cases go Bad' in Davis and de Londras (n 4) 88.

[161] eg continuing detention following habeas litigation, or the non-implementation as yet of rendition judgments requiring effective investigations and accountability.

where litigation's hailed victory for human rights and the rule of law obscure the on-going de facto denial of justice for victims and the complete dearth of accountability.[162]

With this array of positive and negative impacts, so many challenges and diverse opinions, impact analysis is complex. Other forms of investigative, advocacy and political action may well be more useful, and are certainly essential and complementary, such that the impact of litigation is difficult to disaggregate from that of other work. But litigation appears to have played a particular role in an area where political solutions have proved so elusive, changing the context within which the 'war on terror' unfolds. Through judgments, the processes that precede them, and the long and difficult processes of implementation that follow, it has pushed back against executive excess, slipping standards, and the dehumanising of individuals. It has created incentives to respect human rights and increased the costs of violations and of cooperating with violators.[163] By contributing to exposing the truth, to pressure for investigation and accountability, to debate on causes and contributors, and the importance of judicial oversight of executive action within a democracy, it could make a contribution to longer-term non-repetition of the many mistakes of the war on terror, if we are willing to learn.

---

[162] Where courts have a 'light' review, questions can arise in other contexts as to whether they are able to address the substance of the wrong or meaningfully appraise facts at all; see eg *Thomas v Mowbray* (n 57) fn 60, dissent J Kirby.

[163] Ibid; Walker, 'The Reshaping of Control Orders in the United Kingdom' (n 57).

8

Case Study—Justice for Enforced Disappearance in Argentina

I. Introduction

Torture in detention of political opponents was a defining and notorious aspect of the last Argentinian dictatorship (1976–83), to which myriad complex 'transitional justice' processes have been directed in pursuit of truth, justice and non-repetition. The litigation surrounding enforced disappearances in Argentina is a classic example of strategic, multi-faceted and long-term litigation, within a broader campaign and movement, which ultimately led to remarkable results. After many years of impunity and obstructions, the most voluminous human rights trials in history are now underway in Argentina. The journey has been far from linear, revealing an array of inventive and flexible strategies, including the use of diverse types of litigation at different stages, responding to opportunities and dodging obstacles on the long road towards justice and accountability. This case study emerged from a consultancy I conducted between 2015–17 with Open Society Foundations,[1] which provided the opportunity to explore these issues in detail with a range of actors in Argentina.

Section II provides background on the phenomena of systematic enforced disappearance and torture and cruel, inhuman and degrading treatment (TCIDT) in Argentina during the dictatorship and the evolution of political, legal and social responses over time. The importance of litigation has to be understood in this context, alongside and in dynamic relationship with political and democratic transition, and broad-based grassroots and international advocacy. Section III then examines in more detail particular clusters of cases and their impact.

[1] The consultancy was undertaken with the Open Society Justice Initiative between 2015–17 on litigating torture in detention, which contrasted litigation on custodial torture in 3 states. See H Duffy, 'Strategic Litigation Impacts: Torture in Custody' (2017) available at www.opensocietyfoundations. org/sites/default/files/strategic-litigation-impacts-torture-custody-20171114.pdf. The author is very grateful to OSJI colleagues, especially Erika Dailey and Jim Goldston, for the opportunity to do this research, and for authorising the use of this material in this book. She is also very grateful to Anabella Museri who contributed excellent research from Argentina for the original study.

II. Background

The military dictatorship in Argentina (1976–1983) was characterised by systematic human rights violations pursuant to the so-called 'National Security Doctrine'. Democratic institutions were attacked, political opposition repressed, and a key methodology was systematic torture, enforced disappearances and the negation of judicial guarantees to detainees. The use of clandestine detention centres—of which there is estimated to have been at least 340 throughout the country[2]—to detain and interrogate 'subversives', the kidnapping of children of detainees and the refusal to acknowledge their whereabouts characterised the profound impact of what came to be known as the crimes of 'enforced disappearance'. Violations were led by the armed forces, but backed by a range of other influential actors.[3] As so often seen elsewhere, the torture and enforced disappearance unfolded within a political context of the 'state of exception', in which the hypothesis of a global 'war' by the West against international communism was used to justify exceptional measures for the 'protection of national sovereignty' against an internal 'enemy' of *subversivos*.[4] Originally the targets were selected opponents but the focus spread until, as the National Commission on the Disappearance of Persons (Comisión National sobre la Desaparición de Personas, CONADEP) report noted, every dissenter was 'potentially guilty'.

A. Disappearances and Responses during Dictatorship

The fact that many, though not all, of the victims of torture during this period were politically organised meant that civil society resistance and coordination was already well underway during the dictatorship itself. A crucial aspect of the reaction to the torture and disappearances was the formation of now emblematic human rights NGOs, such as the 'Madres' and the 'Abuelas' of the Plaza de Mayo,

---

[2] See CONADEP Report, 'Nunca Más' (1984) available at www.desaparecidos.org/nuncamas/web/english/library/nevagain/nevagain_001.htm; published as a book in English with an introduction by Ronald Dworkin, *Nunca Más: The Report of the Argentine National Commission on the Disappeared* (London, Farrer, Straus & Giroux, 1986).

[3] Property owners, executives and managers of some prominent companies actively participated in the violations committed against workers, and there were high-level connections between the Church hierarchy and the military juntas (M Novaro and V Palermo, *La Dictadura Militar (1976–1983): Del Golpe de Estado a la Restauración de la Democracia* (Buenos Aires, Paidós, 2003); Ministerio de Justicia y Derechos Humanos de la Nación, *Responsabilidad empresarial en delitos de lesa humanidad: represión a trabajadores durante el terrorismo de Estado* (Argentina, Infojus, 2015)).

[4] P Calveiro, 'Formas y sentidos de lo represivo entre dictadura y democracia' in CELS, *Hacer Justicia* (Buenos Aries, Siglo XXI Editores, 2011).

CELS and the Asemblea Permanente, among others.[5] The Argentine human rights movement was in large part born of, and defined by, its emergence from this repression, and its focus on assisting family members to locate the disappeared and to pursue truth and justice for dictatorship crimes.

The repression in Argentina was particularly clandestine, reportedly to guard against the protest, reaction and international pressure that had confronted the dictatorship's neighbour, the Chilean dictatorship of Augusto Pinochet.[6] A key part of early strategies, including litigation, therefore involved securing access to information. Over time, and as access to information grew, the priorities of many victims and civil society groups shifted, and came to focus on accountability.

The fact that many from Argentine civil society organisations and a number of victims were lawyers may in turn have contributed to the natural inclination to use law and the courts as part of their struggle, even during dictatorship, notwithstanding the readily apparent lack of independence and effectiveness of the judicial system at this stage. This was, however, only ever part of the strategy. One description of the tools employed by this nascent civil society movement refers to 'law, discourse and symbolism' as three complementary elements.[7] As regards discourse and symbolism, the labelling of the crime as 'forced disappearance' and the silhouettes of the disappeared and the headscarves of the grandmothers, captured national and international attention. The ability to define and depict the problem, making it comprehensible and compelling to audiences nationally and internationally, was an essential prerequisite to the effectiveness of subsequent legal action to challenge it.

The impact of the courts during dictatorship was extremely limited, if measured against the goals of protecting persons subject to on-going torture and CIDT and arbitrary detention. Indeed, the judicial role at this time has been described as 'legitimisation' of (and the stark refusal to challenge) the status quo.[8] However, in order to legitimise effectively, the courts took seriously their 'bureaucratic'

---

[5] The NGOs included: Mothers of the Plaza de Mayo), Abuelas de Plaza de Mayo (Grandmothers of the Plaza de Mayo), Familiares de Desaparecidos y Detenidos por Razones Políticas (Relatives of Persons Detained-Disappeared for Political Motives), the Centre for Legal and Social Studies (Centro de Estudios Legales y Sociales, CELS), Asamblea Permanente por los Derechos Humanos (Permanent Council for HR) and Servicio de Paz y Justicia (Peace and Justice Service).

[6] Calveiro, 'Formas y sentidos de lo represivo entre dictadura y democracia' (n 4). In 1984, the CONADEP recorded the disappearance of 8,960 people but made clear that it estimated that the number of victims in fact exceeded the 9,000 documented cases and indeed thousands of cases emerged thereafter. Other human rights organisations have maintained more recently that the victim level reached 30,000. See C Smulovitz,'"I can't get no satisfaction": Accountability and Justice for Past Human Rights Violations in Argentina' in V Popovski and M Serrano (eds), *Transitional Justice and Democratic Consolidation: Comparing the Effectiveness of the Accountability Mechanisms in Eastern Europe and Latin America* (United Nations University, 2009).

[7] MJ Guembe, 'Economic Reparations for Grave Human Rights Violations: The Argentinian Experience' in P de Greiff (ed), *The Handbook of Reparations* (Oxford, Oxford University Press, 2006) 21–54.

[8] Ibid.

processing of cases, and as such had some effect. In some respects, this meant little, as habeas corpus applications were formally processed but the executive's denial of all knowledge went unquestioned. But court records did faithfully record judicial approval of the vast numbers of corpses entering the morgue at this time, the signature of those presenting the bodies and the stated cause of death, such as 'armed confrontations'. Although the courts were providing no protection to those who needed it during dictatorship, the court files in these 'morgue cases' became a significant part of the documentary basis for subsequent action.[9]

Given the impotence of Argentinian courts during dictatorship to create pressure on the military, the emphasis by civil society shifted to generating external pressure to impel internal solutions. International visibility was enhanced by seeking monitoring and reporting by human rights organisations, including NGOs such as Amnesty International and others that began to change the perception of Argentina abroad.[10] An important benchmark was the on-site visit of the Inter-American Commission on Human Rights (IACommHR) in September 1979;[11] in one week the Commission received 5,580 complaints from across Argentina, conducted interviews with public authorities and the nascent human rights movement, and generated intense public attention. The resulting 1980 report that revealed the 'alarming' extent of the 'systematic' use of torture, is said to have changed the landscape by making it impossible any longer to simply deny torture and other violations.[12] The report recorded how the clandestine world of the military junta developed to the point where it could engage in such vast human rights atrocities and provided external validation that catalysed the 'organization of the resistance to dictatorship'.[13] This advocacy and monitoring work provided an important reference point in subsequent action, including litigation.[14]

Internal political reactions by the junta to international exposure, including 'disingenuous explanations' and efforts to 'self-amnesty' and destroy evidence prior to leaving office, led to a further 'outcry of repudiation in Argentina and from many western states', and with it the formation of allies for the human

---

[9] See MJS Oliveira, *Poder Judicial y Dictadura. El Caso de la Morgue Judicial* (Buenos Aires, Editores Del Puerto, 2011) available at www.cels.org.ar/web/wp-content/uploads/2016/10/Poder-judicial-y-dictadura.pdf.

[10] Amnesty International, *Report on an Amnesty International Mission to Argentina 6-15 November 1976* (17 March 1977) available at www.amnesty.org/en/documents/amr13/083/1977/en/;/ and the report of NY Bar Association's mission chaired by Orville Schell and Judge Marvin Frankel, published in 1978.

[11] The IACommHR made an *in loco* visit to Argentina. For more information, see *Report on the Situation of Human Rights in Argentina*, OEA/ Ser.L/V/II.49, doc. 19 corr.1 (11 April 1980).

[12] See 'Memoria Abierta' (Open Memory) available at www.memoriaabierta.org.ar/materiales/documentos_historicos.html.

[13] M Pinto, 'The Role of the Inter-American Commission and Court of Human Rights in the Protection of Human Rights: Achievements and Contemporary Challenges' (2013) 20 *Human Rights Brief* 34.

[14] Ibid.

rights movement and for the process of truth and justice that would also prove instrumental following transition.[15]

B. Responses Following the Restoration of Democracy

The dictatorship came to an end and gave way to democratic governance in 1983. Successor administrations have engaged, to varying degrees and in diverse ways, with accountability for torture and enforced disappearance, making use of 'the complete repertoire of procedures included in the transitional justice menu'.[16] A few stages in this process, of relevance to litigation, are worth highlighting.

The first was the creation of the CONADEP by the first democratic government under President Raul Alfonsin. The Commission was more limited in scope, powers and modus operandi than many truth commissions, but nonetheless received and exposed information and complaints concerning disappearances specifically, and in this context, instances of torture in detention.[17] Notably for present purposes, it was explicitly contemplated from the outset that the Commission, which lacked powers to subpoena or compel, would send relevant information it uncovered to the justice system, paving the way for a potentially mutually reinforcing relationship between the Commission and the courts.

Alongside the CONADEP report were the trials of the military juntas in 1985, criminal prosecutions brought against the highest level commanders accused of kidnapping, torture, theft, murder, breaking and entering and forgery of documents.[18] The trials were a moment of enormous political-institutional significance within Argentina and beyond[19]—representing a victory for law over

---

[15] eg Human Rights Watch report on the 'Final Document on the Struggle Against Subversion and Terrorism', Vol 4, Issue 11 (23 October 1992); J Mendez, 'Reluctant Partner: The Argentine Government's Failure to Back Trials of Human Rights Violators', Human Rights Watch Report (December 2001) available at www.hrw.org/reports/2001/argentina/argen1201-04.htm#P218_57995.

[16] Smulovitz, '"I can't get no satisfaction"' (n 6). This included commissions of enquiry, domestic and extraterritorial criminal trials, international human rights cases, public apologies by individuals and institutional actors, reparation schemes and monetary damages, lustration, public commemoration and the establishment of commemorative monuments, spaces and dates.

[17] Its mandate was focused on investigation and documentation of disappearances, but in practice embraced a broader range of torture and CIDT.

[18] L Filippini, 'Criminal Prosecution in the Search for Justice' in CELS/ICTJ Report, *Making Justice: Further Discussions on the Prosecution of Crimes against Humanity in Argentina* (2011) 11, available at www.cels.org.ar/web/wp-content/uploads/2011/10/makingjustice.pdf; JE Mendez 'Truth and Partial Justice in Argentina: An Americas Watch Report' (New York, Americas Watch Committee, 1987) and 'Truth and Partial Justice in Argentina: An Update' (New York, HRW, April 1991) available at www.hrw.org/sites/default/files/reports/argen914full.pdf commenting on the later amnesties and pardons.

[19] Filippini, 'Criminal Prosecution in the Search for Justice' (n 18), eg, describes the conviction of those bearing most responsibility for human rights violations during the democratic government as unprecedented and notes that it marked a turning point in worldwide efforts toward transitional justice. Both the trials and the *Nunca Más* report (n 2), helped consolidate the rule of law in Argentina and, at the same time, gave weight and credibility to the claims of victims and their families for investigating other crimes.

power by demonstrating the ability of the ordinary courts (applying regular criminal offences in the penal code)[20] to judge those who had wielded such enormous destructive power.[21] By focusing on 'paradigmatic cases', the trials exposed the patterns of illegal conduct and the structures used to systematically implement state policy. They authoritatively dismissed the alternative narratives advanced in defence arguments based on the notion of 'just war'. As such, it has been noted:

> In addition to its juridical consequences, the trial gave credibility to the narratives of the past; put beyond suspicion the accounts of the witnesses and became an effective mechanism for the historical and political judgment of the dictatorial regime.[22]

The juntas trial was followed daily on television and newspapers, and had its own paper, *El Diario del Juicio*, specifically dedicated to covering its development, maximising the social impact of the trials.[23]

The National Chamber of Criminal and Correctional Appeals ultimately sentenced the military junta of Jorge Videla and Emilio Massera to life imprisonment based on the analysis of 709 cases presented at trial, and other participants were given lesser custodial sentences, and all were disqualified from office for life.[24] A powerful message emerged as to the possibility, and importance, of high-level individual accountability. Argentina was one of the few countries in the world at this stage that had successfully prosecuted its military in domestic courts following transition to democracy. These measures served as a reference for many later democratic transitional processes in other countries.[25] Internally, one interesting impact of this early litigation was that, instead of closing the accountability question, it fed the demand for justice. Greater available information, increased confidence in the potential of the courts and the rule of law, and enhanced 'weight and credibility' for the claims of victims and their families all contributed to the imperative around further investigation.[26] The Juntas Court itself recommended

---

[20] Torture was criminalised for the first time in 1958 in the Penal Code. It has been noted that 'the trials also demonstrated the capacity of the judicial system to administer justice in the context of political conflict, and its autonomy from political power'; Smulovitz (n 6); Filippini (n 18).

[21] It has been noted that 'the trials also demonstrated the capacity of the judicial system to administer justice in the context of political conflict, and its autonomy from political power'; Smulovitz (n 6); Filippini (n 18).

[22] Smulovitz (n 6).

[23] Ibid.

[24] Orlando Agosti, 4 years and 6 months in prison; Roberto Viola, 17 years; Armando Lambruschini, 8 years; Omar Graffigna and the members of the third junta—Leopoldo Galtieri, Jorge Anaya and Basilio Lami Dozo—were acquitted.

[25] K Sikkink and C Booth Waling, 'Argentina's Contribution to Global Trends in Transitional Justice' in N Roht-Arriaza and J Mariezcurrena (eds), *Beyond Truth and Justice: Transitional Justice in the New Millennium* (Cambridge, Cambridge University Press, 2006); and 'The Impact of Human Rights Trials in Latin America' (2007) 44 *Journal of Peace Research* 427; Filippini (n 18); see also Memoria Abierta, '530 hours: the audiovisual file of the Juntas trials (Argentina 1985)' available at: www.memoriaabierta. org.ar/juicioalasjuntas/ (in Spanish).

[26] Filippini ((n 18) at 13: 'Both the trials and the Never Again [Nunca Más] report helped consolidate the rule of law in Argentina and, at the same time, gave weight and credibility to the claims of victims and their families for investigating other crimes'.

following up on the leads it had gathered about others accused of further involvement in human rights violations.[27]

This momentum towards justice experienced major setbacks in 1986 and 87 however, with the adoption of the *Punto final* (Full Stop) and *Obediencia Debida* (Due Obedience) laws.[28] In an apparent response to perceived threats from the military, the Alfonsin government imposed a time limit for prosecution, on the one hand, and amnestied those who had been 'following orders', on the other. In practice, these laws provided a generalised amnesty and led to the closing of most of the hundreds of investigations that were pending at the time.[29] A further critical blow came between 1989 and 1990 when, again arguing the need for national peace, President Carlos Menem pardoned the military leaders convicted in the 1985 juntas trials and the few individuals who remained under investigation for acts not covered by the amnesties.[30]

C. Evolving Strategies in the Face of Impunity Laws

In the context of the impunity laws, criminal trials ground to a halt,[31] and victims and NGOs sought out 'alternative ways to achieve justice'.[32] Litigation and other strategies had to adjust to the obstacles and opportunities that the reduced legal and political framework presented. First, they focused on exploiting gaps in the impunity laws, by pursuing accountability for the abduction of babies of the tortured and disappeared, which were not covered by the amnesties. This turned out to constitute a critical loophole through which justice would eventually squeeze, as discussed below. Through these cases, civil society actors obtained information and access to disappeared children and, in some cases, the accountability of those responsible.

Second, while the possibility of criminal prosecution for torture and CIDT or disappearance was blocked, creative legal action pressed the courts to accept the 'right to truth' of the relatives and of society more broadly, alongside the right of the relatives to bury and mourn their dead (*derecho a duelo*) and the duty to investigate. As discussed under section III below, the courts accepted these rights,

---

[27] Smulovitz (n 6); Filipini (n 18) at 13–14.

[28] 'The "Full Stop" Law established a peremptory term after which it would not be possible to file criminal complaints for human rights violations, and the "Due Obedience" Law established an irrefutable legal presumption that lower ranking officers were not punishable because they were following orders'; Filippini (n 18) at 14.

[29] Filippini (n 18) at 14.

[30] Smulovitz (n 6).

[31] There were only 12 trials between 1987 and 2000, according to the Fiscal Unit of Coordination. Data available at www.mpf.gov.ar/docs/Links/DDHH/informe_de_la_web_diciembre_2012.pdf. See L Balardini, 'The Long Struggle for Accountability in Argentina. The Role of Civil Society's Activism and State Actors', 2014 Congress of the Latin American Studies Association (Chicago, 2014).

[32] Smulovitz (n 6).

notwithstanding the inability to prosecute or punish those responsible. The 'truth trials' that began in 1995 provided a framework to produce evidence and information that was important in its own right, and which would prove critical when subsequent criminal proceedings were eventually reactivated.

Third, in light of these domestic obstacles, NGOs' work redoubled at the international level and regional fora came into their own. For example, the IACommHR responded to petitions challenging the impunity laws with a 1992 report,[33] finding that the amnesties and presidential pardons violated the obligation to investigate under the American Convention on Human Rights (ACHR). As discussed further under section III, petitions brought to the IACommHR also catalysed state policies on reparation. Although arguably an attempt by the government to appease the discontent that the amnesties and pardons had generated, these reparation schemes were important for victims and families, and they maintained a critical light on their rights and the state's obligations.[34]

In addition, while impunity laws prevented criminal prosecution at home, judicial processes commenced in France, Italy, Germany and Spain under 'universal jurisdiction'. The launching of these cases, and in particular the issuance of warrants of arrest by foreign judges, was described as sending shock waves through the Argentinian judiciary and beyond.[35] The government refused to extradite, but the impact was felt nonetheless. The limits on the ability of the impunity laws to close the accountability question had been clearly exposed, fuelling questions as to whether, if justice was to be done, it would not better be done at home than abroad.

International action was complemented with other domestic strategies such as public demonstrations to foment debate and build collective memory notwithstanding the block on criminal prosecution. Pre-established mechanisms for vetting officials were used to impede promotions and remove implicated members of the armed forces, police, judiciary and elected representatives.[36]

The Argentinian litigation experience to date, the nature and impact of which is described in more detail below, has to be understood in this context. It was only following a long period of national and international activism, further political transitions including failed coups that undermined military power,[37] shifts

---

[33] IACommHR Annual Report (1992–1993) No 28/92, OEA/Ser.L/V/II.83 Doc 14, available at www. cidh.oas.org/annualrep/92span/Argentina10.147.htm.

[34] See further under s III.D: reparation was first offered to comply with recommendations of the IACommHR but the executive branch subsequently decided to extend reparation to embrace more and more victims. Thus, international litigation triggered the adoption of a broader policy of reparation with greater effect.

[35] Interview Daniel Rafecas (Buenos Aires, 2016).

[36] CELS/ICTJ Report, 'Making Justice: Further Discussions on the Prosecution of Crimes against Humanity in Argentina' (2011) available at www.cels.org.ar/web/wp-content/uploads/2011/10/makingjustice.pdf.

[37] Several attempted coups took place in 1986 and 1990. The definitive repression of the 1990 coup is said to mark the end of real military influence in Argentine politics.

in government policy under the first government of Nestor Kirchner, and developments in international law and practice (such as the development of the ICC and the Pinochet universal jurisdiction case in 1998), as well as the incremental litigation steps noted above, that the impunity laws were eventually directly challenged. In this context in the Simón case—discussed below under section III— the Argentine courts ultimately found the laws unconstitutional *ab initio*, based on their incompatibility with human rights obligations.[38] After some back and forth between judicial and executive branches, Congress annulled the laws,[39] and paved the way for the reopening of a massive wave on-going criminal processes against hundreds of persons accused of torture, enforced disappearance and other crimes during dictatorship.[40]

By 2010 a congressional statement described the criminal prosecution of 'the State terrorism' as having become a consolidated and irreversible state practice.[41] Certainly, some controversy surrounding the trials remains, in particular regarding the extent and scope of future prosecutions.[42] However, the fact that within the polarised panorama of Argentinian politics, successive governments of different political complexions have not questioned the continuity or importance of the trials, may be a sign that support for them has become deeply rooted in culture and societal values.[43] Accountability has been described by one

---

[38] Human rights obligations have pre-eminence over statutes under the constitutional since the reform of 1994.

[39] During the De la Rua administration (1999–2001), Congress had debated a law to nullify the pseudo-amnesty laws, but eventually only 'repealed' them, which under the 'rule of leniency' in criminal law left them fully available to defendants. After the decisions of J Cavallo, Congress 'annulled' those laws with retroactive effect, and in turn the Federal Court of Appeals for Buenos Aires upheld Cavallo's decision and the matter went to the Supreme Court. In 2005, the Supreme Court upheld the decision on unconstitutionality.

[40] The trials therefore unfolded in the context of broader social and political processes pursuant to the state policy of 'memory', such as commemoration of sites that had functioned as clandestine centres, or the search for files, the establishment of special entities and programmes to facilitate and support prosecutions. eg establishment of the Procuraduría de Crímenes Contra la Humanidad (a Special Unit on Crimes Against Humanity which coordinated and supported prosecutors); the Program for Truth and Justice within the Ministry of Human Rights (which focused on action within the Executive Branch); and a bicameral Commission for the Identification of Economic and Financial Complicities during the dictatorship established within Congress.

[41] Statement of the Honorable House of Representatives, 57-P- 2010. See 'Diputados declaró "política de Estado" a los juicios por los crímenes de lesa humanidad' p 12 (12 May 2010) available at www.pagina12.com.ar/diario/ultimas/20-145567-2010-05-12.html.

[42] An editorial of the mainstream newspaper *La Nación* entitled 'No more revenge' ('*No más venganza*', 23 November 2015, available at www.lanacion.com.ar/1847930-no-mas-venganza) provoked strong reaction, including from *La Nación* staff themselves: 'We reject the logic that the editorial is trying to build (…). We, the workers of La Nación newspaper say YES to democracy, to the continuity of the trials for crimes against humanity, and say NO to oblivion. For MEMORY, TRUTH and JUSTICE'; 'Fuertes Repercusiones por un Editorial de La Nación' *La Natión* (24 November 2015) available at www.lanacion.com.ar/1848237-fuertes-repercusiones-por-un-editorial-de-la-nacion.

[43] This was somewhat borne out when in 2015 one of the first statements of the incumbent government of a different political persuasion (headed by Mauricio Macri) announced that the trials would continue.

commentator as beyond partisan politics and belonging to the 'common patrimony of the country'.[44]

III. The Nature and Cumulative Impact of Litigation on Enforced Disappearance in Argentina

Litigation of dictatorship violations in Argentina has been varied and versatile. It has utilised diverse methods, tools and fora domestically, while making good use of remedies on the international level to incentivise sluggish domestic institutions to provide solutions. Clustering the cases into several groups, the nature of the litigation pursued and its impact will be described briefly in relation to each group. The clusters of cases correspond to the different stages in the evolution of the human rights situation in Argentina, and the varying demands of victims, prevailing challenges, obstacles and opportunities at each stage. They reveal how the strategic focus, form and impact of the litigation has evolved and shaped the human rights landscape.

A. Laying the Groundwork: Litigation during Dictatorship

As noted in the preceding overview, even while the dictatorship endured there was a considerable amount of litigation which, despite the lack of judicial independence, the cost for lawyers[45] and the lack of success in securing the remedies sought, had significant impact. Offering protection was the key goal, and habeas corpus claims sought to stop the torture and suppress clandestine detention, or at least to create a chilling effect by showing some degree of oversight and pressure. The use of collective habeas corpus action pushed for investigation of disappearances. Over time, litigation evolved to become more politically targeted and strategic. Although broadly considered to have been unsuccessful in their immediate litigation objectives, those processes elicited information which was used inter alia in subsequent litigation, and exposed judicial failure to critical public and international attention.

B. Transition and Trying the Truth

It was, however, post-transition to democracy that litigation assumed a central role, and one that has steadily grown over time. At the outset, a primary goal was

---

[44] R Gargarella, 'El Silencio de los Intelectuales Kirchneristas' *La Nación* (26 July 2016) available at www.lanacion.com.ar/1921757-el-silencio-de-los-intelectuales-kirchneristas.

[45] The CONADEP report speaks to the persecution of lawyers during this period; see n 2 at pt 3 D.

to gain information—most urgently about the whereabouts and fate of missing persons, including babies born in detention and then abducted, as well as those responsible. As that information emerged, accountability became more important. The priority accorded to establishing individual responsibility appears to have been based on firmly enshrined values regarding the importance of criminal law in its own right. Moreover, for many, criminal prosecutions were seen as a means to complete the process of democratisation, strengthen the rule of law and guarantee non-repetition.[46] The litigation experience was not, however (and probably could not have been) the result of a carefully mapped strategy at the outset, so much as a flexible response to evolving priorities and opportunities:

> Mainly it was a quest for justice and knowledge about the truth of what had happened. No one ever thought about the possible consequences of the justice process. With the proceedings making progress, documents and connections were found; and other consequences of the process began to emerge.[47]

The significance of the juntas trials[48] in reasserting the judicial role, opening up democratic space and clarifying facts around the systematic nature of the repression and responsibility, has already been noted. As information unfolded, the trials led to demands for more investigations and ever greater accountability beyond the core hierarchy of the junta. When the investigations and prosecutions that began around the country were however cut short by the amnesty laws of the 1980s, strategic litigation came to the fore as a means of working around these laws and, ultimately, disabling barriers to accountability. This is the focus of the clusters of cases discussed in this section.

The first two clusters reveal ways in which victims and civil society groups adjusted to the narrower juridical space left for litigation after the amnesty laws and, for a time, managed to work *within it*. The third shows the amnesty laws being challenged directly, once the groundwork had been laid, and the time and conditions were adequate. The fourth exemplifies the very many reopened criminal cases that were the culmination of that whole process, these in turn representing the impact of earlier litigation. The chronology demonstrates the incremental approach to litigation impact in this context, before the next section explores the different experience of litigating on-going torture and CIDT in detention today.

Martin Abregu has noted that

> The impossibility of pursuing the authors of these crimes in criminal proceedings did not mean simply the closure of any kind of judicial intervention. On the contrary (...) [i]t was this need to know (in both of its aspects, the personal right of the relatives and the collective right of the whole community) that was presented to the courts, pleading the 'Right to the Truth.'[49]

---

[46] Filipini (n 18).

[47] Interview Carolina Varsky.

[48] CELS/ICTJ Report (n 36), at 8, describes the juntas trials as 'milestones in the collective understanding of the dimensions and impact of State terrorism'.

[49] Former director of the CELS Martín Abregú writing in 1995 CELS Annual Report; see in Human Rights Watch Report (n 15).

During the 1990s, when criminal accountability was blocked, victims and human rights organisations asserted a right of relatives and of society as a whole to know the truth about violations during dictatorship. This built on then nascent references to the right in the Inter-American human rights system (and in turn helped consolidate and entrench a right now recognised internationally).[50] On this basis, several cases pressed national courts to investigate instances of enforced disappearance and torture. As a Human Rights Watch report noted, this was in large part because it was

> the courts that had powers to obtain information from official sources, as well as to summon military and police personnel to testify. For the courts to assume this role, however, they first had to be convinced that the full stop and due obedience laws did not rule out further judicial investigation.[51]

The demands for the truth grew over time. As Hugo Cañón has pointed out, while the main rationale for these processes was the search for the fate of the disappeared, 'this brought with it the complementary and necessary questions of how, where, who, when'.[52] The cases were high in profile, led by respected and politically connected figures and either brought or supported by NGOs. As such, the early cases were selected to show the systematic practice of torture and enforced disappearance.

i. Mignone *Case*

The first was initiated by Emilio Mignone in relation to the enforced disappearance of his daughter Monica Mignone, after detention by the armed forces in May 1976. A judicial process concerning the investigation of her enforced disappearance had been truncated after the adoption of the impunity laws. The case led the Federal Chamber to acknowledge in 1995 that the relatives had a 'right to know the truth' as to the fate of the victims, and they ordered the armed forces to present files to the Court to enable it to reconstruct the necessary information. This would eventually have significant normative impact, paving the way for future cases. The armed forces met this remarkable judicial order with contemptuous silence, and

---

[50] See eg for cases in the Inter-American system, *Velásquez Rodríguez v Honduras* IACtHR Ser C No 4 (29 July 1988); *Barrios Altos v Peru*, Judgement (Merits) IACtHR Ser C No 75 (14 March 2001); *Myrna Mack Chang v Guatemala*, Judgement (Merits, Reparations and Costs) IACtHR Ser C No 101 (25 November 2003) 274–75; see for the right to truth in the European context and internationally eg ECtHR, *El-Masri v Macedonia*, Appl no 39630/09 (13 December 2012); *Husayn (Zubaydah) v Poland*, Appl no 7511/13 (24 July 2014); UNHCHR, Human Rights Resolution 2005/66, 'Right to the Truth' (20 April 2005) UN Doc E/CN.4/RES/2005/66; UNCommHR, Report, 'Study on the Right to Truth' (8 February 2006) UN Doc E/CN.4/2006/91; see also Annual Report of Special Rapporteur on the promotion of truth, justice, reparation and guarantees of non-recurrence, Pablo de Greiff (28 August 2013) UN Doc A/HRC/24/42 at 18–20.

[51] Human Rights Watch Report (n 15).

[52] Interview with Hugo Cañón (2005), prosecutor and part of Comisión Provincial por la Memoria; see Memoria Abierta, 'Juicios por la verdad' Audio-visual archives, available at www.youtube.com/watch?v=q4mx38FYmlA.

the Court was urged by Mignone to reiterate the order. In this context, a second important procedural development emerged, with enduring impact: given the significance of the right to truth, in Argentina and beyond, international NGOs (Center for Justice and International Law, CEJIL, and Human Rights Watch) decided to present joint *amicus curiae*, despite there being no procedure or practice in place in the Argentine legal system for such briefs at the time. The court accepted the *amicus* nonetheless, creating in effect a gateway to the generalised use of *amici curiae* in Argentine courts.

The armed forces still refused to comply with the order, simply asserting that they did not have any information regarding the fate of the victims. In July, the Chamber adopted a confusing resolution that stopped the investigation in light of the obstacles posed.[53] The case had however reopened the judicial process, established the right to know, and exposed the continuing rule of law deficit in which the security forces were beyond the reach of the courts.

ii. Lapacó *Case*

CELS followed up on the recognition of the right to know in the *Mignone* case with a case by Carmen Aguiar de Lapacó, co-founder of the Madres de la Plaza de Mayo and board member of CELS, concerning her daughter Alejandra Lapacó. The same Chamber again recognised the right to the truth, but this time went a step further by articulating the 'obligation' to reconstruct the past and to discover the facts concerning violations during the last dictatorship, based on international standards. It affirmed that the amnesty laws precluded the opportunity to prosecute and punish, but could not imply the culmination of the legal process.

The advance was again short-lived. The armed forces answered once again that they didn't have the information and, following the navy's objections, the Chamber stopped the process.[54] In response, Lapacó appealed to the National Supreme Court. After three years, in August 1998, the Supreme Court held that it would be pointless to allow the inquiry to be reopened. The ruling sent a clear message about the failure of Argentinian justice to deliver on rights that it had, itself, recognised. This required further strategic adjustment by civil society. Among the innovations was a reframing of the litigation (*Urteaga*) and resort to the regional level.

iii. Urteaga *Habeas Data Case*

In light of the limited results of the 'right to truth' cases, relatives of other disappeared persons chose to present the case in different terms: Facundo Urteaga brought a 'habeas data' action to help locate his missing brother. In October 1998,

---

[53] CELS, *Litigio Estratégico y Derechos: La Lucha por el Derecho* (Buenos Aires, Siglo XXI Editores, 2008) available at www.cels.org.ar/web/publicaciones/la-lucha-por-el-derecho-litigio-estrategico-y-derechos-humanos/.

[54] Human Rights Watch Report (n 15).

two months after the *Lapacó* decision, the National Supreme Court allowed victims to claim for information with habeas data actions. Significantly, the Supreme Court accepted the right to information about a relative's death as inherently linked to recognising the right to 'identity', which is in turn closely related to the right to human dignity.[55] The reframing breathed new life into litigation, consolidating and developing the jurisprudence on the right to know and its link with the protection of family members from torture and cruel, inhuman and degrading treatment.

iv. Lapacó *Case before the IACommHR*

In November 1998, Carmen Lapacó filed a petition with the IACommHR, accompanied by a symbolically broad array of human rights organisations.[56] The Commission declared the petition admissible in May 1999, thus creating impetus behind shifting government policy on the right to truth in Argentina. The Commission brokered a friendly settlement of the case with the Argentinian state, in which the state ultimately agreed to 'accept and guarantee the right to truth which consists of the exhaustion of all means to obtain clarification of what happened to disappeared persons'. The state accepted the obligation to continue judicial investigations regarding the fate of the 'disappeared', and the obligation of all arms of the state to cooperate. Thus, ultimately, through negotiations via the Inter-American Commission, the cases led to a policy shift towards recognition of the right to truth while breathing life into the judicial role en route.

In 1998, the Federal Appeal Courts in La Plata followed suit in clarifying that 'the right to truth and information about the victims whereabouts was not foreclosed by the pardons', and that 'investigation should continue to allow relatives to know the circumstances of their disappearances and the location of their remains'.[57]

v. The 'Truth Trials'

Processes to uncover the 'truth' began to take place all over Argentina,[58] with important direct and indirect impact. These processes provided clear recognition of the right to the truth, reasserted the centrality of the judicial role in the struggle over the historical truth, and served to 're-judicialise' the wrongs of the dictatorship era, despite the amnesty laws.[59] Along the way, as most military witnesses who were summoned refused to testify, and the armed forces refused to

---

[55] Human Rights Watch, 'The Truth Trials' (2001) www.hrw.org/reports/2001/argentina/argen1201-04.htm#P218_57995.

[56] The Grandmothers of Plaza de Mayo, Asamblea Permanente por los Derechos Humanos, CELS, CEJIL, Mothers of Plaza de Mayo, Relatives of Detainees-disappeared, Liga Argentina por los Derechos del Hombre, Movimiento Ecuménico por los Derechos Humanos and Servicio Paz y Justicia.

[57] Smulovitz (n 6).

[58] There is no clear data regarding their extent, but they are reported as having taken place in La Plata, Bahía Blanca, Neuquén, Rosario, Cordoba, Mar del Plata Salta, Jujuy and Mendoza.

[59] Smulovitz (n 6).

cooperate, and weak judicial responses, they also exposed the on-going weakness in judicial power and authority and generated debate and resistance concerning this critical dimension of the transition to democracy.

The truth trials contributed directly to revealing important facts and indirectly to identifying those responsible.[60] Through meticulous processes that peeled back 'file by file' the facts around individual cases, they unearthed a wealth of information about detention centres, reconstructed the fate of detainees-disappeared and those who had participated in and facilitated the torture and disappearances.[61] Some of the military who were summoned as witnesses, and were perhaps not fearful of prosecution, revealed important information on the nature of the crimes and perpetrators. The cases provided a framework for the production of evidence and information that would be of critical value in subsequent criminal proceedings. Testimonies given during the truth trials would later be admitted as evidence in the reopened criminal trials and in the challenges to the constitutionality of the amnesty laws.[62]

The testimonies of victims given during the trials, and in interview, make clear how these processes—however limited—catalysed and energised the search for justice. As María Esther Behrensquien, who testified in the truth trials, stated:

> [Y]ou knew they are searching for something positive, the path to justice. You began to readjust, acting with others with the right intentions. To be able to tell, to say the truth (…) that others should know the truth, it was liberating.[63]

Another victim Chicha Mariani described how they 'awakened, in desperate people in their bitter homes, a basis for hope'.[64] The truth trials therefore had an important impact in themselves, providing an alternative road to achieve some kind of reparation and informal justice for victims in the face of obstacles, while also 'set[ting] the foundation for future developments'.[65]

C. Universal Jurisdiction Cases

While those responsible for torture and CIDT in dictatorship were protected from criminal accountability in Argentina by the amnesty laws, judicial proceedings advanced elsewhere based on the principle of passive personality (or victim nationality) and universal jurisdiction. For the most part these processes were 'trials in absentia'.[66] The first was in France of Alfredo Astiz for the

---

[60] For more information, see H Cattani, 'La Llamada "Búsqueda de la Verdad" por los Tribunales Federales de la Ciudad Autónoma de Buenos Aires' (2007) 8 *Revista de Derecho Penal y Procesal Penal* 1461–70; and E Mignone, 'Editorial: El derecho a la verdad' (July–August 1998) 10 *CELS Newsletter*.

[61] Interview with Hugo Cañon (n 62).

[62] Smulovitz (n 6).

[63] Memoria Abierta, 'Juicios por la verdad' (n 62).

[64] C Mariani, 'Madre de Plaza de Mayo', in Memoria Abierta (n 62).

[65] Filippini (n 18).

[66] Such trials are permitted in many, but not all, civil law systems and allow for trial without the presence of the defendant, when he is a fugitive or a resident of another country and extradition is not possible.

torture and disappearance of two French nuns. The particularly insidious facts of the case attracted international attention: Astiz had assumed a false identity and pretended to be the brother of a disappeared person to infiltrate a church group and participate in the kidnapping. Astiz was sentenced to life imprisonment in France, but never served his sentence because the Argentine government rejected his extradition, generating international tensions and pressure.[67]

The major-general in charge of the so-called war against subversion in the capital, Guillermo Suárez Mason, was then investigated in Germany and Italy. In December 2001, the Italian judiciary sentenced Suárez Mason and Santiago Omar Riveros[68] in absentia for kidnapping, torture and murder of Italian citizens. Pressure grew on the Argentine government to extradite or prosecute in accord with the international principle *aut dedere aut judicare*, but it refused.

In 1996, the Spanish Audiencia Nacional (National Court) commenced investigations into Argentine military for crimes of terrorism and genocide (in accordance with the Spanish criminal code) and in 1999, Judge Baltasar Garzón indicted 98 Argentine military officers and issued arrest warrants.[69] In an unexpected and critical development, Adolfo Scilingo presented himself voluntarily to testify before Judge Garzon. Scilingo acknowledged having participated personally in the 'death flights',[70] and provided details of the nature and extent of the state policy of repression. Based on his confession, the Court sentenced Adolfo Scilingo to 640 years in prison.[71] He was the first Argentine military officer present when tried abroad for crimes committed during the dictatorship.

The *Scilingo* judgment had an impact far beyond Argentina or Spain: it made an important contribution to international practice and jurisprudence on universal jurisdiction, albeit emerging from unusual circumstances: an individual presented himself before a foreign court and, along with other cases,[72] helped to catalyse a growth era in universal jurisdiction globally.[73]

---

[67] He was also tried in absentia in Sweden for his role in the disappearance of Swedish citizen Dagmar Hagelin.

[68] Major general and commander of Comando de Institutos Militares (Command of Military Institutes).

[69] Garzón issued international arrest warrants for 48 of them in December 1999 and in September 2001 he continued the pressure by issuing 18 new arrest warrants for Argentine military officers and civilians.

[70] The practice of drugging victims and dropping them from aircraft over the Rio de la Plata and Atlantic Ocean.

[71] It considered crimes against humanity, murder and unlawful detention the School of Naval Mechanics (Escuela Superior de Mecánica de la Armada, ESMA), sentence was April 2005, upheld in 2007.

[72] See eg extradition from Mexico to Spain of Ricardo Cavallo, another navy officer and part of the ESMA task force. Mexico thus recognised the principle of universal jurisdiction. Regrettably Cavallo spent 5 years in prison in Spain without trial, and was later extradited to Argentina, where he has been convicted.

[73] There has been a slowing of that process as universal jurisdiction cases against powerful individuals has caused political backlash and restrictions in the doctrine in recent years.

This litigation once again spurred renewed efforts to secure further 'truth' in Argentina and provided evidence to be used in later criminal processes in Argentina. Together with other universal jurisdiction processes, these cases sent a resounding message that the amnesty laws were not the end of the line and that impunity for egregious crimes could not be guaranteed: 'International cases generated pressure to the national government to judge crimes against humanity, by the threat that if not, other countries could do it'.[74] For victims and civil society the universal jurisdiction cases generated mixed results. On the one hand, not everyone had the opportunity to give testimony before Judge Garzón, and on the other, these processes were inevitably less accessible and further removed from the victims than domestic processes. Nevertheless, one victim noted:

> [T]he trial of Mr. Scilingo gave us a lot of hope. In Argentina, we believed we would never be able to have justice. I must say that after the opening in Spain of the Scilingo case, we knew there would be an impact in Argentina. Why had somebody been tried outside of Argentina, when everything had happened in Argentina?[75]

The timing of the cases was also significant, as they unfolded—awkwardly—alongside broader developments in the system of international justice, including the adoption of ICC statute, in which Argentina had been actively involved as a core 'like-minded' state friendly to the court. The cases therefore created tensions within government, just as the requests for extradition sent shock waves through the judiciary and created tensions between the executive and other arms of the state.[76] As a state proud of its nascent democratic credentials and human rights profile, the international and transnational criticism by regional bodies and foreign courts riled. By way of indirect impact then, these cases contributed to the development of international networks that would assist and strengthen domestic processes in due course. They created pressure and ultimately facilitated the challenging of the amnesty laws and the reopening of the criminal processes in Argentina. The Argentinian experience is a prime example of what Lutz and Sikkink[77] referred to as the dynamic 'boomerang' effect of the transnational justice network, by creating pressure on states from afar and ultimately contributing to justice being brought back home to Argentina.[78]

---

[74] Carolina Varsky interview.

[75] Carla Artes, detained with her mother at 9 months old then transferred to a family; she was a witness in the *Scilingo* case, speaking in 2009. She also noted: 'In my specific case, Mr. Rufa, was condemned to 9 months for forging public documents. Not even for the disappearance of people, or abduction, or being a perpetrator in an illegal camp?'; REDRESS/fidh Conference Report, 'Universal Jurisdiction Trial Strategies: Focus on Victims and Witnesses' (November 2010) 17 available at www.redress.org/Universal_Jurisdiction_Nov2010.pdf.

[76] Daniel Rafecas interview.

[77] E Lutz and K Sikkink, 'The Justice Cascade: The Evolution and Impact of Foreign Human Rights Trials in Latin America' (2001) 2 *Chicago Journal of International Law* 1.

[78] ME Keck and K Sikkink, *Activists Beyond Borders: Advocacy Networks in International Politics* 2 (Ithaca, Cornell University Press, 1998).

D. Pursuing Reparation: Nationally and Internationally

Economic reparation does not emerge strongly in the Argentina litigation narrative, compared to criminal accountability, and less attention has been dedicated to this type of litigation and its impact. While obtaining compensation does not appear to have been a priority for NGOs (who at times showed some resistance to embracing compensation as a key part of reparation[79]) or for victims, the damages litigation in Argentina has nonetheless had important consequences.

Post transition to democracy, many compensation claims were rejected on the basis that civil actions were subject to a two-year statute of limitations. This was challenged by prisoners released before the military dictatorship came to an end, on the basis that they had been unable to initiate legal action before democracy was re-established. This was accepted in some cases, and not in others, leading to considerable uncertainty and inconsistency.[80] The issue reached the Supreme Court, which upheld the statute of limitations running from the moment the prisoner was released. Without justice domestically, the opportunity for strategic engagement of the IACommHR arose, and in 1989 a petition was presented by a group of applicants,[81] arguing that their right to due process had been violated.

Political factors were critical to the way this litigation unfolded. Firstly, a new government came in in the same year in which the claims were made, headed by Carlos Menem, himself a former political prisoner who had won a civil case for damages against the state. In a hearing at the IACommHR, state representatives indicated that the Menem government 'was not necessarily in disagreement with petitioners' and 'wanted to offer adequate compensation'.[82] According to a high-level official at the time, President Menem's intention was,

> on the one hand, to earn the respect of the Organization of American States (OAS) by complying with the decisions of its institutions, and on the other, to implement a policy that would redress his own former colleagues involved in political activism who had been, just as he, victims of the dictatorship.[83]

Not insignificantly, his positive approach to restitution overlapped with the controversial decision to pardon the military officers convicted by the juntas trials in the name of 'reconciliation'. The government agreed to compensate and victims and families dropped their cases. In an example of how litigation gains can have an effect for more than just the immediate petitioners, the laws that were passed to enable the compensation embraced a broader category of beneficiaries, and

---

[79] Guembe, 'Economic Reparations for Grave Human Rights Violations' (n 7).

[80] Ibid.

[81] The first demand was presented on 15 February 1989. The demandants were: Miguel Vaca Narvaja, Bernardo Bartoli, Guillermo Alberto Birt, Gerardo Andrés Caletti,; Silvia Di Cola, Irma Carolina Ferrero de Fierro, José Enrique Fierro, María Ester Gatica de Giuliani, Héctor Lucio Giuliani, Rubén Héctor Padula, José Mariano Torregiani and Guillermo Rolando Puerta.

[82] IACtHR Report 1/93 on the Friendly Settlement Procedure, IACHR Annual report 1992–93, OEA/Ser.L/V/II.83 (12 March 1993).

[83] Guembe ((n 76).

more comprehensive economic reparations have evolved since.[84] Institutions were established to implement the reparatory measures.[85] In an important symbolic as well as practical step, victims received a sum equivalent to the maximum daily wage given to the highest-level personnel of the national government for every day of their detention. In the cases of people who had died or suffered serious injuries during detention, the restitution was higher.[86]

The reparation laws and processes created their own challenges. Some related to practical issues of proof, given the clandestine nature of the detention, torture and enforced disappearances, and the processes were blocked when families insisted that the disappeared person could not be declared dead until his or her body was returned.[87] These obstacles led to laws recognising a status of 'absent by enforced disappearance', enabling the cases to proceed.[88]

But other challenges related to discomfort on the part of NGOs and some victims and survivors themselves, with economic compensation. Reflecting this ambivalence, Martín Abregú, Executive Director of CELS when the law was passed, recalled that:

> Economic reparations were very difficult to conceive and discuss by human rights organizations. For instance, when Law 24.411 was passed,[89] CELS decided to provide legal assistance for the victims who decided to claim for reparation. As Director of the Center, I proposed to the board of directors to make this decision known publicly so that the families knew that they could find technical assistance with us. However, the board decided against it for fear of giving the impression that our center profited from this problem.[90]

The impact of damages processes is necessarily curtailed in a context in which it has been said that 'human rights organizations feared the State was exchanging money for impunity and silence about the past'.[91] It was thus said that damages were considered 'tainted' or 'cursed money' by some of the children of the disappeared.[92] This created a degree of division which has been counter-productive in the restorative process for victims. There does not seem to have been

---

[84] National executive branch decree No 70/91 passed on 10 January 1991. Beneficiaries of this decree were persons who under state of siege had been in the custody of the national executive branch, and who had filed a claim. See also Ley de Desaparición Forzada de Personas (Law No 24.043) of November 1991. Through judicial interpretation, the scheme was expanded to cover persons in exile as well as in detention for example. See Guembe (n 7).

[85] Consejo Federal de Derechos Humanos.

[86] Compensation was paid in the form of bonds of consolidation of the public debt.

[87] Guembe (n 7).

[88] In response to these questions, some human rights organisations proposed as a condition that the victims of this crime not be declared dead, but absent by forced disappearance which was accepted. Law No 24.321 of 11 May 1994 resulted in the creation of a new civil status: absentee by forced disappearance; Smulovitz (n 6).

[89] This law established economic reparation for relatives from enforced disappeared persons during dictatorship.

[90] Interview held on 1 August 2002 and Guembe (n 7).

[91] Smulovitz (n 6).

[92] Guembe (n 7).

the commitment or the ability to address these tensions to maximise the positive impact of reparations.

> Sadly enough, these objections to the reparations policy did not translate into a dialogue or discussion that could have produced a collective way of addressing the issue. The debate within the human rights movement on this subject was shy, cryptic, and hampered by a strong sense of guilt by the families.[93]

Given that economic reparation was not a focus of the Argentine strategic litigation, it is remarkable that just a few petitions by a few individuals, to the Argentine courts and IACommHR, gave rise to one of the largest reparation schemes on the continent—a few snowflakes turning into an avalanche. This reparation policy continued, and the number of victims that qualified for reparation continued to expand, under subsequent governments.[94] Despite the often fraught differences of view regarding compensation, it has been suggested that these reparations have been of key importance, for the individuals affected and beyond:

> Neither truth nor justice, including economic reparations, has the virtue of repairing the loss of a victim, but measures such as these do provide recognition for the victims, and for the pain and suffering experienced by their families. This quality of economic reparations influences both individual and collective processes of addressing the past, and in this sense, it has a fundamental value.[95]

E. The *Simón* Case: Unconstitutionality of Amnesty Laws

The truth trials in Argentina, the orders to proceed to trial in European countries, the arrest of Chilean dictator Augusto Pinochet in London in 1998 and the anti-impunity wave on the international level, reflected inter alia by the adoption of the ICC Statute the same year, are among the national and international environmental factors that paved the way for the reopening of criminal cases in Argentina. The immediate trigger was however a particular piece of litigation challenging the constitutionality of the amnesty laws. The relevance of timing in the decision to pursue that litigation was described in this way:

> Pinochet was arrested in London, the truth trials were making progress throughout the country, Judge Garzón's extradition requests made … at that moment we understood that the conditions were given, and we were coming up on 25 years since the military coup. Then we submitted the repeal request and in March 2001 Judge Cavallo declared the laws null and void.[96]

---

[93] Ibid.

[94] Under Nestor Kirchner and Cristina Fernandez de Kirchner's governments this included persons who were exiled, children born in captivity and babies abducted and illegally adopted. Statutes of limitation came to be overturned in this context too.

[95] Guembe (n 7).

[96] Horacio Verbitsky, journalist and long-time president of CELS (presentation during the VIII Seminario Internacional de Políticas de la Memoria, Centro Cultural Haroldo Conti, Buenos Aires, 24 September 2015) available at www.youtube.com/watch?v=p1dcFIyXpHI. He also notes 'there was going to be a lot of social mobilization on the anniversary of the coup'.

As already noted, the offence of child abduction was not covered by the amnesty laws and the pursuit of legal action for the kidnapping of children born in captivity was one of the ways in which human rights organisations sought to avoid the paralysing effect of these laws. In 1998, the Grandmothers of the Plaza de Mayo filed a case against police officers Julio Héctor Simón and Juan Antonio Del Cerro for abducting eight-month-old Claudia Victoria Poblete[97] and handing her over to an army colonel and his wife. The case sought to recover the identity of the child and reunify the family, and to ensure criminal accountability for Poblete's abduction. But in so doing it also sought to undermine the impunity laws by demonstrating their arbitrariness and absurdity—the authors could be charged for abducting the child but not for the kidnapping, torture and murder of her parents. At the end of 2000, therefore, with the positive environmental factors highlighted above in place, CELS filed a legal action concerning the disappearance and torture of the baby's parents. Arguing that she could not have been abducted without the previous enforced disappearance of her parents, it used the case as a vehicle to request the repeal of the 'Full Stop' Law and the Law of 'Due Obedience'.

In 2001, the Federal Court investigating the case declared the impunity laws unconstitutional and indicted Julio Héctor Simón for crimes against humanity, remanding him in custody. The Federal Court of Appeals upheld the decision, basing its decision on international obligations, citing paragraphs of the Inter-American Court's ruling in the *Barrios Altos* case verbatim. This paved the way for the congressional decision in 2003 that the 'Full Stop' and 'Due Obedience' laws were to be declared null.[98] The Supreme Court subsequently confirmed the nullification of the amnesty laws.

The significance of this decision is clear. Julio Héctor Simón was sentenced on 11 August 2006 to 25 years' imprisonment and absolute disqualification for life. The principal obstacles to accountability were effectively removed, once declared unconstitutional. International standards on the obligation to investigate crimes against humanity and the inapplicability of amnesty provisions and prescription to these crimes was incorporated and consolidated. As such, the case is cited often in national and international cases, as well as in the context of negotiations and discussions on the lawful scope and effect of amnesty laws, as witnessed recently in the Colombian context.[99] The case also had a significant impact on civil society, providing the basis for its active engagement in promoting the criminal trials that it had made possible through it initiative in this case. It has therefore been described as positioning NGOs as leading agents with broad social legitimacy,

---

[97] Her parents were kidnapped in November 1978 and sent to the clandestine detention centre 'El Olimpo'.

[98] Law No 25.779.

[99] Eg ex-president Uribe wrote to the FARC noting the outcome of the experience in the southern cone ('Con Críticas Respondió Uribe a Invitación que le Hizo "Timochenko" para Hablar de Paz' Radio Caracol (16 May 2016) and the Colombian Constitutional Court has also cited this jurisprudence (Expediente D-9499, Sentencia C-579/13, 28 August 2013, available at www.corteconstitucional.gov.co/relatoria/2013/C-579-13.htm).

whose innovative and persistent search for loopholes and possibilities, and refusal to accept the impossibility of justice, had paid off.[100]

The 2005 judgment unlocked the justice process in Argentina. It led to the federalisation of the reopened trials for crimes against humanity. The most apparent quantitative impact of the Simón case is the vast volume of on-going criminal cases referred to below.

F. Reopened Trials and the Expanding Scope of Prosecution

A massive body of criminal trials for torture and disappearance during dictatorship has unfolded in Argentina since the amnesty laws were set aside.[101] Judgment has been rendered in the case of 762 individuals (resulting in 692 convictions and 70 acquittals) and 847 defendants are awaiting trial. As a result, Argentina has had more 'human rights trials' than any other country in the world.[102] Human rights organisations are broadly credited with having provided the impetus behind the trials—making them happen and then effectively acting as private prosecutors, representing victims '*querellantes*' before the courts, as well as investigating, facilitating and supporting the trials from within and without.

This litigation is on-going, and it would be ambitious, and perhaps premature, to seek to evaluate the overall impact of these historic processes. A few observations on the nature and effect of these reopened trials are however merited. Unlike the juntas trials that focused on the leadership core, the current trials have expanded their reach, enabling the exposure and prosecution of a growing number of those responsible—whether as military, civilian, state or non-state actors—for enabling and executing torture and cruel, inhuman and degrading treatment and broader repression during dictatorship. As such, the historical narrative that unfolds is a broader one than that which emerged around the responsibility of the military junta and the policy of disappearance of the CONADEP truth process or juntas trials and embraces a fuller range of responsibility.

The reopened cases have also enabled a more comprehensive look at criminal activity, including the sexual offences that were a systematic practice in detention during dictatorship but not the focus of the first tranche of prosecutions. There were references to sexual abuse presented in the juntas trials and repeated in the

---

[100] Smulovitz (n 6).

[101] As of 2016, judgments have been rendered in the case of 762 individuals (resulting in 692 convictions and 70 acquittals) and 847 defendants are awaiting trial at time of writing. Another 261 suspects have been questioned, charges against 155 defendants were declared without merit, 44 cases were dismissed, 47 are fugitives and 362 died. For updated statistics, see Prosecutor of Crimes against Humanity of the Attorney General's Office, 'Informe Sobre Detenciones: Datos de la Procuraduría de Lesa Humanidad (March 2015–August 2016)' available at www.fiscales.gob.ar/wp-content/uploads/2016/09/Lesa_Informe_detenciones.pdf.

[102] Sikkink and Booth Walling 'Argentina's Contribution to Global Trends in Transitional Justice' (n 25); Smulovitz (n 6).

truth trials, but sexual violence had not been treated as separate crimes under the Argentine Criminal Code until a more gender-sensitive approach emerged with the new processes.[103]

One of the victims who came forward when the processes reopened accused Gregorio Rafael Molina—a former air force sergeant—of rape. The original trial judge found a lack of corroborating evidence to prosecute the defendant, but in September 2006 a ruling held that the victim's testimony could, in these circumstances, be sufficient. With this new procedural framework, in June 2010 Molina was convicted of rape and other crimes against sexual integrity committed in a clandestine detention centre and sentenced to life imprisonment.

The *Molina* case has been described as changing judges' perception and willingness to judge sexual crimes during dictatorship. It opened the courts for the first time to international jurisprudence from international criminal tribunals.[104] It triggered other sexual violence cases afterwards, which also incorporated international jurisprudence on sexual violence as a crime against humanity. Protocols were subsequently established for taking testimony in sexual violence cases, with lasting impact on the prosecution of these cases in other contexts. Notably, by highlighting the systematic practice of sexual violence during dictatorship, this and related cases made an important contribution to a historical narrative that has been lacking to date.[105]

Finally, it deserves emphasis that this new layer of criminal trials brought with it a greater focus on the victims' role:

> In the 1980s the focus of testimonies was aimed at proving the existence of a systematic plan of repression and at legally conceptualizing the notion of disappearance (...). An analysis of this experience has shown that the overall goal of proving illegal repression overshadowed the personal experiences that, while undeniably mentioned clearly remained in second place compared to the broad dimension of the systematic disappearance and extermination.[106]

---

[103] In this case, the traditional barriers to the advancement of sexual violence cases were overcome: the sexist character of the judiciary, the lack of sensitivity on the part of judicial officials, and issues linked to the production of proof, the nature of crime against humanity conception adopted regarding authorship and criminal participation. In addition, it was possible to overcome the tendency of judicial operators to subsume the crime of rape to the use of torture; Balardini, 'The Long Struggle for Accountability in Argentina (n 31); L Balardini, A Oberlin, L Sobredo 'Gender Violence and Sexual Abuse in Clandestine Detention Centers: A Contribution to Understanding the Experience of Argentina' in CELS/ICTJ Report, *Making Justice: Further Discussions on the Prosecution of Crimes against Humanity in Argentina* (2011) available at www.cels.org.ar/web/wp-content/uploads/2011/10/makingjustice.pdf.

[104] It cited the International Criminal Tribunals for Rwanda and Yugoslavia on sexual violence crimes, notably the *Akayesu* and *Foča* cases.

[105] The *Molina* case was recognised by the Gender Justice Observatory of Women's Link Worldwide (Colombian NGO), and selected as gold gavel winner; see Women's Link Wordwide Website, Case Summary, available at www.womenslinkworldwide.org/en/gender-justice-observatory/court-rulings-database/molina-gregorio-case-no-2086-and-joined-cases-gold-gavel-winner-2011.

[106] Balardini (n 31).

Several victims of sexual violence in particular have described the importance of the trials for them in reframing and processing what happened to them. This followed years of having minimised their personal sufferings, especially in relation to sexual violence, and having been labelled as 'traitors' for having had 'sexual relations' with their torturers. The trials provided an opportunity to state their experience, and to finally obtain recognition: 'just recently I could say it. I had never put it into words. We never told our families, to keep them from suffering'.[107]

Survivor statements for the first time focused on personal experience, which included gender-related abuses and harassment suffered. Unlike during the juntas trials, the political history of the victims was also no longer something they were warned to hide. By delinking their political activism from their rights as victims of torture in detention, the reopened criminal cases assume their part in the development of an appropriate approach to victimisation and attribution of blame.

On this journey, criminal law enforcement in respect of crimes of the past has been seen as closely bound up with democratic transition.[108] It has also been closely associated with institutional reform. For the army and navy, individual accountability has been thorough and the institutions themselves purged and reformed.[109] Other institutions have been less in the frame of criminal accountability, and have been subject to little reform. This includes institutions that had a less central, but still notable, role in torture during dictatorship and, sadly, which remain implicated in torture and ill-treatment in police stations and prisons today. The role of other state and non-state institutions—judges, ministers, priests and also businesspeople—who helped sustain the system are now, gradually, being subject to criminal process, opening up a broader panorama of truth regarding responsibility for torture.[110]

IV. Conclusions

The process of historic accountability in Argentina emerged from a confluence of factors, influenced at key junctures by litigation, alongside other strategies around

---

[107] Balardini, Sobredo and Oberlin, 'Gender Violence and Sexual Abuse in Clandestine Detention Centers' (n 112).

[108] Filippini (n 18); Smulovitz (n 6); CELS Annual Report (2015) available at www.cels.org.ar/web/publicaciones/derechos-humanos-en-argentina-informe-2015/; R Gargarella, 'El Contrato del Nunca Más ya no Rige Nuestra Vida Política' *La Nación* (7 July 2017) available at www.lanacion.com.ar/2040424-el-contrato-del-nunca-mas-ya-no-rige-nuestra-vida-politica, has described the issue as beyond partisanship.

[109] See R Diamint, 'El Control Civil de los Militares en Argentina' No 213 Nueva Sociedad (January-February 2008) available at www.nuso.org/articulo/el-control-civil-de-los-militares-en-argentina/. See also MF Saín, 'Las Fuerzas Armadas Frente a las "Nuevas Amenazas (1990–2001)"', Seminario Internacional 'Brasil e Argentina frente às novas ameaças', Universidade Estadual de Campinas (Campinas, 1– 2 August 2001).

[110] Ministerio de Justicia y Derechos Humanos de la Nación, 2015, *Responsabilidad empresarial en delitos de lesa humanidad: represión a trabajadores durante el terrorismo de Estado*, Infojus, Argentina.

memory, truth and justice, carried forward by a core coalition of state and non-state actors backed up by other actors nationally and internationally.[111] It has been a long, multi-staged journey, and far from linear: paths have been blocked, setbacks and diversions created, advances sometimes controversial, and the road ahead is not free from controversies as to the extent and duration of the reopened criminal processes either. But the experience shows how a range of strategies, national, foreign and international fora and actors have come together to produce an impressive cumulative effect over time.

Strategic litigation has been an important human rights tool, albeit among others. It has had an important normative impact, developing for example the right to truth that would later find its way across the continent and on the ECtHR as noted in another case study in Chapter 7. It enshrined international standards, including on the duty to investigate and accountability, in domestic law and practice, in decisions which in turn have been relied upon internationally. The relationship between national and international law was clarified and strengthened en route. Procedures were developed, including the possibility of *amicus* interventions in Argentinian courts, and innovations in the rules of procedure and evidence—designed to meet the challenges of multiple victims and the scale of the reopened dictatorship trials—had lasting (sometimes admittedly controversial[112]) impact on criminal procedure beyond cases of crimes during dictatorship.[113]

The impact on perpetrators, through criminal accountability, has been overwhelming. The sheer volume of individual convictions (2,166 defendants, 622 convicted, 57 acquitted) sends a strong anti-impunity message throughout Argentina and far beyond, symbolising the long arm of the law and its ability to hold individuals to account many years later. The development of the criminal investigations incrementally, to embrace new levels of responsibility beyond the original trials of higher echelons of the army and navy, while at times also controversial, established a fuller historical record as to forms of responsibility, individual, social, institutional and state.

Institutional reform has taken many forms, some clearly associated with litigation. Progressively litigation has strengthened a once shattered image and authority of the judiciary. Some entities were established to support the policy of truth justice and memory and to facilitate the reopened dictatorship cases. Programmes

---

[111] See eg CELS/ICTJ Report (n 36).

[112] One prosecutor in the ESMA cases, Mirna Goransky, resigned citing concern with due process infringements arising from some of these developments.

[113] C Varsky: 'The Judiciary was not prepared to investigate complex crimes and to develop hearings with more than two plaintiffs, so they made changes to adapt the system'. The new protocols and procedures for research and for taking victims' testimonies including in cases of sexual torture and cruel, inhuman and degrading treatment, Acordada 1/12, Reglas Practicas para Asegurar el Debido Proceso (19 March 2012) available at www.pjn.gov.ar/02_Central/ViewDoc.Asp?Doc=67148&CI=INDEX100; see 'Guía de Actuación para los Ministerios Públicos en la Investigación Penal de Casos de Violencia Sexual Perpetrados en el Marco de Crímenes Internacionales, en Particular de Crímenes de Lesa Humanidad', available at www.fiscales.gob.ar/lesa-humanidad/wp-content/uploads/sites/4/2015/06/Gu%C3%ADa-Violencia-sexual.pdf.

within the executive branch established mechanisms and vehicles to, for example, seek out information, accompany victims and stand as plaintiffs in criminal cases.[114] Specialised offices to investigate these cases were created at the General Attorney's Office and some local public prosecution offices,[115] among others.

Victim interviews reveal a range of impacts through the litigation processes at different stages. Along the way the importance of hope, and in providing support and developing networks has been emphasised. The trials themselves have been described as 'having a restorative effect as the victim can talk about the situation … and someone says 'this cannot happen again'.[116] Victims of rape during the Argentine dictatorship, who were labelled as 'traitors' and accused of romantic involvement with perpetrators, have been acknowledged through the judicial process as victims of sexual violence. One victim describes her ability to speak of the violations, and to address the 'guilt', only once the cases were underway. The litigation also led to compensation, and was an important catalyst to establishing (and shaping) economic reparation schemes for victims beyond the applicants in the relevant cases, though this has been hampered by an ambivalent attitude towards this aspect of reparation.

This progress was driven by the determination, and coordination, of victims, human rights organisations, impelled at key stages by sympathetic government and international political, donor and judicial support. These initiatives responded to context, and did what was possible, while influencing that context en route. In different ways, they ensured that at a minimum the pursuit of truth and justice remained at all times part of the Argentinean political scenario, until such times as it became active state policy, and eventually took hold in the fabric of the country. The results thus far have included a remarkable process of individual accountability, a gradual uncovering of a fuller truth, processes in which victims actively engage, in a way that contributes to international norms on accountability globally, and which, while imperfect, are broadly believed to have attributed towards consolidating democracy and the rule of law in Argentina.

There are undoubtedly also limitations in impact. While an impressive range of litigation has borne fruit in Argentina, compensation and disciplinary action tended to be ancillary to criminal cases, difficult to pursue in practice and deprioritised by civil society actors.[117] Where processes *have* been advanced to remove

---

[114] eg Truth and Justice Program, the victim's therapeutic center 'Ulloa', the national and local witness protection programs, among others. Most of these programs were created inside the institutional structure of the National Ministry of Justice and Human Rights, proposed by NGOs.

[115] Procuraduría de Crímenes contra la Humanidad Special Prosecutor office of Crimes against Humanity of the Attorney General's Office, see www.mpf.gob.ar/lesa/; and Special Unit for Child Appropriation During State Terrorism, see www.mpf.gob.ar/lesa/unidad-especializada-para-casos-de-apropiacion-de-ninos-durante-el-terrorismo-de-estado/.

[116] Interview Anabella Museri and Rosa Díaz Jiménez.

[117] Administrative action has been taken by the internal control department of Correctional Services, though this too has tended to follow criminal cases (Arruga; Barros Cisneros cases discussed in Duffy, n 1.).

perpetrators from office they were described as having had a profound impact not only on victims and perpetrators affected, but on other prison officers and on practice. This may suggest that, as some interviewees noted, use of administrative law may be a lesser explored aspect of litigation strategy. Likewise, while the focus on criminal law has been a crucial dimension of the impact of litigation in Argentina, it has also meant that the targets of litigation have principally been individuals, not state institutions. The institutional reform deficit that has been noted may be a by-product of this focus. The contribution to historical narrative is necessarily somewhat limited by the nature of criminal proceedings and the focus on individual responsibility.

A final sobering factor is the stark contrast and disconnect between the experience in relation to torture during dictatorship and torture and cruel, inhuman and degrading treatment in prisons today.[118] In a state that resoundingly asserted '*nunca más*',[119] torture in places of detention continues, and is reported by NGOs and international bodies as frequent and widespread. For some, this is associated with a lack of deep institutional reform;[120] reform was wide-reaching after the transition to democracy in the army and navy, closely linked to the criminal accountability and purging of many within those institutions, but not in the prison system more tangentially involved in dictatorship wrongs. In a country accredited as a champion of accountability, also striking are the levels of impunity in respect of torture today. In turn, the apparent attitudinal disconnect between the repudiation of torture of political opponents and indifference towards often socio-economically deprived 'common criminals' today, reflects the same insidious notions of 'enemy' and 'otherisation' that facilitated past crimes. This raises challenging questions as to the depth of the impact of litigation and other processes on the rejection of torture. Increasingly, there is an attempt by civil society to bridge that gap and to bring the perspective and experience that transformed responses to torture during dictatorship to bear on on-going torture and ill-treatment today.

---

[118] For a fuller discussion of these issues, and the impact of litigation on these issues, see Duffy, 'Strategic Litigation Impacts' (n 1). For an interesting recent analysis, see also DE Rafecas, *La Tortura y Otras Practicas Ilegales a Detenidos*, 2nd edn (Buenos Aires, Editores del Puerto, 2016).

[119] CONADEP report (n 2).

[120] An interviewee from Argentina, Rodrigo Borda, describes how 'the lack of institutional reforms after dictatorship set the conditions that allow torture to persist'.

9

Case Study—Litigating Palestinian Land Rights

I. Introduction

Alaa Mahajna describes Israel as 'among the most litigious societies in the world', noting that:

> Arabs in Israel are no exception [and] this is not a recent development; history shows that since the establishment of Israel in 1948, Palestinians have not hesitated to bring to the Supreme Court cases involving various aspects of their lives, including those connected directly to the core of the conflict, such as land issues.[1]

There has been abundant litigation over Palestinian land rights, among other serious rights-related issues, before Israeli courts. These land-related violations are inherently interlinked with the political issues at the heart of the conflict and the underlying injustice facing Palestinian people. The construction of 'the Wall' through Palestinian land, the on-going settlement expansion, punitive house demolitions, and evictions as part of the annexation of East Jerusalem, for example, have had a devastating impact on individuals, families and communities concerned, and ultimately on the potential feasibility and shape of a future Palestinian state. Understanding the impact of litigation on these issues is a complex, multi-layered endeavour, difficult to dissociate from the frustrations surrounding long-standing failures of political solutions.

While every situation is *sui generis*, it is tempting to speculate that human rights litigation on Palestine is uniquely challenging.[2] Palestinians in the Occupied Palestinian Territories (OPT) of the West Bank and Gaza have no independent judicial system in which to seek protection and redress for violations by Israel, beyond the Israeli court system.[3] While Palestinians frequently have recourse to

---

[1] A Mahajna, 'Litigation Within the Israeli Court System: A Double-Edged Sword' (May 2012) 13 *Jadal* 4, available at www.mada-research.org/en/files/2012/05/Jadal13/Eng/Alaa-Mahajna.pdf.

[2] See the next section on background challenges.

[3] Courts do exist for violations committed by the Palestinian Authority or Hamas in Areas A and B of the West Bank or in Gaza; however; the land rights litigation I explore in this study involves violations by Israel.

those courts, to seek injunctions, restitution or other remedial action, and sometimes compensation,[4] they face a range of obstacles that often entirely block access to court or which result in the judges 'almost never' finding in favour of Palestinian land claims.[5] While the chances of 'success'—favourable judicial resolutions upholding and enforcing Palestinian rights—are minimal, concerns have been expressed for many years as to the potential counter-productivity of litigation, including the legitimising impact of litigation in Israeli courts. Internationally, unlike for most other scenarios explored in other case studies, Israeli refusal to ratify conventions or accept the competence of supranational fora means there is a dearth of human rights mechanisms through which to plead the ineffectiveness of domestic remedies and to seek protection or redress. Where litigation opportunities *are* potentially available the political climate is so fraught that impediments to legal gains are pervasive.[6]

Whether rights litigation makes sense at all this context, and if so how it can be used strategically to create meaningful impact, are contested and complex questions. I had the opportunity to discuss some of these issues during visits to Palestine on consultancy contracts over the past two years, and to explore with some of the many committed survivors, lawyers and activists (Palestinian, Israeli and foreign) engaged in the long human rights struggle their experiences and perceptions of litigation. One of those consultancies specifically focused on reviewing policies and approaches to strategic human rights litigation (SHRL)—by an NGO funding and supporting land and property rights litigation in the West Bank—and offering advice and recommendations on understanding, measuring and improving its impact. Interviews brought to light a range of ways in which litigation has positively influenced change, alongside a depth of controversy around the utility and ultimate impact of litigation. Immediate responses to the question of how people engaged in litigation assess its impact to date varied considerably. There were those who described important and multi-faceted (albeit insufficient) benefits, direct and indirect, while others noted 'none at all', while questioning the legitimising role of litigation as 'possibly sustain[ing] the occupation'. This causes unease for lawyers, for whom the question arises, in litigator Michael Sfard's words, 'Am I a pawn in the greatest swindle of the Israeli occupation?'[7]

---

[4] As in other contexts, some interviewees noted extreme 'sensitivity' around the receipt of compensation from the Israeli state; this is relatively rarely therefore the prime objective of litigation.

[5] Interviewee lawyer in the OPT (2015) described his 'success rate' in winning cases as almost never. See below on obstacles such as non-justiciability as Adalah has released in 2013 a briefing paper explaining some of these. F El-'Ajou, 'Obstacles for Palestinians in Seeking Civil Remedies for Damages in Israeli Courts' (May 2013) Briefing Paper, Adalah—Legal Center for Arab Minority Rights in Israel, available at www.adalah.org/uploads/oldfiles/Public/files/English/Publications/Articles/2013/Obstacles-Palestinians-Court-Fatmeh-ElAjou-05-13.pdf.

[6] Transnational civil or criminal litigation before foreign courts has met with political resistance.

[7] M Sfard, *The Wall and the Gate: Israel, Palestine and the Legal Battle for Human Rights* (New York, Metropolitan Books, forthcoming 2018) Ch 1.

The sections that follow sketch out the background and challenges, and then identify some areas of discernible or potential impact and limitations in relation to human rights litigation on land issues at (1) the national and (2) the international levels. While providing few answers, it is hoped that the overview will help surface questions and contribute to the discussion on the role of judicial responses, and how to maximise them, in a deeply troubling context.

II. Background to Land Rights Litigation in Israeli Courts

The obstacles to litigating such politically charged issues as 'the land grab' in the OPT in Israeli courts are many and varied.[8] People I spoke to described the 'near impossibility' of directly and successfully challenging the legality of settlements, the Wall, the movement restriction regime, punitive house demolitions, and an unjust building permits and planning regime that forces people out of East Jerusalem.

Although according to Israeli law, Palestinians can access Israeli courts in respect of violations in the West Bank or Gaza, the reality is very different as a result of practical and legal hurdles that may block access to courts completely. In one blatant example, would-be litigants from Gaza had access to justice blocked by the simple fact of attendance being required in court proceedings in Israel and the inability to secure a permit to leave Gaza (with court proceedings notably not treated as one of the exceptional grounds justifying permits). Legal hurdles include tight time limits and restrictive statutes of limitation[9] on Palestinians bringing civil action within the OPT—restrictions that do not apply to other legal action in Israeli courts.[10]

Major controversy surrounding applicable law is another form of challenge that strongly influences the potential of rights litigation. Although both IHL and International Human Rights Law (IHRL) apply,[11] the state of Israel denies that

---

[8] These are touched on here but analysed in detail in academic literature and NGO reports: eg the work of academics such as David Kretzmer (*The Occupation of Justice: The Supreme Court of Israel and the Occupied Territories* (Albany, State University of New York Press, 2002)), practitioners such as Michael Sfard (*The Wall and the Gate* (n 7)) and NGOs such as al Haq (eg N Ayoub, *The Israeli High Court of Justice and the Palestinian Intifada: A Stamp of Approval for Israeli Violations in the Occupied Territories* (Ramallah, Al-Haq Organisation, 2004) 111).

[9] The statute of limitations is reduced in such cases to 2 years from the 7 years normally applicable.

[10] eg residents of the West Bank or the Gaza Strip must submit a notice of injury within 60 days of the event.

[11] See eg *Legal Consequences of the Construction of a Wall in the Occupied Palestinian Territory* (Advisory Opinion) [2004] ICJ Rep 136 and F D'Alessandra, 'Israel's Associated Regime: Exceptionalism, Human Rights and Alternative Legality' (2014) 30 *Utrecht Journal of International and European Law* 30.

IHRL applies to the West Bank,[12] and Israeli courts are rarely (and inconsistently) willing to engage meaningfully with international law argumentation.[13] Given the Supreme Court of Israel's ruling in several decisions that, in light of Israeli legislation, East Jerusalem is not 'occupied territory', but part of Israel, the obligations of an occupying power under IHL are also deemed not to apply.[14] Israeli domestic law, applied exclusively throughout the OPT, is in turn substantively weak on the protection of human rights, but weaker still is the military law applied specifically to many situations in which land issues arise in the OPT. This law is applied to Palestinians wishing to lodge claims regarding land and property in the OPT, while Israeli law has curiously been deemed applicable to Israeli settlers seeking to support their rights in the OPT.[15] The result is a weakened and contested legal toolkit for litigation.

Serious allegations arise regarding the independence and impartiality of the judiciary, and systemic discrimination in access to justice. In a context in which settlement expansion is a major source of violations, with which courts have refused to engage, the fact that several judges on the High Court are settlers is one striking manifestation of the judicial deficit.[16] On the other hand, it is often noted that there have been both extremely positive and extremely poor decisions on human rights issues in the past, as a result of which Israeli courts enjoy a strong reputation internationally on the grounds of some well-known principled judgments; some within the judiciary do still value their erstwhile international reputation.

---

[12] See eg Norwegian Refugee Council (NRC) Report, 'Driven Out: The Continuing Forced Displacement of Palestinian Residents from Hebron's Old City' (July 2013) 48, available at www. nrc.no/globalassets/pdf/reports/driven-out-the-continuing-forced-displacement-of-palestinian-residents-from-hebrons-old-city.pdf.

[13] The courts have taken a selective and very narrow view of the state's obligations under IHL: see Kretzmer, *The Occupation of Justice: The Supreme Court of Israel and the Occupied Territories* (n 8) 35–40. O Ben-Naftali and Y Shany describe the courts' approach to applicable law and human rights as 'intriguing', and resorting to one of the following options: unequivocally espousing the position of the military; citing international humanitarian law but not international human rights law; referencing human rights without specifying whether the source is international human rights law, Israeli administrative or constitutional law; or referencing international human rights law only in order to show that it is irrelevant. They note that its jurisprudence to date has 'quite resolutely managed to leave unresolved even the question of the applicability and enforceability of the Fourth Geneva Convention'; 'Living in Denial: The Application of Human Rights in the Occupied Territories' (2003–04) 37 *Israel Law Review* 17, 87–93.

[14] The Supreme Court of Israel has ruled in several decisions that, in light of Israeli legislation, East Jerusalem is not occupied territory, but part of Israel and uniquely governed by Israeli law; see Law and Administration Order (No 1) 1967, Israeli Collection of Regulations No 2064, 28 June 1967, p 2690 and Basic Law: Jerusalem, Capital of Israel, Laws of the State of Israel No 980, 5 August 1980, p 186.

[15] eg Israeli settlers being evacuated from the Gaza Strip have been held to possess constitutional property rights under Israel's Basic Laws and were entitled to compensation for their eviction, while Israel's Basic Laws are not applicable to OPT Palestinians; see eg *Adalah—The Legal Center for Arab Minority Rights et al v Minister of Interior et al*, HCJ 7052/03, Judgment of 14 May 2006 in al Haq report 'Legitimising the Illegitimate? The Israeli High Court of Justice and the Occupied Palestinian Territory' (2010) 24, available at www.alhaq.org/publications/publications-index/item/legitimising-the-illegitimate.

[16] There were 3 judges when I enquired there in 2015.

This coupled with the fact that military commanders for their part still argue the rule of law as a basis for action and inaction, provide glimmers of hope as to the role of law, and litigation, as a means of engagement.

So how have courts responded when Palestinian land rights issues have come before them? In practice, while courts often find in favour of the government and against applicants, and may do so in ways that amount plainly to a denial of human rights, more commonly justice is more subtly denied. Sharon Weill analyses the various functions played by the Israeli High Court as (1) apologist (a legitimating agency for the State's actions); (2) avoidance (of exercising jurisdiction over a case); and (3) deferential (maintaining a dialogue with the political branches of government, but deferring to the state's discretion).[17]

Through judicial avoidance and deference,[18] litigation is kept out of court in various ways. One of these is when the government settles cases, which can reap positive results for the applicants concerned, though invariably will not involve addressing the underlying wrongs. The *Cliff Hotel* case was an unusual case, where Palestinian hotel owners were absurdly accused of being 'absentee property owners' as their hotel had been 'zoned' into East Jerusalem following annexation while their home was 200 metres away across the line; the applicants refused to settle on a point of principle and the Israeli Supreme Court was forced to rule in an awkward and revealing case.[19] The Court found that the Absentee Property Law did apply to Palestinian properties in East Jerusalem, but that the government had discretion over the use of the law which should only be exercised in rare and exceptional cases to confiscate the Palestinian property.[20]

Beyond settling cases, a second crucial way in which judges avoid adjudicating on human rights issues that *do* proceed to court is through the broad doctrine of 'non-justiciability'.[21] This has been invoked to avoid determining 'political' issues, irrespective of the fact that they also happen to be fundamental human rights issues. The decision that settlement expansion was non-justiciable is perhaps the most striking instance of abdication of the judicial role through the non-justiciability doctrine. The decisions on non-justiciability, while doing nothing with the claim at hand, are not without effect so far as they embody and provide irrefutable evidence of denial of justice.

---

[17] S Weill, *The Role of National Courts in Applying International Humanitarian Law* (Oxford, Oxford University Press, 2014).

[18] Ibid.

[19] The Ayyad family ran the hotel, on the eastern border of Jerusalem, from 1961. The hotel was zoned into East Jerusalem by Israel when East Jerusalem was annexed in 1967. The owner, who lived 200 m behind the hotel, was declared an Absentee Property Owner, despite the fact that neither he nor his hotel moved. A long legal battle contributed, eventually, to the restoration of the hotel. See case summary in the NRC Report (2015) NRC Report, 'The Legality of the Wall Built by Israel in the West Bank' (January 2015) 8, available at www.nrc.no/globalassets/pdf/reports/the-legality-of-the-wall-built-by-israel-in-the-west-bank.pdf.

[20] Ibid.

[21] See n 13.

A third and perhaps more insidious way in which human rights issues are effectively avoided is through the treatment of these issues as banal procedural or technical planning issues. Instead of siding with the government on policies that plainly violate international law or reaching patently rights-unfriendly decisions,[22] courts appear to have evolved a practice whereby they decide on facially innocuous procedural grounds.[23]

The courts have also demonstrated extreme deference to the state in less direct ways, particularly when the 'security' card has been played. This deference is seen in cases concerning 'The Wall', in which the courts have for the most part left the 'delicate balance' of security to the government, without meaningful review of the lawfulness of decisions purportedly taken on security grounds.[24] Cases show that the security doctrine has not only been invoked extremely widely, but also at times under plainly false pretences; one example was a case in the Jordan valley in which land was seized from Palestinian farmers on national security grounds, then taken over or transferred to settler farmers, who interviewees suggested had the Palestinian former owners subsequently work their land.[25] In another case, the government's argument in court that there was a 'security' imperative was contradicted by public statements (when under pressure regarding the slow progress of the Wall, indicated that there was no real security problem in that particular area).[26]

Courts have, however, also increasingly shown themselves willing to engage in what is presented as a 'balancing' exercise in respect of the proportionality of harm caused.[27] Courts have refused to question underlying policy, but in some cases at least, required the authorities to implement it in ways that are more consistent with human rights, including a minor rerouting of the Wall to mitigate harmful effects. Examples include the well-reported *Cremisan* case, which challenged the route of the Wall through the Cremisan valley that would separate a Palestinian village from the land off which it survives, and a Salesian convent from the local community it served.[28] Judicial intervention ultimately resulted in a rerouting that

[22] As held by international bodies, see next section.

[23] There are many examples in practice, which might include issues related to procedural irregularities in a planning process, permits, apparently innocuous issues of tenancy rules etc, effectively ducking rights-related arguments of substance.

[24] eg Israeli Supreme Court, *Beit Sourik Village Council v The Government of Israel et al*, HCJ 2056/04, Judgment of 30 June 2004.

[25] Interviews Jordan Valley 2015; for other examples and judicial rebuke, see C Levinson, 'Settlers Farming Land Israeli Army Has Closed Off to Its Palestinian Owners' *Haaretz* (26 April 2015) available at www.haaretz.com/.premium-settlers-farming-land-closed-to-its-palestinian-owners-by-army-1.5355048.

[26] See *Battir* case, further discussed below; for a summary of the facts and the decision of the Israeli High Court, see NRC Report (n 19) at 11–12.

[27] Sfard notes how as the Court has shifted its analysis in recent years to issues of 'proportionality' in construction of the wall and settlements, in these areas judicial interventions may be significant; M Sfard,' The Price of Internal Legal Opposition to Human Rights Abuses' (2009) 1 *Journal of Human Rights Practice* 39, 41–42.

[28] The Wall will separate the West Bank city of Beit Jala from the settlement of Har Gilo and the village of Walaja. Critics claim its real purpose is not to increase security but to allow settlement

still separated the community from its land but kept the convent intact,[29] resulting in media reports of the constraining role of the courts.

III. Impact of Litigation on Land Rights before Israeli Courts?

Despite the obstacles and frustrations highlighted above, litigation work has continued apace before Israeli courts driven by the commitment of applicants and key repeat players such as NGOs and a cadre of human rights lawyers. In a context in which many advocates plainly feel extremely doubtful as to what they have achieved, and frustrated at most turns, perhaps it should be unsurprising that there is considerable uncertainty and different views around litigation goals. At one end of the spectrum, some Israeli organisations have identified the end of occupation as a goal, given its centrality to rights protection and restoration of the rule of law.[30] At the other end, the humanitarian goal of protecting clients intent on staying in their homes as long as possible is another. Simply 'sustaining the status quo' and halting the advancement of settlements was cited by some as perhaps a more realistic strategic goal, among others.

Naturally, the identification of short- and longer-term goals, and processes of change, is for local actors and allies, and a complex one. Discussions in Palestine included how clear but flexible litigation goals may assist strategic development, and their absence certainly influences the approach to impact assessment and evaluation. It may be the case that focus on long-term ambitious goals has led to a sense of litigation achieving nothing, where it may be that litigation processes have had a range of positive effects that fall below the radar. On the other hand, impact may go beyond very narrowly defined goals. The next section therefore highlights some of my discussions on the many different levels of impact of litigation in this field for those directly and indirectly affected by displacement in Palestine. It also exposes the severe limitations (and negative effects) of litigation, raising the

expansion. For coverage, see eg P Beaumont, 'Israel Resumes Work on Controversial Separation Wall in Cremisan Valley' *The Guardian* (18 August 2015) available at www.theguardian.com/world/2015/aug/18/israel-resumes-work-controversial-separation-wall-cremisan-valley.

[29] See for the decision of the Israeli High Court in this case, *Beit Jala Municipality et al v Ministry of Defense (Cremisan Valley Case)* HCJ 5163/13 (2 April 2015); translated by Society of St Yves—Catholic Center of Human Rights, available at www.saintyves.org/uploads/files/Cremisan%20 Final%20Ruling.pdf; see for more details about the case, Society of St. Yves, 'The Last Nail in Bethlehem's Coffin: The Annexation of the Wall' (July 2017) available at http://www.saintyves.org/downloads/reports/20171010045710.pdf.

[30] See eg B'TSELEM—Israeli Information Center for Human Rights in the Occupied Territories, available at www.btselem.org/campaignlist; Bat Shalom Advocacy Goals, available at www.batshalom. org/files/about_us.html and www.batshalom.org/files/Declaration.html.

question of its role as at best one contributor to broader solutions, and certainly not as an alternative to them.[31]

A. Delay as Success? Slowing the Displacement of Palestinians

'Buying time' might be described as one of the major tactics and successes of displacement litigation in Palestine. While this at first sounds distinctly underwhelming as a goal or achievement, the significance of delay as impact must be understood in context.

Litigation has contributed to significant delays that have thus far stopped hundreds of eviction and demolitions orders, notably in East Jerusalem. While temporary, suspensions of the violating orders have in some cases been for specified lengthy periods, with a court deciding in one 2014 case which I discussed with lawyers that an eviction should be suspended for a noteworthy nine years.[32] In many cases, it appears that the duration of the suspension is unspecified, pending determination of the matter by the courts. While the vast majority of cases will not ultimately be 'successful', in terms of vindicating the rights of individual communities to remain, the delays generated by the cases have important implications.

Firstly, there is the impact of this delay on lives of human beings and communities, who benefit from remaining in their homes for extended, if generally indeterminate, periods. While this generates what must be excruciating uncertainty, it may give some applicants space to try (despite obstacles) to regularise their situation if at all possible. By the time that a case is ready for adjudication, the facts may have changed, causing the court to seek further information from the state.[33] In practice it allows families to continue to live in their homes, and for communities to remain intact, for many years.

Secondly, the impact of delay has added significance, given the implications of eviction on a range of other rights. In the particular cases where eviction contributes to an individual's 'centre of life' moving outside East Jerusalem, it is likely to be accompanied by a loss of residency rights in East Jerusalem. This carries serious ramifications for a host of related rights to welfare, work, education, family and social dimensions of life that go beyond the immediate right to property and to a home, given restrictions on access to Jerusalem imposed on Palestinians in the West Bank.[34] Once removed, there may be no access back into their communities.

---

[31] See further the possibility of negative impact at section III.K below.

[32] This was the case in the area of Im Haroun in Sheikh Jarroh in East Jerusalem, an area where displacement is a mounting risk: www.ochaopt.org/content/significant-increase-risk-displacement-east-jerusalem.

[33] Sometimes the case is no longer a priority owing to changed circumstances and the demolition order can be cancelled.

[34] A person who is evicted from their home may still be a legal resident of Jerusalem and be allowed to live somewhere else in the city, but if his or her 'centre of life' moves outside Jerusalem, or he or she is suspected of having committed security offences, Israel will revoke their residency with the serious implications noted.

This has particular resonance for many of those currently challenging eviction orders in East Jerusalem who have lived in the area since 1948, when they were displaced from land elsewhere in what is now Israel. They are seeking to avoid repetition through recognition of their rights and status.

Thirdly, the broader political significance of the delays is key to understanding the impact of what seem like fairly pedestrian land and property disputes. The strategic, political, economic, cultural and religious significance of Jerusalem for Palestine is well known and its potential to constitute the capital of Palestine in the future depends on halting the removal of Palestinians from East Jerusalem and the creation of the 'buffer zone' around Israeli-controlled areas. The slow takeover of East Jerusalem, at odds with international agreements and international law, takes place case by case and house by house.[35] This may be done by employing arguments that appear at face value to be banal and procedural, concerning planning rights and inadequate documentation, but as one experienced lawyer said of 'planning and property' cases in East Jerusalem, 'the whole of east Jerusalem is a public interest case'.

Fourthly, buying time is also relevant on a macro level so far as the plausibility of an eventual two-state solution is jeopardised by on-going settlement expansion and displacement. Delays in settlement expansion or in the removal of Palestinians from East Jerusalem for example do not provide solutions, but they may create time and space for other solutions from wherever they might emerge.

B. Occasional Direct Recognition of Rights and Implementation of Orders

Although infrequent, it would be wrong to lose sight of the fact that there are cases in which courts have directly found in favour of victims. In rare situations, such as where property rights have been incontrovertible through clear documentation and a lack of any basis for countervailing legal claims under Israeli law, courts have directly recognised the right to property of Palestinians.[36] Likewise, in some—albeit rare—cases, concrete measures have been ordered by the court to protect Palestinians' rights. For example, in a case in which settlers in Hebron built a synagogue on the estate of the indefatigable Mr Ja'abaari, whose estate is now sandwiched between two settlements intent on expansion, the case was clear and the Court ordered the synagogue's removal. Plainly unlawful settlements have been ordered dismantled.

Such apparent 'successes' are both rare and partial, however, for various reasons. Judgments depend on implementation, which in some of these cases has

---

[35] See eg NRC Report, 'The Legal Status of East Jerusalem' (December 2013) available at www.nrc. no/globalassets/pdf/reports/the-legal-status-of-east-jerusalem.pdf.

[36] Many reasons, including the absence of documentation, and the inability to get such documents, contribute to this situation remaining exceptional.

been lacking. In the *Ja'abaari* case, the synagogue built by settlers on Mr Ja'abaari's land has been demolished and rebuilt multiple times. When he stood his ground, and the courts ruled in his favour, the pressure assumed new forms, less suscep-tible to legal challenge, such as violence and intimidation from settlers to which the police have failed to respond. Even litigation 'successes' of this type can hardly be seen to solve any problem as such. Litigation gains have also led to prompt setbacks in legislative form. The widely reported *Arnona settlement* litigation was an unusual court success that led to the dismantling of one settlement.[37] However, it was followed by legislative changes whereby the Knesset legalised the unlawful expropriation of private Palestinian land even if the owners could prove their ownership to the satisfaction of the Israeli legal system.[38] This controversial Settle-ment Regulation Law is itself currently before the courts and has caused division within the government's own team.[39]

Other concrete victories have responded to extreme military or executive orders without even an arguable legitimate basis—such as school closures ordered in the Jordan Valley to force the Bedouin to leave land, which was lifted, protecting the schools and open space.[40] Other cases involving demolition orders of Bedouin homes have not been won, however, and the problem is persistent. The victories assist Bedouin to keep pushing the agenda, while their rights are still in constant jeopardy. Preventing the destruction of schools allows particular children's rights to education, among others, to be respected at least a bit longer. Arguably, even if it has done little to solve the problem, it contributes directly and indirectly to an environment in which the on-going struggle over land and property can continue.

C. Challenging, Modifying and/or Frustrating Policies?

The broad goal of much public interest litigation is 'policy change'. As noted above, achieving this directly through litigation,[41] as happens elsewhere in com-parative practice, is extremely difficult in Israeli courts at this time. Litigation appears to show little direct impact on policies of displacement and control, set-tlement development and the construction of the Wall, among others.

Several people I spoke to in Palestine, however, described the impact of cases as 'frustrating policies', rather than necessarily tangibly changing them. One also

---

[37] 'Supreme Court orders removal of Amona outpost' *Times of Israel* (25 December 2014).

[38] See Law on Regulation of Settlement in Judea and Samaria, 5777-2017 SH No 3604, p 394 at 410 (13 February 2017).

[39] See Press Release of Adalah Legal Center for Arab and Minority Rights (10 February 2017) available at www.adalah.org/en/content/view/9030.

[40] Examples from communities I visited in Palestine include the schools linked to the Bedouin communities in Fasayel or near the settlement in Hebron city centre, both of which remained open following litigation.

[41] Policy may be challenged in many ways and through intermediate steps; eg other levels of impact identified below in this section, such as exposure of the policy and shaping the discourse around it, may indirectly contribute to modifying policy.

sees change in the way in which policies are *implemented*. In a handful of cases, extreme effects of those policies may have been softened through litigation, such as the rerouting of the Wall to minimise its impact and the decision to adopt the least harmful way of implementing the policy.[42] The *Cremisan Valley* case mentioned above was a key example of how litigation shaped the wall, albeit to a limited degree.[43] Other cases include the *Bil'in* case where the army offered to put a gate in the Wall to minimise harmful impact.[44]

Litigation in this context might be seen as nibbling at the edges of policies that cannot be directly changed, to bring about minor changes in their effects, but falling far short of meaningful policy change. As noted below, some argue that shaving the rough edges off policies through minor changes comes with a cost that must be taken into account so far as it serves to 'beautify the occupation'.[45] On the other hand, the real effect for individual rights and livelihoods is clear. The result can be enormous tensions and strain on those most affected and on the litigators who represent them who can feel like 'collaborators in the management of a human rights violation', but unable to confront it head on.[46]

D. The Preservation of Culture and Heritage

The significance of several land rights cases must also be understood in terms of the preservation of cultural property and Palestinian cultural heritage. The importance of this is increased in the context of what was described as an attempt on the part of some within the Israeli establishment to rewrite history or reflect only one aspect of it, through the cultural or religious justifications recently put forward for the seizure of land.

Cases such as the *Battir* case concerning the 500-year-old Palestinian terraces, or the Cremisan monastery and convent, demonstrate how the rerouting of the Wall

---

[42] eg the decision of the Israeli High Court in 2013 in the *Battir* case (case summary in NRC Report (n 19) at 11–12) or its 2015 decision in relation to the *Cremisan Valley* case (n 29) further discussed below.

[43] In August 2014, the Supreme Court instructed the Israeli government to consider new alternatives in the construction of the Wall so as to leave the Silesian convent and monastery on the Palestinian side of the Wall, with another decision handed down in February 2015 (n 29). The case achieved international attention, exposed the gruesome nature of policy, and has had an apparent influence, to some degree at least. See eg P Beaumont, 'Israel's Top Court Blocks Extension of Separation Wall through Cremisan Valley' *The Guardian* (2 April 2015). However, in 2016, the Court refused claims in respect of the Wall dividing the community from their land and the devastating socio-economic, cultural and social impact of the Wall remains. See B'Stselem—Israeli Information Center of Human Rights in the Occupied Territories,' Barrier to Separate Beit Jala Residents From Their Lands, Laying Groundwork for Annexing Settlement' (12 November 2015) available at www.btselem.org/separation_barrier/20151112_beit_jala_separation_barrier.

[44] See for discussion with regard to *Bil'in* case, Sfard (n 7) Ch 5.

[45] See section III.K below.

[46] Sfard (n 7) noted in Ch 1 that 'asking the army to put in a gate to give the farmers better access to their land would mean putting ourselves exactly in the position the army would like human rights activists to be: collaborators (…)—in this case, the fence'.

has real historical and cultural significance, and plays a role in avoiding irreparable harm.[47] The multiple cases seeking to protect the housing rights of the Bedouin in the Jordan valley or the Negev are, in essence, about the survival and the cultural life of a people. Even if presented by the state as property cases wherein reasonable attempts have been made to provide suitable alternative 'accommodation', these cases can challenge and expose relocation to fixed concrete pods as an end to the Bedouin way of life.[48] As a result of hundreds of planning objections in the *Nweima* case, the Court asked the state to respond to a very detailed list of planning, social, cultural and anthropological considerations concerning Bedouin lifestyle, which in turn proved fertile ground for new challenges and the introduction of a wide range of evidence on social and cultural issues.[49]

UNESCO accreditation of certain Palestinian sites, such as the Jerusalem Old City and Battir as World Heritage or Endangered Cultural Heritage sites, has helped litigation efforts. Israeli courts have shown some sensitivity to the perception that they are damaging the environment of places of 'international' cultural interest.[50] As such, beyond the immediate impact on those directly affected, litigation also has an indirect impact by slowing and limiting the erosion of the religious and cultural heritage of Palestinians and minorities within that group.

E. 'Holding a Mirror' to the Problem: Exposure of Unjust Policies, Practices

It was also suggested by many of those I spoke to that a key area of impact, and for some *the* main added value of public interest litigation in this context, lies in exposing injustice. This includes highlighting unjust laws, policies and practices, in terms of both the Knesset's role and judicial complicity. Land rights cases in Palestine provide a prism through which the true nature, motivation and impact of unjust policies can be seen, with a view to some other form of social or political responses. Some cases, such as the long-standing struggle of the Sheikh Jarrah community in East Jerusalem, highlights the legal hypocrisy that means that Israeli Jews can have their properties restituted to them but Palestinians cannot.[51]

---

[47] eg in July 2013 in the *Battir* case Israeli High Court of Justice issued an injunction against extending the separation barrier through the Palestinian village of Battir given the 500-year-old terraces and aqueduct. See for case summary NRC Report (n 19) at 11–12. Similar issues arise in relation to the *Cremisan Valley* case (n 29).

[48] See Reframing at section III.G below, highlighting the importance of how these cases are communicated.

[49] See Israeli High Court of Justice, *Wadi Al Qteyf (Sateh al Bahar) Community v No 8115/12.*

[50] UNESCO accreditation has drawn international attention to such cases, forced the courts to find compromises that take account of cultural/environmental considerations and drawn in cultural/environmental legal arguments. The historic nature of the caves in Susiya has a similar focus. Source

[51] The Legal Status of East Jerusalem, Norweigian Refugee Council, 2013.

In some instances a particular case may epitomise and personify the impact of policies on human beings, while often the exposure comes by showing how seemingly innocuous state application of rules on planning, landlord and tenancy reveals a state policy of displacement when multiple cases are considered together. Whether such messages are heard, and acted upon, depends on receptivity and is undoubtedly an advocacy challenge that groups in at least some selected strategic cases are trying to meet.[52] But as one interviewee put it, litigation can be one way of 'holding a mirror to the problems in Palestine'.

i. Exposing Fallacies in Official Positions

As noted under section III.H (Information Gathering), litigation in Palestine also goes some way to exposing the government, and in particular fallacies behind its positions and justifications for violations. This includes exposing lies told to the courts themselves. For example, in the context of the *Battir* case, the government's arguments in court as to the real and immediate security imperative behind the Wall were contradicted by political statements made by the Minister of Defence to the media (in response to criticism of the delays, he noted that the Wall was not in fact needed for defence reasons). As noted above, in the Jordan Valley the security card had been played and accepted by the courts, yet subsequent events revealed the true motivation to have been settlement expansion or indeed financial benefit (for example where the land has then been let back to Palestinian residents for gain).

ii. Exposing Discrimination and Deficiencies in the Justice System

The frustrating litigation story in Palestine shows the myriad obstacles facing Palestinians and how they are presented to appear anodyne. The issue is complex, however, and requires careful analysis and explanation to targeted audiences. Exposing and challenging the lack of independence and impartiality is notoriously difficult, even where international standards and fora are clear and available, but analysis of cases demonstrates the indirect discriminatory impact of policies. The cases, considered together, show the stark lack of available and effective remedies in Israeli courts, and have a myth-busting role as regards official justifications and misrepresentations.

It may also have repercussions for international jurisdiction. There are few international remedies for victims of violations, and it remains to be seen whether international criminal accountability will ever be forthcoming in relation to the OPT. It may, however, be the case that this exposure will prove significant to assessments of the 'willingness' of domestic courts, in the context of the International

---

[52] See eg the NRC campaign around the *Cliff Hotel* case noted in section II.

Criminal Court (ICC) admissibility criteria[53] or potentially where subsidiarity operates in relation to universal jurisdiction proceedings.[54]

iii. Demonstrating Victim Impact and Resilience

Exposure also enables targeted audiences to better see and understand the human beings behind the injustice. Cases expose the impact of abstract policies on concrete individuals and situations, individualising each policy and enabling others outside to empathise, which can be critical in mobilising broader based support.

Litigation in Palestine also tells a compelling tale about human resilience and the sheer determination of individuals not to give into injustice but to use legal mechanisms to defend their rights. The cases enable others to see victims as individual human beings, to understand and identify with their human story, as well as see them as believers in the rule of law (which may be relevant to generating a sympathetic understanding, influencing international opinion and garnering support). A case in point might be Mr Ja'abaari's persistent resort to the authorities to document attacks on him and his family by settlers, and the police's failure to protect. So far as litigation is aimed at influencing public opinion, much depends again on messaging and communication strategy. For some clients this backfires and can have quite the opposite effect.

The importance and ultimate effectiveness of exposure depends on what happens with the information or awareness brought to light, for example, where it is used alongside targeted advocacy. Nonetheless, exposing myths, influencing the debate and opening up the democratic space for discussion nationally and internationally may be a key measure of the difference made by litigation.

F. Psycho-social Impact on Victims and Communities

Crucial questions concerning the impact of land rights cases relate to the empowerment of individuals and communities. The positive psycho-social impact of these cases emerged palpably from discussions with affected persons. Several

---

[53] On 16 January 2015, the ICC Prosecutor announced the opening of a preliminary examination into the situation in Palestine (ICC Press Release, ICC-OTP-20150116-PR1083); the ICC operates under 'complementarity' according to Art 17 ICC Statute. The impact of the 'losing case' is seen quite graphically then in a context in which international engagement by the ICC depends on a functioning national judiciary.

[54] Numerous states increasingly adopt a model of subsidiarity in their approach to assuming jurisdiction only over cases not being adjudicated by courts in the territorial state able and willing to do domestically; see eg Netherlands, Belgium, Germany and Spain. For more information see REDRESS/FIDH, 'Extraterritorial Jurisdiction in the European Union: A Study on The Laws and Practice in the 27 Member States of the European Union' (December 2010) 25–27, available at www.fidh.org/IMG/pdf/Extraterritorial_Jurisdiction_In_the_27_Member_States_of_the_European_Union_FINAL.pdf.

people gave voice to the importance of litigation as one way of 'doing something',[55] countering the powerlessness generated by the occupation and their general situation of persistent victimisation.[56] In this context, litigation was described by some as providing a 'form of resistance'. Each minor or intermediate victory may empower at least some to continue in different ways to fight within a rule of law approach. The power of the legal process is particularly apparent in a context in which it is clear that so many people have a strong sense of the potential broader political and historic significance of their cases, beyond winning or losing the legal action in question.

The sense of the significance of engaging in the process itself was captured by one applicant in the *Ja'abaari* case, who proudly displayed copies of the hundreds of unanswered complaints lodged in respect of intimidation by settlers. When asked why he takes action with no obvious outcome, he stated that: 'There is an Arab proverb that "Even the bullet that misses makes a noise." If they do nothing, I have a record'.[57]

So far as litigation serves to invigorate the struggle to protect rights, it is closely linked to the question of mobilisation more broadly. In some cases I discussed (though not others), the litigation in Palestine has facilitated, and fed into, social mobilisation. The creation or strengthening of social structures within affected groups or communities focused on litigation can also contribute to the effectiveness of other, non-litigation strategies.[58] One example of the above may be the Sheikh Jarrah communities in East Jerusalem, where a local committee engages with international litigation with international partners and the advocacy conversation is focused around enabling community advocacy. While some cases involved engaged victims and communities, others revealed more of a handing off by victims or communities to lawyers, as if the litigation processes were not entirely matters for them, which may in turn influence impact. Many international studies identify politically-aware, mobilised and organised groups as key factors to longer-term strategic success of litigation initiatives. Litigation and mobilisation have a symbiotic relationship as seen in this example, where the community initiative, coordination and support networks impel the work; international partnerships make it possible, and the litigation appears to contribute to the cohesion and impulse.[59] (Conversely, as discussed further in section III.K below on the negative

---

[55] Jaábarai interview; despite his defiance and determination to exploit litigation, it also reflects a lack of alternatives, as he asked 'What else can I do?'.

[56] As one applicant said 'it is humiliating to complain to anyone but Allah, but what else can I do? So I have to keep complaining'.

[57] See below on record-keeping as a goal and additional level of significance of these cases.

[58] As noted below several analyses of public interest cases internationally have noted the significance of mobilisation for litigation. Beyond that, the formation of these groups can itself be most important to the broader benefit to the community, as noted in Ch 6 on Guatemala.

[59] See eg study on why litigation on rights issues in US and India reaped differential results in C Epp, *The Rights Revolution* (Chicago, University of Chicago Press, 1998) and the Atlantic Philanthropies report analysis of the factors contributing to impact in eg the well-known *Grootboom* housing case in South Africa, which includes social mobilisation as a key factor; see 'A Strategic Evaluation of Public

impact, if litigation distracts from mobilisation rather than feeding into it, it can have very detrimental effects on the human rights struggle.)

G. Reframing the Problem

Litigation has exposed the nature of violations in the OPT in a way that may help to 'reframe' the problems, highlighting features that may otherwise be obscured beneath the apparent subtlety of some forms of violation. This may include disclosing the de facto discrimination in the administration of justice or in the impact of facially neutral laws, which can be very difficult to prove without reliable statistics. Series of cases, taken separately but considered together, such as the mass of land and property right litigation brought by NRC in East Jerusalem, can reveal systematic displacement, persecution, and therefore a dual system of discrimina-tory justice for example.

The decision to argue in Israeli courts in 2004 that the violations amounted to 'apartheid' were unlikely to be based on calculations that such arguments would prosper in court, but on their anticipated impact on shaping international perceptions. The CERD committee has used its reporting function to classify the situation in these terms, thereby highlighting the discrimination behind poli-cies and practices in Israel. This positive reframing—through legal arguments or resolutions—may also be relevant to the historical narrative. They may in the full-ness of time be relevant to international accountability should processes such as the ICC gather momentum.

On the other hand, legal argument and proceedings can occasion an unhelpful reframing of issues as legal when in fact they are intensely political. It has been suggested for example that litigation has, at least on occasion, neutralised a 'more radical' conversation through the tone and framework imposed by the litigation process.

H. Documentation and Historical Records

Accessing information on state policy has been a goal of some human rights litiga-tion in the OTP and a by-product of others. The direct use of litigation to secure access to information through the Israeli Freedom of Information Act has given rise to useful information, though a broadly framed and interpreted security excep-tion seriously curtails its impact. Some lawyers therefore appeared unconvinced

Interest Litigation in South Africa' (June 2008) 104ff, available at www.atlanticphilanthropies.org/app/uploads/2015/09/public_interest_litigation_sa.pdf. My analysis of Guatemala highlights how one of the most important outcomes of the litigation processes was the longer-term social organisation and mobilisation; see Ch 6. See also Maria Jose Guembe's analysis of dictatorship-related litigation in Argentina; see Ch 8.

as to the utility of the litigation process to secure the most vital information in this context and gains have been less direct.

Litigation in Palestine has, however, gone some way to drawing out the authorities' positions, creating information and opportunities, or litigation 'stepping stones'. While relatively contained, there are examples of statements being made to the court by government lawyers that reveal something about their plans, relationships with others or motivation that can prove useful for human rights protection. For example, in the *Ja'abaari* Hebron litigation, government lawyers explained to the Court that where the case concerned *certain* (influential) settlements or settlers, decisions, including the implementation of the Court's judgment, had to be taken at the highest level of government. Indications of government relocation plans have occasionally emerged indirectly from litigation, as in the settler-led litigation seeking destruction of the school.[60] Such elucidation of government policy and plans can help clarify the relationship between government and non-state actors, and the nature of policy in relation to settlements in general or target groups in particular. Where the authorities have shown disdain for the administration of justice and are seen either to be effectively lying to a court, or failing to implement its judgments, there may also be an impact on judicial dynamics between state and judiciary, potentially opening up tensions and encouraging more liberal judges to be more robust in their oversight function.

Closely linked to the question of exposure is the significance of this litigation for the purposes of documentation and recording. I was struck by the extent to which Palestinians see 'keeping a record' as a key motivating factor, as reflected in Mr Ja'abaari's phrase cited above.

Of course, records may serve many different purposes. Each of them may carry different requirements of the 'recording' in question, with obvious differences between advocacy or political goals, and legal or accountability ones. Strategic documentation is therefore important, just as is SHRL. But undoubtedly the process of preparing litigation on land rights has generated vast information on patterns of violations, perpetrators, justifications offered and justice denied, which are 'potentially' valuable records of relevance to other historical and individual accountability processes. Comparative experience suggests that documentation produced for the purposes of litigation can be vital for other processes in the future, some of which may not yet be foreseeable.[61]

---

[60] The litigation in this example had been brought by a settler litigation organisation against the Khan al Ahmar community's school, demanding that the Israeli state exercise its 'duty' to demolish the school. In April 2012, the Israeli state responded that the demolition of the school was inextricably linked to the 'relocation' of the entire community. See B'Tselem—Israeli Information Center for Human Rights in the Occupied Territories, 'Israel Moves to Advance Forcible Transfer of Khan al-Ahmar' (14 September 2017) available at www.btselem.org/press_releases/201700914_khan_al_ahmar.

[61] See Chs 3 and 4 on impact; eg the thousands of petitions filed by the Vicariate of Solidarity (La Vicaría de la Solidaridad) in Chile requesting release of detained and disappeared persons during Pinochet's regime, which were predictably 'unsuccessful' but exposed and documented facts and failures; likewise the Argentina litigation during dictatorship at Ch 8.

Looking at the issue in a broader frame, Feldman describes as a 'win-win' situation litigation trying to get judges to rule on settlements; even a judicial ruling by an Israeli court that the settlements were legal, was considered a step forward in the fight against them and the occupation. This corresponds with his belief that 'a regime of evil writes itself to oblivion', and the role, in that context, of the High Court of Justice's case law as 'the great library of the occupation'.[62]

I. Impact on Legal Culture and the Rule of Law?

Some people I spoke to discussed the importance of sustaining a focus on courts, and a belief by the population in resort to rule of law approaches towards ending violations now and in the future. Once again, similar analysis and debate has been advanced in relation to other situations, including the South African system under apartheid, which are resonant in this context.

So far as litigation work, and funding of and support for such work, contributes to building capacity of local advocates and lawyers, shaping legal culture, and positively influencing the approach of courts and other bodies (however slightly), it was suggested by those working on the ground that it may be investing in the future justice system. The focus on developing sustainable systems of lawyering may make a particularly important contribution to the creation of functioning legal services systems. While the counter-argument that undue confidence in the rule of law in Israel would be misplaced and distracting must also be taken into account, the importance of investing in a 'rule of law culture', influencing the approach of lawyers, courts and public perception for the future, is compelling.

J. Paving the Way for International Litigation?

As noted above, the Israeli courts have not been willing to give effect to international law and enforce international obligations, nor save in exceptional cases to have close regard to international law. In the avoidance of their judicial oversight role, they have been unwilling to review the lawfulness of Israeli policy on fundamental rights issues. A number of people in the OPT referred to these decisions as serving to exhaust domestic remedies and paving the way for international recourse. The absence of international fora makes the extent of this questionable, given the lack of courts as such before which individuals can take Israel internationally. It remains the case, however, that in the monitoring function of human rights bodies within the UN framework, it is by reference to judicial decisions that international human rights bodies have found Israeli to be systematically violating rights in its approach to land and property in the OPT. Of particular

---

[62] A Feldman, 'Which Side Are You On, Grandpa Weinstein?' *Haaretz* (25 July 2013).

current relevance is the role that 'failed' judicial cases may have in establishing the jurisdiction of ICC, either on account of evidence relevant to understanding state policy, and more pertinently to establishing that national courts are unwilling and unable to provide justice at home.

K. The Cost of Litigation: Negative Impact and Managing Risk

The crucial distinction between the goals of SHRL and its impact is, of course, that impact may be positive or negative. Concern over negative consequences is particularly prevalent in discourse on the role of Israeli courts. Negative impact takes many forms in this context.

i. Reprisals and Accelerated Violations

Most directly, are the *reprisals or accelerated violations* under litigation's shadow; demolitions have proceeded on an expedited basis in light of the prospect of litigation, with a view to ensuring that when the litigation unfolds the issue is moot or the state avoids being bogged down by litigation. The cost of litigation has also included arrests and harassment of applicants or of their family members. Legal action may bring attention to communities and highlight their vulnerability, which can be both positive and negative, triggering direct reprisals, and also internal tensions and divisions that can be disempowering.

ii. Policy Impact?

The refusals of the courts and the inability of litigation to confront and change unjust policies, such as settlement expansion, has been noted. It has also been suggested that litigation has contributed to 'policy setbacks'. The courts have been described as feeding the overuse of security justifications and arguments; by accepting carte blanche the government's arguments under the security card, the courts encouraged overreaching resort to such rationale, contributing to the 'security thesis' that settlements and the permanent presence of Israeli civilians in the OPT served Israeli security, which in turn is said to have enabled the creation of numerous settlements during the 1970s.[63]

iii. Regressive Legal Standards

Legal standards have been undermined in various ways through litigation in this context. They have arisen in the few cases in which courts have directly reached

---

[63] Sfard (7), noted in Ch 3 the evolution thereafter: 'The court bowed its head to the argument that settlement activity is guided by security considerations and, as the security argument grew weaker, that the settlements are a political question in which the court has no business meddling, despite its clear legal aspect'.

decisions with wide-reaching implications, for example on non-justiciability. If we see the striking exposure of denial of justice that such an open decision represented as impact, this has to be offset against its negative precedential value that may reduce prospects in future cases. The passage of the Settlement Regulation Law following the *Arnona* judgment against the state is a striking example of legislative pushback.[64]

Several commentators alert us to the incrementally negative legal consequences of litigation over time, in clarifying and consolidating the worst or in expanding the very powers or practices that the litigation sought to challenge.[65] Israeli jurisprudence in occupation-related cases has been described as, almost without exception, strengthening the powers of the Military Commander and leaving basic human rights unprotected.[66]

iv. The Risk of 'Legitimation' and 'Beautifying the Occupation'

Such concerns loom large in discussion on litigation impact in the OPT. Several commentators have noted the price that may be paid for the impact highlighted above whereby, as Sfard puts it, 'internal opposition legitimises the abusers' narratives and their claim for sole authority over the subject at hand; viewed from this perspective, the Wall or barrier cases contributed to the occupation's durability'.[67] The mere possibility of litigation—and its use by respected lawyers—suggests that those subject to occupation have access to justice, and that 'this regime speaks the language of the rule of law and human rights and is committed to them, at least officially'.[68] Weill's analysis also outlines the 'apologist' role of courts, according to which they serve as a legitimating agency for the state's actions.[69]

Alaa Mahajna likewise describes legitimation as one of two outcomes of the adoption of 'a litigious approach', taking the example of constitutional challenges to the Citizenship and Entry into Israel Law (2003, amended 2007), which prohibited Israeli citizens who marry Palestinians or spouses from other 'enemy states' from unifying with their spouses in Israel. He claims that the legal challenges 'grant[ed] a measure of legitimacy to the legal system and its institutions, mainly the Supreme Court', notably in the eyes of Arab Israelis who placed their faith in judicial solutions to the detriment of other forms of advocacy for change.[70]

---

[64] See legislation on expropriation following the *Amona* litigation, above.

[65] Michael Sfard wrote in 2009 of the 'price of internal legal opposition to human rights abuses' (n 27); Weill, *The Role of National Courts in Applying International Humanitarian Law* (n 17).

[66] Ibid.

[67] Sfard,' The Price of Internal Legal Opposition to Human Rights Abuses' (n 27) at 47.

[68] Ibid, 18.

[69] S Weill (n 17).

[70] He refers notably to 'legitimation' of the Israeli legal system through evidence of increased 'approval' of and 'confidence' in the Israeli courts. He acknowledges the difficulties in proving this, and it is not entirely clear on what basis he so concludes, though he cites the fact that more cases were brought over time and the answers (which he admits were to dubious questions) in the 2011 Israeli Democracy Index. See Mahajna 'Litigation Within the Israeli Court System' (n 1) at 3.

The suggestions by respected Palestinian and Israeli lawyers such as Kretzmer, Sfard, Weill and Mahajna among others that the judicial role may have contributed to sustaining and legitimising the situation underpinning the violations is sobering to say the least. It raises many questions. Does use of the court system in the OPT (or during South Africa's apartheid, or Argentina's dictatorship), *necessarily* send the message that those engaging in litigation believe it to be just and fair? Can this be mitigated in the way litigation is conducted, messaged outside the courtroom, or connected to the broader range of advocacy, outreach and education work? How can the judicial approach be exposed as not a 'meaningful' review? On balance, *have* the courts legitimised the situation in the eyes of Palestinians or internationally or has this been offset by international action against Israel at UN level or in the International Court of Justice (ICJ) discussed below? If the legitimation is too high a price to pay, what is the acceptable alternative to engaging within the legal process, and what is its cost?

v. Complicity or Boycott

These issues were at the heart of discussions by a group of lawyers that proposed, in 2008, a one-year boycott of the courts. Although the proposal was circulated to all relevant groups, it was not ultimately adopted.[71] While the need for 'alternatives' to litigation was broadly understood, the idea of boycott could not be endorsed by the human rights groups and lawyers operating in the OPT.

It is also noteworthy that none of the commentators who, as noted above, are wisely critical of the impact of the judicial process, seem to conclude that litigation should not be done. They raise issues that must be taken seriously and at a minimum have an impact on *how* it is done, to minimise potential negative impact. Their analysis calls on those conducting public interest litigation and others to make efforts to ensure that this legitimising function of the Supreme Court is minimised; seeking justice from the courts, while working to expose their injustice, to highlight the unjust laws, policies and practices, strengthen civil society, and appeal for more meaningful, engaged and informed support from the international community.

vi. Distraction and Disempowerment

The key related concern is the danger of law, and litigation, as distraction. Perhaps reflecting the extent to which laws are used and manipulated in relation to the occupation, it has been suggested that the Court has become the 'major arena for the struggle against human rights abuses by the occupation forces'.[72] To the

---

[71] Sfard (n 7) ch 1, describes the 'High Court Assessment Team' grappling with the tough question 'given our disturbing experience, was it right to continue to petition the High Court on behalf of the occupied? And if not, what alternative avenues of legal activism could we pursue (…)?'.

[72] Sfard (n 27) at 38.

extent that this depletes energy from pursuing (or perhaps identifying) alternative strategies it may be counter-productive.

The second outcome of the Citizenship cases was described as follows:

> the adoption of a strategy of litigation against the Citizenship Law counteracted efforts by advocates and grassroots organisations to mobilise political campaigns against human rights violations committed by this law. By pursuing litigation, individuals and groups may also have unwittingly legitimised, directly or indirectly, unjust institutions and systems, thereby weakening extra-legal resistance.[73]

This raises an important question concerning the potential negative impact of rights-related litigation that has resonated in conversations about civil rights litigation in the United States, for example: namely, law and litigation as distraction at best or an agent of disempowerment at worst.

Mahajna describes how a 'continuous battle within the walls of the Court' ensued for years after petitioning the Supreme Court of Israel but that there was no 'significant form of political action or opposition against the Citizenship Law during the several years of litigation starting in 2003'.[74] She further noted:

> People, including the affected families [...] relied solely on the Court to bring them justice, and they neglected other forms of opposition,' concluding that 'The more Palestinians rely on litigation for achieving socio-legal change and the more confidence they show in the Supreme Court, the less they will try extra-legal forms to achieve this goal.[75]

In part, this calls for realistic recognition of the time and resources taken to litigate, which may pose a serious risk of depletion from other strategies. But so far as possible, litigation and political strategies might be seen not as alternatives but either as complementary or indeed integrated. The extent to which litigation necessarily distracts from other non-legal means of mobilisation or pursuit of change may depend on litigation goals and strategy: how the litigation is perceived, its role within a broader struggle and how it is carried out. In short, is it pursued as a solution or as a tool. The real danger in this respect may lie not in litigation per se, but in seeing it in isolation and as an alternative to political solutions, which underlines the importance of trying to locate the role of litigation (as many in Palestine clearly do), as part of a much broader process of change. As noted, those astutely critical of the role of litigation—often themselves involved in the frustrating practice—do not conclude that it should not be done but in the words of one of Mahajna's conclusions that 'Palestinians and human rights organizations should be extremely careful (...) before making the decision to adopt a strategy

---

[73] Mahajna, 'Litigation Within the Israeli Court System: A Double-Edged Sword' (n 1) discussing the Citizen and Entry cases, at http://mada-research.org/en/files/2012/05/Jadal13/Eng/Alaa-Mahajna.pdf.

[74] Ibid, 4.

[75] Ibid.

of litigation'.[76] The key points that emerge may relate more to concerns about *how* to do litigation, rather than *whether* to do it.

vii. Financial Strain and Vulnerability

Finally, a related area of risk and potential negative consequences of cases is the financial dimension. Litigation is extremely costly for Palestinians litigating in Israeli courts and is only possible where funded by NGOs: besides legal fees, engineering experts are required for many eviction cases, fines can be charged for the period when people remain in their homes and conduct the legal challenges, and so it goes on. The prohibition on foreign funding of NGOs poses very serious additional challenges and uncertainties in this context. Without the continued support of financial backers, the litigation would be impossible, flagging a major challenge ahead.

IV. International Litigation on Palestinian Land Rights

It is normally when national mechanisms fail that supranational human rights litigation comes into its own. As regards resort to international mechanisms, however, (almost) unique challenges arise in respect of violations in the OPT. Quite apart from political issues and obstacles arising in relation to Israel/Palestine, there is a remarkable dearth of international human rights courts or mechanisms available in relation to violations by Israel, on account of the largely consensual nature of human rights jurisdiction and Israeli refusal to be subject to external review. Suffice to recall here that while some softer human rights review or monitoring mechanisms can be used, such as the UN Special Procedures, or perhaps recourse to support from specialised agencies, international human rights litigation opportunities in the sense of complaint mechanisms are simply not available. Although Israel has ratified many relevant treaties, and treaty bodies have found IHRL to be applicable in the OPT, Israel has not accepted the right of individual petition.

There are however other litigation-related developments worthy of note, though some of them with as yet questionable impact.

Worthy of brief preliminary note is the potential impact of ICC proceedings in circumstances where the crimes in question fall within the Court's jurisdiction. Although premature to consider the impact of the existence of the ICC

---

[76] Ibid, 5. He notes clearly '[i]n case there is any doubt, this article by no means intends to underestimate the legal work of Palestinian advocates or to call for a halt (…) [in case] [m]aking political struggles into legal ones could further strengthen confidence in the Israeli court system and result in the abandonment of other forms of political struggle against the state'.

mechanism and the Palestinian referral to the prosecutor of 2015, it may yet be the case that even before or without ICC litigation, the spectre of ICC engagement may make the authorities, and national judiciaries, take note. As already noted, the existence, or not, of effective domestic litigation remedies impact in turn on admissibility before the ICC.

This section will focus on other litigation: first transnational proceedings in foreign courts—including on universal jurisdiction—and the role of the ICJ through the well-known Advisory Opinion on the Wall. A few observations on each are noted below.

A. Foreign Courts and Universal Jurisdiction

Given the political impediments, obstacles in Israeli courts and lack of international courts with jurisdiction, it is no surprise that victims, lawyers and activists have sought to use foreign courts, invoking various bases of jurisdiction, including universal jurisdiction (UJ).[77] For the most part these cases have focused on the most egregious acts of violence as war crimes and crimes against humanity, rather than land rights claims (though such claims certainly could fall within the crimes covered by UJ). Claims have been brought in multiple states in relation to a host of violations. Invariably problematic and politically fraught, they have given rise to political interference and legal backlash, revealing varying degrees of impact— positive and negative—as a few cases illustrate.

Cases against Israel have contributed to considerable political backlash, and to restrictions in UJ laws in Europe.[78] Cases have been thrown out by foreign courts,[79] governments have intervened[80] and prosecuting authorities have refused to take

---

[77] See eg the Palestinian Centre for Human Rights (PCHR) report on 'The Principle and Practice of Universal Jurisdiction: PCHR's Work in the Occupied Palestinian Territory' (2010), which maps developments and its efforts in bringing UJ to use on the Palestinian situation, specifically pp 113–38, available at www.pchrgaza.org/files/Reports/English/pdf_spec/PCHR-UJ-BOOK.pdf.

[78] Cases in Belgium in relation to the Sabra and Shatila massacres (*Ariel Sharon et al* case) caused significant diplomatic pressure and led to the Belgian government tightening its law. The complaint was eventually thrown out by the Supreme Court; see *Haaretz* (24 September 2013) www.haaretz.com/news/belgium-s-highest-court-throws-out-case-against-sharon-1.101075. In the UK in December 2009, a London judge issued a warrant for the arrest of former Israeli Foreign Minister Livni in relation to war crimes during Israel's 2008–09 Gaza offensive, reportedly prompting procedural changes in its universal jurisdiction law in 2011; see D Machover and R Sourani,' Changes to UK Law Didn't Protect Tzipi Livni' *Al Jazeera* Opinion (10 October 2011) available at www.aljazeera.com/indepth/opinion/2011/10/201110912402659549.html.

[79] See *Sabra* and *Shatila* case (n 80) and *Bennjamin Ben Eliezer et al* case (Spain), AFP and R Sofer, 'Spain's Top Court Closes Gaza Bombing Case' *y net news* (13 April 2010) available at www.ynetnews.com/articles/0,7340,L-3875490,00.html.

[80] eg *Moshe Yaalon* case (New Zealand): arrest warrant issued on 27 November 2006 against former IDF Chief of Staff during the Al-Daraj assassination, on the basis of grave breaches of the Geneva Conventions criminalised by local statute. Within 24 hours the New Zealand Attorney General directed the district court to stay prosecution permanently, ostensibly on the grounds of insufficient material supporting the allegations. See D Eames and R Berry, 'Government Overrules War-Crimes Arrest Order' *New Zealand Herald* (1 December 2006).

them forward on grounds of the lack of presence of the accused,[81] or immunity, sometimes creating problematic precedents en route.[82] To the rare extent that foreign courts have relied on the effectiveness of domestic investigations, under a 'subsidiarity principle' incorporated into Spanish law for example, the exposing role of domestic litigation becomes relevant.[83] Sometimes delays in implementation have simply meant the individuals had left, and the issue became moot.[84]

Despite this, claims at least look set to continue, and the relevance of the role of 'foreign courts' in exercising sometimes more restrictive versions of universal or other extra-territorial jurisdiction remains. Recent examples include calls to investigate the notorious shooting by an Israeli-French officer in a French court,[85] and requests to Argentinian courts to investigate crimes committed during military operations in Gaza during 2014.[86] Certainly universal jurisdiction was very much cited as a key aspect of a strategy still considered viable at an International Meeting on the Question of Palestine supported by the United Nations.[87] Litigation has also begun to fan out to focus on the international obligations of third states, through their support for or failure in respect of corporations registered on their territories.[88]

---

[81] *Benjamin Ben Eliezer et al* case (Switzerland): in September 2003, 2 criminal complaints were submitted to the Swiss Military Attorney General on behalf of Palestinian victims in respect of war crimes by a former Israeli Minister of Defence and other IDF officials. The Prosecutor decided not to prosecute the cases, as none of the accused were on Swiss soil at time; PCHR Report (n 78) at 118–19.

[82] In the UK, in December 2009, a London judge issued a warrant for the arrest of former Israeli Foreign Minister Livni in relation to war crimes during Israel's 2008–09 Gaza offensive; the Foreign and Commonwealth Office attributed diplomatic immunity to her visit retrospectively, preventing an arrest. See also *Matar v Avraham Dichter* case (US) where a US civil class action claim brought against Dichter, the director of Shin Bet at the time of the attack on Al Daraj, was dismissed on immunity grounds; PCHR Report (n 78) at 123–24.

[83] The Spanish Appeals Court in *Bennjamin Ben Eliezer et al*: Spain voted 14–4 in favour of closing the investigation, upheld on appeal by the Supreme Court, on the grounds that the Israeli authorities had investigated the bombing; PCHR Report (n 78) at 130–31.

[84] See eg *Ami Ayalon v Netherlands* case (Netherlands): torture complaint filed with the Dutch prosecution authorities against the director of Shin Bet during the time of an alleged torture; the Public Prosecutor did not initiate an investigation, pending the result of a delayed decision regarding Ayalon's status in relation to immunity. By the time the decision had been reached, Ayalon had left Dutch territory; PCHR Report (n 78) at 126–28.

[85] See J Moore, 'Groups Call For France to Investigate IDF Shooter for "War Crime" if Israel Absolves Him' *Newsweek* (30 March 2016); he was ultimately tried in an Israeli court.

[86] Primera denuncia en Argentina contra Israel por genocidio en Gaza, www.palestinalibre.org/articulo.php?a=52321.

[87] UN Press Release, 'Experts Suggest Invoking Universal Jurisdiction among Legal Options to Address Israeli Settlements, as International Meeting on Palestine Question Continues' Meeting Coverage of the GA Committee on the Inalienable Rights of the Palestinian People, GA/PAL/1346 (8 September 2015).

[88] eg a case brought against Canada to the Human Rights Committee (HRC) on 28 February 2013 involved claims by residents of Bil'in village, alleging Canada's failure to regulate or prevent the extra-territorial actions of a Canadian registered company breaching the Geneva Convention by building settlements. See complaint at www.globalinitiative-escr.org/wp-content/uploads/2014/03/130228-Individual-Complaint-ICCPR-Canada-ETOs-FINAL.pdf; see further for judgment by Québec Superior Court, *Bil'in Village Council et al v Green Park International and Green Mount International et al*, Case No 500-17-044030-081 (18 September 2009) available at www.internationalcrimesdatabase.org/Case/938/Bil%27in-v-Green-Park/ (in English).

Arguably various negative repercussions also emerge from this practice. In the *Benjamin Ben Eliezer* case in Spain, the principle of subsidiarity was used to subvert the effectiveness of UJ by allowing Israel to conduct its own internal (and inevitably exonerating) review. In the *Dichter and other* cases, the agitation of UJ proceedings had the negative effect of setting a broader precedent for immunity from common law principles. In the *Livni* or *Sahra* and *Shatila* cases, it resulted in tightened laws, further restricting the application of jurisdiction.

That said, there may still be elements of 'success without victory' so far as such cases, while not proceeding, have nonetheless had an impact. Some arrest warrants have been issued, sending a clear message, and the spectre of such litigation has caused those accused to shift travel plans.[89] The cases have also raised the underlying issues for political, diplomatic and civil society reaction. As one writer (opposed to UJ action against Israelis) observes:

> Lawfare [UJ claims] can achieve significant goals even if the complaints fail, in fact even if the complaints fall far short of the standard for conviction. In addition to media coverage, 'universal jurisdiction' prosecutions, including those that are unjustified, can potentially influence the decision-making calculus of Israeli commanders; contribute to Israel's delegitimization and demoralization; and reduce Israel's ability to conduct diplomatic relations and communicate effectively with foreign audiences.[90]

B. The Wall Advisory Opinion

i. Background to the Opinion

The background to the *Wall* Advisory Opinion is well known. Israel began building a barrier, ostensibly for security reasons, which was said to reflect the course of the Green Line running between Israel and the occupied West Bank but in practice ran virtually completely within the Palestinian areas occupied by Israel, causing serious hardship and rights violations to many Palestinians.[91] The UN General Assembly (GA) in 2003 adopted a resolution requesting an advisory opinion from the ICJ in respect of the 'legal consequences arising from the construction of the wall' by Israel.

---

[89] See eg *Almog* case (UK): an arrest warrant for a retired Head of the Israeli Gaza Division was issued in London for war crimes, but the British police made no effort to board the aircraft upon Almog's landing on 11 September 2015. In 1 demonstration of impact, following a tip-off from the Israeli embassy, Almog decided to return to Tel Aviv (rather than continue with his trip and risk arrest); see 'Israel General "Avoids UK Arrest"' *BBC News* (12 September 2015) available at www.news.bbc.co.uk/2/hi/uk_news/4237620.stm.

[90] O Kittrie, *Lawfare: Law as a Weapon of War* (Oxford, Oxford University Press, 2016) 262.

[91] For background, see eg E Vallet (ed), *Borders, Fences and Walls: State of Insecurity?* (Farnham, Ashgate, 2014); H Ibhais and K 'Ayed, *The Separation Wall in the West Bank* (Beirut, Al-Zaytouna Centre For Studies and Consultations, 2013); D Abdullah and I Hewitt (eds), *The Battle for Public Opinion in Europe: Changing Perceptions of the Palestine-Israel Conflict* (MEMO Publishers, London, 2012); NRC Report (n 19).

The ICJ's reply, in a 14-1 majority, to the question put by the GA was that the Wall built by Israel, the occupying power, is contrary to international law.[92] On the merits[93] the Court made a number of important conclusions. Firstly, and unsurprisingly, the ICJ confirmed Israel's status as an occupying power under international law, holding:

> [t]he territories situated between the Green Line ... and the former eastern boundary of Palestine under the Mandate were occupied by Israel in 1967 during the armed conflict between Israel and Jordan ... All these territories (including East Jerusalem) remain occupied territories and Israel has continued to have the status of occupying Power.[94]

The Court noted the applicability of a number of important international law sources, principles and instruments to the OPT, of relevance given Israel's rejection of applicable law. This included (1) the principle of self-determination of peoples relating to the Palestinian people;[95] (2) the Hague Regulations (which, it said, have become part of customary law);[96] (3) Geneva Convention IV, which, it argued, was applicable owing to the armed conflict which arose between Israel and Jordan when the 1967 conflict broke out,[97] and (4) international human rights conventions such as the ICCPR and ICESCR.[98]

The Court found not only that the construction of the Wall violated the above-mentioned rules and principles,[99] but that the Israeli settlements in the OPT had also been established in breach of international law. It noted that if the Wall and its associated regime became a permanent fact, this would be tantamount to unlawful annexation. The Court considered the Wall and its regime to violate numerous human rights, including freedom of movement, right to work, health and education.[100]

Normatively, and perhaps in legal advocacy terms, the terms of the Advisory Opinion were perhaps most innovative and therefore significant in clarifying the obligations of *other* States. The ICJ observed the violation of certain *erga omnes* obligations, namely the duty to respect the right of the Palestinian people to self-determination and certain obligations under international humanitarian law. It held that states were therefore under an obligation:

> not to recognize the illegal situation resulting from the construction of the wall in the Occupied Palestinian Territory, including in and around East Jerusalem. They are also

---

[92] *Israeli Wall* Advisory Opinion (n 11) at 201–02.

[93] On the question of jurisdiction, it held both that it had jurisdiction to give the Advisory Opinion which had been requested (n 11 (at 156, 201)) and that it was appropriate, in the circumstances, to exercise that jurisdiction (n 11 (at 164, 201)).

[94] Ibid, 167.

[95] Ibid, 171.

[96] Ibid, 172.

[97] Ibid, 177.

[98] Ibid, 180.

[99] Ibid, 180–94.

[100] Ibid, 191–92.

under an obligation not to render aid or assistance in maintaining the situation created by such construction. It is also for all States, while respecting the United Nations Charter and international law, to see to it that any impediment, resulting from the construction of the wall, to the exercise by the Palestinian people of its right to self-determination is brought to an end ... [and] to ensure compliance by Israel with international humanitarian law.[101]

Assessing and in turn rejecting potential defences to these breaches, such as necessity or right of self-defence, the ICJ ultimately found that Israel should accordingly cease the construction of the Wall in the OPT and dismantle the parts that had already been built.[102]

ii. The Wall Advisory Opinion's Impact?

Some 11 years since the Court's pronouncement, it is clear that the ICJ's Advisory Opinion remains unfulfilled; the Wall still stands and has been further developed, and Israel's settlement regime has continued to expand and encroach on further areas of the OPT.

However, impact and implementation are not coterminous. It is noteworthy that there does not seem to be any comprehensive review of impact (and much of the commentary was made relatively shortly after its release)—reflecting a common deficit in impact analysis that needs to be addressed if we are to fully appreciate and build on the advances that litigation may represent. A few observations from the material available and the conversations I engaged in regarding possible levels of impact are offered for further discussion.

a. Declaratory and Normative Impact?

As set out above, the Advisory Opinion provides an authoritative interpretation of a number of points that have remained controversial in the Palestine context. It provided an authoritative statement on applicable international law. It provided unequivocal findings in law as to the nature of Israel's violations, and its obligations to stop and remedy them. It enshrined also a clarification of the obligations of *other* states in a context in which Israel is unresponsive and other states may guard their human rights reputations more cautiously. In an area where international law is developing as regards the obligations of non-cooperation of third states, the Opinion itself makes an important normative contribution as reflected in prolific citation in international academia and practice. While far from the first condemnation of illegality, the Opinion provided the imprimatur of the highest international legal institution.

---

[101] Ibid, 200.
[102] Ibid, 195.

b. Reframing and Grounding 'Political' Issues in Law, Supporting
    other International Initiatives

Responses to the Opinion tend to focus on the Israeli rejection of the decision and refusal to cooperate. However, as Sir Arthur Watts noted:

> Although Israel and a handful of other States rejected the advisory opinion, the great majority of the international community accepted it as a valuable statement of the legal position—an outcome which was helped by the fact that the ICJ adopted its conclusions with overwhelming majorities (…). [T]he Court's advisory opinion was more than just a restatement of pre-existing positions adopted by political organs of the UN: it was a legally reasoned exposition, lending the full weight of the UN's 'principal judicial organ' to propositions which hitherto had been grounded almost as much in politics as in law.[103]

The case has certainly been reflected in the subsequent work of international institutions, which have routinely referred to it and called for it to be given effect. These include the Conference of High Contracting Parties to the Fourth Geneva Convention, which refers to the *Wall* Opinion to 'reaffirm the illegality of the settlements in the said territory and of the expansion thereof and of related unlawful seizure of property as well as of the transfer of prisoners into the territory of the Occupying Power'.[104] Other recent examples include strongly worded Resolutions of the General Assembly, noting the ICJ's conclusion that 'the Israeli settlements in the [OPT] have been established in breach of international law', demanding that Israel comply with its legal obligations set out in the ICJ's Opinion, and requesting Secretary-General follow up.[105] During 2016, there were multiple resolutions by the Human Rights Council,[106] and a report of the Secretary General pursuant to GA Resolution 70/89 with an extensive update on the status of the Israeli settlements on the OPT and their impact,[107] referring to the Opinion.

There had been many strongly worded criticisms before 2004, which have also gone unheeded. Nonetheless, it certainly gave greater legal authority and support to the international community's myriad demands on Israel to comply with

---

[103] A Watts, 'Israeli Wall Advisory Opinion (Legal Consequences of the Construction of a Wall in the Occupied Palestinian Territory)' *Max Planck Encyclopaedia of Public International Law* (February 2007) para 43.

[104] Declaration of 17 December 2014, available at www.news.admin.ch/NSBSubscriber/message/attachments/37764.pdf.

[105] Resolution 70/89 of 9 December 2015, UNGA Res 70/89 (9 December 2015) UN Doc A/RES/70/89.

[106] On 24 March 2016, several resolutions were issued. These call on Israel as Occupying Power to end its occupation of the OPT (UN Doc A/HRC/31/L.36); demand that Israel, as Occupying Power, cease all practices violating the human rights of the Palestinian people including the construction of the Wall and its settlement activities; (UN Doc A/HRC/31/L.37); and demand that Israel cease all settlement activities and comply with the legal obligations in the Advisory Opinion (UN Doc A/HRC/31/L.39).

[107] 'Israeli Settlements in the Occupied Palestinian Territory, Including East Jerusalem, and the Occupied Syrian Golan' (2016) UN Doc A/71/355; see also GA Resolutions and there have been times where strong language and unequivocal assertion of violation of international law has been put forward, eg Res 37/123 regarding occupation of Golan Heights (16 December 1982) UN Doc A/RES/37/123.

international law, providing force to its condemnation. As such, it forms part of an incremental journey of many steps towards a situation in which the egregious nature of the violations is ever more blatant and indisputable.

c. Catalyst to other Responses, Discourse and Public Opinion?

The Opinion is often thought to have been ignored by the Israeli judiciary, just as it was rejected by the government, but indications suggest otherwise. The fact that Israeli courts handed down a judgment that would be seen to be addressing some of the more disproportionate impacts of the Wall just before the Opinion came out, has itself been deemed a reaction of sorts.[108]

The decision has also been described as having a mobilising and catalysing effect on advocates working on the OPT, 'breath[ing] new life into the principled fight against the fence in Israel, which had been beaten down by defeats in Israeli courts'.[109] It impelled more litigation, and submissions reflecting the judgment, in Israeli courts. It led to questions from the courts themselves and provoked the convocation of a panel extended from three to nine justices 'a rare number reserved for particularly far-reaching cases'.[110]

Finally, the decision has served as a rallying point, vindicating the demands of those advocating for Palestinian rights. Certainly, civil society organisations frequently have recourse to the Advisory Opinion in their information and advocacy materials. It has also, arguably, opened up debate on the possibility of further exploitation of this mechanism—for example, in relation to the crime of apartheid—suggesting in some sense that the existing ICJ Opinion had added value to the struggle for Palestinian rights.

The symbolic function of litigation in the reframing and relabelling that has been noted, and along with 'The Wall' case has had some impact on the terminology used to define the problem. Israel has continually referred to the Wall as a 'security fence', the UN Secretary-General (and many reports in the media) have referred to it as a 'barrier', while Palestine and the Arab States have referred to it as a 'wall'. The latter came to be adopted by the UN through, in particular, the work of John Dugard as Special Rapporteur on the Palestinian Territories, and was given

---

[108] *Beit Surik* case before Israel's Supreme Court, in Sfard (n 7) at Ch 3. He notes that on 25 June, the secretariat of the ICJ in The Hague issued a communiqué that the Court would issue its Advisory Opinion on the separation wall on 9 July; 2 days later the Israeli court summoned parties and announced its decision would come down 9 days before that of the ICJ. Its decision did not challenges lawfulness, of course, but it did introduce elements that suggest a balance between security and the need to avert a human rights catastrophe, to address disproportionate impact, thereby strengthening the argument that Israeli courts were dealing with the issue.

[109] Ibid.

[110] Sfard (n 7) at ch 3, notes the '[the judge] Barak instructed the parties to submit briefs on the impact they believed the ICJ ruling had on the rules set forth in the Beit Surik case. Was it necessary—he appeared to be asking—in light of the ICJ ruling, to change the High Court's ruling on the authority to build a fence inside occupied territory? Because the discussion was so important, Barak extended the panel from three to nine justices, a rare number reserved for particularly far-reaching cases'.

judicial endorsement by the ICJ in the Advisory Opinion, influencing to some degree at least narratives that may in time make a more substantive difference.

As to public opinion, it is at least arguable (but difficult to meaningfully assess) that the Advisory Opinion and its declaration of Israeli legality has influenced international public opinion in some quarters. In such assessments it is always difficult to separate the timing of the decision from other public opinion shaping events, such as the more recent widely reported Israeli actions in Gaza, that may have had a much more prominent impact.[111] But there is no doubt that it raised the profile of attention to the Wall and shaped the way in which the issues were discussed. Arguably other work of human rights courts and bodies has been even more significant in this respect; CERD's labelling of dual systems within the West Bank as 'segregation' in 2012 was described as having an impact on the way issues were thought about by some and discussed domestically and internationally. The big difference with the Wall case was the extent of coverage, and the perceived authority of the ICJ.

The Advisory Opinion has been the subject of extensive discussion in legal and academic circles, on the egregious nature of the violations and their implications, including for the responsibilities of third states. These debates and respected legal opinion expressed on the issue, emboldened by the ICJ, may influence perspectives on the relationship between foreign states and Israel, shifting matters of political opinion into the realm of legal obligations.

The ICJ Opinion may also be seen as a symbol of the powerlessness of the international judiciary, and the state's dismissive response as a basis for further frustration, demoralisation and sense of injustice for Palestinians. But it may also be seen differently as an authoritative judicial rebuke that at a minimum contributes strengthened legal tools with which to keep chipping away at the injustice it exposed.

V. Conclusions

The structural biases in the Israeli legal system, the ineffectiveness or apparent counter-productivity of much litigation of land rights before Israeli courts, the lack of binding international mechanisms and relative disregard for international legal authority within Israel, among other factors, call for a long, hard look at litigation goals and impact. The need to examine carefully whether and how to litigate, and how to reconsider 'success' is perhaps clearer in the context of Palestine than anywhere else, in light of the virtual impossibility of frontal challenges blocking unlawfulness and redressing injustice. 'Failure' before Israeli courts has meant not only petitions rejected, but also the consolidation of bad law

---

[111] See eg this argument in 'Israel and the World: Us and Them' *The Economist* (31 July 2014).

and the triggering of further violations in response. The 'success' of the ICJ Opinion, in the face of the continuation of the Wall, can be seen as a symbol of Israeli defiance and of the powerlessness of litigation and international justice. Each can contribute to a sense of hopelessness.

Inevitably, impact is closely associated (but not coterminous) with political opportunities, and the negativity shrouding litigation is closely linked to feelings about the desperate failure of political solutions. It would be fanciful to think that litigation will bring legal solutions in place of political ones, and much scepticism surrounds the question regarding how much closer to such solutions litigation (or indeed international engagement) has brought Palestine. Perhaps one key danger to emerge is that of privileging legal approaches over political ones.

But that is not to say litigation cannot and has not made any difference, albeit alongside other processes of community empowerment, advocacy, information dissemination and education among others. As highlighted above, litigation may have bought time, stymied the flow of violations, exposed realities, mobilised communities, increased pressure and helped maintain crucial issues on a tired international agenda. It may have forced perpetrators, governments and judiciaries to at least consider the cost, and perhaps sometimes to modify behaviour, or at least their travel plans. It has forced into the open government policy, and isolated Israel in respect of its violative policies in the OPT. It may change the cost-benefit analysis forcing it to modify policies even if it cannot attack them frontally. Through the keeping of historical records, and influence on historical narrative, it may be that, as people on the ground have often noted, litigation processes that reap little results today may contribute to other political and legal processes, and greater impact, in the future. Comparative experience of challenging injustice through the courts in other once 'hopeless' situations—equality issues during apartheid in South Africa, freedom of movement in the Soviet Union or disappearance under Argentinian dictatorship—provide reminders of the slow, subtle and sometimes immediately imperceptible ways in which frustrated litigation may advance or prepare for longer-term change.[112] It remains to be seen whether, in the fullness of time, the underwhelming nibbling at the edges of injustice will be considered futile or prove more significant than now meets the eye.

---

[112] Examples include the South African experience challenging apartheid pass laws, where exceptions were found within discriminatory laws, and expanded, or the litigation during dictatorship in Argentina in Ch 8 and the experience of Russian NGOs challenging permits or PROPOISKA system discussed in E Rekosh, KA Buchko and V Terzieva (eds), *Pursuing the Public Interest: A Handbook for Legal Professionals and Activists* (New York, Public Interest Law Initiative, 2001) 90–91. Litigation originally failed, but eventually a critical body of cases were won. They in turn were not implemented. Over time, despite this, they contributed to growing independence of the Russian judiciary and distance from the state.

Part III

10

Litigating Strategically
and Meeting the Challenges

There is no blueprint for the development of litigation strategy. It is even difficult to generalise about what constitutes 'good strategy' in the abstract, without regard to the particular situation or case, that is, to the range of goals pursued, the legal, political and social context, the particular issue at the particular time, the resources available and the obstacles (likely to be) encountered, among other considerations. So much depends on so many variable factors and conditions, that this chapter does not attempt to set down a general framework for a good strategic case. Rather, it seeks to highlight some of the many strategic considerations relevant to advancing change through SHRL and some of the ethical, professional and practical challenges that we need to meet. It suggests ways in which we may be able to create or influence the conditions most conducive to the types of impact flagged in Chapters 3 and 4, to maximise the potential of SHRL to advance human rights goals.

In as far as the goals and impact of SHRL are multi-faceted and long term, planning and investment must match this. Clearly, this involves strategic thinking beyond that of preparing, presenting and winning the case. It may include how to frame the case(s), where and when to present them, which strategies to use inside and outside of the courtroom, how to identify possible partners and allies, and to develop momentum towards a long-term multi-faceted process of change of which litigation is often but one part. There can be no formulaic approach, resulting in a magic 'strategic toolkit' but strategy can be informed by considerations of what has and has not worked, and why, in other contexts.

Discussions on developing litigation strategy often occur in the abstract, with a certain disregard for reality that should be acknowledged at the outset. Though developing strategy is an inevitably speculative exercise, it cannot be an abstract one. It is not, or perhaps should not be, an exercise where lawyers sit around a polished table with a blank sheet of paper and map out the long road to justice (though these conversations may be important and useful if part of something bigger). Strategies, like the need for litigation, emerge in various ways, and may be in large part dictated by the context and driving forces from which they emerge.

Rather than an exercise that takes place in a vacuum, context, as ever, determines how the development of strategy arises in the first place and what is likely to work. In some cases—some may say in the ideal scenario—it may emerge in the context of a broader social movement; as South Africa litigators Dugard and Langford have noted: 'advocacy and mobilisation, rather than litigation, might drive an overall long-term strategy in which litigation only plays a small, though critical, part'.[1] Indeed, it has been noted by an increasing range of commentators that in so far as SHRL pursues broad social change, SHRL is most effective when used as a tool *by* and *for* those social movements.

That said, in the real world cases do not always emerge from a broader social movement. Often violations happen, urgent needs arise and litigation responds. The *Hadijatou Mani* case, despite its wide-reaching impact on others, nonetheless emerged from the urgent need to provide a detained woman with protection rather than from a long-term litigation strategy. The same reality was reflected in the comments of the late and greatly respected Turkish advocate Tahr Elci, in response to questions regarding 'strategic litigation' on torture in detention in Turkey a couple of years ago: 'I do not know what you mean with "strategic"; in our case people who were tortured came to us and we took their cases'.[2] Moreover, in some contexts, civil society can hardly operate at all, impeding the development of broader strategies for change domestically.

The approach to the development of strategy will also differ according to the nature of the organisations or individuals involved. Even among legal actors engaged in the litigation themselves, NGOs focused on strategic litigation are more likely to develop a broad strategy for change, and seek out or respond to cases, and develop litigation strategies, within that broader framework, while private lawyers may be more inclined to be reactive and to keep a narrower focus on strategy within the case itself. Varying models of service delivery and organisational focus, different mandates and funding, are all considerations that make it impossible to generalise about how litigation strategy is, or indeed should be, developed.

Across the spectrum, it is often the case, however, that lawyers often find themselves engaged in a planning process much later than would be ideal. It is also true that it is in the nature of SHRL, that sooner or later, the need to plan for impact must be confronted. This chapter reflects on strategic choices and considerations that may positively influence impact in particular situations, offering suggestions as to how goals might be advanced, impact enhanced and potential impediments minimised.

---

[1] J Dugard and M Langford, 'Art or Science? Synthesising Lessons from Public Interest Litigation and the Dangers of Legal Determinism' (2011) 27 *South African Journal on Human Rights* 39.

[2] H Duffy, 'Strategic Litigation Impacts: Torture in Custody' Open Society Justice Initiative (Open Society Foundations, 2018).

I. Strategic Planning (and its Limits)

'If you want to make God laugh, tell him your plans'.

Woody Allen

Timely strategic planning is extremely important. It is essential to identify goals, evaluate realistically the potential contribution of litigation and other forms of action to change, and assess risk and capacity, before deciding to take on a case or cases. Identifying the means of litigation, the framing of the facts, useable evidence, the clients, the law and a forum, are the obvious basic elements that need to be taken into account and planned for in any case. With SHRL, in addition, a broader identification of longer-terms strategies is needed to enable movement towards the range of legal, political and social goals that may be pursued, the partners—and allies—that may be needed and the resources for long-term commitment that the enterprise entails.

A mistake sometimes made is to delay thinking about impact, and also implementation, until too late in the day. At its most extreme this can happen only once the 'legal' part of the case has run its course and judgment is anticipated, when lawyers may turn to advocates for help with implementation, whereas decision-making *at each stage of the process* should be influenced by an understanding of the potential impact of the case and related strategic considerations.

It is true that goals may shift, as may the nature of strategic considerations, and decisions will need to be reviewed and revised at different stages in the process to reflect these shifts. It is nonetheless important to start the process with the end in mind, and a clear commitment to a flexible and responsive approach. If the pursuit is mainly of restorative, victim-centred goals, then the greatest emphasis may be put on evaluating the process of litigation itself, and the extent to which it gives victims a degree of satisfaction through participation, for example. If, on the other hand, getting access to information is important, more emphasis will be placed on identifying the best avenues for obtaining it. If changing entrenched attitudes is among the goals, media strategy and developing communication partnerships and strategic messaging may be as important as any legal filing.

Most organisations that engage in SHRL will develop broad strategic plans, which may reflect particular theories of change to account for the ways in which litigation may contribute to change on various dimensions. They will generally also have case selection criteria to facilitate decision-making on specific cases. Strategic plans, considered case selection criteria and an adequate internal process, can be very valuable for litigating organisations on various grounds. They provide a framework to assist in the process of identifying the goals and potential impact of case, as well as more managerial functions of ensuring efficient allocation of resources, helping prevent organisational overreach, facilitating transparency and equity to ensure that the decisions are fair and justifiable, and of course engaging and reporting to funders. Available resources, and expertise, compliance with funders' conditions and organisational constitutional requirements, will all play a role for organisations in decision-making.

Inevitably however, strategic plans, pursuant to theories of change, and case selection criteria are frameworks rather than checklists. To begin with, there is a limit to what we control, or can even anticipate, in the journey towards long-term social change for example, and myriad factors will influence the array of impacts as set out in Chapter 4. In fact, SHRL is, in practice, often *opportunistic*: timing and the ability to respond to unanticipated windows of opportunity is one of its essential features, because cases sometimes emerge 'spontaneously' or the landscape changes in a particular way that may suddenly make the time right for a particular argument or approach to prevail. The case studies are replete with examples where litigation was responsive and adjusted to such moments of political and legal opportunity.[3] Indeed, adjusting to immediate crises, as well as opportunities, is the staple of human rights litigators and has led to some of the most significant litigation.

Perhaps surprisingly, this does not make strategic planning any less important. But it informs how we plan for and conduct litigation; plans do not provide a detailed road-map, but they offer at least a 'framework' to guide the litigation effort. To avoid the danger that unrealistic plans become a straitjacket that impedes action rather than aiding it, flexibility remains key. In other words, perhaps we need to plan strategically, but also know that God will laugh—and be prepared to laugh with her.

II. Identifying Goals and Realistically Assessing Risks

Assessment of goals, risks and foreseeable impact is an essential starting point for any litigation. In very broad terms, the goals pursued determine strategy and inform plans and tactics.[4] in line with the emphasis placed on understanding impact throughout this study, goals should be considered and defined in terms of the diverse and broad-reaching ways in which litigation can have an impact you seek to achieve as set out in Chapter 3. Having a clear sense of goals (and whose goals they are), and monitoring and re-appraising them throughout the process, is critically important.

Firstly, careful scrutiny of goals is a prerequisite to giving responsible and realistic advice to clients, and to responding effectively to their decisions and

---

[3] eg the Argentinian experience in the case study (Ch 8) exemplifies the extent to which litigation strategy adjusted all the time, though each of the studies illustrates this quite clearly in different ways.

[4] While closely interrelated, strategy may be understood as the broader identification of goals/potential impact and the development of the theory by which the relevant impact can be achieved, while planning may go more specifically to how and when this will be done.

instructions. This provides the basis for managing the expectations of victims and survivors—unmanaged expectations being one of the greatest dangers of SHRL.

Goals may vary between victims and other affected individuals, supportive NGOs and other actors. Difficult ethical questions—noted below—can arise when goals conflict, and these must be confronted and addressed as transparently as possible. Multiple actors may *each* have multiple goals; some may be identified as primary goals, others secondary, and indeed one goal may simply be not to act inconsistently with the goals of others. Success in an individual case may mean achieving its own goals while seeking to ensure that these do not impede, for example, broader policy aims. At the same time, the task of correctly understanding and interpreting what affected persons want, in the face of massive human rights violations, may itself require considerable insight into complex cultural and psychological issues.[5]

Secondly, it is also worth recalling that goals are fluid, and that in practice they do shift over time. By way of example, victims' priorities shift as violations cease and knowledge increases: a primary goal while violations are unfolding will often be pursuit of information, and cessation of the wrongs, yet when the information is received in the course of litigation, and perhaps hope of cessation or restitution fades, compensation or accountability become more significant.

Thirdly, especially given the enormity of some human rights challenges and underlying sustaining factors, it may be considered important to identify short- or medium-term objectives, which are more specific and attainable,[6] alongside longer-term goals. Goals and priorities will also shift in line with what is achievable politically, as the broader landscape changes. Clear examples of such shifts emerge in the case studies from Latin America. In post-dictatorship Argentina for example, families of victims of enforced disappearance most wanted information that might lead to the location of missing loved ones, and only once information was forthcoming did the accountability goal come into sharp focus. Clearly articulated, but realistic and flexible goals can provide a beacon as the process unfolds.

Finally, goals—together with our assessment of the potential for positive and negative impact—may affect the cases we select, where we litigate them, the way we argue them and with whom we partner, and will strongly influence strategy, tactics and plans. Goals provide one measure against which we ultimately evaluate 'success' and learn from litigation. Like impact, they are about so much more than a narrow view of what it is to 'win' or 'lose': a judgment that finds against

---

[5] See eg work of anthropologists on interpreting the reparation goals and objectives of indigenous groups in some parts of Guatemala in the case study on Guatemala (Ch 6). The work of psychologists and anthologists should, ideally, inform legal work at this stage.

[6] Funders may require that these are 'SMART' goals: Specific, Measurable, Attainable, Realistic/Relevant and Time Bound. Limits on measurability, and the importance of funder flexibility and sensitivity, are noted below.

victims may nonetheless constitute positive impact, and meet some victim goals, while conversely the 'success' of a judgment in the victim's favour, that ultimately makes no obvious difference in bringing about the change he or she pursued, is questionable.[7] Evaluating different levels of impact and assessing 'success' is best done in light of a clear understanding of evolving goals; what was and is important to whom and why.

The Hippocratic oath applicable to physicians should apply with equal force to human rights lawyers and advocates. 'First, do no harm' may seem like a very minimal baseline, but, in practice, litigation will often be inherently risky in diverse ways, and avoiding harm cannot be taken for granted. Those most affected by the risks will face sometimes excruciating decisions as to whether the risks to themselves and perhaps others are ones they are willing and able to countenance. To do so they obviously need sound advice (not necessarily only from lawyers) based on as full a risk assessment as possible. Responsible lawyering entails guarding against disappointments, disempowerment and despondency, as well as against the harassment or security implications, that may ensue during or after the litigation process. The risk of manipulation or re-victimisation, compounding the original wrongs, deserves much more careful attention than it is sometimes given in practice.

The challenges to understanding and evaluating risk are considerable, but it is ethically important to ask whether those of us involved in litigation, or the various legal systems, do enough to ensure we do no harm, and to minimise risks that are assumed.

Risks in respect of one set of goals may be offset by gains in others, but the weight to be afforded to different goals and risks is often far from obvious in practice. When, for example, it appears likely that a court will rule unfavourably on a case, difficult questions include how to weigh the potential value of moving forward with litigation (eg public education, shaming the government, establishing a public record of violations) against the risk of creating bad precedent or other harm, including the financial costs of litigation.

Any risk of a litigation backlash—like any other form of impact—should be assessed in the short and longer term and from diverse vantage points. A current case in point relates to sexual orientation rights in parts of Africa, where a difficult and at times fraught debate relates to whether, and if so how, to confront egregious homophobia within the African system. While some favour an approach that confronts the inequality head on, many are mindful of the potential for negative results and favour an incremental approach that builds towards the same goal over time (see section IV below on incremental approaches). In this connection, it is also crucial to long-term human rights change to keep in mind the possible impact of the planned litigation on relations between activists and other groups,

---

[7] The difference between impact and winning is more fully explored in Ch 4.

and on broader movements for change. At the same time, just as impacts often surprise us by surpassing goals or expectations, so do litigators show remarkable strength in deciding to venture forth despite the potential risks, and in doing so make possible positive strides forward for human rights for others. It may be that with an extremely risk-averse approach, few would litigate serious human rights violations at all. What is clear is that the decision to do so must be taken by those most affected, based on sound advice, involving sometimes impossible personal decisions and tricky political judgement calls.

III. Litigating in Context: Understanding, Naming and Framing the Problem

It perhaps goes without saying that it is essential to understand and confront the nature of the violations at the heart of the litigation. This includes understanding the political and social context in which violations occur and what influences the way they are seen, including the prejudices, preconceptions, or sustaining factors that may underpin the violations.[8] Violations are often accompanied by numerous justifications: for example, law enforcement agencies have justified what may be discriminatory treatment by suggesting that certain groups are 'disproportionately criminal' or 'dangerous' in the context of broader security concerns. Similarly, 'health and safety', tourism or planning considerations have been used to justify evictions in Palestine, in an attempt to make the violations seem like innocuous administrative measures in the general public interest.

As such, the nature of the phenomenon may not be plain on its face, and exposing and reframing, as already noted, can be critically important, not only within the courtroom but also beyond it—legally, politically and symbolically. The *Identoba v Georgia* case before the ECtHR provides a neat example. The state's failure to prevent or investigate the violent obstruction of an anti-homophobia demonstration assumed greater significance when categorised by the Court not merely as a violation of the marchers' rights to freedom of expression and of assembly and association, but also of their rights to be free from degrading treatment and discrimination.[9] Several of the case studies highlight the significance of reframing an issue—the OPT land violations as apartheid,[10] the Guatemalan massacres as

---

[8] Most cases concern inequality and social prejudice—the resolution of which, if it ever comes, will be generational. This will often involve addressing discrimination that is deeply embedded in the social fabric, which is especially challenging.

[9] *Identoba v Georgia* Appl no 73235/12 (12 May 2015) (ECtHR) was a ground-breaking case involving harassment of anti-homophobia demonstrators. I was adviser to counsel of Identoba in the case along with a colleague from Interights.

[10] Ch 9.

genocide,[11] or the Argentinian detentions as enforced disappearances[12]—as significant on many levels. Framing may also matter for the identification of potential allies and intersections, jurisdictions and available fora, and more broadly for the strategies or tactics employed (some of which are identified below).

The question of whether any piece of litigation could not only aim to redress the immediate wrong in a narrow sense but also seek in the longer term to change the underlying conditions is a perennial challenge for SHRL. It compels litigators to consider in each case who the relevant audiences are likely to be, and which arguments—presented where and by whom—are most likely to be influential. This is especially important and challenging when cases concern, at their core, inequality and prejudices that are deeply embedded in the social fabric and which many people may consider normal (as in perhaps all of the case studies). Change, if it comes, like the problem, may be multi-generational.

IV. Litigating for the Long Term: Incremental Change and the Question of Timing

Understanding the political and social context at any particular point in time is therefore inextricably linked to a realistic assessment of potential possibilities and risks. Practice shows that it is crucial to stay alert to how these may change, presenting opportunities that were not previously present. Although systems vary in their approach to 'precedent' or the weight to be given to previous decisions, practice reminds us that, across systems, rejection by a court at one point in time does not necessarily mean the same approach will be taken later.[13] As things change so do litigation opportunities, perhaps as a result of previous litigation alongside many other factors.

Argentina provides an example of how environmental factors changed gradually over time, influencing and influenced by litigation. The truth trials in Argentina, the orders to proceed to trial in European countries, the arrest of Chilean dictator Augusto Pinochet in London in 1998 and a broadly trending discontent with impunity on the international level, as reflected (among other things) in the adoption of the ICC Statute the same year, are among the international

---

[11] Ch 6: the Commission in *Plan de Sanchez* (IACtHR, *Case of Plan de Sánchez Massacre v Guatemala*, Judgment (Merits), IACtHR Ser C No 105 (29 April 2004)) recognised 'genocide; of the indigenous groups victimised by the scorched earth policy, while this was not legally relevant it was very significant. One objective of this case was to have the nature of genocide recognised, which it had not yet been at that stage in Guatemala in 1995.

[12] Ch 6.

[13] See below on the value of sequential cases on this basis, and comments in section III on cumulative impact.

factors that paved the way for the reopening of criminal cases in Argentina. The immediate trigger was however a particular piece of litigation challenging the constitutionality of the amnesty laws.[14] The relevance of timing to the political gamble of pursuing litigation has been described in this way:

> Pinochet was arrested in London, the truth trials were making progress throughout the country, Judge Garzón's extradition requests made ... at that moment we understood that the conditions were given, and we were coming up on 25 years since the military coup. Then we submitted the repeal request and in March 2001 Judge Cavallo declared the laws null and void.[15]

This corresponds with what has been discussed in relation to the cumulative impact of litigation in Chapter 3 (and the advantages of clusters of cases later in this section). Consistent with the incremental, long-term nature of change, strategies need to be flexible and incremental, pursuing perhaps modest impacts at each stage of a longer journey. Understanding evolving contexts and shaping strategies on the move, with the flexibility to respond when a confluence of factors indicate there may be the possibility for change, are key.

V. Strategic Nibbling at the Edges of Injustice v Judicial Confrontation?

How we choose to frame an issue, and when and how to challenge it, are therefore crucial strategic decisions that involve careful consideration. Relatedly, and perhaps ironically, it is often in the face of the most extreme systemic injustice that frontal attacks on the unlawfulness of violations are least viable. As Geoff Budlender noted of the use of the courts during apartheid South Africa:

> In reviewing those areas where there was success in this enterprise it is necessary to analyze what distinguished the successes from the failures. In the first instance, there was clearly no possibility of success if the legal attack threatened the very foundations of the system. A technically valid attack on the legality of racial discrimination per se, or on the constitutional foundations of the state, would have been either rejected in the courts or (if upheld) promptly reversed by legislation[16]

---

[14] The famous *Simón* case finding amnesties incompatible with human rights under the Constitution and international law, discussed at Ch 8.

[15] Horacio Verbitsky journalist and long-time president of CELS (presentation during the VIII Seminario Internacional de Políticas de la Memoria, Centro Cultural Haroldo Conti, Buenos Aires, 24 September 2015). He also notes 'there was going to be a lot of social mobilization on the anniversary of the coup'.

[16] Geoffrey Budlender, Foreword, in R Abel, *Politics by Other Means: Law and the Struggle Against Apartheid (After the Law)* (New York, Routledge, 1995).

Richard Abel explains the gradual erosion of apartheid legislation, specifically legislation limiting freedom of movement (the '*dompas* system') and land rights, through 'technical' arguments that could be upheld and slowly make holes in the laws, to allow a little light in. He sets out how the *dompas* system was challenged first by arguing that women should be allowed to stay with their husbands in 'white areas', and then their children also. After that, again on technical arguments, litigation advanced an interpretation of the law that changed the rules that had made it impossible for black workers to secure the benefits normally attached to continuous employment.[17] The litigation did not displace the offending underlying principle, nor did it give rise to legal briefs that could be used as resounding advocacy documents. It may even have left a bad taste in the mouths of rights-minded lawyers. But, by doing what was feasible and useful in the particular context, it helped, gradually, to carve out exceptions and, in doing so, to expose the weakness in the underlying law or policies, paving the way for further change at other moments of opportunity and in other ways.

The litigation of Palestinian rights in Israeli courts has at times presented a similar spectacle: where frontal challenges to unlawfulness are rendered impossible by the law or the courts, including through a broad doctrine of 'non-justiciability', strategies may involve frustrating policies, finding exceptions that narrow their scope and impact, modifying their implementation and the like. Some feel that the gains of this nibbling at the edges of injustice are slight, and the costs considerable in terms of potentially legitimising the system (arguments that surfaced in South Africa too). Reference in the Occupied Palestinian Territories context to litigation as a form of 'resistance' is also reminiscent of the fact that in many of the most challenging situations it may not be possible to confront justice head on, or to press for the most progressive advances in rights protections, but instead strategic litigation may at times be defensive, preventing or slowing deterioration in standards or protections.

VI. Exploiting Litigation Synergies: Movement Building, Legal Advocacy and Reaching beyond the Court

There has been growing recognition of the relationship between litigation and the social movements of which it will often—perhaps ideally—form part, as already highlighted above.[18] An awareness of how litigation emerges from

---

[17] The law provided that every year employment of black people commenced afresh—denying black workers the benefits that accrue from continuous employment. This was all based on the wording of the legislation and small ways of defeating the practical impact of it.

[18] J Cavallaro and S Brewer, 'The Virtue of Following: The Role of Inter-American Litigation in Campaigns for Social Justice' (2008) 8 *SUR Journal on Human Rights* 85, 88–89.

broader human rights agendas and movements, and how it might feed into them, should be an aspect of strategic litigation planning from the outset.[19] Similarly, experience suggests that an active role for organised civil society in litigation efforts will be one crucial factor enhancing many of the levels of impact flagged in Chapter 4.[20]

Sometimes enabling or removing obstacles to social mobilisation, or empowering social movements, might be one of the objectives, or consequences, of SHRL. The importance of this level of impact to long-term investment in change is clear. But so too are the associated challenges in building movement and constituency around certain types of rights issues and certain groups of 'victims'.[21] As the case studies show, the nature of affected groups of victims and their support group may make an enormous difference to the ability to constructively engage the public, influential political actors or indeed the courts themselves through SHRL. Quite different considerations arise for example in the 'war on terror' context, in terms of the identification of 'target groups', or the ability of those most affected to mobilise, develop and direct strategies of response, compared with the politically organised and supported Latin American domestic human rights movements around accountability for example. This is linked to the importance of understanding and confronting the challenges posed by context, including inequality, fear and prejudice—all of which must be taken into account in shaping litigation and advocacy responses. Other challenges may arise where victims and survivors are non-residents, and perhaps even excluded from the state by the government, making change through SHRL extremely difficult. In such circumstances, bringing them into the judge's, policy-makers' and public's consciousness is more important and more challenging.

A. Litigation and Advocacy

It follows from the nature of most of the multi-faceted and broad-reaching goals or impacts discussed in Chapter 4—such as catalysing political solutions or bringing about gradual social cultural or attitudinal change—that if it is to achieve its potential it will much more often than not have to be part of much broader action

---

[19] It should not only arise, as can be the case, when the case requires broad-reaching 'implementation' by other actors if it is to be given effect.

[20] Many of the research efforts in this field referred to in this book point to the role of organised civil society groups: see eg S Budlender, G Marcus SC and N Ferreira, *Public Interest Litigation and Social Change in South Africa: Strategies, Tactics and Lessons* (New York, Atlantic Philanthropies, 2014); Charles Epp's study on US, Canadian, UK and Indian courts; Garavito's study of Colombian courts and Duffy, 'Litigating Torture in Custody' (n 2) on the impact of litigation in Argentina, Kenya and Turkey.

[21] *cf* political torture in Argentina in Ch 8, and security-related violations in Ch 7 for example; identifying a group, and its ability to organise for change is hampered. Duffy (n 2) contrasts Argentinian torture and ill-treatment of victims during democracy with those marginalised groups subject to TCIDT in detention centres today.

for change. The case studies provide ample support for the view that litigation can have broader impact if there is a focus beyond the strictly legal and practical case-building, to other complementary tools, notably monitoring, campaigning, advocacy, and exposing, education and capacity building, legislative reform initiatives, media and communications. Some have gone so far as to call litigation so understood '*politics by other means*'.[22]

It should also be recalled that litigation has its limits as an agent for political and social change, and associated tensions can arise. Some of the goals of litigation (for example, rule of law goals) may warrant caution in this respect, ie it will be important to locate the case within, yet—as appropriate—set it apart from, political processes, if it is to fully realise its particular potential. Litigation is, in significant part, about giving effect to the law in particular contexts and its 'rule of law' function should not—and need not—be compromised by its strategic political use. Professional constraints, ethical obligations and in particular careful respect for judicial independence and impartiality—actual and perceived—both contribute to and reflect the integrity and legitimacy of the process, and ultimately therefore have an effect upon on its impact. Particular sensitivities can arise as to the cohabitation of advocacy and litigation roles within organisations, as well as from the respective roles of legal representatives and NGOs where goals may be quite different and clarity in respect of priorities and obligations is essential.

Strategic human rights litigators are increasingly aware of how what happens within the courtroom or legal procedure can have broader repercussions. Effective and targeted communication of litigation's message to a wider audience is one of the challenges, and not one that necessarily comes naturally to lawyers.

Where possible, the use of other vehicles to tell the story behind the case, most obviously engaging the press, but potentially also story tellers, artists, playwrights and film-makers for example, can maximise the reach and effect of legal work.

Legal documents and presentations in court may well themselves serve a useful broader advocacy function too, for some audiences, provided they are used consistently with relevant legal and procedural constraints such as confidentiality. Strategic introduction of expert evidence, including expert legal opinions but also multi-disciplinary perspectives such as from historians and anthropologists, can help to tell a fuller story. With a savvy media and advocacy strategy, a renowned expert can constitute a newsworthy hook, as well as drawing in valuable voices to the internal legal deliberations. Statements and attendance by international public figures can also raise the profile of a case, drawing greater interest into the process. Use of independent *amicus* interveners are also a way to profile a particular issue— such as the focus by the Special Rapporteur on terrorism and human rights on the right to truth in the rendition hearings at the ECtHR. Ben Emmerson intervened in the hearing of the Al Nashiri and Abu Zubaydah cases at the ECtHR, discussed in Ch 7. In various ways, what goes on within a case can perfectly appropriately

---

[22] Abel, *Politics by Other Means* (n 16).

and usefully be given a life outside the case, and can be used also by others in their litigation strategies.

There are also limits on the extent to which what happens in court can, or should, be shaped by a broader advocacy agenda that should be borne in mind; not least, it would be unstrategic to push too far such that judges may react if they feel 'manipulated' in a way that *they* consider inappropriate. This is partly about careful adherence to rules, procedures and professional standards, but also legal and judicial cultures will vary considerably in this respect. Conversely, attention should also be paid to how litigation may affect the advocacy agenda, and vice versa. Litigation may in certain circumstances, whether directly or indirectly, impede advocacy and thereby affect the realisation of some of its goals, such as fomenting debate and catalysing political solutions. The fact of pending litigation may, depending on the system, render issues '*sub judice*' and subject to reporting constraints during the case. There has recently been debate for example in the Netherlands, on whether the undoubtedly significant litigation on the Srebrenica massacre hampered activism and debate in this way.[23] Questions may also arise as to whether the whole range of relevant interests, perspectives and issues can stay in the discussion once a litigation process has started. For example, it is often difficult to ensure that attention is still paid to broader issues such as underlying causes, contributors and non-repetition, and that the debate does not narrow unduly to the responsibility of defendants in a particular case. Litigation *can* contribute to that broader debate but this will generally not happen alone.

It also deserves emphasis here that while litigation may be a useful complementary tool, it is also in some quite obvious ways a more restrictive one and its utility should not be assumed. This includes the narrow jurisdictional limitations that require that only limited types of cases, by persons who meet limited criteria, can be brought before particular fora, that will in turn apply the applicable law within the constraints of accepted discourse of rights in the relevant judicial-legal culture. Together with limitations on the types of evidence and voices that can be brought into the process, this may further restrict the utility of the process. In determining the power of litigation alongside other forms of advocacy and pressure for change, all of these limitations and the challenges, as set out in Chapter 2, must be kept firmly in mind.

The effectiveness of human rights litigation has been described as largely dependent on the '*extra-legal skills of the lawyers involved*'.[24] The challenges for many lawyers in meeting professional and ethical obligations, while having an eye on larger social and political issues, are potentially enormous and positive experience-sharing and support from formal and informal networks is of vital

---

[23] Comments Amsterdam roundtable March 2017.

[24] B Kingsbury, 'Representation in Human Rights Litigation' (6 April 2000) Carnegie Council for Ethics in International Affairs available at www.carnegiecouncil.org/publications/archive/dialogue/2_02/articles/611.

importance. It should also be acknowledged that lawyers are not always the best people to do many aspects of this work, and many NGOs—whose role, if available, is likely to be crucial—will not have the capacity to assume the burden of all aspects of SHRL. This makes it critical to identify a range of relevant local, national and international partners, allies or supporters, experts from other disciplines beyond the law too, whose timely engagement may be a crucial factor in maximising impact (see section D on partnerships and roles).

B. The Role of the Media

The role of communications, and the constructive use of the media by litigators (whether lawyers, victim groups or both) has proved critical to impact in many cases. To achieve the levels of impact identified above—exposure, education, shaping discourse, debate and influencing attitudes—this is clearly central. The development of a communications strategy, however modest, and nurturing ties with interested media contacts to ensure the quality of coverage are now common features of NGO work around SHRL.

There is no shortage of examples of communications strategy making a positive difference. The role of media in reporting in detail on the *Hadijatou Mani* case was critical in catalysing debate, empowering other women to assert their rights and eroding the state of denial surrounding slavery in Niger—among the most important levels of impact of the ECOWAS case. There are however, also many examples of unfavourable coverage, at times demonising individual victims and the courts.[25] In political environments hostile to human rights, such as those in which many security-related violations occur, the role of the media can be extremely important, with the risk that it can also be counterproductive, depending on the nature of the coverage. In the Litigating the 'War on Terror' study, we see litigation that prompted varying coverage, but which contributed to ensuring that the stories of individuals—which were meant to remain secret—are known around the world.

Depending on the case and context, part of the value of litigation can lie in its ability to create newsworthy events and hooks—which may arise at various stages from the lodging of the case, to a hearing, to its conclusion or follow-up. It can, however, often be a challenge to generate sufficient media and public interest in litigation, and creating accessible explanations of why apparently remote and lofty legal proceedings matter can be a crucial skill to develop in SHRL. Where

---

[25] See eg the UK example of Abu Qatada and the controversy surrounding the ECtHR decision to block his extradition to Jordan (*Othman (Abu Qatada) v UK* Appl no 8139/09 (9 May 2012) (ECtHR)); and the negative attention surrounding the case brought by Gina Miller concerning Brexit and the triggering of Art 50 (*R (on the application of Miller and another) v Secretary of State for Exiting the European Union*) [2017] UKSC 5).

an independent media is compromised, as may often be the case in situations of massive violations, the impact of SHRL is often neutered.

While generally an important dimension of outreach, media engagement is time-consuming and its value should not be assumed in all cases. Beyond directly poor coverage, or very limited coverage that may have required disproportionate investment of time, certain solutions may be taken off the table once the case is in the public eye. In the rendition context, reparations settlements—which have been extremely rare—were made explicitly conditional on non-disclosure. More subtly, media attention may back a government into a position in which it adopts less favourable but more politically palatable positions.[26] The role of pressure through the media may be a useful tool, and the challenge is therefore to ensure sufficient interest and adequate reporting, but its utility cannot be taken for granted.

C. Complementary (Non-litigation) International Processes?

As noted already, human rights litigation is one of many regional and international processes that exist to give effect to human rights standards. Developing the inter-relationship between litigation and *other* mechanisms that are not specifically connected with it can amplify impact. These would include the dynamic relationship between litigation and monitoring processes through, for example, the UN or regional special procedures, state reporting processes, or the Universal Periodic review, as well as civil society campaigns and various public and private media initiatives, among others. This inter-relationship can be seen in the momentum of mounting condemnation of Israel for violations of Palestinian land rights, through the construction of the wall, preceding the Advisory Opinion (see Chapter 9) or the rendition litigation (Chapter 7) wherein Special Rapporteurs among others have provided a form of follow-up through their repeated references to the cases, thereby keeping the issue on the table and the conversation alive. Some bodies have multiple functions within their institution, such that there may be even greater scope for complementarity in the exercise of the multiple roles. For example, the UNHRC, and the African and Inter-American Commissions all hear individual cases as well as compiling state reports. The case studies in Latin America show how pressure has consistently been maintained through the procedures of state reporting, monitoring and enquiry, alongside litigation. Advocates and others should consider engaging those entities effectively to maximise the various levels of impact of litigation.

---

[26] See examples in Duffy (n 2) regarding prisons roundtable discussions as part of friendly settlement and negotiations in Argentinian prisons cases.

D. Developing the Right Partners, Networks and Coalitions

Developing a holistic approach to litigation advocacy and other forms of action is closely linked to the identification of key partners. The people best placed to advance the strategy will depend, among other things, on the goals and context, audiences to be accessed and obstacles to be neutralised. The most obvious partners are civil society partners who are often at the heart of, or somehow connected to many SHRL successes—whether or not directly involved in the cases themselves. The role for parliamentarians, politicians, professional entities in the relevant field such as law associations, medical experts and service providers or unions, and the role of academia and the media, referred to above, may all be key.

The right partners may be essential for access and trust. There are good reasons why affected communities may feel naturally untrusting towards legal organisations swooping in on litigation 'opportunities'. In this situation, it may be that natural partners for those most affected, and bridges to other actors—including lawyers, will be civil society organisations that provide social services or humanitarian assistance, not legal ones. Needless to say, where state partners can be harnessed, as in Argentina when the state became a partner once it developed the policy of 'truth, justice and memory', the litigation had wind in its sails. Garnering cross-party political support may help the reframing of issues, generate trust, and build towards long-term social and democratic goals, as opposed to political opportunism which may provide shorter-term gains.

The composition of the legal team itself is also an important part of the equation. Many factors are relevant, including legal skills, knowledge of and respect from the relevant court, broader experience, identity and profile. There may then be advantage to the engagement of 'repeat player litigators' with knowledge of systems and courts.[27] This does not mean that the same organisations should litigate all the cases, and there is also much to be gained from broadening the base of those litigating internationally for example—as has happened in recent years—by bringing litigation closer to the ground, and victims closer to the court. Issues of client representation are complex and trust is crucial. Having representatives from among affected communities, where possible, may enhance the relationship of trust, but at other times it will not. There are many examples throughout history of 'landmark' litigation where relatively inexperienced lawyers have achieved great things, either despite or maybe even because of their relative inexperience and willingness to take risks.[28]

---

[27] Dugard and Langford, 'Art or Science?' (n 1). There has been some discussion again in the South African context with regard to 'repeat player litigators', which might have an advantage over one-shotters. The repeat player advantage can be achieved in a number of ways, such as through providing litigation support to a range of similar organisations (eg social movements).

[28] The famous Somerset slavery case of 1772, in which the judge Lord Mansfield is generally attributed with changing the law on slavery in England, is an example of a case where the role of an inexperienced but determined lawyer has been said to have been a significant factor in contributing to litigation impact. See interesting analysis of the factors that enhanced impact, with remarkable

At the same time, in a growing field, experience within the relevant system, and of comparative systems (for comparative arguments and identifying alternative approaches that have prevailed elsewhere) lend obvious value. Ideally, it may well be that what works best is a small complementary group of partners that can draw on various strengths and characteristics. The Mani team was, in my experience, a positive example of one such well-functioning international legal partnership. There was a strong, leading role for civil society, consisting of a local network working closely with the applicant, and a committed international network led by Anti-slavery International, with a legal team comprising Nigerien, regional and international men and women with diverse backgrounds, expertise and areas of focus.

As in any other litigation, careful attention should be paid to ensuring that it is the clients who make the choices as to their representation, and that the profile of the whole legal team in the particular context is not overlooked. In addition to the core litigation team (whatever the particular model), it is no less important that this team be supplemented by a coalition or 'constituency' of support. Sometimes, challenging questions arise as to how we effectively build consensus and coalition while ensuring effectiveness in the litigation and other work. But what is clear from my experience, is that waiting until the implementation stage—hoping that 'advocacy' actors will then spring into action to ensure full implementation of litigation—rarely works well. Developing a sense of ownership by a broader range of actors is likely to significantly define litigation's impact.

E. Educating Judges and Improving Human Rights Literacy

Numerous cases show how judicial education may be a positive impact associated with litigation, whether directly or indirectly. If judges are unaware of rights or unwilling to give effect to them, providing judicial training and education programmes—ideally before litigation—may be a crucial complementary activity. Given the ethical and professional consideration linked to the integrity and weight of the judicial function, questions may arise concerning the closeness of, for example, advocates and judges involved in a capacity-building relationship during litigation processes. Some caution may therefore be due, in order to avoid any perception of inappropriate influence that could undermine the litigation.

Human rights conscious judges may and often do also provide invaluable partners and interlocutors, with various key roles beyond the obvious judicial one. They may play roles in the judicial trainings or 'cross-judicial dialogues', in monitoring, commenting on, or potentially intervening in cases that raise important

resonance today, in SM Wise, *Though the Heavens May Fall: The Landmark Trial That Led to the End of Human Slavery* (Boston, DeCapo Press, 2005). There are many contemporary examples, eg *Marcx v Belgium* which shaped standards before the ECtHR or the landmark *Roe v Wade* case argued by a lawyer in her 20s on her first appearance before the Supreme Court.

human rights issues of common concern. In a context in which judges look with increasing interest to the work of their global peers, engaging judges—again in an appropriate and non-compromising way—in SHRL is worthwhile.

VII. Case Selection, Sourcing and Tactics: Is there a Right Case at the Right Time?

One of the challenges faced by organisations that seek to pursue change through law is the sourcing and selection of cases ripe for productive litigation. Various models of 'sourcing' cases exist in practice. At one end of the spectrum are the cases that happen without any particular strategic objective, so that the first challenge for other actors may simply be to know about the case in a timely way, spot its potential and find an appropriate way of supporting it so as to maximise its strategic impact.[29] At the other end are cases that are in a sense 'manufactured' by international interest groups, with a view to strategic goals, whereby victims would usually have to be found who are willing to have a case pursued in their name.[30] This may even involve advertising for anyone in that category who was thinking they may wish to bring a case to get in contact.[31] In between, there is a range of ways to identify and pursue SHRL, through networks, education and ongoing mentoring: the 'litigation surgeries' that Interights ran were an example that combined these strategies, in order to develop relationships with and to support partners, while identifying potentially significant cases.

Each of these examples raises questions as to the most effective and appropriate approaches to strategic case sourcing and selection, and views about it differ. Much depends—as ever—on goals, but the actors from which cases emerge, and those engaged in and committed to them from the outset, are likely to influence litigation's ultimate impact. Strategic litigation cases that pursue broad social change but do not emerge from, or have a close connection to, the affected communities may not make the same difference on the ground as those that do, nor perhaps should they be expected to. As was observed of successful litigation within the South African anti-apartheid context 'the legal work was most successful when its strategies were used in support of mass movements'.[32] Put differently, where those movements impel the strategies in the first place, the impact will naturally be particularly pronounced.

---

[29] Issues include the effectiveness of access to information concerning on-going case docket before regional and international courts, which varies between bodies.

[30] This depends on the system: where *actio popularis* is possible, no such victim may be needed but this is rare and a victim in whose name the case is brought is usually a prerequisite.

[31] The NGO Process for Change advances this approach.

[32] Geoff Budlender—leading South African activist and lawyer.

SHRL cannot lose sight of the fact there is, after all, a right to a remedy on the part of those whose rights have been violated, and human rights litigation is in large part about treating human beings as rights bearers and making their rights a reality.[33] Care must be taken to ensure that these rights are not undercut by SHRL. It is also worth emphasising that the ideal case may be an illusion. A key message in this study is that there is a limit to what we control in litigation: cases happen, and when they do, the question for those interested in SHRL may be whether to lend weight to the case, how to assist or what role to assume, to maximise positive and minimise negative impact, rather than whether it is a 'best case scenario'.

A. Single Case, Sequential Cases or a Series?

Understanding impact as cumulative was emphasised in Chapter 3 and above in this section. Cumulative impact may emanate, as the case studies show, not from a case but from multiple cases or, as just noted, more often from the interaction of litigation with other processes. There are several ways in which this might be reflected in tactical litigation choices.

The bringing of *multiple* contemporaneous cases may serve to expose the systematic nature of the wrong in an effective way, and/or to create a helpful dynamic between cases that approach strategy slightly differently. Lithuanian rendition cases provide an example of this.[34] Our case proceeded to the ECtHR when it became plain that the national investigation had been closed and there were no meaningful remedies domestically; another applicant's case continued to press domestically for change. The former case arguably created a pressure on the latter to work, while the continued inadequacy of the steps taken by the state in response to the latter provided further evidence of ineffectiveness to support the former case. (See also the case studies from Guatemala (Chapter 6), and in particular the dynamic created between the *Plan de Sanchez* and *Dos Erres* cases).

There are many examples of how *sequential* litigation has, in turn, led to unfolding impact over time in a range of different ways. The seminal *Brown v Board of Education* in the US was itself a sequential case: the first round focused on principle, the second on securing implementation. Gradually advances were consolidated, even if they remained notoriously incomplete. The significance, both positive and negative, of sequential cases in the Guantanamo context is discussed in Chapter 7. This and other case studies illustrates how judges may adjust their approach over time, towards more robust engagement, in light of sequential cases. The impact of the series of seven cases litigating different aspects of LGBT rights in South Africa provides a further impressive illustration of litigation's steady gains,

---

[33] See representation versus *amicus* role discussed below—a key way to avoid tensions.
[34] Ch 7: see the *Abu Zubaydah* and *al Hawsawi* cases.

with more challenging gains arguably being made possible building on those that have gone before.[35]

In some cases sequential impact arises as judges' frustrations grow with the state's failure to address the issue, or with its non-compliance with previous orders. A good example is the series of cases challenging the Soviet permit laws; relatively conservative judgments (by broadly compliant judiciaries rendered on narrow technical grounds) prompted firmer judicial responses at later stages as the state refused to comply and the issue was returned to the courts repeatedly.[36] Returning to court may also allow judges to expand on previously restrictive approaches in light of more favourable facts or evolving 'scientific or societal' developments for example.[37] The Guatemalan and Argentinian examples show clearly how the significance of the wrongs was exposed, and gradual gains were made, through a series of cases brought by different civil society organisations over time. These were not generally strategically planned and coordinated, but they did drive in the same direction, bringing with them a sense of momentum, and paving the way for litigation victories that no one case could have achieved. This points once again to the importance of timing, and of taking the steps that *can* be taken at the relevant point, while being mindful of the potential for greater strides forward in the future.

The *Hadijatou Mani* case, by contrast, shows how much can be achieved through a single case. In some ways, its exclusive nature made it stand out more, while being clearly presented as an illustration of a pervasive problem. As a single case involving one woman's story, it presented a whole complex social political phenomenon in simple human terms. It may nonetheless be that impact could have been deepened through follow-up litigation.

B. Paradigmatic or Unique Cases?

Cases that typify a widespread or prevalent practice can have particular strategic importance. If, for example, the goal is to expose a persistent injustice, or to effect systemic change, the logical step would seem to be to look for a case that presents

---

[35] 7 cases brought by NGOs and individuals are discussed in the Atlantic Philanthropies report on litigation in South Africa (n 20) 27–36. The report suggests it would have much more challenging had, eg, same-sex marriage come before decriminalisation of sodomy.

[36] E Rekosh, K Buchko and V Terzieva (eds), *Pursuing the Public Interest A handbook for Legal Professionals and Activists* (Chicago, PILI, 2001).

[37] See the journey in the transexuals recognition cases before the ECtHR where the Court notably went from finding the refusal to recognise was not a violation, to a narrower majority finding there was no violation a few years later, and stronger dissents, to another case with similar facts being upheld: from *Rees v UK* Appl no 9532/81 (17 October 1986) (ECtHR), *Cossey v UK* Appl no 10843/84 (27 September 1990) (ECtHR) to *Goodwin v UK* Appl no 28957/95 (11 July 2002) (ECtHR). Similar evolutions and subsequent cases have 'righted' poor findings: contrast *Ireland v UK* Appl no 5310/71 (18 January 1978) (ECtHR) and *Selmoni v France* Appl no 25803/94 (28 July 1999) (ECtHR) regarding changing approaches to what constitutes torture.

facts that are typical of the unjust situation, and not easily to be dismissed as merely an 'aberration'. It should also be recalled though, that in some situations it may be desirable to effect change through a case that is in some respect *untypical*. Litigation can then expose the violation as out of step with regional or international standards, more effectively isolating the wrongdoer. The ECtHR has often considered whether the facts of a case are out of step with currently accepted norms and practice, by referring to the 'European consensus' for example.[38] Moreover, 'exceptional' cases will often be more feasible. Courts seek—not infrequently—to present findings as fact-specific and exceptional. In particular, as the case studies show, there are many examples of compliant judiciaries that were unwilling to challenge practices and policies, but willing to recognise exceptions to them.[39] It may then be the advocates' job to roll those gains out into other situations and perhaps, gradually, to show that the exception is in fact the rule.

C. The Sympathetic Victim?

The role of 'sympathetic' victims in case selection deserves exploring, particularly in light of the role that media representation and public opinion play in hindering or supporting human rights advancements. There can be little doubt that telling compelling human stories can be deeply influential within court and beyond. This can be of great importance to many levels of impact, such as the challenging goal of shifting public opinion. Obviously, facts are all important in litigation, but what role can and should the 'sympathetic' victim play in a system where human rights are at stake? Victims of violations may already have been presented in an unsympathetic light, such that sympathy for him/her is likely to be dangerously scarce: if litigation is conducted for violations committed in the context of anti-terrorism measures or immigration controls—where rabid antipathy for victims already abounds, the reframing of their situation can be a core objective and, as noted in Chapter 4, SHRL can play an important role.[40]

   In such cases, it can, however, be particularly challenging to elevate the discussion to one of law and principle, and this difficulty should not be overlooked. Yet, it is precisely this seeing behind the labels to the human beings affected in this context that is all-important.[41] Sometimes the debate must evolve, and litigation may foreshadow this. Take the cases of torture in the war on terror; torture is always prohibited and always abhorrent, but it may be no coincidence that one of the first pieces of litigation exposing torture in the war on terror concerned an

---

[38] The significance of a 'European consensus' is recognised specifically in the jurisprudence of the ECtHR, but most courts have regard to this factor directly or indirectly.
[39] See section V above, with examples from apartheid South Africa; others from Argentina, or the Soviet Union, are highlighted in Chs 3 and 7.
[40] Ch 4.
[41] See Ch 7.

innocent man and mistaken identities. Presenting an innocent victim to a frightened American public may have proved critical to changing the discussion from one about the 'rights of terrorists' to one about the tragic consequences of abandoning the rule of law.[42] Over time, and much public debate, the 'innocence' card may have become less of an issue in rendition litigation.

The questions may be: what can be achieved by the litigation process, as a tool to move beyond prejudices that sustain human rights violations, and when and how is the human (rights) story best told? At the same time, the answers are rarely clear and considerations of principle must remain in the foreground. Human rights do not depend on people being likeable, and rights cannot be forfeited. Indeed, among the goals of SHRL may be the reassertion of the universality of those rights, and education in this respect.

VIII. Strategic Use of Fora

Where multiple available jurisdictions make such a choice possible, many factors influence strategic litigation decisions on the choice of fora. Some of these were highlighted in the *Hadijatou Mani* slavery case where there was the possibility of bringing the case to either the ACHPR, the UNHRC or the ECOWAS Court as the state of Niger had ratified all three relevant instruments. That case, in which the choice of forum was decisive to its impact, is suggestive of certain factors that may be influential in other cases. These include the binding force of decisions rendered by the body or court, the record of compliance with the court's orders in practice, the capacity and experience of the judges on the issues in question, the speed of the process, the involvement of the victim and whether hearings are public, providing opportunities for media engagement for example. The existence of strong practice or 'precedent' to date is certainly an important question, but one amongst many others. In practice, very practical questions like time limits may also play a role. For example, the rule in the ECtHR—stipulating that applicants must have brought their complaints within a period of six months from the violation or date of the final domestic decision—contrasts with the more flexible 'reasonable time' rule in UN Human Rights Committees.

On the national level, whether there is a choice of forum at all may be less clear but worth considering. Choice of forum will depend, among other things, on the goals, the remedies sought, and on whether the framing of the issue opens up jurisdictional possibilities. Whether criminal law measures are appropriate and can be fully utilised as 'strategic' will obviously depend in part on the nature of the wrong, as well as other factors including available evidence and standards of proof,

---

[42] Interview Steven Watt ACLU.

and whether there is an active role for victims and NGOs in the criminal process (which is generally a feature of civil law rather than common law systems).[43] On the other hand if, as in some systems, the possibility of pursuing civil remedies is likely to be suspended pending the criminal process, this may also have a bearing on litigants' decisions.[44]

Choice of fora is closely linked to choice of defendants, which may range from state, non-state and individual defendants, or all of the above, depending on the impact sought. Interesting examples from the rendition context before US courts illustrate how litigation against or between private parties may in certain circumstances be allowed to proceed, perhaps under the radar, and to bear fruit, where similar action against the state would be curtailed on state secrecy grounds. As Chapter 7 notes, this was the case for claims against psychologists involved in designing torture techniques for the CIA (which eventually settled in 2017), while the 'Richmor litigation' of contractual disputes between flight companies involved in the rendition programme gave rise to reams of information, which could in turn be used in subsequent human rights litigation.

The choice of forum may also be influenced by the effective independence of the judiciary, which can rarely be taken for granted: how likely is it that the particular court will be willing to decide against the government where the law and facts so indicate? In general, in pursuit of greatest impact, it may make sense to try to bring the case in a way that will enable the case to proceed to the apex court. But this may not necessarily be the best strategy where independence is compromised. In such cases, it may be that lower courts, less focused on the broader political issues, would be more likely to find in favour of an applicant in the right case, or to let information seep out. In the Palestinian Occupied Territories the choice has sometimes had to be made between bringing relatively innocuous 'planning cases' in the hope of achieving narrow victories before lower courts, or—if the lower courts are either not hearing the cases or not providing remedies—trying to address the problem as a question of fundamental human rights (and a political issue) and seeking to advance the claims through the higher courts. Sometimes, smaller victories on technical grounds may be what is feasible, and hopefully can be used to move incrementally towards a broader goal. Thus, the relationship between the (strategic) choice of forum, the framing of the issue and the broader strategies, is symbiotic.

As well as alternative fora, consideration should be given to the potential use of *multiple* fora. If several cases fall to diverse bodies at the same time, might this influence the approach, and generate positive results? Where there is the

---

[43]   Ch 2: criminal law processes are more open to and controlled by victims and civil society in civil systems, but there are also trends towards greater engagement in common law systems.

[44]   See eg Turkey study in Duffy (n 2).

possibility of using several fora alongside one another,[45] there may be the potential to create a dynamic relationship, or perhaps even healthy human rights competition, that may be beneficial to the more effective protection of rights in particular contexts.[46]

IX. The Victim in the Human Rights Process: Whose Case is this Anyway?

Many questions arise regarding the role of victims and their relationship with the litigation process. These concern, among other things, their relationships with their representatives, with other victims, with any NGOs or civil society actors involved, with the media and with the court process, and the implications for their protection and/or empowerment.

A. The Representative/Client Relationship

The professional and ethical obligations of human rights lawyers, and the 'lawyer/ client' relationship on the international and regional levels, are surprisingly neglected and largely unregulated. In the first place those pursuing structural change through strategic human rights litigation may have goals that differ from, and could ultimately even conflict with, those of their clients. While not *necessarily* problematic, these co-existent agendas need to be identified and managed.

Various tensions may arise at any stage of the process: pressure on clients to pursue litigation or decisions by clients to withdraw from it, pressure to engage, or not, in friendly settlements, differing positions on how the case should be argued or on the public profile to be given to a case, can all put strain on the advocate/ client relationship.[47] In this context, developing strategies (see below) that mean that the overall goals do not depend on the one individual being willing to proceed—for example, collectivising complaints or running sequential cases— becomes more important in SHRL. While advisers must advise, decisions must remain with the clients in whose name the processes are brought. In practice, this is less recognised in relation to SHRL than one might assume.

---

[45] Rules often indicate that a case cannot go to alternative international fora at the same time or successively; but see HR Committee where a case that has been dismissed on procedural grounds by other international mechanisms may be brought before the Committee.

[46] An example may be the sanctions cases in the security context in Europe, brought first to the ECJ (not exclusively a HR court) and later to the ECtHR (see the *Kadi* cases at the ECJ or the *Nada v Switzerland* and *al Dulimi v Switzerland* cases before the ECtHR).

[47] A classic example may be arguments in relation to the death penalty, or other penalties that may be desired by some applicants but conflict with the values or mandate of representing human rights organisations.

There may be good reasons for the dearth of specific rules setting out require-ments for representation—to keep open the possibility of *any* representation, which in practice in many contexts can be in very short supply and to ensure representation of choice. National regulations through bar associations may apply to legal representatives, but often do not in practice. An overly regulated approach may well not be conducive to ensuring that victims are supported and represented and that cases can be brought. It is important, however, for closer consideration of the accountability of international representatives and principles of good prac-tice that transcend contextual variables, to avoid conflicts and ensure that cases can be brought, while guaranteeing effective representation and that affected persons rights remain centre-stage. As foreshadowed in Chapter 3, where the pro-cess remains the victims' process, it can be empowering, in ways that can ben-efit both them and society more broadly. But practice suggests this is often not the case.

B. Victim Protection

The security and protection of victims, witnesses and those associated with them is a pressing issue, yet—perhaps ironically—somewhat neglected in international human rights practice. Litigation has had horrific security implications for many, as noted in Chapter 4 under negative impact. That said, there are examples of the international litigation process, and its profile, having a positive protective effect: the *Hadijatou Mani* cases illustrates the potentially terrible consequences of bring-ing legal action domestically, yet once the issue went to international litigation harassment by both the state and private entities ceased. Other studies suggest a similar chilling effect from domestic litigation.[48]

Protection from exposure may also be needed where the matter litigated is an inherently controversial one, such as access to abortion.[49] It is essential to ensure networks of real support for those that may be rendered vulnerable by litigation on either level. Nevertheless, given the inadequacy of currently available mecha-nisms for protection, care must be taken and honest reflections made as to the cost to individuals of litigation. As well as broader sharing of experience, more thought is necessary about how to provide protection for witnesses, and about the role that institutions themselves can play in this. The experience of national systems and of international criminal law may also inform our considerations of how best

---

[48] Duffy (n 2) contains several examples; Ms Akkoc's case, which formed 1 of the key ECtHR cases against Turkey for sexual violence, is one. Note though that this report also contains examples of litiga-tion provoking reprisals.

[49] *Tysiac v Poland* Appl no 5410/03 (20 March 2007) (ECtHR) was a case, in which Interights was somewhat involved, where the applicant had been denied an abortion to which she was entitled in law on health grounds, after which she went blind; as a result of the litigation, both she and her daughter were exposed to excessive media attention, positive and not, which created personal difficulties for her.

to address the current deficit in human rights processes. In addition to more practical and material forms of support, are issues related to approaches to confidentiality and protection of witnesses from the negative effects of exposure.[50] Lessons might also be learned from cases where judicial processes and media campaigns have had adverse effects.[51]

C. Managing Expectations and Effective Communication

As noted above, perhaps the greatest risk of human rights litigation, and one that comes to pass with great regularity, is unrealised, and unmanaged, expectations. This may arise from disappointment at the judgment or remedies, or lack of implementation, or an undermining process in which applicants feel marginalised, ignored, manipulated or even re-traumatised. The identification of these risks, and exploring how to avoid them in the particular context of litigation, is essential at the earliest stages of any human rights litigation. This includes the need for time to be taken, where possible, for early discussions with victims and relevant support groups. Consideration of the nature and the form of communication is due, to ensure sensitive and effective communication with victims at the outset and throughout the process. Adequate recording of meetings and advice is important, while at the same time ensuring a comfortable and secure environment. Effective communication may also involve non-legal specialists where possible. Making communication work within the litigation team, with the applicants at the centre, is one of the most important challenges in SHRL.

D. The Victim's Role in the Process

As noted above, litigation can be empowering or disempowering. It can contribute to repairing, or reinforcing and entrenching, the underlying wrongs. One dimension that influences the impact of the process is the role of victim participation in the process itself. The extent to which victims and those affected participate in, and gain satisfaction from, the process is variable. This may depend on whether they are kept informed of the progress of the case in an appropriate and timely way, whether proceedings are transparent and inclusive, and indeed whether there are actual hearings (increasingly de-emphasised in international practice), and, if so, what their role is.

---

[50] The identity of the victim (and/or complainant) must be revealed in the communication; this exposes them to potential negative effects and raises the question of how best to protect against this type of impact.

[51] The rule that communication must not be anonymous is enshrined in most rules of procedure based on the state, like any party, having the right to defend itself. But rules often allow in principle for the applicant's name not to be made public if so requested.

Regrettably, supranational courts and bodies' procedures have often been lacking in respect of effective victim participation. While there have been positive developments in some systems, regressive steps have been taken in others. The victims' role in the Inter-American system has been transformed over time, due to direct participation and an autonomous role (from that of the Commission) in proceedings before the Court. In a different type of forum, the ICC's rules enabling victim participation throughout the process marks a stark departure from those of the ad hoc international criminal tribunals that preceded it. By contrast, at the ECtHR, there is a negligible role for victims. This could be considered as out of step with the Court's essential purpose, and undermining of its impact. It is above all consistent with efforts to streamline procedures and cut costs.

In general, the lack of public hearings undermines various types of potential impact. As some of the cases studied here suggest, public hearings, including meaningful and safe victim participation, can form an essential part of the restorative process. With regard to the *Hadijatou Mani* case, I have suggested that the profound impact of that case—on the victim, on social attitudes and behaviour and institutions within Niger—can largely be attributed to the ECOWAS Court's willingness to sit in public session in Niger. The fact that the victim herself was heard, among others, and that coverage was extensive, changed the way the issue was framed and discussed in Niger. Experience at the African Commission also suggested that the most effective type of evidence was often victim-impact evidence, given orally, which appeared to contribute to favourable, and more rapid, findings for plaintiffs. Commitments to restorative measures made at public hearings in the *Plan de Sanchez* case provide another example. Finally, as mentioned in Chapter 4, the possibility of a (public) hearing sometimes prompts governments to make commitments ahead of it: by way of one example, in a case before the ACHPR, an Egyptian victim of arbitrary detention, represented by Interights, was released by the Egyptian government immediately before the hearing.[52]

E. Multiple Victims and Survivors

Particular issues arise from the role and representation of multiple victims, where litigation either addresses mass atrocities or systemic human rights problems affecting groups as a whole. Identifying victims, and possible clients, and establishing their relationships with other affected groups or communities, can be extremely challenging. Investing in the organisational dimensions of representing massive numbers of victims is complex but essential. The organisation of victims' groups can be critical to achieving many of the goals identified above—ensuring

---

[52] eg the immediate release of Mr Metwalli before the hearing in Egyptian litigation at the ACHPR, amongst others (*Metwalli v Egypt* before the AfCommHR).

that victims remain central, reframing perceptions of victims, giving them a voice (while making sure it is not dominated by some members of the group in a way that may underscore systemic inequalities) and providing for their security and support.

The formation of representative groups may itself be one of the ways in which litigation has a positive impact, bringing people together in response to egregious wrongs, forming associations and helping establish a long-term community commitment. The formation of the Asociacion por la Justicia in the context of the Guatemalan genocide cases provides an excellent example of this. As mentioned above, engaging multiple victims can also ensure that the litigation does not entirely depend on the continuing commitment of any one individual who may well drop out of the case as complications arise, or their situation changes— as victims quite often do for many reasons, and are entirely within their rights to do so.

F. Collectivising Complaints and Working around Victim Standing?

Given the individual burden that bringing litigation can represent, claims that are brought on behalf of a group can have important advantages. As noted above under multiple complaints, one such advantage is the opportunity to demonstrate and embody the widespread and systematic dimension of the problem and its wide-reaching effects. On the other hand, in some cases the opposite may be true; a single case involving one person can shine a light on the human story in a way that collective action cannot.

While collectivising complaints will often be beneficial, it is not always possible. First group claims may be enormously time-consuming and burdensome, and there may not in practice be the resources to support such claims. Where there are, systems vary as regards the ability to present 'collective complaints'. Notably, the European, Inter-American and UN individual complaints procedures generally do not provide for such complaints[53] (though, as noted above, multiple victims can file together).[54] The African system and the committee established under the European Social Charter do not have the same requirements regarding victim standing. This offers distinct advantages for cases falling within the geographic and subject matter jurisdiction of these bodies. Attention

---

[53] eg the UN HR Committee has held that an individual can only be a victim if he/she is actually and personally affected: 'If the law or practice has not been concretely applied to the detriment of the individual, it must in any event be applicable in such a way that the alleged victim's risk is more than a theoretical possibility' (*Aumeeruddy-Cziffra v Mauritius* HRC 35/1978 (9 April 1981, para. 9.2). The IACommHR 'receives a communication or petition alleging a concrete violation of the human rights of a specific individual' (I.A. Court, OC-14, p 45).

[54] They may present complaints together as one, or file separately, and the court may join the cases.

should also be paid to whether, through creative litigation, a right to bring such collective complaints can be advanced where it might not, at first, seem possible.[55] As mentioned in Chapter 4, bringing collective complaints or actions on behalf of victims—previously considered impossible—has gradually became accepted practice in the ACHPR.

It is essential if SHRL cases are to be heard that a broad approach to standing is adopted. To some extent, most if not all systems have developed flexible approaches to victim status over time. For example, allowing those *potentially* affected by a measure to bring a case, was one way in which the Inter-American system expanded the category of those with standing.[56] Particular difficulties have arisen when the victim is dead, and has no next of kin to represent him or her, yet the issue at stake raises fundamental rights issues that need to be heard. Interights faced this challenge in the *Campeanu* case,[57] which ultimately opened the possibility of NGO representation where there was no applicant or next of kin to bring crucially important human rights cases that affect the most vulnerable and unrepresented. This principle may be ripe for further development, expanding exceptions through future litigation.

X. Additional Litigation Roles: *Amicus,* Expert or Observer?

As set out in Chapter 2, many national and supranational systems have opened up to *amicus* interventions in recent years. These interventions can provide an extremely effective way to achieve some of the more straightforward and ethically less complex goals of SHRL, such as jurisprudential development or clarification. If any conflict is anticipated between the requirements of legal representation— including the prioritisation of the victims' goals, and the clearly strategic objectives of NGOs, it may well be wiser to engage in the case as a third-party intervener rather than as a representative.

The functions of third-party interventions to which courts have been receptive include contextualising the case, explaining the impact or significance of the case and how it affects people other than the parties to the case. Third parties can also be used to provide a comparative perspective on how the issue is handled in other

[55] See Ch 2. eg the African Commission is well known for having no requirement of victim status; a great majority of communications brought under Art 55 have been brought by NGOs, but this decisive aspect of the Commission's procedure is not enshrined in the rules. Rather it emerged from a vague rule on standing that was taken advantage of by petitioners and became practice.

[56] *María Eugenia Morales de Sierra v Guatemala,* Case 11.625 (2000) (IACommHR); *Emérita Montoya González v Costa Rica* Case 11.553 (IACommHR); *Klass v Germany* Appl no 5029/71 (6 September 1978) (ECtHR).

[57] *Centre for Legal Resources on behalf of Valentin Câmpeanu v Romania* Appl no 47848/08 (14 July 2014) (ECtHR).

jurisdictions, domestic or international. Their interventions are one of the key vehicles for the cross-fertilisation of strong standards between systems, as they commonly provide international and comparative law surveys, including bringing in 'soft law' standards relevant to the topic at hand, as an aid to interpretation.[58] The nature of third-party interventions continues to evolve rapidly as the practice proliferates. Nonetheless, challenges emerge as some courts seek to restrict interventions, for example by imposing stricter time limits and reducing the number of pages that may be submitted.[59]

Amicus briefs can be particularly valuable at the early stages of a tribunal or system (as in the early days of the ECtHR when its jurisprudence was being shaped) and for novel legal issues (such as the recent example of the definition of modern slavery).[60] As always, their value should not be assumed. Care is due to ensure that they do not impede the process in any way, or that their impact is not in practice limited to enhancing the profile of those intervening.

Where they are used, it should be recalled that a*mici curiae* are, however, friends of the court, not of the parties. There has been some backlash against overly 'coordinated' approaches between parties and interveners, which litigators would do well to be sensitive to. Even if—as on the international level—it is not clearly regulated, interventions may be more effective and more readily received if they are different in content, tone and approach from the parties' briefs. For example, an *amicus* intervention should generally address specific, identifiable issues relevant to the case, but not the facts of the case, and it should not express support for either of the parties.

Another related possibility to consider is the use of 'expert witnesses', who may address a court or body on issues of fact and occasionally of law.[61] *Amicus* interventions or expert witnesses can also be an important way of drawing greater attention to a case, in court or in the media, and engaging authoritative voices. Either of these types of intervention can provide a vehicle for NGOs to address the issues of strategic importance to them, while avoiding the potential conflict of interest that a representation role might create for the organisation.[62] Such interventions have clearly had significant impact on human rights standards, and sometimes on the outcome of cases.[63] Careful consideration should therefore be

---

[58] See eg *amicus* on domestic violence comparative standards and approaches by Interights in in *Opuz v Turkey* Appl no 33401/02 (9 June 2009) (ECtHR).

[59] See changes to ECtHR rules of procedure and the practice of asking for interventions of 8–10 pages.

[60] An example in this field from my practice was the intervention in the *Fazenda Brazil v Brazil* case, noted in Ch 5, rolling out gains from other systems, in identifying elements of modern-day slavery.

[61] See *Garzon* case before the UN HR Committee in which I am counsel. I used expert witnesses such as multiple high-level judges and academics to comment on the underlying legal issues, of relevance to the determination of the facts.

[62] NGOs are increasingly involved as representatives as well as supporters and interveners.

[63] eg several examples of my practice, like other lawyers and NGOs, show *amicus* arguments on standards directly replicated in human rights judgments.

given to the roles assumed. It is worth noting that high-level interventions from, for example, judges, may have a particular impact.

Finally, trial monitors should also be considered as a complement to human rights litigation strategies. Appropriately done, monitoring is potentially another way of bringing oversight to domestic judiciaries. In states where judicial independence is under threat, this can increase their sense of being part of an interested, international, legal community, while enhancing the visibility that is so critical to the achievement of some of the levels of impact discussed in this report.

XI. Effecting Change in Real Time: Litigating to Stop or Prevent Violations

Worthy of closer analysis, are the ways in which international and regional litigation can be used more effectively to prevent or to stop violations, as well as fulfilling their traditional role of providing redress after the fact. Litigation is in part inherently reactive, but the preventive potential of SHRL arguably transforms its significance, and can be given effect in various ways.

A. Precautionary or Urgent Measures

Depending on the system, there are various ways in which human rights processes might provide urgent protective measures. On the supranational level, through the use of interim, precautionary or provisional measures, courts and human rights bodies sometimes have the power to order (or otherwise urge) states to take urgent measures to prevent imminent, irreparable harm to human rights. This is usually pending a resolution on the merits of a claim of violations before the human rights court or body.[64] This is particularly pertinent given how delays and varying records of implementation threaten to undermine legitimacy in many systems today. However, it should also be recalled that the last thing that many victims of state-sponsored abuse want is 'protection' from the state.

This protective power has, however, been effective in many cases to prevent transfers—in the face of allegations that serious rights violations would arise in the transferee state, or the imposition of the death penalty—pending determination of whether there had been a fair trial, for example. However, the authority behind such orders is not always acknowledged and compliance with such

---

[64] Most major HR instruments and mechanisms have such a power attached, though it has been invoked to varying degrees. eg ECHR, ACHR, ACHPR, ICCPR optional protocol, CEDAW, UNCRPD Optional Protocol, Art 4 and the International Covenant on Economic Social and Cultural Rights Optional Protocol, which recently entered into force.

measures is, in practice variable.[65] There are several notorious cases, including—to my regret—some that I have been involved in with Interights, or previously in Guatemala, where orders for precautionary or interim measures have been completely ignored, and may even have expedited the use of the death penalty to avoid international oversight.[66] On the other hand, in numerous cases, such measures appear to have had a direct positive impact; one example may be the *Taba* case before the ACHPR, which I argued for Interights on behalf of three individuals sentenced to death by state security courts in Egypt, where interim measures were followed by stays of execution, which were ultimately never carried out.[67]

A further problem, which litigation strategies may, in time, help to overcome, relates to the limited scope of protective measures: it is often unclear to what extent they may be used to protect interests beyond risks to life and risk of torture, for example, though comparative practice seems to suggest a broadening out of the category of relevant interests. It is important to persuade courts to see the connection between violations such as attacks on the media or on human rights defenders and risks to the life and safety of the population more broadly.[68]

B. Systemic Change and Non-repetition

The analysis in Chapter 4 makes clear that strategic litigation's broader goals can include changing systems, institutions, policies, practices and laws with a view to avoiding violations in the future. Accepting the preventative potential of IHRL raises the question how most effectively to bring about lasting change through SHRL. This would require addressing underlying causes and contributory factors, so as to see where the need for structural, institutional reform, education and shifting of cultural attitudes and habits (see Chapter 4) can most effectively be aided by SHRL. By looking at litigation as one contributor to change, alongside others, it is no longer unrealistic or fanciful to see such things as susceptible to the influence of litigation.

In particular, arguments on remedies and reparation could more often be framed around non-repetition—a key dimension of reparation that is largely neglected in international practice. It is also important for advocacy purposes that the link is made between litigation of past violations and its significance for the

---

[65] eg the HR Committee has characterised the violations of its r 86 concerning interim requests as 'grave breaches of its [a state's] obligations under the OP' (*Piandiong et al v The Philippines* Comm No 869/1999 (2000), para 5.2). The r 86 provision is now contained in r 92 (see UN Doc CCPR/C3/Rev.8).

[66] *Bosch v Botswana* AHRLR 55 2003; *Pedro Castillo Mendoza and Roberto Girón v Guatemala* 1996. An earlier example from before my time at Interights was *Ken Saro Wiwa v Nigeria* AHRLR 212 1998.

[67] I was counsel for Interights, alongside Hossam Baghat of EIPR.

[68] Some rules refer to 'irreparable harm' or to 'grave breaches' of obligations. eg r 92 of the Human Rights Committee's Rule of Procedure, where the performance by the state of certain actions would cause irreparable damage to the author, the Committee issues a request addressed to the state to take interim measures to preserve the status quo.

future. By highlighting that significance more clearly, its impact may ultimately be greater. Obviously, though, there are no easy answers as to how strategy can be developed to ensure that the remedies sought include effective guarantees of non-repetition, and lasting structural change such that the same violations would be avoided in the future. We may pursue strategies that recognise a more modest role—not in changing policy as such but in changing the space within which such policy change is pursued. Litigation may simply alter the cost benefit analysis of those in positions of power, or create spaces for dialogue within which issues are discussed and policy might be shaped.[69]

C. Litigation as a Measure of (almost) Last Resort?

It is often said, quite wisely, that litigation is a matter of last resort where other solutions prove ineffective. This is generally true, but certainly not always, and deserves more careful consideration.

First, it perhaps goes without saying that in some of the urgent circumstances that present themselves in human rights litigation specifically, such as where a client faces the risk of execution or other harm, or is imprisoned unlawfully, there is an ethical obligation to use litigation immediately.

Moreover, as reflected in the 'exhaustion of domestic remedies' rule (whereby most international systems require deference by supranational to national remedies),[70] early recourse to supranational courts is permissible where such remedies are not effective and it would be demonstrably futile to wait. While the domestic remedies rule should be taken seriously, there may also be situations where, notwithstanding arguable remedies pending, embarking on international litigation may make sense. It may send a clear signal to domestic authorities and judiciaries to ensure that justice is done at home, so as to prevent the need for supranational action. It may avoid the possibility of courts determining that you waited too long (and have fallen foul of time limits) after it became plain that remedies were ineffective. These are exceptions though, and it is generally true that international litigators should take care not to interfere with (emerging) legal, or indeed political, solutions that may contribute more effectively to long-term rights protection.

For both national or supranational litigation, this book has underlined the importance of sensitivity to the dynamic between the litigation process and political progress. This will often require a cautious approach to the use of litigation, but it also includes awareness that the spectre of litigation can be used as a catalyst or contributor to other political solutions. Sometimes this also militates in favour of intervention litigation as early as possible, to help prompt or usher in timely solutions, rather than risking that the moments of opportunity for such solutions domestically may have passed.

---

[69] Ch 4: see the platforms for dialogue created by structural Latin American litigation.
[70] Ch 5: it does not apply before the ECOWAS Court, as the *Mani* judgment reiterated.

This corresponds with thinking about litigation as one part of a range of strategic approaches that may (or may not) be complementary, such that it runs alongside and interacts with other forms of advocacy. This may be preferable to a strictly linear mentality, where one approach fails and another arises. While litigation should not jeopardise political solutions, the inter-relationship is often more nuanced than is commonly recognised: litigation can help to draw attention, frame, catalyse and influence political debate, engage allies and exert pressure to achieve those solutions, by providing an alternative if they fail. If used strictly sequentially, such dynamic capability may in certain circumstances be lost. If an issue becomes moot, litigation's potential impact may likewise be lost. Strategic litigation is therefore usually, but not always, a matter of last resort.

XII. Creative Remedies and Implementation

Closely linked to the question of impact is that of the remedies that international and regional courts and tribunals can order and pursue, and the question of how to maximise the processes of implementation and follow-up. Practice in relation to remedies and reparation varies strikingly between bodies.[71] At one end of the spectrum, the IACHR has taken the lead in devising inventive and wide-reaching approaches to remedies; at the other, the ECtHR has traditionally taken a narrow view of the 'just satisfaction' it will award by way of pecuniary and non-pecuniary measures. Looking across all the systems surveyed here, there is an apparent lack of legal principles and/or transparency attaching to the determination of damages, leading to the perception of arbitrariness. This has to be taken into account, and can cause difficulties in advising clients and managing expectations. It also limits the ability of victims and lawyers to make responsible decisions as to impact. This is, however, an area where law and practice are in a state of considerable flux, with novel approaches to damages and implementation continuing to emerge, and with them opportunities for those involved in SHRL to play a role in helping shape them.

The African Commission provides a good example of a somewhat mixed approach to awarding reparations: it has been willing to give specific instructions for equitable remedies on occasion, such as re-granting citizenship, setting up truth commissions, undertaking environmental impact studies and revising legislation, all of which may be further developed. However, it has on occasion neglected compensation, possibly reflecting the broader ambivalence towards this form of reparation[72] or has deferred to national courts to determine quantum.[73] By contrast, the *Plan de Sanchez* case shows how far reparations

---

[71] See Ch 2.

[72] See Ch 4 on various types of victim-focused impact.

[73] The first decision in which this principle was articulated was *Emgba Mekongo Louis v Cameroon* Comm no 59/9, ACHPR/59/91:2. The Commission found that the complainant 'had in fact suffered

orders can go: here the litigants successfully pursued a broad range of material, non-material, collective social-economic and cultural reparations. Even in the much more conservative ECtHR system, specific remedies have sometimes been awarded, indicating exactly what the state had to do to meet its obligations under the Convention.[74] It remains to be seen whether attempts to encourage the ECtHR to incorporate non-material and symbolic forms of reparation such as apology, and measures of non-repetition, will be successful.[75]

Experience from across systems indicates that the increasingly creative use of remedies is becoming an important tool for trying to bring about the strategic goals discussed in this report.[76] As already mentioned, this suggests that it is worthwhile for litigators to try to influence the approach to remedies. One way to do this is by ensuring adequate focus on remedies at an early stage. In practice, this sometimes gets neglected, as remedies generally don't need to be argued at the outset of the case. Another, is by identifying carefully those remedies that correspond to the goals and potential levels of impact discussed in Chapter 4. Requesting remedies that may not yet have been endorsed by the system may bear fruit, as practice has shown.[77] In national and some international systems—such as the European one, which tends to be conservative—too much of a creative push may not be well received and, as ever, it is a judgement call as to how far to push, and when, and the nature of any possible cost. However, requesting specific remedies from the court, sometimes even where there is no precedent for it, should certainly be considered.

As noted in Chapter 2, a major challenge is presented by the relatively poor record of implementation across bodies.[78] This is an area to which increased resources and analysis have been dedicated in recent years, helping to identify the many impediments to effective implementation. While the focus of the current study is on the broader question of impact, poor implementation also creates a credibility deficit for the system, as well as a debilitating effect on the pursuit of victim-related and systemic goals.

How then, can SHRL be conducted so as to increase the likely effectiveness of implementation towards the end of the process? The prospects for

---

damages. [But] Being unable to determine the amount of damages, the Commission recommends that the quantum should be determined under the law of Cameroon'. See also *Antoine Bissangou v Republic of Cong* Comm no 253/2002, ACHPR.

[74] *Assanov v Bulgaria* Appl no 24760/94 (28 October 1998) (ECtHR), an early Interights case and the first case where the Court ordered release of the individual as there was no other way for the rights to be remedied.

[75] In the very recent litigation *Abu Zubaydah v Lithuania*, I called for the ECtHR to adopt a broader approach and recognise the critical role of recognition and apology as part of just satisfaction in rendition cases, but whether this will bear fruit is not yet known.

[76] See eg the creative use of collective habeas corpus cases in Argentinian courts, or the Colombian courts examples in Ch 2, among many others. See eg P De Grieff, *The Handbook of Reparations* (Oxford, Oxford University Press, 2006).

[77] See Ch3, and the evolving African practice referred to above.

[78] See eg OSJI report, 'From Judgment to Justice' or the *Interights Bulletin on Implementation* in Ch 2.

implementation can be improved by attending to certain things right from the outset of the process. Firstly, the chance of good implementation is greater if the litigation is part of a broader process for change. Secondly, partnerships of particular relevance to implementation should be cultivated early on. These might include the parliamentarians whose support will be needed for legislative reform and advocacy, and other politically influential partners willing to move for political change. Actors engaged from the outset are more likely to feel invested and willing to respond at the implementation stage. Thirdly, the request for clear and specific remedies at an early stage may impact positively on the implementation of a successful judgment down the line.

What is clear is that there are processes in place—and some new ones have evolved in recent years—to monitor implementation, which themselves provide potential opportunities to enhance impact and should in fact be seen as part of the litigation process. The newfound procedural openness—however slight—of the Committee of Ministers of the Council of Europe to involvement of applicants' representatives is worthy of note,[79] as is the growing amount of work done by NGOs in the field.[80] An example of the contribution of monitoring processes is highlighted in the Guantanamo and Rendition case studies. In other systems too, the follow-up mechanisms should be exploited as fully as possible, though they often provide limited opportunity for meaningful engagement as presently constructed. Implementation sometimes follows automatically, but rarely does it happen alone. Much depends on how advocates use the systems, and gradually, through practice, shape those systems, increasing their openness and their effectiveness as additional tools to enhance SHRL's impact.

XIII. The Economy of Human Rights Litigation

Resourcing human rights litigation is a serious challenge. This book has suggested the importance of the thorough investigation of violations, patterns and perpetrators, the availability of lawyers and other actors who play crucial complementary roles, their long-term investment in SHRL, victim protection and particpation, and the capacity and even the independence of courts and other human rights bodies themselves, all of which stand to be jeopardised by a lack of funding. Human rights litigation is not and should not be a 'gravy train' to enrich lawyers, but the

---

[79] Under r 9 of the Rules of the Committee of Ministers for the supervision of the execution of judgments and of the terms of friendly settlements, the Committee is entitled to consider any communication from NGOs, national human rights institutes and international organisations with regard to the execution of judgments.

[80] The work done by NGOs like OSJI in this field in recent years to facilitate dialogue between victims, NGOs and the relevant institutions, and the establishment of a new NGO initiative to monitor ECHR compliance in 2016 is promising.

real cost of bringing and conducting effective litigation should be understood. If SHRL lawyers (especially those specialised in these type of human rights cases) need to work pro bono on a regular basis, not only is the sustainability of their work questionable, it renders the whole SHRL enterprise inherently precarious, and reduces its ability to meet its potential as a tool for human rights change. It is therefore crucial to find ways to make the funding of SHRL more secure. Clearly then, funder fatigue and funder uncertainty as to the true value of strategic human rights litigation, pose daunting challenges to effective SHRL.

It is also very important that the management of the costs of litigation be addressed right at the outset of litigation. These include the legal and court costs, the liability to pay costs to the other party if the case is lost, which will vary between systems and may inform whether—or where—litigation is pursued. A client confronted with the requirement to provide 'security for costs', ie to come up with a large amount of money upfront in order to show the bona fides of his claim, may decide not to seek redress at all. It may, however, be possible to argue for costs to be reduced or suspended—including by reference to creative comparative arguments which have prevailed in some states where advocates have persuaded courts of the insidious impact of the potential burden of costs in public interest cases.[81] Solutions may also arise, for example, by means of some kind of indemnity or insurance, or by exploring whether a different jurisdiction might be available with less cost-vulnerability. In some states, such as the UK, contingency fees have replaced the legal aid system as the principal method of facilitating access to justice, at least in some areas of the law. Conversely, even in supranational litigation, it may be possible for a client to recover fees against the state when it wins litigation—an avenue that should certainly be explored.[82]

Almost regardless of the particular circumstances, funding invariably has a huge influence on the way litigation is conducted, sometimes on power-relationships between relevant actors, and the ability to adopt the sort of holistic approach set out as most favourable in this report. One challenge is for those engaged in SHRL to articulate its importance to potential funders and supporters. It is also essential that responsible funders acknowledge that genuinely strategic litigation may be a slow and underwhelming process of resisting setbacks or making painstakingly small advances, requiring a commitment to flexibility and long-term vision and investment.

---

[81] The general rule on costs is that costs follow the event, to compensate the winning party for the vindication of its position and dissuade less compelling litigation. This rule is a strong deterrent to public interest litigants and there have been exceptions made to the general rule, eg where courts have discretion not to award costs against an unsuccessful litigant. In the USA, some jurisdictions have established systems in public interest cases where the public interest plaintiff can recover costs if successful and not be liable for costs if unsuccessful (eg California Private Attorney General Statute CCP 1021.5 (1977)).

[82] This is so in the ECtHR; while lawyers often have to take cases pro bono, they may recover some (rarely all) costs at the end of the process and they should be prepared to account for those costs in the course of litigation and not leave it too late or they may forfeit their opportunity.

11

Conclusion: Appreciating and Demythologising Strategic Human Rights Litigation

The overriding purpose of this study has been to explore and explain the many ways in which strategic human rights litigation can and does contribute to the advancement of human rights protection. To be sure, litigation is only one, relatively discreet form of legal action. When it plays a role, it mostly does so alongside and in dynamic relationship with other legal and non-legal processes. It is a tool, not a magic wand.

One interviewee for this study noted that we should 'demythologise the power of judicial solutions generally'.[1] Careful consideration is certainly due as to whether other more traditional human rights tools are available and might advance many of the goals discussed in this report more quickly, cheaply and effectively. *A fortiori*, it is imperative not to automatically privilege legal responses to the detriment of other effective strategies. At the same time, however, the judicial role makes a particular type of contribution to human rights, that is not readily equatable or interchangeable with others. It embodies a unique legal authority and a particular democratic function—that of guardian of the rule of law—that is interlocked with rights protection and often needs reasserting in the face of widespread or systematic violations. Without sanctifying the judicial role, we do well therefore to recognise its intrinsic value and to consider how best to make use of its particular power and symbolism.

It is also important to demythologise the 'strategic' element of SHRL. This study has offered reflections on the extent to which we really can predict, plan for and realistically control the trajectory of any piece of strategic litigation, or strategic plans more broadly. Careful analysis of goals and planning for impact are essential for effective and responsible litigation, but flexibility is also essential, to adjust and respond to opportunities and obstacles that arise when life happens, as it will, outside the lines of a strategic plan. Likewise, a realistic view of the ability to measure and demonstrate impact is essential for all who engage in and support SHRL. We can acknowledge the lack of precision tools for meaningfully 'measuring' the

---

[1] Gaston Chillier, CELS, interview Buenos Aires, January 2016.

contribution of litigation within a broader human rights effort, without precluding efforts to understand its potential for responding to, influencing and reinforcing other desirable developments in the field.

Finally, demythologising litigation means also recognising its limitations, attendant dangers and negative impact. It implies the need for those engaged in SHRL to create the time and space to enquire into the real impact that cases have had, on those in whose names they were brought and more broadly on the multiple levels of change highlighted in this study.

There is a saying that *'the only sure thing is change'*.[2] Human rights litigation changes things in a multiplicity of ways, and the types of change achievable, which this study has sought to illustrate, are more diverse and wide-reaching in nature than may at first meet the eye—even to those of us who have been involved in SHRL for many years.

The premise of this book was the need to set aside our assumptions about the importance of SHRL, in favour of careful enquiry into whether it makes a difference or not, when and why. When examined through the lenses set out Chapter 2, multiple dimensions of impact emerge. SHRL rarely provides complete solutions; even where it can provide remedies for a problem it will not resolve the entrenched underlying realities that often manifest themselves in human rights violations. However, as the case studies demonstrate, litigation can be a catalyst or contributor in the changing of laws, directives, guidelines, policy statements, the terms of the debate, the voices heard in it, the labels and language employed, media coverage, narratives, attitudes and insights. It can therefore change the landscape within which the struggle for human rights continues to take place, strengthening movements and empowering forms of resistance and forces for change that will be essential to greater impact down the line. For all its precarity, it can have a truly transformative impact on people's lives.

The need to understand strategic human rights litigation in context is a thread that runs throughout this book. Part of this is the broad international context, as set out in Chapter 2, which reveals the extraordinary expansion and development of the field of human rights law and litigation in recent decades. This brings with it challenges, but also the exponential growth of opportunities for individual or multiple victims of violations to litigate strategically.

Our understanding of impact, and the dubious meaning of success, explored in Chapter 3, demonstrates the need to see change over time. It is important to burst the bubble on the 'champagne moment' that is too often seen as the culmination of the litigation journey, in favour of assessing *impact* on multiple dimensions, at different stages of the process, from diverse perspectives, over a prolonged period of time. There can indeed be 'success without victory'[3]—lost cases that

---

[2] An adaptation from Heraclitus, 'The only thing that is constant is change'.
[3] J Lobel, *Success Without Victory; Lost Legal Battles and the Long Road to Justice in America* (New York, NYU Press, 2004).

nonetheless have their own potency by contributing to longer-term change—just as the victory of a winning case that is never implemented, fails to impel change or produces a backlash, may be pyrrhic.

The experience captured in the case studies in Chapters 5 to 9 demonstrates how litigation may influence change at many points in time, not only (or even principally) upon judgment. The mere spectre of litigation can trigger significant change (as can the power of the on-going process), while gradual shifts in practices, attitudes or culture may develop in response to litigation a very long time after judgment is rendered. In the ebb and flow of change in which litigation plays a part, it should be borne in mind that today's negative impact may transform into tomorrow's positive outcome.

The case studies also show that litigation is not a panacea, nor a sole operator, but one potential contributor or catalyst to many forms of change. The question is not what any particular piece of litigation achieved itself, but whether and how it contributed to many forms of change as part of a broader strategy with several parallel and interconnecting dimensions.

Chapter 10 explored the implications of these findings on impact for the development of strategic litigation in the future. While there is no blueprint for good litigation strategy, there are identifiable factors exposed in the case studies that have been influential in enhancing impact in particular scenarios which may inform the development of effective strategies elsewhere. The case studies demonstrate the need to understand the myriad complex political and socio-economic factors that inevitably shape litigation possibilities and impact: in Argentina during its transitioning to democracy, in Guatemala during its peace process, in occupied Palestine under Israeli rule, and in pursuit of reparation and accountability for torture in the context of the 'war on terror'. Strategies must reflect, and may seek to influence, the particular social, political and historical context.

The way cases are brought forward, and by whom they are driven and supported, invariably affect strategies adopted at all stages of the process, and their impact, as do the partnerships and alliances formed and the level of civil society investment. The role of applicant groups, and their overarching organisation, coordination and the compatibility of their objectives with those of strategic partners, are also likely to be influential. Effective communication of human rights stories, and the non-legal skills of the litigation team and its allies, may be as determinative of success as winning the legal argument. In many ways, what happens outside the courtroom may be at least as important as what happens inside the legal process.

The structure of the litigation itself is another variable: at times, sequential, follow-up or collective cases have had particular impact while on other occasions isolated powerful cases can have had a vastly disproportionate impact, depending on the particular applicants, the power of their story and the ability to communicate its underlying message to a broader public. Many other strategic considerations of relevance include choice of forum, framing of arguments, selection of counsel, witnesses and experts, interlocutors inside and outside the courtroom. While there is no necessary conflict between client goals and strategic ones, recognising potential tensions and ensuring an ethical and human rights based approach to client representation, is among the key challenges in principle and practice. These are amongst the broad array of considerations that feed into cautious strategic litigation that seeks to maximise impact and minimise risk.

It is clear that we should avoid applying a 'mechanistic logic' in trying to identify 'best practice'[4] as there is certainly no one size fits all strategy to ensure or enhance impact. But at the other extreme it would be wrong to consider any situation so *sui generis* that we cannot learn from our own and others' past experience. Even in what may appear to be the most exceptional set of circumstances, inspiration can nevertheless come from the long-term observation and understanding of the role that litigation has been able to play on other continents, at other times. There is a need to consider how those engaged in SHRL can learn more naturally from their own practice, and share positive and negative experience comparatively, to enhance the impact of SHRL in the future.

SHRL is not subject to a checklist whereby ticking off a specified number of impact boxes will add up to maximal function or measure predictable success. Nor is it about a magic formula. Litigation rarely resolves human rights problems. However, it can and does make a difference, sometimes directly and dramatically, but more often subtly and even imperceptibly, changing the human rights landscape. Perhaps what we look through is a kaleidoscope, with litigation as the hand that turns it one degree to reveal a new context, within which advocates will continue to work to give real effect to human rights. Litigation is an 'imperfect but indispensable'[5] tool in that endeavour, the power of which depends in large part on how it is used. In an era in which human rights are under particular attack in many parts of the world, as is the role of the courts, the use of strategic human rights litigation looks set to be more challenging, and more important, than ever.

---

[4] J Dugard and M Langford, 'Art or Science? Synthesising Lessons from Public Interest Litigation and the Dangers of Legal Determinism' (2011) 27 *South African Journal on Human Rights* 39.

[5] S Cummings and D Rhode, 'Public Interest Litigation' (2009) 36 *Fordham Urban Law Journal* (in 'Public Interest Legal Services in South Africa Project Report' (2015) *Socio Economic Rights Institute of South Africa* 10).

INDEX

Note: Alphabetical arrangement is word-by-word, where a group of letters followed by a space is filed before the same group of letters followed by a letter, eg 'legal teams' will appear before 'legality'. In determining alphabetical arrangement, initial articles and prepositions are ignored. Page numbers followed by the letter 'n' refer to footnotes on the quoted pages.

CPSIA information can be obtained
at www.ICGtesting.com
Printed in the USA
LVHW012005250720
661520LV00002B/5